Library of
Davidson College

VOID

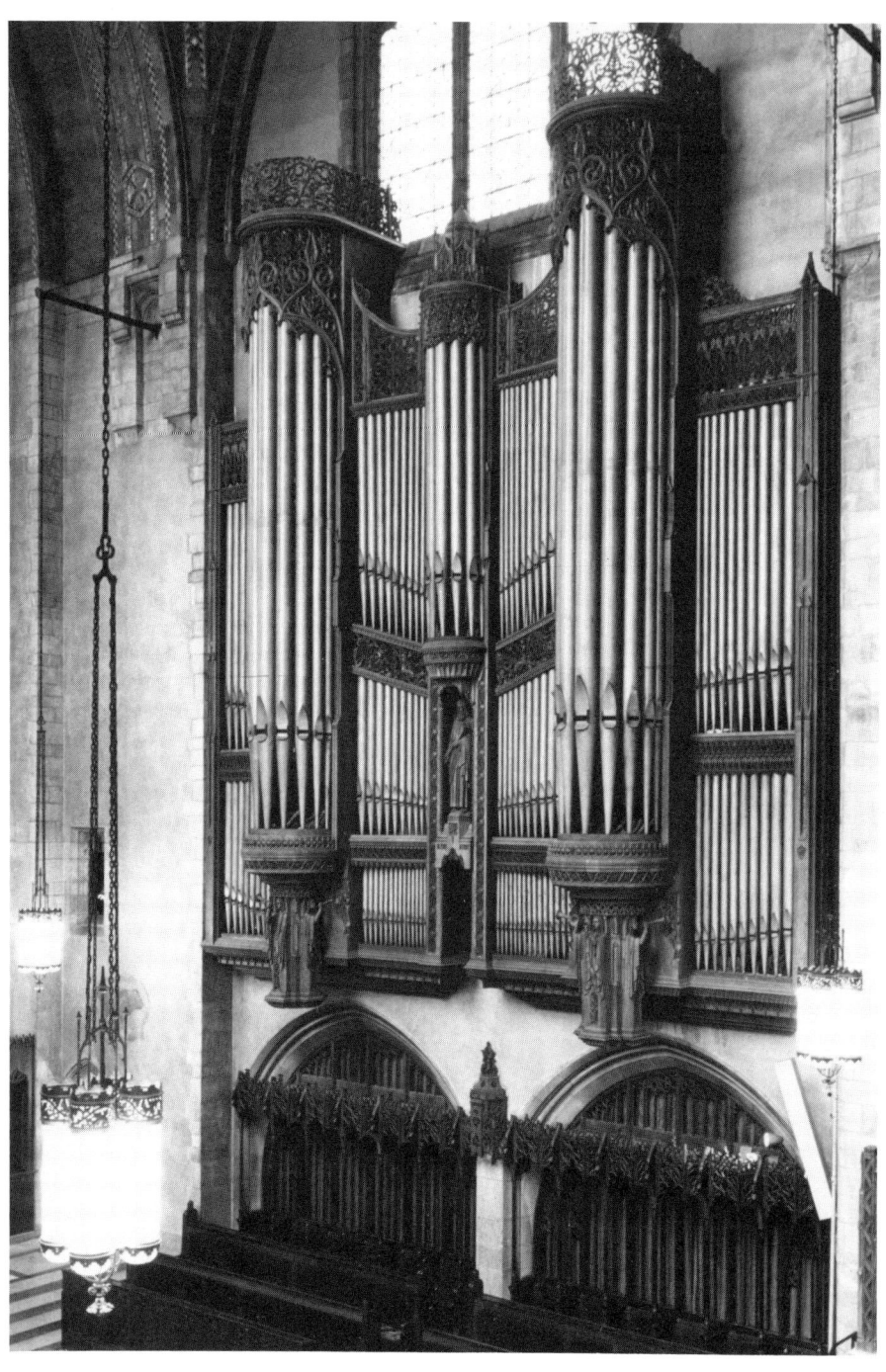

The Facade of Opus 634 built in 1927 for the Rockefeller Chapel, University of Chicago. Carving by Alois Lang; Bertram Goodhue, Architect; Photograph by Thomas A. Burrows.

The Life and Work
of
Ernest M. Skinner

by
DOROTHY J. HOLDEN

The Organ Historical Society
Richmond, Virginia
1985

Opus 475 of 1924, Jefferson Avenue Presbyterian Church, Detroit
Photograph courtesy of Dr. Allan A. Zaun

ISBN 0-913499-00-5
Copyright © 1985 by The Organ Historical Society, Inc.

With deep appreciation to
Kenneth H. Holden
and
Evelyn M. Beach
whose support and understanding
made this book possible

ACKNOWLEDGMENTS

I am indebted to the many people who have assisted me in the preparation and writing of this book by their contributions of data, anecdotes, pictures, specifications, advice, editing and proofreading. They are: Henry Karl Baker, Robert Baker, William H. Barnes, Wheeler Beckett, Homer Blanchard, Edgar A. Boadway, John J. Bolten, William Bunch, George W. Collins, Joseph F. Dzeda, William J. Deveau, Sydney F. Eaton, Edward W. Flint, Edward B. Gammons, Catharine and Harold Gleason, Edward H. Hastings, Stanton A. Hyer, I. L. Jones Jr., J. R. Knott, Elfrieda Kraege, Arthur Lawrence, Alexander McCurdy, Hugh L. Murray, Joseph Musser, Robert Noehren, Edwin D. Northrup, Barbara Owen, Francois Paradis, Richard Purvis, Robert J. Reich, John A. Schantz, Robert Schuneman, George and Ruth Scott, Eugenia S. Shorrock, Richmond H. Skinner, John Stenberg, the Taunton Historical Society, Frank H. Taylor, Paul W. Townsend, Donald R. Traser, William T. Van Pelt, William Francis Vollmer, Allan A. Zaun, and Alle D. Zuidema. I thank each and every one of them for their part in helping to make this biography of Ernest M. Skinner become a reality.

Dorothy J. Holden

The Photographs in this book are reproduced in loving memory of Nancy Elizabeth Quimby by a gift of her husband, Michael.

The Organ Historical Society acknowledges with appreciation the funds contributed by many of its members to the publication of this book. The Society is especially grateful for the exceptional generosity of Mr. Wesley C. Dudley, and for the special gift of Mr. David L. Junchen.

SUBSCRIBERS

Leland Abbey
Herbert D. Abbott
Daniel F. Abrahamson
Elizabeth J. Adair
A. Elbert Adams, MD
Mark Adams
Robert W. Addison
Aeolian-Skinner Organ Company
Dennis H. Akerman
Nita Akin
G. W. Aland, Jr.
Richard Alexander
Jack R. Alexander
Marlan Allen
Dean H. Allen
Ludwig Altman
Douglas J. Amend, MD
J. Theodore Anderson
Barry Fitzgerald Anderson
Dr. Robert T. Anderson
Karl F. Anderson
Herbert R. Anderson
Norman A. André, Jr.
David B. Andrews
Daniel L. Angerstein & Assoc., Ltd.
John Apple
Lawrence Archbold
David H. Archer
Mrs. Nonato Arcila
Joseph Armbrust
A. H. Arnold
Gordon S. Auchincloss
Kenneth R. Aultz
Gilbert G. Avilla
William C. Aylesworth
Richard M. Babcock
William L. Bagileo, Jr.
Mary William Baines
Howard J. Baitcher
Henry Karl Baker
William Baker & Co.
MaryAnn Crugher Balduf
Christopher A. Ballad
Ballard Pipe Organs, Inc.
Nelson Barden
G. Dene Barnard
David M. Barnett
Donald Curtis Barnum, Jr.
J. Michael Barone
Wilson Barry
Benjamin S. Basile
Merton O. Bassett
Peter L. Bates
Paul Batson
Evelyn M. Beach
Paul R. Beavin
Robert A. Beck
George E. Becker, MD
John E. Becker
Martin G. Becker
Allen Paul Bedrick
Charles D. Beeler
Donald P. Belben
Diane Meredith Belcher
Jerry T. Bell
Richard J. Beltle
Vincent and Esther Benitez
Glenn R. Benson
James S. Benzmiller
Corinne M. Berg
The Rev. Mark G. Bergman
Philip N. Bergstresser
Christopher J. Berke
Roger E. Berube
Howard P. Best III
B. G. Bevenour
James R. Biery
Keith Bigger
James Wesley Biggers, Jr.
David A. Billings
Dean W. Billmeyer
Fred W. Billmeyer, Jr.
Edgar Billups
James Bisbing
David A. Bishop
Lawrence E. Bishop, Jr.
Gustav Bittrich
Charles W. Blair
Ralph Blakely
Dr. Homer D. Blanchard
Ted W. Blankenship, Jr.
Thomas A. Bloom
E. A. Boadway
Willis Bodine
Charles F. Boehm
Bruce P. Bogert
David Bohn
Bob Boin
Samuel S. Bond
Terrill W. Borne
Boston University Libraries
David A. Bottom

Steve C. Bournias
Larry W. Bowers
Marlyn Michael Bowman
Raymond C. Boystel, Jr.
William E. Brach
Doug Brady
William F. Brame
G. Brandenburg
James M. Bratton
Robert Breihan
David W. Breneman
Henry L. Brengel
Frederick H. Brewer, Jr.
Colver R. Briggs
Richard G. Brode
David A. J. Broome
William J. Brosnan, EdD
David Burton Brown
George B. Brown
Kyler W. Brown
Peter A. Brown
Vernon Brown
William P. Brown
Dwight J. Bruce
Mr. and Mrs. Raymond Brunner
John E. Bryant
Fred N. Buch
Charles E. Buchner
George M. Buck
Nelson E. Buechner
Dr. John Moore Bullard
Bill Bunch
Bunn-Minnick Organ Company
Hugh E. Burdick
Roger F. Burg
Thomas A. Burrows
Lawrence S. Burt
William G. Burt, Jr.
John A. Busack
Dr. Jerome Butera
J. Melvin Butler
Donald G. Butt
Neal Campbell
Lynn C. Canny
Roy H. Carey, Jr.
Michael W. Carlyle
Douglas C. Carrington
Fr. Thomas J. Carroll, SJ
Brian Carson
Gordon C. Carson
Edgar Lysle Carswell
Edward L. Carter Jr.
Paul S. Carton
Ralph E. Carver, RN
James G. Casey
Robert H. Caskey
Raymond L. Chace
Mr. & Mrs. Jack Chadwell
David Chalmers
Gerald Chalupka
A. R. Chapman
Terry Charles
Charles M. Ruggles Pipe Organs
Robert Chase
Sidney Chase
Dr. Thomas J. Chase
Marc F. Cheban
The Rev. James J. Chepponis
Michael Chervenock
Mr. & Mrs. George A. Choban
Mrs. George Christ
Michael Christiansen
George E. Chubb
Church Organ Sales
R. Harold Clark
Dr. Thomas R. Clark
Charles H. Clarke
William B. Clarke, Jr.
Newell H. Claudy
Dan Clayton
Kevin M. Clemens
Marion L. Clemens
Richard Cockerham
David W. Cogswell
Ralph C. Colburn
Robert E. Colberd
Gary Coleman
Michael Coleman
P. D. Collins
Dr. Adrian A. Collins
Edith Connelly
Henry M. Cook
C. W. Cooke
Giles Buckner Cooke
Dean P. Coombs
Harris E. Cooper
Scott G. Corey
Hubert Corina
William T. Corkery
Kent Cormack
Robert R. Cornelison
Cornell University Library

Ray Cornils
G. Dale Cornor
Douglas W. Craw
John R. Crew, Jr.
Robert H. Crilley
Jerry J. Critser
Douglas C. Crocker
H. Proctor Crow, Jr.
J. Warren Culp
J. E. Cummings, Jr.
Richard Cummins
Carlo Curley
Donald D. Curry
Christopher R. Cusumano
William F. Czelusniak
Thaddeus J. Czerkowicz
Kenneth G. Danchik
Ivan E. Danhof, PhD, MD
George W. Daniels
George A. Darling
Cleone C. Davidson
Miss Beverli Davis
Dwight Davis, FAGO, CHM
Forest K. Davis
Merrill N. Davis III
Walter W. Davis
Davis Memorial Library
John DeCamp
George V. DeGruccio, Jr.
Harold de LaChapelle
Victor R. de la Torre
Franklin A. de Lespinasse
Richard P. DeLong
William De Turk
Dr. Alfonso J. DeVino
Francis P. Dean
A. David Deery
James L. Dennis, MD
Thomas A. Densel
Mrs. D. H. Dent
Preston H. Dettman
Douglas R. Dexheimer
Matt L. Dickerson
Robert C. Dickinson
William D. Dickinson
Steven A. Dieck
Lynn A. Dobson
Kenneth P. Dod
Mary Ann Dodd
Dr. Phillip C. Dodson
Harold Owen Doering
John Doney
Harold E. Donze
Tom Doub
Alan Douglas
George Downes Jr.
Brock W. Downward
Tim Drewes
Allen G. Dreyfuss
Hugh L. Dryden, Jr.
Brantley A. Duddy
Mr. and Mrs. Wesley C. Dudley
Francis E. Dugal
Malcolm D. Dutton
Joseph F. Dzeda
E. B. Hanford and L. W. Paré
Terry Byrd Eason
Leonard East
Harry J. Ebert
W. Thomas Edwards
Dr. Steven Egler
C. R. Eichhorn
George Benson Eichler
Bradford H. Elker
Larry D. Ellis
Alice L. Ellsworth
Gregory Brooks Elmore
Dr. Roger P. Elser
Stephen Emery
Leo Allan Endel
Ronald K. Englund
Benjamin R. Epstein
Thomas Erickson
Robert M. Estes
Broocke Eubank
D. V. Evans
Robert Eversman
Frank E. Fairchild Jr.
Cliff & MaryAnne Fairley
Elbert W. Fanter
Dr. Barry B. Farmer
David Farr
Tom Farrell
Mr. and Mrs. Kenneth I. Farrell
George Faxon
William Fearnley
David E. Fedor
Frederick W. Feedore
James H. Felten
James A. Fenimore, MD
John Fenstermaker
James H. Ferguson

William E. Ferris
Jerry Field
David A. Fielding
Thomas F. Fierro
Shirley M. Finney
First Baptist Church, Savannah, Ga.
Norman Z. Fisher
Marty Fisher
Mary and Joseph Fitzer
Mike Foley
John V. Fondo
Wilbur W. Forschler
Tom Fortier
David H. Fox
Michael Fox
David Fuller Fraley
Brian Franck
Glen Robert Frank
Gerald Frank
Richard M. Frary Jr.
James E. Frazier
Rubin S. Frels
Roy E. Frenzke
Michael and Susan Friesen
Wayne J. Froelich
David L. Furniss
Gary W. Gabert
Michael J. Gaffney
Douglas A. Gammage
Thomas E. Garbrick
Steven L. Garbus
George B. Gardner
James E. Gardner
Dan R. Garland
Oland P. Gaston
Daniel E. Gawthrop
Richard M. Gayhart
John Gebhard
Richard M. Geddes Jr.
Hugo Gehrke
M. W. Randy George
George Bozeman Jr. & Co.
Charles W. Gibson
The Rev. Robert K. Giffin
Vincent & Cheryl Gilbert
Randolph Gilberti
L. Brent Giles
Donald M. Gillett
Mark Gilliam
Rod Glasgow
Robert Glasgow
James W. Glass
Mr. and Mrs. Donald F. Glover
Sebastian Matt. Gluck
Gary and Ann Gold
Cliff Golden
David Gooding
Robert S. Goodwin
Larry Gorjup
Philip F. Gottling, Jr.
Grafton Piano and Organ, Inc.
Carl Gravander
Arthur G. Green
John Powell Green
Alexander E. Greene, Jr.
Robert B. Greene
Richard F. Gremlitz
Richard E. Groves
Wm. M. Grunewald
Lance S. Gudmundsen
Walter J. Gundling
Thomas W. D. Guthrie
Paul N. Haggard
Robert A. Halleman
Richard C. Hamar
David L. Hamblin Jr.
Dr. Bengt Hambraeus
Joel D. Hamers
Ernest F. Hamilton, Jr.
James J. Hammann
Gerre Hancock
E. B. Hanford & L. W. Paré
LeRoy K. Hanson
William D. Hargett
James Wiley Harker
Daivd and Iris Harris
David S. Harris
Raymond Allen Harris III
James K. Hartman
Richard S. Hartman
John W. Harvey
Greg W. Harwick
Dean Edward H. Hastings, Curry College
William L. Hatzenbuhler
Nelson E. Hayes
Mac Hayes
Bryant S. Hazard
Will O. Headlee
Roger W. Heather
James Hecht
William F. Heefner

Pat Heflin
Tim W. Hemry
W. Lee Hendricks
John Wynn Henshall
Douglas Herbst
Frederick P. Hermes
Stephen Hermes
Scott P. Herpick
Christian Herrmann, Jr., MD
Michael B. Herzog
Paul S. Hiebert
Leon Hiett
Walter F. Hildebrand
Alfred G. Hill
George R. Hill
Mr. and Mrs. Joseph R. Hill
Stephen L. Hill
Edgar B. Hilliar
Carl L. Hillyer
Robert Hinson
George Hipkins
Maeva H. Hipps
James A. Hodges
Michael B. Hoerig
Otto Hofmann
Kenneth H. Holden
David W. Holland
Walter H. Holtkamp, Jr.
Lloyd R. Holzgraf
Kathleen Hoopman
John Hopkins
Philip B. Horton
James R. Houston
Allyn Hoverland
Richard T. Howard
Michael S. Howe
H. A. Howell
William L. Huber
W. Robert Huey
David O. Huffstetler
Dana Hull
Paul A. Humiston
D. R. Hunsberger
W. A. Humphries
Douglass Hunt
Donald C. Hunt
Brian Hunt
Richard F. Hurley
Mark C. Hutchison
D. Deane Hutchison
Stanton A. Hyer
Kary Wilson Hyre
Charles E. Ingram
Stevens Irwin
Alfred Q. Isaacson
Karen Hite Jacob
Paul A. Jacobson
Robert E. Jacoby II, MD
Dennis James
Gary James
Robert A. James
David M. Jeffers
S. David Jennings
Paul Jernigan, Jr.
Lee Jessup
James K. Jobson
Brian S. Johnson
Henry C. Johnson
Homer R. Johnson
Lance E. Johnson
Leonard B. Johnson
Lawton C. Johnson
Lowell E. Johnson
Mrs. Ralph H. Johnson
Richard M. Johnson
Dr. Roy A. Johnson
David G. Johnston
James H. Johnston
Michael Johnston
William Johnston
William W. Johnston, MD
Gregory M. Joly
Bradley E. Jones
Brian Jones
Clarence Jones
Gary W. Jones
Robert A. W. Jones
W. Thomas Jones
David L. Junchen
Alfred C. Kaeppel, FAGO
Dr. Wayne Kallstrom
Anne Louise Kazlauskas
Michael Keeley
Roy F. Kehl
Marguerite E. Keil
Scott Kent
Lawrence M. Kerecman
Joseph R. Kibler
Ruth E. Killian
Brenda Jean King
E. Peter King
Lamar R. King

Robert Burns King
Daniel Kingman
James T. Kingston
Norman Kinnaugh
Norman L. Kinsey
Bertram Y. Kinzey, Jr.
Mark R. Kirchenberg
K. Bryan Kirk
Otis B. Kittle
Hans Gerd Klais
Philip A. Klann
Peter J. Knapp
Richard W. Knapp
August E. Knoll
Robert A. Koch
Mark A. Konchan
Samuel H. Koontz
Stephen Paul Kowalyshyn
Gregory P. Koziel
Joel Kremer
Charles Krigbaum
Frederick J. Kruse
John Joe Kuriger
Ivan J. Kuster
Ken Ladner
Dr. John W. Landon
Allen Langord
Stephen Fuller Larrabee
Brion N. Larson
Mark E. Laubach
Alan M. Laufman
Irving B. Lawless
Sand Lawn
Arthur Lawrence
Fred B. Le Compt
Dr. E. Dale Lee
Gilbert Lemieux
David R. Lenington
Robert G. Lent
Laurence W. Leonard
Wayne Leupold
John M. Levick Jr.
David Lewis
David W. Lewis Jr.
Jeffrey L. Lewis
Jim Lewis
Kim William Lewis, DD
Wesley L. Lewis
Lewis & Hitchcock, Inc.
Larry Liggin
C. Alan Lightcap
Phillip G. Lighthall
The Rev. Thomas Lijewski
Richard A. Lind
William Lindberg
Jody W. Lindh
Joseph Marvin Linger
A. K. Lipchak
Harry W. Littman
Mark W. Lively
Richard A. Locher, Jr.
Bruce K. Lockhart
Robert J. Lockridge
John R. Long
Dr. Page Long, FAGO
Stephen E. Long
Mrs. Nancy O. Longley
David R. Lornson
Major Stephen M. Lott
Harry M. Lowell, MD
Jon M. Lowell
Ken Lundberg
Linwood D. Lunde
Alfred E. Lunsford
M. L. Bigelow & Co. Organ Builders
M. P. Möller, Inc.
Anna G. N. MacGregor
Forrest Mack
Charles E. Majure, PhD
Warren G. Marble
Susan Marchant
Nancy Marema
T. L. Marks
Edward F. Marra, MD
K. C. Marrin
H. Winthrop Martin
John J. Martin
Edward Mason
Edwin E. Mason
Kenneth Matthews
Dr. Thomas Matthews
Lorenz Martin Maycher
John Suel E. Mayers
Robert R. Mayo
David M. McCain
Dr. Charles S. McClain
Robert K. McConnell Jr.
Thomas L. McCook Jr.
Lloyd L. McGaughy
Gerald F. McGee
Mark E. McGuire
John S. McIntosh

Wm. R. McMahon
Charles W. McManis
Michael W. McMullen
Robert McMullin
McNeely Organ Company
Donald McPherson
David McVey
Gary S. McWithey
Arthur Means
Stephen L. Mehler
Christopher E. Mehrens
Richard G. Mendenhall
Jesse B. Mercer
Herbert E. Merritt
Messrs. Czelusniak et Dugal, Inc.
Messrs. Hunting & Boggs
Gordon L. Meyer
Grant Meyers
D. Michel Michaud
Edward T. Mickey, III
Arthur Middleton
Midland Lutheran College Library
Bradley F. Millard
Earl L. Miller
Gordon L. Miller
June Miller
Marion Miller
The Rev. Ralph H. Miller
Robert G. Miller
Robert R. Miller
Taylor K. Miller
Miller Pipe Organ Co.
W. R. Milligan, Organbuilder
Franklin Mitchell
John H. Mitchell
John S. Mitchell
Walter J. Mitchell
Rosalind Mohnsen
David L. Molvik
Theodore A. Montgomery, MD
Dirk W. Mooibroek
Robert E. Moonan
Richard I. Morel
Richard Morgan
Roch L. Morin
Hector B. Morneau
Clayton L. Morris
Richard Morrison
Joe Motley
Mount Holyoke College Library
Vernon R. Mouw
Culver L. Mowers
Jon Moyer
Helen Mueller
Randall S. Mullin
Michael Murray
Thomas Murray
Joffrey Murrell
Music Curio Repair Shop
Andrew L. Mutti
Milford H. Myhre
Don Myers
Nashotah House Library
Carl Natelli
John R. Near
Charles L. Neill
A. Scott Nelson
Mark Edward Nelson
The Rev. Mark R. Nemmers
John D. Newall
James F. Neumann
New Orleans Baptist Theological Seminary Music Library
Nicholas-Bradford Organ Co., Inc.
Thomas C. Nicholson
Clarence John Nielsen Jr.
Robert R. Nielson
Noel W. Nilson
William J. Noll
Keith E. Norrington
Mrs. R. Ronald Norwood
The Rev. Claudius S. Nowinski, MS
David R. O'Steen
Dr. Orpha Ochse
Harold D. Ocker
Gerald E. Oehring
John Ogasapian
Thomas L. Oliphint
Alvin M. Olson
Gerald L. Orbaner
Organ Clearing House
Organ Design Technology
Organ Supply Industries, Inc.
Freeman R. Orr, Jr.
Henry A. Orszvlak
Barbara Owen
Ruth L. Palmer
John A. Panning
Dorothy Jean Papadakos
James A. Parisi
Margaret L. Parker
Robert E. Parr
Perry G. Parrigin

John R. Parsons
Donald R. M. Paterson
William W. Payne
Ronald J. Pearson
Nelson B. Pease
Pelland Organ Co.
Michael D. Pelton
Harley A. Perkins
H. W. deB. Peters
Rodney M. Petersen
Joan Peterson
David R. Petty
Petty-Madden Organbuilders
Lawrence Phelps
John D. Phillippe
Adrian W. Phillips
Dr. Peter V. Picerno
D. Lynn Pickering
Mrs. Mary Eleanor Pickle
Hugh M. Pierce
Charles F. L. Pierpont
Harley Piltingsrud
Stephen L. Pinel
Paul M. Pinkosky
Pipe Organs by Muench
Keith F. E. Pittman
Louis Playford
Joseph W. Pool, III
John O. Porbeck
Dorothy E. Poschen
Charles E. Potter
John J. Potter
Stephen D. Potter
Thomas V. Potter
Warren L. Potter
Melvin Potts
Prairie Organ Company
Richard B. Price
M. E. Prokopchak
Theodore J. Purchla
Richard Purvis
Michael Quimby
Ted Quinton
R. A. Colby, Inc.
Douglas L. Rafter, AAGD
James G. Raimond
J. C. Randall III
John L. Randolph
Mac Range
Stephen Rapp
Doris & Dave Rasche
Keith Rasmussen
Miss Jeanne Reed
Lois Regestein
Robert Reuter
C. Thomas Rhoads
E. Craig Richmond
Blaine Ricketts
Rowland Ricketts, MD
Robert C. Riehl
Eric R. Riley
Frank Rippl
Vincent D. Ritzert
Eugene Roan
Earle D. Robbins
Joseph G. Roberts
Stephen Roberts
Eric N. Robertson
Albert F. Robinson
Lawrence Robinson
Roche Organ Co., Inc.
G. W. Rohrer
William M. Rokes
Melvin T. Rollema
Rosales Organ Builders, Inc.
Manuel J. Rosales, Jr.
Paul Alan Rosendahl
John R. Ross
Michael A. Rowe
David Oakley Ruberg
Wolfgang Rübsam
Alice Rucker
Michael Rudd
David C. Ruler
Stephen A. Rumpf
David C. Rutford
Carl E. Rutz
Lee S. Rynder
Paul Sahlin
Mr. and Mrs. Wilbur T. Sanford
Gerald A. Saunders
Allen R. Savage
Scarritt College Library
Stephen G. Schaeffer
Schantz Organ Company
The Rev. Alfred von Schendel
Russell Schertle
Arthur E. Schlueter, Jr.
Elmer A. Schmahl
Elizabeth Towne Schmitt
Hans Schmidt
J. Paul Schneider
Schneider Pipe Organs, Inc.

Schoenstein & Co. Organ Builders
Harold Dennis Scholl
William Schoppenhorst
Carl E. Schroeder
Suzanne B. Schroeder
Schudi Organ Co., Inc.
The Rev. Frank J. Schultz
Gordon A. Schultz
John Preston Schultz
E. H. Schuricht
Jeffrey A. Scofield
Robert E. Scoggin
Elizabeth R. Scott
Mark Scott
Robert A. Scott
Ruth Alden Scott
David C. Scribner
Horace W. Sellers
Victor P. Serresseque
Ronald T. Severin
Gerard & Nancy Shamdosky
Don Shaw
Ronald P. Shepard
Carol Shepardson
J. Allen Shivers
Mrs. Eugenia Skinner Shorrock
Richard and Lois Shorrock
Ned Siebert
Donald E. Silvius, MD
Kenneth F. Simmons
George-Lee Singleton
Paul Singleton
Gerald R. Skeels
Mr. and Mrs. J. P. Skentelbury
E. F. Small
Richard A. Smid
Arnold E. Smith
Bon R. Smith
Charles P. Smith
Gale E. Smith
Graham W. Smith
Dr. James E. Smith
Mark Timothy Smith
Rollin Smith
Stoddart Smith
Nicholas Snow
Richard C. Snyder
Murray and Hazel Somerville
Mme. Sarah Soularue
Paul Spalla
John L. Speller
The Rev. Norman Spicer
Harry Spring
Henri M. St. Louis
St. Thomas Church, New York
Jack Staley
Brad K. Starcevich
Kenneth Starr
Michael E. Stauch
Peter P. Stearns
Stephen A. Steely
The Rev. John W. Steiner
J. H. Steinkampf, Jr.
C. Martin Steinmetz
Sonia P. Stiklius
John A. Stokes
Francis M. Stone
Edward Millington Stout
Daniel I. Streeter
Nelson A. Streett
Hans W. Stumpf
John Suhr
B. Frank Summers
Robert C. Sunkel
Dr. Thomas W. Surber
Michael E. Sussman, MD
Frederick Swann
Jon Atwood Swanson
J. Richard Szeremany
Paul Szymkowski
Frank M. Tack
Esther L. Talcott
Robert Tall
Thomas L. Tallentire
John B. Tanner
James H. Tate
Frank H. Taylor
Homer S. Taylor
The Choir, Presbyterian Church of Dover, Delaware
The House of Hope Presbyterian Church
The Noack Organ Co., Inc.
The Reuter Organ Company
Mark Thewes
Frank L. Thomson
John Tiedtke
Timothy J. Tikker
Rowena B. Tingley
Mr. and Mrs. H. Kenneth Tonak
William H. Traver
Ruth J. Trexler
William A. Troup

Robert M. Turner, Organbuilder
Thomas F. Turner
Kenneth V. Turvey
Alvin L. Uhlman
William A. Ulco
Richard Unfreid
Dennis J. Ungs
Union Theological Seminary in Virginia
University of California Library
University of Canterbury, New Zealand
University of Georgia Library
University of Louisville Music Library
University of Puget Sound Library
Charles J. Updegraph
Hollis R. Upson
Samuel E. Urmey
John H. Vandiver
Henry Van Dyke
John W. Van Laak
William T. Van Pelt
John V. Van Zanten
Robert Van Zweden
Aran Vartanian
Nancy W. Vernon
William M. Via
James Vinson
Arie M. Voskuil
Barbara Vukich
Dan Wagner
David Wagner
Randall E. Wagner
D. Edward Walker
David E. Wallace
Joseph Wallace, Jr., MD
Robert E. Waller, AAGO
E. J. Walling
John Powel Walsh
Martin R. Walsh
Norman M. Walter
Lawrence R. Walters
Norene Walters
Richard J. Warchol, MD
Philip Hulse Warner
Sally Slade Warner
Wayne T. Warren
K. M. Watson
Gerald R. Weale
Harold W. Weaver
Lucile Hammill Webb
Robert M. Webber
Richard R. Webster
Henry Wehmeyer
James J. Weisenborne
Thomas D. Weisflog
John H. Welch
R. W. Welch
Frederick Wells
Dexter M. Welton
Lowell B. Wendell
John Robert Wenta
William R. Whipple
Robert W. White
Vernon H. White
Donald White
Franklin F. White
John S. Whiteley
Robert Bruce Whiting
Russell G. Wichmann
Bard B. Wickkiser
Harold Wiebe
Martin Weigand
David K. Wigton
Robert J. Wilcox
James O. Wilkes
Wilkes College, Farley Library
Dr. Harry Wilkinson
Warren H. Williams
David Williamson
Edmund Wills
Richard E. Willson
Todd Wilson
Burton D. Witham, Sr.
Robert G. Withers
Jerry R. Witt
Edward P. Wood
James A. Wood
Douglas M. Woodard
Susan Carol Woodson
Charles Woodward
Robert Eugene Woodworth, Jr.
H. L. Wormhoudt
David Garth Worth
Jonathan A. Wright
Michael Wells Wright
Robert L. Wyant
A. W. Yeats
Dr. Stanley E. Yoder
Larry Young
The Rev. Carol Henry Youse
Donald D. Zeller
Richard B. Zentmeyer Jr.

CONTENTS

Acknowledgments v
Chapter 1. Childhood and Apprenticeship (1866-1890) 1
Chapter 2. Courtship and Marriage (1893) 9
Chapter 3. Romanticism and the Orchestral Ideal (1894-1898) 13
Chapter 4. Ernest Starts His Own Business (1900-1907) 24
Chapter 5. The Skinner Orchestral Organ (1906-1913) 37
Chapter 6. Personal Life (1906-1915) 49
Chapter 7. World War I and After (1914-1919) 58
Chapter 8. The Roaring Twenties 69
Chapter 9. An Impressive Year (1921) 80
Chapter 10. Theater and Residence Organs 88
Chapter 11. The Skinner Reputation (1922-1924) 99
Chapter 12. The New Skinner Organ (1924-1926) 110
Chapter 13. G. Donald Harrison Joins the Skinner Firm
             (1927-1929) 121
Chapter 14. Tensions Build at Skinner Organ Company
             (1929-1930) 138
Chapter 15. Serlo Hall and the Five-Year Contract (1929-1932) 147
Chapter 16. The Aeolian-Skinner Organ Company (1932-1933) . 156
Chapter 17. A New Start (1933-1938) 178
Chapter 18. Problems and More Problems (1938-1941) 190
Chapter 19. World War II: The Fire and After (1941-1947) .. 208
Chapter 20. Last Years in Business (1947-1949) 221
Chapter 21. Loneliness and Despair (1951-1956) 227
Chapter 22. Ernest's Last Years (1956-1960) 243
Chapter 23. Epilogue 250
Organ Specifications 253
Bibliography 283
Index 293
Photographs 301

Ernest M. Skinner
photograph by C. H. Freeman, Wakefield, Massachusetts
courtesy of Edward H. Hastings via Joseph Dzeda

CHAPTER 1

Childhood and Apprenticeship, 1866-1890

IN NORTHWESTERN PENNSYLVANIA, among the rolling foothills of the Appalachian Mountains, is a small city named Clarion. Aside from a modern college campus, a scattering of gas stations, and other obvious landmarks of the twentieth century, much of this pleasant community, with its century-old store buildings, churches, and charming gingerbread-trimmed houses, is not appreciably different from the little mid-Victorian town that it was when Ernest Martin Skinner was born there in the winter of 1866.

The center of Clarion is dominated by the large, dark-red sandstone City Hall which dates back to the 1880s, replacing the previous one which was destroyed by fire along with all the birth records. Among them undoubtedly was that of Ernest Skinner. Consequently, there is no way of knowing the house where he was born or whether it exists today. This event most likely took place in a hotel or rooming house, for his parents, Washington and Alice Skinner, who were both concert singers, were on the road staging an opera in Clarion at the time, moving on soon after his birth. The very name of his birthplace, an organ stop, foreshadowed his destiny. Within half a century Ernest Skinner would become one of the greatest and most influential organ builders in America.

Among Ernest's ancestors are several who foreshadow his talents. They include Otis Brett, his maternal grandfather, who was an itinerant teacher, and Nathan Skinner, a skilled craftsman who worked as a trunk maker. But most illustrious was John Alden, whose name was immortalized by the poem "The Courtship of Miles Standish," and who, by some accounts, was the first man to step ashore when the *Mayflower* arrived at Plymouth in 1620.[1] Skinner's ancestral connection with John Alden was through his mother, with young Ernest being the tenth generation descendant. This lineage was to be a source of considerable pride to him in his later years.[2] John Alden was evidently skilled with his hands, for he was originally a cooper in his home country of England and was employed in making repairs on the *Mayflower* during her voyage to the "New World." Alden was also a man of integrity, keen intelligence, and determination, a man "highly esteemed for his probity, sagacity and resolution." Another trait which was to be inherited by Ernest's mother and by Ernest himself was John Alden's long life span. Alden lived to be eighty-eight years old, an exceptionally advanced age for those days, being at the time of his death the "last surviving signer of the *Mayflower* Compact."

Ernest's father, Washington Martin Skinner, was born on 7 November 1836 in Lowell, Massachusetts. His mother, Alice Francis Brett, was born on 30 August 1844 in Houlton, Maine. Alice Brett was twenty years old and Washington Skinner was nearly twenty-eight years of age when they married on 5 November 1864 in Marlboro, Massachusetts. A little over one year later their first child, Ernest M. Skinner, was born on 15 January 1866. When Ernest was two years old, a brother, Harry Clifford Skinner, was born on 30 August 1868 in Craftsbury, Vermont. As in the case when Ernest was born, the Skinners were apparently on a concert tour.

Ernest had a great uncle, his paternal grandfather's brother, who was a music teacher. In addition to this uncle and Ernest's parents, there were also other musical members of the family. With so much musical talent in the Skinner family, it probably was not much of a surprise when, as a young child, Ernest began to show a fascination with producing musical sounds. When the Skinners went to visit relatives or friends, the young Ernest delighted in running his fingers around the rims of tumblers to make music (undoubtedly, much to the hostesses' chagrin!). He would try to get music out of everything he could get his hands on. This was no doubt an omen of the direction his life was to take. Ernest's musical sensitivity was destined to find expression not in the composing, performing, or teaching of music, but in the creation of musical tone through the medium of organ pipes.

It was well that Ernest did not seek his creative fulfillment in the playing of keyboard instruments. The little fingers of both of his hands had no joints and were unusually small. This condition, no doubt, would have been a handicap to fluent playing of the piano or the organ.

Ernest did, in fact, have difficulty in reaching an octave on the keyboard.[3]

By the time Ernest was seven years old, his parents had given up their nomadic way of life as touring concert artists and settled down to a permanent home in Taunton, Massachusetts.[4] This may have been due to the fact that their two boys were now old enough to attend school. Ernest's childhood home, a large two-and-a-half story frame house at 10 Spring Street in Taunton, is still standing.[5]

According to his daughter, Eugenia Shorrock, Ernest Skinner talked very little about his early life. However, from Mrs. Shorrock and her sister, Ruth Scott, we learn a little of early relationships between the young Ernest and his family. His brother Harry did not share Ernest's musical inclinations and the two of them did not get along very well. Ernest also disliked his father and his grandfather. He particularly hated his father, whom Mrs. Shorrock describes as being very pompous and abrupt. His dislike probably accounted for the fact that he always refused to use their common middle name "Martin."

In spite of the hostility Ernest felt toward his father, it was his father who introduced him to the world of music. Washington Skinner organized an opera company in Taunton when Ernest was about ten years old. He took his son with him to rehearsals and performances of the Gilbert and Sullivan operas which the company presented, thus creating in Ernest a "great love for these operas. This great love went a bit further and included the prima donna."[6] Of this first romance, Ernest recalls, "I fell violently in love with the star Ida Mulle, who was engaged for the principal solo part." This obviously one-sided romance did not last, for the object of Ernest's affections left his father's opera company, making the young boy "sick at heart."[7] Ernest sent her a Maybasket full of candy as a token of his regard. Thus ended this affair of the heart. But that period of his life marked the beginning of a much more enduring love affair. The hearing of those Gilbert and Sullivan operas instilled in Ernest a consuming love of music which was to be the motivating force behind his entire creative life.

When Ernest Skinner was about fourteen years old, he and his family left Taunton, taking up residence in West Somerville, Massachusetts, where he attended high school for about six months.[8] According to his autobiography, which appeared in the March 1951 issue of *The Diapason,* Ernest left high school because he "made no progress in Latin." However, there was also a more practical reason why his formal schooling ended prematurely. Hard times came to the Skinners, and Ernest was obliged to go to work to help support his family.[9]

Little is known about Ernest's teen-age years, following his departure from school, except that he "worked in various places, two of which were mercantile . . ." Work as a shopkeeper apparently had little appeal for him, for he then found employment in a candy factory where he ate his fill of candy the first day. That, likewise, was merely a job to Ernest, and so he struggled through these uncertain years when he "couldn't see much ahead and couldn't seem to get anywhere."[10]

During these teen-age years of aimlessness, Ernest apparently was troubled by prevailing concepts of God and religion. Like most of the Victorian period, the early 1880's were characterized by moral seriousness and its attendant concern with propriety and virtue. Specifically, Ernest had a great deal of exposure to the strongly Calvinistic doctrines emphasized by the Baptists, since he served as a bellows pumper in a Baptist church for several years. His home life reinforced these attitudes and doctrines. His father was remote and authoritarian; his mother was very stern and allowed no liberties.

It is hardly surprising, then, that Ernest conceived of God as a stern and remote judge. But his intelligence and sensitivity led him to struggle with this conception. We know that he had great difficulty accepting the line, "lead us not into temptation," from the Lord's Prayer. To Ernest, this implied that God would deliberately tempt one to do evil, and, throughout his life, he refused to use the phrase. Instead, he substituted, "deliver us from temptation and from evil."[11] Ernest's struggle against the stern image of God culminated in a dream, which profoundly affected his outlook. This intensely vivid dream remained indelibly imprinted upon his mind. Later, as a very old man, Ernest described this dream:

> I dreamed that I died and met the Most High who took me up in his arms as 'tho *[sic]* I were an infant and talked to me for quite a long time and finally answered a question I asked in so witty a manner that I had to laugh and laughed so heartily that I woke up laughing and was grieved beyond words to realize it to be a dream which . . . I have never forgotten . . . It has really influenced my whole life. I think it was really a vision and every detail of what happened is as alive today after sixty eight years as the day after it happened . . . The landscape, people and what happened is as vivid as when it came to me.[12]

Ernest Skinner's dream-vision apparently led him to perceive God as having warmth, love, and a sense of humor—an image which was a sharp contrast to the current Victorian concept of God. No doubt, the religious beliefs Ernest acquired as a result of this dream were to be what would guide and sustain him throughout the rest of his long and eventful life.

Some of Ernest's adolescent ennui, and certainly his dissatisfaction with the jobs he had, must have come from his lack of opportunity to pursue "the absorbing passion of his life."[13] That passion was conceived at the Unitarian Church in Taunton, where Washington Skinner was employed as the tenor of a quartet. It was there that Ernest saw his first pipe organ.[14] "It was a clumsy instrument operated by a hand-blown bellows," but young Ernest was fascinated by it.[15] At that time, the ten-year-old boy was unable to move the bellows handle owing to his "small strength and height."[16] A few years later, Ernest had grown big and strong enough to be engaged as bellows pumper for the practice hours of Mr. Edward M. French, who was then organist of the Baptist Church (now Winthrop Street Baptist Church) in Taunton.[17] In exchange for his labors, he was given fifteen cents per hour and was allowed by Mr. French to arrive early and go inside the instrument to study its mechanism to his "heart's content." *The Pipe Organ Pumper* calls him "a conscientious pumper. On difficult numbers he insisted that the organist give him a copy of the music so he could time his minimum and maximum effort to a fine point."[18] He also did his first organ repair. Ernest recalls: "One day when something went wrong with the bellows I found the hinge of an entire fold had broken loose. I was very proud at having found unaided the cause of the difficulty."[19] Once having diagnosed the cause of the problem, Ernest repaired it himself.[20]

When he was twelve years old, Ernest made his first attempt to build an organ. "It was to be a self-playing organ operated by a drum with pins in the surface to strike the notes." He constructed small wooden pipes for this instrument, but could not get them to speak. For assistance in this matter, he went to Mr. S. M. Tinkham, piano tuner and salesman in a piano store. Mr. Tinkham was unable to give Ernest much help, so his first organ building venture remained uncompleted.[21]

During the time that he served as bellows pumper at the Baptist Church, Ernest also assisted the organ tuners, Mr. Cadwater and Mr. Lahaise, when they would come to tune and make repairs on the organ.[22] Erasme Lahaise, upon his retirement from the Hook & Hastings Organ Company in 1931, tells of this encounter with Ernest many years before:

> I recall with pride that fifty years ago in November I was tuning the organ in the First Baptist Church, Taunton. My assistant at that

time was only a boy, but he was a genius. He was no other than Ernest M. Skinner.[23]

Ernest's genius and inclination, however, were frustrated for the five years when he moved aimlessly and indifferently from job to job. Finally, when Ernest was twenty (1886), his father arranged for George H. Ryder, "a small organ builder of Reading, Mass," with whom Washington Skinner was "personally acquainted," to take on Ernest as a shop boy.[24]

> My first duty was to sweep the shop after which I wound trackers. After a little while I wound them with a hand operated machine, which I contrived, at about twice the ordinary speed.[25]

Ernest soon developed a growing interest in the art of voicing, a process by which organ pipes are manipulated to give them a desired tonal quality. However, the possibility of acquiring this skill was to remain out of his reach for the time being. Later on Ernest spent part of his time as an assistant to Ryder's voicer and tuner, Wm. H. Dolbier, who apparently was not very willing to share his knowledge with his inquisitive apprentice. But Ernest did not let this stop him from learning:

> I desired to know the theory of setting a temperament but found it was a secret. "Charlie" Moore, a reed voicer for Samuel Pierce, finally told me to sharp the fourths and flatten the fifths and this is all the instruction I ever had in the art of tuning. I bought a piano hammer and practiced on my father's piano by putting it out of tune. I remember my joy the first time I succeeded in killing the "wolf." As time went on and my small experience found opportunity I hunted tuning methods and possibilities to a finish.[26]

In the later years of his employment with Ryder, Ernest spent many months exclusively in tuning, during which time "he developed a practice of setting the temperament on every class of register, including mixtures, by ignoring the octave and using fourths and fifths alone." He developed this into a process which was both speedy and accurate.[27]

After four years of working at Ryder's shop, Ernest was "fired one morning by a new Irish foreman . . ."[28] According to Ernest,

> The foreman was Mr. Horace Marden who was a fine man and very helpful, but he got a position soon after I was there with Geo. S.

Hutchings and was followed by an Irish foreman who not only knew nothing but was an iltempered idiot whos [sic] manner soon drove me out of the place . . .[29]

His firing proved to be a blessing in disguise, for Ernest immediately was employed as a tuner by George S. Hutchings of Boston, probably through the good graces of his former foreman, Mr. Marden.[30]

Shortly after he commenced his employment with Hutchings, Ernest left to work for Jesse Woodberry of Boston, who offered him a job traveling as an outside man, installing organs, and promised to send him with "an organ going South." Ernest had a great desire to travel and was "somewhat crestfallen to learn that said organ was going to South Boston . . ."! Since that was as far south as he was to travel at that time, Ernest went back to work for Hutchings. By now, his greatest ambition was to become a voicer, and he returned to Hutchings with the promise of a voicing job. This desire was to remain unfulfilled, however, for in the meantime Hutchings' draftsman left and Ernest was given this position instead. Nevertheless, his association with Hutchings proved to be most valuable. Ernest Skinner was to remain with that firm for the next eleven years, during which time his duties would expand to include those of mechanic, tuner, and eventually factory superintendent.[31]

FOOTNOTES

[1]This account of John Alden is entered in *Encyclopedia Americana,* 1966 ed.
[2]Ernest M. Skinner, Letter to Alexander McCurdy, 26 August 1954.
[3]This genetic trait was shared by Ernest's father and brother and later transmitted to Ernest's son, Richmond.
[4]Arthur Hudson Marks, "A Biography of Ernest M. Skinner," *Stop, Open, and Reed,* 1, no. 4 (December 1922), p. 2.
[5]Taunton Historical Society, Taunton, Mass.
[6]T. Scott Buhrman, "Ernest M. Skinner: Organ Builder," *The American Organist,* 8, no. 5 (May 1925), p. 173.
[7]Marks, p. 2.
[8]Marks, p. 2; see also Ernest M. Skinner, "Ernest M. Skinner Recalls the Past on 85th. Birthday," *The Diapason,* March 1951, p. 4, and Buhrman, p. 173.
[9]Personal interview with Ruth Scott, 10 October 1972.
[10]Marks, p. 2.
[11]Ernest M. Skinner, Letter to Alexander McCurdy, 22 July 1954.
[12]Ernest M. Skinner, Letter to Alexander McCurdy, 19 June 1954.
[13]Helen Hulett Searl, "Wizard of the Pipes," *Christian Science Monitor,* 5 June 1943, p. 6.
[14]Skinner, "Ernest M. Skinner," p. 4.
[15]Searl, p. 6.
[16]Marks, p. 2.
[17]Marks, p. 2.
[18]Chet Shafer, *The Pipe Organ Pumper* (New York: Greenberg, 1926), p. 52.

[19] Marks, p. 2.
[20] Buhrman, p. 173.
[21] Marks, p. 2, and Skinner, "Ernest M. Skinner," p. 4. Quotation from Marks, p. 2.
[22] Marks, p. 2.
[23] "Boston News," *The American Organist,* 14, no. 12 (December 1931), p. 751.
[24] Marks, p. 2, and Buhrman, p. 174.
[25] Buhrman, p. 174.
[26] Buhrman, p. 175.
[27] Buhrman, p. 175.
[28] Buhrman, p. 176.
[29] Ernest M. Skinner, Letter to Barbara Owen, 16 April 1957.
[30] Skinner, Letter to Barbara Owen, 16 April 1957.
[31] Marks, p. 3-4.

CHAPTER 2

Courtship and Marriage 1893

ERNEST SKINNER was by now in his mid-twenties and well established in his chosen career. Fairly slim and about five feet ten inches tall, he was a handsome young bachelor with dark brown hair and blue eyes. Ernest had left his parents and was living alone in Somerville, Massachusetts. While attending a concert, he saw a beautiful young woman who was soon to become an important part of his life. A petite girl in her early twenties with light brown, curly locks and blue eyes, Mabel Hastings was just the sort of vision to captivate immediately the fancy of a romantic young man such as Ernest Skinner.

Mabel was born in Bethel, Maine, on 29 August 1869.[1] Her father, D. S. Hastings, was a civil engineer. He was surveyor for the laying out of the Northern Pacific Railroad, the first northern rail route to link the east and west coasts of the United States. While Mr. Hastings was working on this project during the 1860s, he fell in love with the state of Montana. Later he bought land near Ubet and set up a sheep ranch. On this ranch Mabel spent much of her childhood. She was still living there when, as a young woman, she became engaged to be married. The subsequent death of her fiancé left Mabel suffering from a nervous breakdown. Her parents decided that the best way to help her recover from her grief was to send her to work in Boston.

After coming to Boston, Mabel was employed as a secretary at Sprague & Hathaway, a portrait artist and framing concern. A Mabel Skinner (no relation to Ernest Skinner) was also a secretary at Sprague & Hathaway. Eventually, Mabel Hastings went on a blind date along with Mabel Skinner, whose date was Harry Skinner, Ernest

Skinner's brother. Mabel Hastings' date turned out to be none other than Ernest M. Skinner. It is a matter of conjecture whether Ernest had engineered this meeting himself. However it happened, this date marked the beginning of a flourishing romance.

Mabel was quiet and reserved, with a "gentle personality that blossomed after a slow beginning with strangers."[2] Her quiet, unassuming disposition was a perfect complement to Ernest's rather outgoing and aggressive temperament. Also, having graduated from Fryeburg Academy in Maine when she was about eighteen, Mabel was well-educated for a woman in those days and was obviously intelligent. Possessing brains as well as beauty, this gentle young lady evidently inspired Ernest's unbounded admiration. In a very short time, Ernest knew that he wanted Mabel for his wife and thereafter waged an intensive campaign to persuade her to marry him.

The date on which Ernest proposed to Mabel is unknown, but it was apparently during a season when the weather was fairly warm and pleasant and conducive to staying outside. During the nineteenth century, there were few public parks. Instead, Victorian cemeteries, which were beautifully landscaped, served this purpose for those who desired a pleasant place to walk and enjoy the out-of-doors. Mount Auburn Cemetery in Cambridge is just such a place, and it was there that Ernest asked Mabel to marry him. Time flies for those who are deeply in love, and before they knew it, it was sundown and the gates of the cemetery had been locked for the night. Upon discovering their predicament, Ernest and Mabel yelled for help. Fortunately someone heard their calls and let them out.

According to Ruth Scott, her parents' courtship and betrothal did not span more than two years. It was most likely in the year following his proposal that Ernest married Mabel. Their wedding took place on 29 March 1893 in the parlor of the Hastings' spacious old home in Bethel, Maine. The ceremony was at eleven o'clock in the morning, and the wedding party, which consisted of the bride and groom, the best man, and the maid of honor, entered the parlor to the strains of of the "Bridal Chorus," from Wagner's *Lohengrin*. Following the ceremony a light meal was served for the bridal party and the thirty-five relatives and friends who were present for the occasion, after which the bride and groom, with gifts "choice and numerous," departed "for their home in Boston amid a shower of rice, old slippers, and the best wishes of their friends" to begin their married life together.[3]

Ernest and Mabel's first home, a two-and-a-half story frame house at 293 Savin Hill Avenue, located near Dorchester Bay in the Dorchester district of Boston, was relatively simple as Victorian houses go. This house, which they rented, was to be their home for the first two years of their married life.

As with all newly-wed couples, Ernest and Mabel each had to make certain adjustments as they became accustomed to living as husband and wife. One particularly frustrating problem that they encountered stemmed from the fact that Ernest snored. He could fall asleep "at the drop of a hat." He also slept soundly and was apt to sleep late in the morning. Unfortunately, he snored so loudly that no one else could sleep in the same room with him. Consequently, it was not long before Ernest and Mabel were sleeping in separate bedrooms. Ernest felt very bad about his snoring and even submitted to an operation with the hope of curing it. However, this operation failed to produce the desired result, for he still snored as noisily as ever. There was nothing else Ernest and Mabel could do except continue to sleep in separate rooms. Years later, when the Skinner family acquired a summer home at Alton Bay, New Hampshire, Ernest was segregated in his own room in the back of the cottage, on the first floor, while other members of the family and guests slept in the upstairs bedrooms.

Mabel was devoted to Ernest and would do almost anything to please him. She always wore blue because it was his favorite color. According to one account, she also served Ernest his breakfast in bed on a tray. It always consisted of two fried eggs, sunny-side up.[4] Ernest was not hard to please when it came to meals. He was content to eat well-prepared but ordinary food. One of his great weaknesses was strawberry jam. He was also very fond of coffee. Ernest loved to brew coffee and, with the same thoroughness with which he approached everything else in life, was forever trying new ways to make that perfect cup of coffee. However, he had no aptitude for cooking. Fortunately for him, Mabel was an excellent cook.

After two years of marriage, Ernest and Mabel moved to a larger house at 7 Evandale Terrace, only a few blocks from their first home on Savin Hill Avenue.[5] Located on Savin Hill, one of the best neighborhoods in Dorchester, the house was at the end of the street, overlooking Dorchester Bay. The Skinners lived so close to the Bay that they had their own beach right next to the house. Ernest's love of the water was probably one of the main reasons they bought that house. Every house that he and Mabel were to own throughout their long married life would be near the water.

Ernest and Mabel were to spend the next thirty-three years of their lives at 7 Evandale Terrace, and it was there that she was to give birth to all three of their children. Their first child, Eugenia Skinner, was born on 21 July 1896, about a year after they moved to Evandale

Terrace. Richmond Hastings Skinner, their second child and only son, was born two years later on 10 August 1898. Ernest was very proud of his children, but he would not be around much to enjoy them while they were growing up. Other concerns were vying for his attention during these years.

FOOTNOTES

[1] Letter received from Edward H. Hastings, 10 July 1972.
[2] Letter received from Edward H. Hastings, 12 April 1972.
[3] Skinner-Hastings wedding announcement, from unidentified newsclippings, 1893.
[4] Letter received from Alexander McCurdy, 24 April 1974.
[5] The house at 7 Evandale Terrace is still standing today. However, a large portion of Dorchester Bay that it once overlooked is now filled in, and the Skinner family's beach has been replaced by a freeway.

CHAPTER 3

Romanticism and the Orchestral Ideal, 1894-1898

BY 1894 ERNEST SKINNER had worked in the organ business long enough to have some fairly well-defined opinions. At this point in his career he became preoccupied with the concept of an ideal organ. This ideal organ was to have "a complete tonal resource" along with perfect mechanical equipment that was designed for the maximum convenience of the organist. This ideal organ not only would contain all the traditional organ voices that were characteristic of the pipe organ throughout its long history but would also incorporate the sounds of many orchestral instruments such as the French Horn, Saxophone, and Oboe. It was to be what Ernest termed "a *practical* organ," which would be "suitable in every way for any purpose for which a pipe organ can be utilized."[1]

Ernest's concept of the ideal organ had its roots in the Romantic Movement which began in Europe and England during the later part of the eighteenth and early nineteenth century. Prior to this time, objectivity, clarity in presentation, perfection of form, and the emotional restraint which characterized the classic ideal were the standards by which literature, music, and all other artistic works were judged. The new romantic spirit, which affected every phase of artistic expression, was a progressive spirit which rebelled against established conventions and traditions. This romanticism was marked by subjectivity, a desire to express one's personality, feelings, and ideals without being restricted by external rules or standards.

Beginning primarily as a literary movement, romanticism soon extended its influence to the musical world. Indeed, many romantic composers of the early to mid-nineteenth century derived much of their inspiration from literary works. This resulted in new forms of music as programmatic orchestral works and romantic operas based on folk-lore, mythology, and poetry of the Middle Ages. The most outstanding examples of this new subjective type of music were the symphonic poems of Franz Liszt, the symphonies of Hector Berlioz, and the operas of Richard Wagner.

The wealth of programmatic music composed during the romantic era demanded a more expressive medium for its interpretation. An improved and enlarged symphony orchestra was developed to meet this requirement. It was not long before the symphony orchestra and its literature assumed great importance and popularity in the musical world.

The romantic movement and the ensuing popularity of symphonic music soon began to affect the organ. Romantic influences were first noticeable in the organs of Germany and France. Prior to the romantic era, the pipe organs of those countries had been bright, clear, and silvery in tone, with a predominance of upper work in the form of mixtures and mutations. The brilliant reed stops of these organs were rather coarse in tone and often imitative of various early instruments such as krummhorns and sackbuts, forerunners of modern instruments. In the mid-1800's, however, the tonal character of European organs began to change perceptibly. Upperwork decreased as a greater proportion and variety of 8' stops were included. The over-all sound of these instruments became richer, heavier, and more massive, with some stops being introduced which vaguely suggested the tone of clarinets, oboes, and orchestral strings.

The romantic idea of the symphonic organ reached the United States in the 1860s. Prior to this time, American organs had not been very different in tonal character from their earlier European counterparts, although, because American churches were smaller, so were the organs. Like the European organs of the eighteenth and early nineteenth centuries, the tone of the early American organs was bright and clear, but these instruments had proportionately fewer reed stops and their tonal resources were limited.

The trend toward orchestral sound in American organs began in 1863 with the importation of the German-built Walcker organ for the Boston Music Hall, Boston, Massachusetts. This organ, of four manuals and eighty-four registers, was probably the largest instrument to be installed in this country to that time. Compared to existing American organs, its tone was much heavier and it had a greater variety of 8' voices.[2] This instrument was subsequently to have a great influence on American organ builders.[3]

The establishment and growth of high caliber symphony orchestras in the United States during the later decades of the nineteenth century did much to stimulate interest in orchestral music.[4] As a result, orchestral transcriptions became quite popular in organ recital programs. This, of course, affected the tonal design of organs during that era. American organ builders began to build instruments with less upperwork and an increasing proportion and variety of 8' tone. But American organists and organ builders were not content to stop with the approximation of orchestral sound which was characteristic of the European romantic instruments. They desired an organ which would, as closely as possible, imitate the symphony orchestra. In order to interpret efficiently the orchestral transcriptions which were now much in vogue, they needed an instrument which not only had massive tone, but also possessed a variety of color in the form of stops which imitated the sounds of symphonic instruments, together with the dynamic flexibility of the symphony orchestra.

If the state of technology had remained as it was in the 1860s this ideal of an imitation symphony orchestra would have remained forever out of the reach of American organ builders. In order to approach imitating the smooth and full-bodied tone qualities of orchestral instruments in an organ, it was necessary to have higher wind pressures. Before the 1860s all American organs had tracker action, which consisted of a direct mechanical linkage between the keyboards and the pipe chests. One great disadvantage of this action was that the more stops employed or the higher the wind pressure used, the more difficult it became to depress the keys. Thus, the wind pressures, as well as the size of the organ, were limited by mechanical action.

Even if it had been possible to utilize higher pressures, thus acquiring the means to produce orchestral sounds, there was no way of conveniently playing a wide-compass pedal keyboard while simultaneously controlling dynamics via the swell pedal, which was not balanced until later in the nineteenth century. The swell boxes of most organs built during the first three-quarters of the nineteenth century were controlled by an unbalanced pedal which may have hitched in the open or closed position, or may have been held at a position in between or variably manipulated by the right foot, leaving the left only to play the pedal keyboard, which may have been of short compass.

Some mechanical improvements had been introduced to this country with the import of the Boston Music Hall organ in 1863. The balanced swell pedal, which was introduced with this instrument, "greatly increased the tonal flexibility and expressiveness of the organ."[5] The Boston Music Hall organ also had a register crescendo device whereby individual stops could be successively added by the use of a foot pedal.[6]

The wind supply for the Boston Music Hall organ was provided by a hydraulic blower which depended on water rather than man-power for its operation.[7] This was probably the first hydraulic blower to be used in the United States. By 1876 organ builders began to experiment with electric motors for supplying wind.[8] However, the electric rotary fan, which is used today, did not come into use until 1900.[9]

The first step toward overcoming the limitations that mechanical key action imposed on wind pressures and organ size came in the mid-1860s in America when builders began using in their larger organs a pneumatic lever invented in 1832 by the Englishman Charles S. Barker. Somewhat later, the adoption of tubular-pneumatic action further enhanced options in tonal design and voicing. Toward the end of the 1860s, American organ builders Hilborne Roosevelt and John C. B. Standbridge began to experiment with electric action.[10]

By the early 1890s American organs had changed considerably from what they had been in 1860. These later organs had a greater proportion of 8' stops, with relatively little upperwork. They were now much larger, more powerful, and more orchestral in sound. Greater dynamic control and easier registration changes were possible as a result of improvements in action and console controls.

Nevertheless and despite the progress made during the preceeding quarter century, organs built with electric action during the early 1890s were unreliable and slow in response.[11] Also, the various stops of American organs still lacked the smooth, refined tone of the orchestral instruments after which they were named, and which they were presumably voiced to imitate.

It was at this point in the evolution of the symphonic organ that Ernest M. Skinner became much interested in the orchestral ideal. Significantly, Ernest was the embodiment of the romantic spirit which had given birth to this ideal. A strong individualist, possessing an unfailing optimism and a powerful creative drive, Ernest took up where others had left off in working toward the romantic orchestral ideal. It was he who was to play a central role in bringing this concept to its fullest realization. Essentially, Ernest's ideal was that of an all-purpose organ which combined a traditional tonal structure, including mixtures, with the variety in color, tonal refinement, and musical flexibility of a symphony orchestra. In 1894 many features of Ernest's projected ideal existed only in his imagination. The fulfillment of his ideal was dependent upon mechanical equipment which was fast, reliable, and convenient to use. But the mechanism of the organ, as it existed at that time, was still inadequate for the kind of organ Ernest envisioned.

During most of his sojourn with Hutchings, Ernest Skinner's creative work was devoted primarily to the refinement of his electric action and to a general improvement in the mechanical equipment of the organ. By 1892 he had developed a pneumatic swell pedal action which was instantaneous in response, giving the organist perfect control over expression.[12] This was his first patented invention.[13]

In 1893 Ernest designed the first electric action that Hutchings built. This action, which was used in the organ installed in St. Bartholomew's Church in New York City, "proved unreliable, but two years later was successfully reconstructed by the company according to Skinner's design with a different magnet."[14]

By 1896 Ernest had made many improvements in his electric action. These included a permanently adjusted armature valve; a high resistance magnet using the permanently adjusted armature valve; a coupler action employing multiple windings on key action magnets to take the place of extra key-contacts for each coupler to a given keyboard; a highly efficient closed-circuit stop action; a crescendo pedal which added stops in succession by means of a "master contact sequentially completing circuits actuating stops," made possible by the closed-circuit stop action; an electric sforzando device which engaged all stops at once by closing all register circuits simultaneously; and a movable, compact console with stop knobs on hinged stop jambs which swung out for use when being played, closing up to receive the roll-top when not in use.[15]

By 1896 Ernest Skinner was Hutchings's factory superintendent.[16] During the following two years, he supervised the installation of numerous organs for the Hutchings firm. Among these were many Massachusetts installations: Harvard Church, Brookline; Mission Church, Roxbury; Union Congregational Church, Worcester; Pilgrim Church, Dorchester; and Arlington Street Church, Boston. All of these were made with Ernest's new electric action, incorporating his electrical and mechanical improvements as they were developed.[17]

The most notable installation supervised by E. M. Skinner during these years was the organ built by the Hutchings firm for South Congregational Church, New Britain, Connecticut, in 1896.[18] This instrument consisted of sixty-five stops and, according to a description furnished by organ historian Barbara Owen, was "the largest organ in Connecticut, and with one exception, the largest in New England." This description goes on to quote an "impartial expert," who stated that it was "the embodiment of the most advanced organ building in the world today." The New Britain organ contained all of Ernest's recently developed improvements, including his coupler action which used single contacts and multiple wound magnets. This instrument also had the distinction of being the first installation using Ernest's new movable console. The action in this organ was described as being "lighter in touch than that of a grand piano," having "a marvelous capacity for repetition," being "instantaneously responsive," and having "met the most crucial tests." Another description of the New Britain organ states that "the entire instrument is wonderfully under control of the player and the conveniences supplied for the rapid change of combinations are almost bewildering at first sight."[19]

The New Britain organ also showed evidence of tonal innovation. In this instrument, certain tonal characteristics emerged which were to be identified with Ernest Skinner's work from then on. The description in the dedication program furnished by Barbara Owen includes these tonal resources:

> Particular attention will be directed to the voicing of the instrument, which is as beautiful and unusual as is the action unique and complete. The single aim of both builder and those having the work in charge has been to produce a *musical* organ, and to that end neither pains nor expense has been spared. Many organs are forced even in the diapasons, and especially in the mixtures in order to "fill the church." This organ is so resourceful, owing to its comprehensive scheme, that forcing is entirely unnecessary. The full organ effect, therefore, is dignified, massive and brilliant, completely filling the church, yet without harshness.
>
> Especially noteworthy is the great number of reeds in the scheme, there being no less than sixteen stops of reeds, four of them being sixteen feet pitch. The brilliancy of the organ is secured by this generous use of reeds, as in the modern foreign organs, while the screaming mixtures often predominant have been subordinated, as instanced by the five rank mixture in the swell, which is so subdued and silvery as to be available as a solo stop in combination even with the vox humana.
>
> The string stops are seldom equalled in any organ. The Swell Vox Celestis when heard with the Pedal Orchestral 'Cello (itself tuned with a wave) gives one the impression of a large body of strings in an orchestra.
>
> In the fundamental tone of the organ, the diapasons, there is no lack, the tone being especially churchly, full and mellow, and strongly suggestive of the celebrated English diapasons.
>
> The effects that can be produced by the softer combinations are

> simply wonderful. The tone seems to come from no particular place, but pervades the entire church, and has the peculiar floating quality of music heard in large cathedrals.

It was this non-directional, "floating" tonal quality which was to become particularly characteristic of Ernest Skinner's work. These descriptive notes pertaining to the New Britain organ also make mention of its "unusually large and complete" pedal organ and "the variety and uniqueness of orchestral effects which can be produced upon it."

Sometime around 1898 Ernest Skinner invented his high-speed pitman windchest action which was first used in the organ in the Dutch Reformed Church, Flatbush, Brooklyn.[20] By this time he had improved and refined his electric action to a considerable degree. It was to be further improved and modified within the next fifteen years, but he had come a long way. His newly developed pitman chest not only afforded greater speed and fluency in organ playing, but was also capable of operating on far higher wind pressures than were possible on the old mechanical action slider chests. This opened up a whole new world of possibilities in the realm of pipe voicing and organ tone. As Skinner himself stated, ". . . the modern organ, with its magnificent power and wealth of orchestral color and perfection of mechanism, is made possible wholly through the disassociation of the touch and the wind pressure."[21]

By 1898 Skinner had heard of the English organist and electrician-turned-organbuilder named Robert Hope-Jones, who was doing much experimentation with electric organ action and had recently made some important improvements in this field. News of Hope-Jones' work naturally aroused Ernest's interest and curiosity, and he developed a great desire to travel to England "for the express purpose of seeing the great Worcester Cathedral organ built by Hope-Jones, the reputation of which was filling all England and reaching out to America."[22] Luck was with Ernest. At that time he did the tuning and tone regulation of a residence organ belonging to Mr. Montgomery Sears, a wealthy Boston patron of the arts. Mr. Sears was so pleased with Ernest's work that he offered to send him abroad to learn what he could from the foreign builders.[23]

Ernest made his journey abroad in February of 1898, the entire round trip costing him $250.00. In an autobiographical sketch written in 1922 he tells about his voyage across the Atlantic:

> I went on a cattle steamer from Boston. It took ten days and I didn't see the sun once the whole trip as it was a howling hurricane from

start to finish. The ship heeled 39 degrees—the only other passengers were three horsemen who were taking over some horses to sell.[24]

Upon landing in Liverpool, Ernest "immediately went across to Birkenhead to the Hope-Jones factory." Hope-Jones was not there, but Ernest met his brother, who directed him to a Hope-Jones intallation in the Blind Asylum in Birkenhead. The only thing that impressed Ernest about the organ there was that "the strings seemed rather strident."[25]

It was only after he returned to London that Ernest actually met Hope-Jones. In his letter to C. A. Van Buskirk, he gives this account of his meeting:

> I then went to London and registered at the Thackery Hotel on Great Russell Street opposite the British Museum. Here Hope-Jones walked in on me one day while I was at lunch, after which we went up to my room and I showed him some of my patented compound wound magnets in which the coupling was done by winding on the magnets instead of by extra contacts. That evening he took me up to St. George's Church, Hanover Square . . . The first thing he showed me was the combination action which worked from the street current with such force that it could be heard all over the church. It was simply impossibly noisy, after which he played the organ to me. The tone was so brutal and harsh that I was much impelled to rush out of the church and get away from it. Afterwards in Liverpool he took me to see a very small organ of four manuals in which there were not more than four stops in the Swell organ—a Phonon and a powerful reed, and I don't remember what the others were, but the whole thing was simply brutal and destitute of musical value. I was so disgusted and disappointed with the whole business that I never went near the Worcester Cathedral . . .

However, Ernest's stay in England was not wasted. Soon after his arrival in England he attended an organ concert at St. George's Hall, an event which was to make a lasting impression on him in more ways than one. In his autobiographical sketch in *Stop, Open, and Reed,* Ernest tells of this experience:

> Dr. Peace played operatic airs on a big Vox Humana to a crowd that filled the hall. After each number there was clapping and yelling and a spontaneous expression of enthusiasm in full keeping with what we hear in these United States at a ball game. There was no doubt whatever that Dr. Peace played to that crowd just what

would please them most and that they thoroughly enjoyed it. I then and there acquired an overwhelming sympathy with the idea of music for the common public as well as for the musician.[26]

That night at St. George's Hall, Ernest Skinner was also to make the acquaintance of another English organ builder, Henry Willis Jr., who, along with Henry Willis Sr. (known as "Father" Willis), was to exert a great influence on Ernest's methods of reed pipe construction and voicing:

> At St. George's Hall I was very fortunate in meeting Henry Willis, Jr., who was most agreeable to me. He sent a man with me to look at one of his organs and permitted me to take measurements of reeds and a fine tremolo which was fine in effect and noiseless. Afterwards at the dinner table he showed me where I had overlooked much of importance and further instructed me in the fundamental principles of reed voicing which were unknown in America as far as my experience goes.
> I had read of the Willis Tuba on 22" wind in St. George's Hall. When I heard it I was wild with enthusiasm. It was so incredibly fine and superior to anything I had ever heard. I owe everything I know of the trumpet family to Henry Willis, Senior and Junior. I was given the freedom of the St. George's Hall organ and I made the most of it.
> Later in London, I met Willis, Senior and his superintendent who thought I had something to sell and was on that account somewhat aloof. When he found I was just an admirer of the Willis work he sent me with an attendant to see one or two instruments in churches and he was very hospitable.[27]

Upon departing from England, Ernest went to Holland, which he found quite disappointing as far as the organs were concerned. He "found the touch of the organs abominable and the tone impossible," and described the ensemble as being "an aggregation of strident mixtures." Ernest's next stop on the continent was Antwerp, where he took the opportunity "to hear the celebrated chimes." From there, he traveled to Paris, where he met organists Charles-Marie Widor and Louis Vierne. The latter was to become a life-long friend. During his stay in France, Ernest also visited the factory of the leading organ builder in that country:

> I visited the factory of Cavaillé-Coll but did not see him as he was very old and seldom came to the factory. I saw a small instrument of his in an auxiliary showroom with the swell pedal in so awkward a position that when the foot was on the shoe the knee was two or three

inches above the great keys. I think he must have been experimenting with a balanced swell shoe.[28]

After another brief stop in England, Ernest returned to America, again in a cattle boat, and in another hurricane. Upon his return, he made his first replica of the Willis 16′ Trombone in the Hutchings factory.[29]

English methods of voicing high pressure reeds had probably not been totally unknown to Ernest prior to his trip to England. He may have initially been introduced to English reed voicing by Carlton Michell, an English organ builder who came to America in the mid-1880s. Michell became associated with Hutchings as a voicer in 1890, the same year Ernest began his work with that firm. In 1894, after leaving Hutchings, Michell designed an organ for St. Luke's Church, Germantown, Pennsylvania, incorporating many new features which were copied by other American builders. These features included the use of heavy pressure reeds and harmonic reeds.[30] Despite any possible influence from Carlton Michell, the importance of Ernest's visit to England cannot be minimized. There is no question that after his meeting with the Willises his high pressure reeds of the trumpet family showed a great improvement and refinement.

FOOTNOTES

[1] E. M. Skinner, "An Ideal Organ," *The Organ,* 2, no. 12 (April 1894), 290, quoted in Homer D. Blanchard, "The Organ in the United States: A Study in Design, Part II," *The Tracker,* 25, no. 1 (Fall 1980), p. 37.

[2] Orpha Ochse, *The History of the Organ in the United States* (Bloomington & London: Indiana University Press, 1975), p. 204.

[3] William Harrison Barnes & Edward B. Gammons, *Two Centuries of American Organ Building* (Melville, N.Y.: Belwin-Mills Publishing Corp., 1970), p. 32.

[4] Ochse, p. 197.

[5] Barnes, p. 117.

[6] Ochse, p. 203.

[7] Ochse, p. 203.

[8] Ochse, P. 268.

[9] Barnes & Gammons, p. 32.

[10] Ochse, pp. 208, 265.

[11] Barnes, p. 249.

[12] "A Pneumatic Swell Pedal," *The Organ,* 1, no. 7 (November 1892), 164 (courtesy of E. A. Boadway).

[13] T. Scott Buhrman, "Mr. Ernest M. Skinner's Record," *The American Organist,* 19, no. 4 (1936), p. 126; Patent no. 500,040, *Specifications and Drawings of Patents,* 20 June 1893; This device was later replaced by Skinner's "Whiffle-tree" swell engine (Patent no. 1,076,069, *Specifications and Drawings of Patents,* 21 October 1913).

[14] Barnes & Gammons, p. 45.

[15] "Inventions and Tonal Developments of Ernest M. Skinner," *The Diapason,* February

1946, p. 17; Patent no. 595,660, *Specifications and Drawings of Patents,* 14 December 1897.

[16]Arthur Hudson Marks, "A Biography of Ernest M. Skinner," *Stop, Open, and Reed,* 1, no. 4 (December 1922), p. 4.

[17]Ernest M. Skinner, "Communications" (Letter to the Editor), *Pianist and Organist,* 3, no. 11 (November 1897), p. 283.

[18]Buhrman, p. 126; The Ernest M. Skinner Organ Company rebuilt and added an Antiphonal Organ to this instrument in 1910 (E. A. Boadway, "The Skinner & Aeolian-Skinner Opus List," *The Boston Organ Club Newsletter,* July & August 1972; Blanchard, pp. 40-41.

[19]Everett Truette Scrapbooks, Boston Public Library, MS.

[20]Buhrman, p. 126; According to a "List of Inventions and Tonal Developments of Ernest M. Skinner," *The Diapason,* February 1946, p. 17, Skinner's pitman chest was an adaptation of the "Casavant system of pneumatic valves supplying the pipes," given to him by that firm.

[21]Ernest M. Skinner, *The Modern Organ* (New York: H. W. Gray, 1917), p. 1.

[22]Ernest M. Skinner, Letter to C. A. Van Buskirk, 18 October 1932 (courtesy of Henry Karl Baker).

[23]Marks, p. 3.

[24]Marks, pp. 3 & 4; According to this autobiographical sketch, the first thing E. M. Skinner heard upon his arrival in England "was that the Maine had been blown up," thus starting the Spanish-American War.

[25]Skinner, Letter to C. A. Van Buskirk.

[26]Marks, p. 3.

[27]Marks, p. 3.

[28]Marks, p. 3 & 4.

[29]Barnes, p. 72.

[30]Ochse, pp. 235 & 258.

CHAPTER 4

Ernest Starts His Own Business, 1900-1907

IT WAS NOW 1900, the dawn of a new century. The first decade of the twentieth century was known as the "Age of Optimism," and Americans had good cause for their self-confidence.[1] This was an era of general and widespread prosperity. Food was plentiful and cheap. In recent years many new and useful devices such as the telephone, the sewing machine, the typewriter, the self-binding harvester, and the automobile had been invented and were now coming to be used by an increasing segment of the population. Over the preceding century, this country had grown from a little more than a dozen states along the eastern coast to a vast nation which spanned the entire North American continent, and it was now being drawn together by expanding railroad networks and newspaper chains. Thanks to the increasing use of mass production methods, the United States had become the leading industrial power of the world. Moreover, America had recently emerged from the Spanish-American War as a major military power. All this came about largely as a result of the driving energy and individualism which was characteristic of the American people during the nineteenth century.

This was no less a time of optimism for Ernest M. Skinner, for, at the beginning of the new century he saw his own horizons rapidly expanding. During the tenth and eleventh years of his association with Hutchings, Ernest "sold almost the entire output" of the firm, in addition to his "duties as superintendent, and draftsman and development work in tubular and electric actions."[2]

In 1900 Ernest took out a patent on a device which provided "greater facility of expression" in automatic piano-players.[3] He called this invention the *themodist* and described it as "a device applied to mechanical piano players which accents certain notes and makes it possible to bring the melody forward by mechanical means about as well as it can be done by the human player."[4]

One of the more important and most publicized installations he had supervised to date was the organ built by Hutchings in 1900 for Symphony Hall, Boston. This instrument was intended primarily for the purpose of supporting the "great choral works . . . given there by the Cecelia and Handel and Hayden [sic] societies," and had a "movable and detachable console."[5] This installation also incorporated the new Willis type reeds of the trumpet family. In the Everett Truette scrapbook at the Boston Public Library is this description of its tonal resources:

> The pedal trombone is voiced on the method developed by Willis, the celebrated London builder, giving power without sacrificing quality. The trumpet stops of the great and swell, in addition to the trombone, are voiced on a high air pressure and are made double length to middle F: in other words, they are what is called harmonic stops, which insures a proper balance between the bass and treble, the treble with old methods of voicing always being thin and weak, as well as more or less disagreeable in quality . . .
>
> The scales of the pipes in this organ are from 15 to 30 per cent larger than the scales usually employed in organs of this size, resulting in great solidity and firmness. This latter applies more particularly to the diapasons and flutes, which form the foundation tone of the organ.
>
> The pedal organ is very large in proportion to the balance of the organ, it having 14 stops . . .
>
> The voicing, on which mainly depends the success of the instrument . . . includes all the best points of European and American schools. The great delicacy and characteristic quality of tone in the different stops, the dignified power of the full organ, without harshness, and the perfect blending of the whole into one agreeable and massive tone, yet not lacking in brilliancy, are all successful features of the voicing of the organ.

In 1901 the Hutchings firm acquired the Votey Organ Company, subsequently forming the Hutchings-Votey Organ Company, with George Hutchings as the president of this new concern and Ernest Skinner as vice-president.[6] Now a partner with Mr. Hutchings, Ernest described their association as being "most pleasant" and "one of mutual confidence."[7] However, not all was well.

After sixteen years of experience in the organ business, Ernest "was still at arm's length" from that which he "longed to become, a voicer."[8] Also, his inventive genius had aroused the envy of some of the older men in the shop who "were extremely jealous" of all his new accomplishments.[9] This jealousy held Ernest back in his creative work and added to his dissatisfaction with the current situation. In his letter to Barbara Owen, he tells of the final events at Hutchings which led to his departure from that firm:

> I was with the Hutchings people for twelve years but they eventually got a so called business man into the office who not only had a domineering disposition but was so mean financially that some lumber people wouldn't sell us lumber because Plummer, the business man, found fault with it hoping to get a reduction in price. His treatment of clients also was so disrespectful that I frequently had to go and apologize to them and things finally got so bad that I was forced to tell Mr. Hutchings that he would have to choose between Plummer and myself. He chose me and told Plummer to get out, but had to pay him $15,000. for his stock in the Company. Well I don't seem to remember just what happened after that except that some very disagreeable thing happened, I think it related to design of mechanism which made repair work over necessary, but anyway I finally resigned . . .

Upon resigning from the Hutchings firm Ernest was on his own and, at last, was free to pursue his heart's desire—that of becoming a voicer. He started his own organ company with $4,300.00 capital, part of which was provided by the royalties on his piano accenting device.[10] In 1901 he began building and rebuilding organs in an unpretentious shop at 387 East Eighth Street in South Boston.[11] This factory, which Ernest described as a "shack," had formerly housed the Hale Rubber Works plant.[12] His first employee was William I. Hitchcock, who had been foreman of the chest department at Hutchings during the time that Ernest had been superintendent there. Hitchcock was to serve as Ernest's factory superintendent for the next thirteen years.[13]

The first organ to be built by Ernest's newly formed company was a two-manual instrument of seven stops which was installed in the Unitarian Church of Ludlow, Vermont.[14] The installation was completed by mid-July of 1902. A news item appearing in *The Vermont Tribune* on Friday, 18 July 1902, described the new Skinner organ as being "a handsome instrument; not gaudy or showy, but neat and attractive." According to this report, the organ case was constructed of quartered oak and mahogany, with show-front pipes "done in gold with a stippled surface."[15]

Shortly before this time Ernest had developed a duplex pitman chest which made it possible to draw each stop on this chest independently on two different manuals without the use of couplers. The duplex chest considerably increased the versatility of the small two-manual organs which constituted much of the new firm's output during the first years of its existence. The organ at the Unitarian Church in Ludlow, Vermont, was most likely the first instrument to contain Ernest's duplex action.[16] However, this instrument was not equipped with his electric action, but was built with tubular-pneumatic action.[17]

By the middle of 1902 Ernest Skinner's organ building business showed every indication of being a success. He had acquired several new contracts including the installation of a teaching organ in the new building of the New England Conservatory of Music; the installation of a two-manual tubular organ in San Salvadore Church, Broome Street, New York City; and extensive repairing and rebuilding of the organ in Grace Church, New York City. The reconstruction of the organ in prestigious Grace Church was the largest job undertaken by the firm to that time, and it added considerably to Ernest Skinner's growing reputation as an organ builder. This rebuild involved the installation of a new four-manual console which featured a concave-radiating pedal board designed and patented by Willis. This was a radical departure from the old flat pedal boards used previously by American organ builders. The old action was replaced by Skinner's own single contact electro-pneumatic action, developed while he was still with Hutchings. Also, a new Solo organ, consisting of an 8' Stentorphone, an 8' Grosse Flute, a 4' Flute, and a Tuba Mirabilis, was added.[18] Ernest was quite proud of this instrument and took great delight in showing off its capabilities to interested visitors.[19]

Also during 1902, Ernest Skinner became associated with Walter E. Young, an accomplished musician who had a number of years of experience in the piano and organ business and who was "ably fitted to look after the artistic side of a pipe organ manufacturing business."[20] Skinner's new firm became known as Ernest M. Skinner & Co.[21] By late that year, Charles A. Ryder, son of Ernest's first employer George Ryder, had been appointed as New York representative of the company "in order to take care of their constantly increasing business in the metropolis."[22]

The next year, 1903, promised to be even better for Ernest M. Skinner & Co., which, for a firm barely two years old, had an impressive number of contacts. At the beginning of that year, Ernest's new contracts included the rebuilding of a "large old organ" in the First

Dutch Reformed Church of Kingston, New York, and the construction of a new two-manual instrument for First Congregational Church of Brewer, Maine, both of which were to have "tubular pneumatic action throughout." Also, Ernest contracted to build three organs for private residences: a three-manual instrument for the home of J. Mitchell Clark of Newport, Rhode Island; an organ with a self-playing attachment for the home of Mrs. H. N. Slater of Readsville, Massachusetts; and a two-manual tubular organ with self-playing attachment for the home of T. Clarence Hollander of Wenham, Massachusetts.[23] The self-playing attachment employed in the last two residence installations was a very recent invention of Ernest Skinner, the first demonstration of this device apparently having been in 1901. At that time, "an interesting exhibition was given at the South Church, in New Britain, Conn. . . when the Aeolian was attached to the pipe-organ, and a well selected program was presented by Ernest M. Skinner."[24]

It is interesting to note that even though Ernest had developed an electric action which was reliable and quick in response, many of his first instruments were outfitted with the much older tubular-pneumatic action. This could have been for economic reasons, since the comparatively new electric action was barely out of the experimental stage and was probably much more expensive than the more widely used tubular-pneumatic action. Also, no doubt, there were many conservative customers who, wary of anything new and relatively unproven, did not trust those "new-fangled" electrical devices.

Sometime prior to May of 1903 Ernest Skinner took on James Cole as a partner, forming the Skinner & Cole Organ Co. Ernest was president of this new concern, with Cole serving as vice-president and Walter Young as secretary and treasurer. James Cole came to the Skinner firm with twenty-five years of experience in the organ business.[25] Both a voicer and an organist, he originally came from England and was said to have been trained in the art of voicing by Carlton Michell.[26] It was probably from Cole that Ernest learned to build the fine diapason chorus which was to become an important feature of his future creations.[27]

At the time the Skinner-Cole partnership was formed, contracts were signed for the construction of several two-manual organs. These included the Main Street Baptist Church in Saco, Maine; the Union Church in North East Harbor, Maine; and the First Methodist Episcopal Church in Atlantic City, New Jersey.[28] It is known that the North East Harbor organ had a Skinner & Cole nameplate, and it is most likely that the other two instruments were constructed during this brief partnership.[29]

The last Skinner & Cole organ was a three-manual instrument which was installed in the Evangelical Lutheran Church of the Holy Trinity, New York, Opus 113, in 1903.[30] The reason for the dissolution of the partnership is unknown. It has been hypothesized that Cole may have been too conservative to get along with the dynamically progressive Ernest Skinner.[31] The fact that in his writings Ernest never mentioned his association with Cole may mean that either he did not attach much importance to Cole's artistic contributions, or did not care to admit their value. Ernest was a very independent soul, and it has been said that when he saw someone else do something, he'd get the notion that he could improve on it—and he usually did![32] Anyway, by the end of 1903 James Cole had parted company with Ernest Skinner, remaining in relative obscurity until his death in 1934, while Skinner's fame continued to grow.[33]

On 16 January 1904, *The Music Trades* reported that Ernest Skinner's organ building firm, now called E. M. Skinner & Co., had "many good prospects for the year just entered," and that it had "built up a splendid trade, which extends into many states."

That year, Ernest introduced his Erzähler, the first of the many new stops which he was to develop over the next few decades.[34] The tone of the Erzähler is characterized by having a fundamental and an octave harmonic of equal strength, and it has the unusual property of blending with and re-enforcing the tonal quality of any stop with which it is combined. It was first used in the organ built for Christ Church, Hartford, Connecticut.[35] According to a letter written to Alexander McCurdy on 18 May 1954, Ernest did all his own flue voicing at the time the Erzähler was invented. In this letter he tells how this stop came into being:

> I rebuilt an organ in N. Y. state somewhere which has a bell gamba which they wanted made into something else as it was not of much value musically. Well I cut off the bells at the tie top of the lower conical part then transposed it to the proper pitch and noted a very pleasant character in its tone. I took note of its scale characteristics and when I got to the factory I made some pipes which exaggerated these peculiarities and had a most interesting tone which in my imagination seemed to be talkative, or trying to say something. I had a German working for me and asked him the German word for storyteller and he replied Erzähler, and there it was, an ideal name for a new tone . . . The Erzähler named itself.

An important contract secured by the Skinner firm during the year of 1904 was the $30,000 rebuilding of the organ at Plymouth Church,

Brooklyn.[36] This work resulted in what, except for the case and the old wood pipes, was virtually a new instrument. The new organ was "built according to the most modern ideas," incorporating electric action "with movable console, new wind chests, and new blowing plant."[37] The following quotation from an unidentified newsclipping conveys some idea of its sound:

> The instrument has been voiced with all due regard to the Church building and its acoustic properties. Every pipe is allowed to speak with ease, and as a result there are none of the ill-effects of overblowing or forcing the tone.
> A feature of the new organ will be the absence of the ear-splitting noise of the former tuba and stentorphone. There is no suggestion of harshness in the present organ, but the tone is round and full with plenty of reserve power. There are a great number of soft stops for endless variety of *nuances,* something that never before has been heard in Plymouth Church.

The newsclipping ends with these comments:

> When Mr. Skinner was given the contract he expressed the desire to build in Plymouth Church an organ that would loom up and surpass anything of its kind in this vicinity. Those who have heard the instrument feel that Mr. Skinner has more than kept his word. He has put his heart and soul into the work, and being a man of refined taste with a keen sense of artistic effect and musical balance, he has succeeded in impressing on the Plymouth organ his own personality.

In all truth, it was this ability to infuse his instruments with all the vitality, warmth, and charm of his own personality that created the very essence of the Skinner organ. This intense quality of personal expression in his instruments was the very thing which was to bring about Ernest's outstanding success as an organ builder in the succeeding decades, but in later years was to be his downfall.

In 1905 Skinner's organ building business was incorporated as a stock company "with subscriptions from Mr. George Foster Peabody of New York and from business friends in Worcester, Mass."[38] This new organization was called the Ernest M. Skinner Company and Ernest Skinner himself was its president.[39] One of his subscribers from Worcester became treasurer of the firm and, in addition to E. M. Skinner, the entire "office force at this time consisted of . . . one bookkeeper, one stenographer, and one draftsman."[40]

Meanwhile, the notorious English organ builder Robert Hope-Jones had come to America in 1903, first taking employment with the Austin Organ Company of Hartford, Connecticut, and then attempting to organize his own factory.[41] In spite of Ernest's disappointment with what he had seen and heard of Hope-Jones' work when he went to England, he began to doubt his own judgment after he returned to the United States and continued to hear praise of the Hope-Jones organ.[42] After Hope-Jones' attempt to establish his own firm did not materialize due to lack of capital, he approached Ernest "saying that his work had been a commercial failure, but an artist's success."[43] In 1905 Ernest took Hope-Jones into the Skinner organization, where he became vice-president and served "in the capacity of salesman."[44]

During his fifteen-month association with the company, Hope-Jones sold several organs. One of these instruments "was bought by Park Church, Elmira *[New York]*, which was built under his supervision."[45] Two other contracts signed by Hope-Jones were for the organs built for First Congregational Church of Collingwood, Ohio (Opus 131), and St. John's Church in Bridgeport, Connecticut (Opus 137).[46] Hope-Jones also sold the organ which E. M. Skinner built in 1906 for Trinity Cathedral, Cleveland, Ohio (Opus 140).[47]

When Ernest took Robert Hope-Jones into his organization, he had one hundred percent confidence in the man and thought him to be "a genius of whom people were jealous."[48] However, he soon thoroughly regretted forming this alliance. In a short time Hope-Jones proved to be a man who was not above resorting to deceit and trickery in order to get what he wanted—at Ernest Skinner's expense. In a letter written to C. A. Van Buskirk on 18 October 1932, Ernest recalls:

> The organ for the Cathedral of St. John the Divine was contracted for while he was still with me, but I was put to some difficulty to assure them that he would have no influence whatever on the organ. The contract excluded Hope-Jones, and was phrased that the organ should be built under the supervision of Ernest M. Skinner and of him only, but for reasons originating with the authorities of the church, the document was not delivered to us for sometime afterwards, but the next day after I told Hope-Jones that we had received this contract, articles appeared in Boston papers saying that the "Cathedral authorities" had given the contract to the Skinner Company on account of the admiration of the work of Hope-Jones, which under the circumstances was very embarrassing to me, and made necessary some further explanations.[49]

Hope-Jones continued to undermine Ernest Skinner's authority, until Ernest came "very close to losing *[his]* position with the Skinner Company on account of the influence of Hope-Jones" on his backers.

Fortunately for Ernest, "they got on to his game just in time to prevent this." Meanwhile, when he was still on the Skinner payroll, Hope-Jones organized a company of his own in Elmira, New York. Ernest "got wind of this and confirmed it with decoy letters."

The situation finally came to a head while the organ which Hope-Jones sold to Park Church in Elmira was being installed. Ernest relates the details of this incident:

> During the progress of this instrument we built an English Horn from his dictation, and gave it to the voicer, whose name was Brockbank, to voice. It had a very flaring bell and a perfectly impossible blatancy. Mr. Brockbank told him that the church would not accept this stop, and I agreed with him. When the stop was placed in the organ the church refused to accept it, as I expected, and then Mr. Hope-Jones claimed that the stop was mine, and was put in under his protest.[50]

This episode proved to be the last straw for Ernest, and he immediately fired Hope-Jones.

Robert Hope-Jones' dismissal from the Skinner Company apparently did not put an end to his subversive activities. According to the letter quoted above, two of the organs which Hope-Jones sold were not yet built when he left the Skinner firm. He subsequently prevailed upon these clients to break their contracts with the Skinner Company and give them to the Hope-Jones Organ Company in Elmira. As a result, he received his commission from his own company on these two instruments plus the Park Church organ, which was built while he was still associated with Skinner.

Fortunately, Hope-Jones' tactics did not have any lasting effect on Ernest's career. As for Hope-Jones, his firm continued with increasing financial difficulties until 1910, at which time the Rudolf Wurlitzer Organ Company of North Tonawanda, New York, acquired the patents and plant of Hope-Jones Organ Company. It was through the legendary "Mighty Wurlitzer" that most of Robert Hope-Jones' ideas were to achieve immortality, but not until after his suicide in 1914.[51]

Probably the most useful of Robert Hope-Jones' contributions to organ building were the improvements he made in the electric action, including round wire contacts to replace the old flat spring contacts. Other significant improvements included the use of coil springs instead of weights on reservoirs to regulate wind pressure, and the adoption of the horseshoe style of console with stop tabs.[52] He is also credited with the exploitation of the unit system, by means of which variety in sound was obtained by utilizing a comparatively few ranks of pipes and making them available at several pitches (ranging from 16' to 2' or 1-3/5') and on all manuals by the use of electrical relays.

Some of Hope-Jones' tonal developments were highly controversial, to say the least. He advocated the use of high wind pressures, employing "pressures as high as 50 inches," and never using less than a five inch wind pressure.[53] The exaggerated scaling in his pipework produced very big flutes, dull and heavy "Phonon" type diapasons, keen "frying bacon" strings, and highly colorful and individualistic reed stops. Also, Hope-Jones considered mixtures and mutations unnecessary and advocated their elimination from tonal schemes. The Diaphone, a valvular foundation stop with little harmonic development and an exceptionally quick attack and release, which was used as a bass to diapasons at 16' and 32' pitch, was Hope-Jones' best-known tonal innovation. It is interesting to note that the Diaphone was adopted for use in fog horns by the U. S. Coast Guard![54]

Ernest Skinner claimed that "the voicing and action of the Skinner organ were not changed in any respect" by Hope-Jones' influence, and that "his influence on the tone was limited to the voicing of the organ in Park Church, Elmira."[55] On the other hand, many authorities contend that Skinner was substantially influenced by Hope-Jones. Ernest's viewpoint was no doubt colored by the rather unpleasant relationship which developed between himself and the other man. In all fairness, though, it should be stated that the truth probably lies somewhere between these two opinions.

Ernest did adopt the use of coil springs on reservoirs and the use of round wire contacts. He did not, however, abandon the use of drawknob consoles, which he strongly favored over the Hope-Jones horseshoe stop-key consoles, and he vehemently disapproved of the unit system, except for its limited application in manual Solo stops and pedal stops. In the latter case, he would unify, or "augment," a few basic ranks (Diapason, Bourdon, Trombone, etc.) at various pitches (16', 8', 4', and sometimes 2' or 32') in order to provide a bigger pedal division in a limited space. His justification for this practice was that, since one seldom played chords in the pedal, unification was far less objectionable in that division than it was when applied to manual stops.[56] He undoubtedly unified Solo stops for the same reason, since they, like pedal stops, were generally played one note at a time. He often unified the Solo Tuba to play at 16', 8', and 4' pitches in his earlier instruments.

With respect to tonal matters, Ernest never used the extreme wind pressures and exaggerated pipe scales advocated by Hope-Jones. The only discernible influence in the Skinner organ was the employment of high, narrow mouths and, sometimes, leathered upper lips in the diapasons, and the presence of a rather thick sounding flute called the Philomela. For the most part, though, Skinner's diapasons and flutes never became as dull or heavy as the Hope-Jones variety, and the Philomela vanished from his tonal schemes by 1920. Until the 1920s, Ernest did use some rather small-scaled, keen-toned string stops, but this could just as well have been due to Carlton Michell's influence. As for his reeds, Ernest may have utilized some of Hope-Jones' ideas, but the Willises were an equally important influence in the construction and voicing of these stops. Ernest did not adopt the Hope-Jones Diaphone, and he never completely eliminated mixtures from his organs.

Ernest's innate artistic sensitivity was no doubt one reason why he was less willing than many organ builders of the day to accept the tonal concepts of Robert Hope-Jones. Another reason for his moderation in tonal matters may well have been his friendship with organ architect George Ashdown Audsley.[57] Audsley published his well-known two-volume work, *The Art of Organ Building,* in 1905, the same year that Hope-Jones joined the Skinner Organ Company. Audsley was totally opposed to Hope-Jones' ideas on upperwork, unification, and wind pressures. He advocated fairly low wind pressures, and insisted on the use of mixtures and other high pitched stops to reinforce the natural harmonics of the fundamental tone, which, on manuals, was usually the 8' Diapason.[58] At any rate, Audsley's friendship with Ernest probably acted as a counterbalance against Hope-Jones' extreme ideas, and it was fortunate for Ernest and the Skinner organ that this was the case.

FOOTNOTES

[1]*This Fabulous Century* (New York: Time-Life Books, 1969), I, 29.
[2]Arthur Hudson Marks, "A Biography of Ernest M. Skinner," *Stop, Open, and Reed,* 1, no. 4 (December 1922), p. 4.
[3]Patent no. 663,368, *Specifications and Drawings of Patents,* 4 December 1900.
[4]T. Scott Buhrman, "Ernest M. Skinner: Organ Builder," *The American Organist,* 8, no. 5 (May 1925), p. 178.
[5]Ernest M. Skinner, Letter, *The Organ,* 23, no. 132 (April 1954), p. 199.
[6]Orpha Ochse, *The History of the Organ in the United States* (Bloomington & London: Indiana University Press, 1975), p. 296.
[7]Buhrman, p. 178; Marks, p. 4.
[8]Ernest M. Skinner, "Ernest M. Skinner on Fine Organ Tone Versus 'Ritualism'," *The Diapason,* August 1933, p. 21.
[9]Ernest M. Skinner, Letter to Barbara Owen, 16 April 1957.
[10]Marks, p. 4.
[11]Unidentified newsclipping from the scrapbook of Mabel Hastings Skinner.

Ernest Starts His Own Business (1900-1907) 35

¹²Marks, p. 4; unidentified newsclipping from the scrapbook of Mabel Hastings Skinner.

¹³"Organ Builder Hitchcock Dead at 91," *The Diapason,* April 1967, p. 38; In 1915, upon leaving the Skinner Organ Co., Hitchcock, along with Theodore C. Lewis, then voicer and finisher for E. M. Skinner, formed the Lewis & Hitchcock organ building firm in Washington, D. C.

¹⁴Buhrman, p. 178.

¹⁵"A New Church," *The Vermont Tribune,* Friday, 18 July 1902, quoted in E. A. Boadway, *The Boston Organ Club Newsletter,* January & February 1978, p. 9.

¹⁶T. Scott Buhrman, "Mr. Ernest M. Skinner's Record," The *American Organist,* 19, no.4 (1936), p. 126; According to a Skinner Organ Company advertisement which appeared on p. 9 of the January 1915 issue of *The Diapason,* a later and much improved form of this duplex action was printed by E. M. Skinner in 1905 (Patent no. 807,510, *Specifications and Drawings of Patents,* 19 December 1905).

¹⁷"A New Church," quoted in Boadway, p. 9.

¹⁸"Rebuild Grace Church Organ," *The Music Trades,* New York, 2 August 1902 (courtesy of E. A. Boadway).

¹⁹Unidentified newsclipping from the scrapbook of Mabel Hastings Skinner, written around January 1905.

²⁰"New Concern Starts Well," *The Music Trades,* New York, 1903—exact date unknown (courtesy of E. A. Boadway).

²¹"Ernest M. Skinner Takes a Partner," *The Music Trades,* New York, 4 October 1902 (courtesy of E. A. Boadway).

²²Letter received from E. A. Boadway, 15 February 1977; "E. M. Skinner & Co. in New York," *The Music Trades,* New York, 8 November 1902.

²³"Boston Builders' Contracts," *The Music Trades,* 31 January 1903 (courtesy of E. A. Boadway).

²⁴Patent no. 667,039, *Specifications and Drawings of Patents,* 29 January 1901; Some "new and useful Improvements in Tracker-Boards for Automatic Musical Instrument Players" were patented by E. M. Skinner in 1902 (Patent no. 715,307, *Specifications and Drawings of Patents,* 9 December 1902) which were quite likely incorporated in the "self-playing attachments" of these residence organs; quotation from *The Music Trades,* New York, 11 May 1901 (courtesy of E. A. Boadway).

²⁵"New Concern Starts Well."

²⁶Letter received from Barbara Owen, 15 November 1976.

²⁷Personal interview with Edward B. Gammons, 3 May 1976.

²⁸"New Concern Starts Well."

²⁹Letter received from E. A. Boadway, 15 February 1977.

³⁰E. A. Boadway, "The Skinner & Aeolian-Skinner Opus List," *The Boston Organ Club Newsletter,* July & August 1972, p. 2; this installation was also the first opus in the Skinner file. It is believed by some that Skinner began numbering his organs at 100.

³¹Letter received from E. A. Boadway, 15 February 1977.

³²Personal interview with Edward B. Gammons, 3 May 1976.

³³"Good Prospects For New Year," *The Music Trades,* 16 January 1904 (courtesy of E. A. Boadway); according to this news item, the firm was now called the E. M. Skinner & Co.; Letter received from Barbara Owen, 15 November 1976.

³⁴George Ashdown Audsley, *Organ Stops and their Artistic Registration,* 2nd. ed. (New York: The H. W. Gray Co., 1941), p. 119.

³⁵William Harrison Barnes, *The Contemporary American Organ,* 3rd. ed. (New York: J. Fischer & Bro., 1937), p. 73.

³⁶*The Music Trades,* New York, 16 June 1904.

³⁷Unidentified newsclipping from the scrapbook of Mabel Hastings Skinner.

³⁸Buhrman, "Ernest M. Skinner," p. 178.

³⁹Skinner, Ernest M., *Who's Who in America,* vol. 30 (1947).

⁴⁰Marks, p. 4; Buhrman, "Ernest M. Skinner," p. 179.

36 The Life and Work of Ernest M. Skinner

⁴¹Dan Barton, "A Genius Who Failed . . . Why?" *The Bombarde,* 3, no. 1 (Spring 1966), p. 4.

⁴²Ernest M. Skinner, Letter to C. A. Van Buskirk, 18 October 1932 (courtesy of Henry Karl Baker).

⁴³Barton, p. 4; Skinner, Letter to C. A. Van Buskirk.

⁴⁴Ochse, p. 334; Skinner, Letter to C. A. Van Buskirk.

⁴⁵Skinner, Letter to C. A. Van Buskirk.

⁴⁶E. A. Boadway, "The Skinner & Aeolian-Skinner Opus List," *The Boston Organ Club Newsletter,* July & August, 1972, p. 3.

⁴⁷Letter received from Edwin D. Northrup, 4 July 1978; Boadway, "The Skinner & Aeolian-Skinner Opus List," p. 3. The tonal design of this instrument was revised by E. M. Skinner when Edwin Arthur Kraft was appointed organist at Trinity Cathedral in 1907, following Hope-Jones's departure from the Skinner firm.

⁴⁸This account of Skinner's dissatisfactions with Hope-Jones, including the quotations, are from Skinner, Letter to C. A. Van Buskirk. The firing is discussed in Ernest M. Skinner, "Mr. Skinner in Rebuttal," *The Diapason,* September 1949, p. 25.

⁴⁹Skinner, Letter to C. A. Van Buskirk.

⁵⁰Skinner, Letter to C. A. Van Buskirk.

⁵¹William Leslie Sumner, *The Organ,* 2nd. ed. (London: Macdonald & Co., Ltd., 1955), p. 231.

⁵²William Harrison Barnes & Edward B. Gammons, *Two Centuries of American Organ Building* (Melville: Belwin-Mills Publishing Corp., 1970), pp. 51, 52, 139.

⁵³"The Story of Robert Hope-Jones," *Theater Organ,* VI, no. 1 (Spring 1964), p. 23.

⁵⁴Barnes & Gammons, pp. 51 & 52.

⁵⁵Skinner, Letter to C. A. Van Buskirk.

⁵⁶Ernest M. Skinner, *The Modern Organ,* 6th. ed. (New York: H. W. Gray Co., Inc., 1945), p. 14.

⁵⁷Personal interview with Eugenia S. Shorrock, 11 October 1972.

⁵⁸Ochse, pp. 339, 340.

CHAPTER 5

The Skinner Orchestral Organ, 1906-1913

BY NOW Ernest Skinner had already invented the Erzähler, which was a distinctly new non-imitative voice. He also had recently discovered that, by abandoning the customary voicing practice of sharpening the upper lip of metal flue pipes, he was able to make a "great improvement in the speech" of all these stops, particularly the strings.[1] As a result, his diapasons and string-toned stops possessed great richness, fullness, and warmth that received much admiration. By combining all the knowledge acquired from his former associates and adding his own touch, he developed a diapason which bore little resemblance to any others built to that time. This new Skinner diapason had a very pronounced octave harmonic, giving it a warm, singing quality, and possessed what Ernest termed a "cheerful buoyancy."[2]

The organ built for Old Cabell Hall at the University of Virginia is probably quite typical of Ernest Skinner's work around 1906.[3] The electric action and console of this instrument (which is extant and was restored in 1983) are, for the most part, almost identical to the type built by Hutchings under Skinner's supervision and according to his design during his last few years with that firm. Although this organ was under construction while Hope-Jones was with Skinner, it shows little evidence of his influence. The wind pressure and pipe scaling are not extreme, and the over-all tone of the stops, individually and in combination, is moderately light and bright. For the size of the instrument, the diapason chorus is fairly complete, with a mixture in the Swell division.

A variety of 8' tone, some of it orchestral, is present in the University of Virginia Skinner. The Swell strings (the Salicional and Voix Celeste) are rather keen, but also quite big and full, giving them the tonal quality of a 'Cello. The Choir Dulciana and Unda Maris, in contrast to the Swell strings, are soft and delicate, yet harmonically rich, suggesting muted violins in an orchestra. This instrument also contains Ernest's recently invented Erzähler. The reed stops show Willis and nineteenth-century French influences. The Swell Oboe, however, which is capped, has a sweet, haunting, covered quality, foreshadowing Skinner's English Horn, not to be developed for several years.

The Skinner organ, as exemplified by the University of Virginia instrument, shows evidence that by 1906 Ernest Skinner had already progressed beyond the symphonic organs of late nineteenth-century Europe. It had the weight and warmth which characterized the European romantic instruments, but the 1906 Skinner organ had a proportionately greater variety in 8' tone than its European counterpart and, because of its improved mechanical equipment, was far more flexible. However, the orchestral organ, as Ernest envisioned it, was yet in its infancy. He was now entering an intensely creative stage of his life when he was to develop the many orchestral imitative stops which were to become the trademark of his work.

The new voices which Ernest was to create during the next two decades found their inspiration in "the lovely voices" he heard in the orchestra; the grandeur of scenery in Yosemite Valley, which he loved and visited at every opportunity; and, occasionally, "in the company of one or another of the wonderful people who [gave him] their friendship."[4] Above all, though, it was the symphony orchestra that was to provide the greatest stimulus for Ernest's creativity. Two decades later, Ernest Skinner was to state:

> What I have done in creating the Skinner Organ is due almost wholly to a love of music, plus a mediocre inventive faculty, plus an unbounded belief in the possibilities of the organ. The symphonic orchestral colors have always seemed to me to be as necessary to the organ as to the orchestra and so under the stimulus of some great orchestral or operatic work I have worked out all the orchestral colors and have included them in the Skinner Organs.[5]

The Orchestral Oboe was the first orchestral imitative stop to be developed by Ernest Skinner.[6] It was inspired by "some lovely passages on the oboe" in Wagner's *Parsifal*.[7] Soon after Ernest heard this work, he faithfully captured its "plaintive pastoral quality."[8] According to a list Ernest furnished for a biographical sketch which appeared in the May 1925 issue of *The American Organist,* the first example of his Orchestral Oboe was placed in Opus 145 at Tompkins Avenue Congregational Church, Brooklyn, which was installed in 1907. However, it also appeared in the slightly earlier Opus 135 installed in the Great Hall, City College of New York in 1906.[9]

Two other recent tonal developments of Ernest Skinner were included in the City College of New York organ. The first example of his 32′ Bombarde appeared in this instrument.[10] In the Skinner Company brochure *The Skinner Organ,* Ernest states:

> The 32′ Bombarde is the only tone having definition both with regard to pitch and quality that will adequately support modern chorus manual reeds of 16′, 8′ and 4′ pitch. The pitch of the pedal organ is normally one octave below that of the manual. The modern organ is rich in 16′ chorus reeds, which are not adequately supported by either 16′ pedal reeds or 32′ Diapason. The 32′ Bombarde affords a magnificent foundation for chorus reeds of whatever power, and possesses a dignity unapproached by other means.

Unlike many 32′ Bombardes, which are constructed entirely of metal, the Skinner Bombarde has large wood resonators in the lower two octaves.[11] As a result, these Bombardes are very full and resonant and can be felt as much as heard.

Also appearing in the City College of New York Skinner is the two-rank Dulcet, which belongs to the family of string-toned stops. This is the earliest known appearance of the Dulcet. Again, we turn to the Skinner Company brochure for a description of this stop:

> The Dulcet is a stop having two ranks of pipes, of very slender scale, and etherial quality of tone. Either of the ranks would be cold of themselves, with respect to quality. This is due to the slender scale, and the fact that it is necessary to blow them rather forcibly to obtain the desired quality. The two ranks identical in character, impart warmth and the shimmering silvery effect peculiar to this stop.

It is quite probable that the two rank Dulcet was a direct result of Hope-Jones' influence. This influence may have been present, to a lesser extent, in the development of Skinner's Orchestral Oboe, as well. The 32′ Bombarde, however, was most likely a result of "Father" Willis' influence.

During 1906 the Skinner firm extended its field into the international market with the installation of a two-manual organ in the Cathedral in Tokyo, Japan.[12] Although all of the instruments designed and built by E. M. Skinner to this time had used electro-pneumatic action, the Tokyo Skinner was made with tracker action. This was because of the likelihood "that adequate servicing of electric action could not be guaranteed there . . ."[13]

At this time Ernest Skinner's ingenuity was called upon to solve an unusual problem for the Boston Symphony Orchestra. Its conductor, Dr. Karl Muck, was planning to perform Richard Strauss' *Also Sprach Zarathustra,* and wanted a striking 32' effect for the big C major chord opening this work. The 32' Open Wood Diapason in the organ at Boston Symphony Hall did not produce enough 32' tone to suit Dr. Muck, so he had Ernest make one 32' reed pipe for bottom C only, wiring it in with the 32' Open Wood. It was a small and insignificant reed compared to the big, high-pressure 32' Bombardes that Ernest usually built,

> . . . but it was there. So, when that piece came on, and old John Marshall, then the organist of the symphony . . . put down that C major chord and put his foot down . . . they say that Ernest Skinner jumped right out of his seat on the center aisle and said: "Thar she blows!"[14]

Ernest Skinner's reputation as an organ builder was spreading, and he was now building organs for customers all over the United States. Among the more notable instruments that he built during 1909 through 1913 were the organs in Trinity Church, Toledo, Ohio; Sage Chapel, Cornell University, Ithaca, New York; Cathedral of St. John the Divine, New York City; Grace Chapin Hall, Williams College, Williamstown, Massachusetts; Fifth Avenue Presbyterian Church, New York City; St. Thomas' Church, New York City; and Fourth Presbyterian Church, Chicago, Illinois.[15]

Ernest was a conscientious and dedicated artist and built instruments of consistently high quality. However, in his striving to build the finest organ of which he was capable, he often was unable to meet deadlines. Elfrieda Kraege, historian of Fifth Avenue Presbyterian Church, New York City, relates the problems encountered by Ernest Skinner while his organs for that church were under construction:

> In the summer of 1912, the church officers began to talk about a new organ for the church . . . St. Thomas' Episcopal Church, two blocks away, was investing in a Skinner organ, and on February 19,

1913, the chairman of the Trustees wrote to Ernest M. Skinner that we wanted one too . . .

Before signing the contract, one careful trustee checked the experience of others and found that Mr. Skinner had occasionally been unable to deliver his organs on time because of limited personnel to handle the large number of contracts he was given, and his having money tied up in the building of a new factory. On the other hand, the man wrote: "From all I can learn, Mr. Skinner builds the best organs in the country, is a man of artistic temperament and apparently of high character and great professional pride. I have no doubt that he would do his best to give us fine organs and that he would probably come through all right."

Because of the concern that Mr. Skinner might not be able to meet deadlines, the contract included a clause concerning the dates of completion, with the church agreeing to pay $20. a day additional if the organs were completed ahead of time, and Mr. Skinner agreeing to pay $20. a day if the organs were not completed by that date, October 15, 1913 [*The contract was signed on March 20, 1913*] . . .

Both of our careful trustee's predictions came to pass. Ernest Skinner did in fact do an excellent piece of work, and he wasn't on time! One cannot but sympathize with him and with the church alike, when three months after the scheduled completion date, one of the most powerful stops in the organ, the Tuba Mirabilis, was still in Boston waiting to be voiced, while Mr. Skinner's one and only reed voicer was busy at the church on other matters connected with the organ. The ordinary delays of industrial life plagued Mr. Skinner, too. When he tried to ship some large pipes, the bill of lading came back marked "delayed on account of lack of a car of sufficient length."

In the 160 pages of correspondence in church archives . . . we see an artistic and dedicated man struggling to complete the organ with many difficulties—mainly the delay in his new factory being completed, and his lack of sufficient staff. In a letter of October 14, 1913, a day before the deadline, Ernest Skinner ruefully admitted that he was a victim of his own ambition to create a masterpiece, both in the organ and its case. He had especially wanted to build the casework, an opportunity he seldom had, and to create a beautiful case such as some European organs have . . . Apparently the Trustees understood Mr. Skinner's problems, since the penalty clause for lateness does not seem to have been carried out.[16]

Meanwhile, Ernest Skinner's new tonal developments were coming in rapid succession. By 1910 his Flute Celeste, English Horn, and Celesta stops began to appear in Skinner organs. A Flute Celeste, consisting of two ranks of Spitz Flute pipes, made its first known appearance in the Skinner installed in Trinity Episcopal Church,

Toledo, Ohio. Although there is no description of a Spitz Flute Celeste in the Skinner Company brochure, there is one of the Flauto Dolce Celeste, which, aside from having a smaller scale and a tone that is somewhat softer and brighter than the Spitz Flute Celeste, is essentially the same in general quality and function:

> The Flauto Dolce and the Flute Celeste occupy the same relationship to each other as do the Salicional and Vox Celeste. The Flute Celeste imparts a wave to a combination of the two. This stop is a specialty. Of all the organ stops it is the most beautiful. It is full of dramatic suggestion, in spite of its dreamy non-aggressive characteristics. It is closely allied to the muted strings of the orchestra.

In comments printed on page 21 in the August 1933 issue of *The Diapason,* Ernest Skinner recalls his inspiration for the creation of this stop:

> The flute celeste was the result of hearing the muted strings in the slow movement of the orchestral accompaniment of the B flat minor piano concerto of Tschaikowski, which seemed to me to be the most heavenly sound I had ever heard.

The English Horn was presumably first used in the City College of New York Skinner at both 16′ and 8′ pitches.[17] However, no such stop appears in the specification of this instrument at either pitch. According to an item found on page one in the December 1957 issue of *The Diapason,* the first English Horn appeared in the Choir division of Skinner Opus 174 at the Church of Christ, Congregational Church in Norfolk, Connecticut, which was built in 1910. This stop is described in the Skinner brochure as having "the mournful covered quality peculiar to its orchestral prototype."

As an old man, Ernest Skinner told organ historian Barbara Owen this story of the English Horn's conception: Ernest and some friends went to a concert at Boston Symphony Hall where he heard the Prelude to Act III of *Parsifal*. After hearing the English Horn solo, he could not get the sound out of his mind. When the concert had ended, Ernest sent his companions home by one taxi and went directly to his factory in another. He found some oboe pipes around the shop and experimented with them until about three or four o'clock in the morning, attempting to reproduce the English Horn tone in pipes while his memory of it was still fresh.

What Ernest accomplished during the night following that concert was only a beginning. Nearly two decades were to pass before Ernest would succeed in building an English Horn stop which, to his critical ears, truly captured the tone of its orchestral counterpart.[18] Of all the many new voices he created, the English Horn "took the longest time to develop to a satisfactory degree."[19]

The Celesta made its first known appearance in 1909 in Skinner Opus 175 at Sage Chapel, Cornell University.[20] For all practical purposes, the Skinner Harp and Celesta were the same stop. During the 'teens, the two names were often used interchangeably, although, later on, the terms were generally used to designate the stop at 8' and 4' pitches, respectively. This stop was "based in principle on the orchestral instrument of that name" and took twenty years of development before Ernest "was satisfied as to its quality."[21] Most builders produce a Harp or Celesta tone by means of a felt-covered wooden mallet striking against a tuned metal bar which is mounted on a metal tube-shaped resonator. Skinner, however, obtained an unusually sweet tone by using piano hammers in place of mallets and wood resonators instead of metal ones.

The Skinner Opus 150 completed in 1910 at the Cathedral of St. John the Divine, New York City, was distinguished by the introduction of several of Ernest's new tonal developments.[22] Among those stops were the French Trumpet, Gamba Celeste, and 32' Violone.[23] The French Trumpet is somewhat brighter than the usual Skinner Trumpet or Cornopean. It is generally voiced on lower wind pressure than Skinner customarily used. The Skinner Company brochure has this description of the Gamba Celeste:

> The Gamba Celeste belongs to the String family. It is the largest in scale of all the String tones. By a special treatment of scale and voicing, great breadth and power is obtained. This stop imparts extraordinary richness, both to the String division and to mass effect.

The 32' Pedal Violone was described by Ernest Skinner as being "a voice of profound depth, having both an impressive character and definition."[24]

The Cathedral of St. John the Divine organ was the first Skinner installation known to contain a Flügel Horn, also called Cor d'Amour or Corno d' Amour. Although the Flügel Horn was used in the Solo division of this instrument, it is customarily located in the Swell division of most Skinner organs, taking the place of, and serving the same function as, the usual Swell Oboe. It is described in the Skinner Company brochure as being "acoustically an Oboe with the defects removed." It is constructed like a small-scaled Trumpet and is capped. The resulting tone is a very smooth-sounding cross between an Oboe and a Cornopean.

According to Ernest Skinner, the Tuba Mirabilis was first used by him in the St. John the Divine organ.[25] This stop, an extraordinarily loud and brilliant reed stop of the Trumpet family, is usually included in Solo divisions of larger Skinner installations. It is interesting to note that Ernest had used a stop bearing this name as early as 1897 in the Hutchings organ in South Congregational Church, New Britain, Connecticut.[26] A Tuba Mirabilis also was included in the Solo organ added to the Grace Church, New York City, rebuild in 1902, and appeared in the specification of the City College of New York Skinner, built in 1906.[27] The Tuba Mirabilis in the Cathedral of St. John the Divine organ may have been a new and improved form of the stop. Its construction and voicing are based on the Willis examples utilizing very high wind pressure, generally about twenty inches. Ernest obviously could have devised this stop much earlier, but this was probably his first installation where the organ and the building were large enough to accommodate such a powerful stop.

Ernest Skinner's most famous creation, his French Horn stop, was introduced in Opus 195 installed in Chapin Hall, Williams College, Williamstown, Massachusetts, in 1912.[28] This was the only one of E. M. Skinner's tonal developments to be patented.[29] Ernest gives this account of how his French Horn came into being:

> When the organ was planned for Williams College, Mr. Salter insisted on a French Horn and so one was written into the specifications. Before that time Richard Strauss' Salome was given by the Manhattan Opera Company and I had heard eight French Horns in unison in the Salome Dance and was from that time on determined that the French Horn should be added to the voices of the organ if I could ever get the opportunity to work it out.
>
> The opportunity came and after much research the French Horn took its place in the Skinner Organ.
>
> I had a better French Horn than I really expected for the tone was not only there but the so-called bubble was present.[30]

Also making its first appearance in the Williams College Skinner was the Corno di Bassetto.[31] It is described in the Skinner Company brochure as being "in effect a powerful Clarinet," with a tone that is "cool, authoritative and of great richness and purity." The Corno di Bassetto generally was included only in the Solo divisions of larger instruments, although there is one example of the author's acquaintance, taking the place of the customary Clarinet, in the Choir division of a medium-sized three manual Skinner of fewer than forty ranks.[32]

Ernest's first 32′ Sub-Bass was built for the Skinner Opus 205 installed in St. Thomas Church, New York City in 1913.[33]

Shortly thereafter, the Kleine Erzähler was introduced in Opus 210 at Fourth Presbyterian Church, Chicago, Illinois, also built in 1913.[34] The Kleine Erzähler consists of two ranks of small-scaled Erzähler pipes, with one rank tuned sharp so as to form a celeste with the other rank, which is tuned to unison pitch. It has a lovely and subtle sound, and usually appears only in the Choir divisions of large Skinner organs of fifty ranks or more. In a letter to Mrs. Emmons Blaine, donor of the Fourth Presbyterian Church organ, Ernest tells how this stop came about:

> I have invented a new stop through my study over this case. I wanted to put in a Flute Celeste of which I am very fond. It takes up considerable room, and I set about finding a way to take less. I wanted to make the stop softer than usual, so I had some pipes made up to a small scale from the model of my Erzähler. The result is a most beautiful combination . . .[35]

By now, the Skinner organ was a radically different instrument from that which was built by the firm in 1906, just seven years earlier. However, more orchestral imitative stops remained to be invented before Ernest Skinner's orchestral organ would be complete. While the development and improvement of tonal resources had been Ernest's primary preoccupation during the past fifteen years, he had continued to modify and improve his consoles and electro-pneumatic action. By 1913, both had pretty well attained their final form.

By this time, Ernest Skinner's original 1893 pneumatic swell pedal action, his first patented invention, had been replaced by an even more sensitive and efficient electro-pneumatic "whiffle-tree" swell engine.[36] Also, in recent years, he had eliminated the multiple windings on his key action magnets, instead employing pneumatic switches in the console to operate the couplers. His old compact and portable console with swing-door stop jambs was no longer in use. In its place was a massive, elegant console which was the last word in convenience and comfort for the organist. In *The Modern Organ,* Ernest describes the modern Skinner console:

> The console of a high grade modern organ is a very handsome affair. The interior finish is in polished mahogany. The drawstops are of solid ivory of a size to permit clear and distinct lettering.[37]

The exterior of Skinner consoles was usually made of oak, although at least one console was constructed of solid mahogany, stained light to complement its high-gloss, dark, wine-colored mahogany interior.[38]

These exceedingly attractive Skinner consoles were designed with more in mind than mere beauty. E. M. Skinner maintained that "the convenience of the organist should be made the first consideration of the organ builder, regardless of fads, hobbies, or economics."[39] The distance between keyboards, the position of the pedal board, the placement of the drawknobs, and the location of all mechanical devices (expression pedals, combination pistons, etc.) on the Skinner console were designed for maximum convenience, and the manual keys of most of these consoles were now equipped with "tracker touch."[40] Ernest Skinner has this description of the latter feature:

> The keys have "tracker touch," *i.e.* four-oz. initial and one and one-half oz. when depressed. This makes the organ and piano touches almost identical, so that practice on either instrument is of equal value and not an interference, as was the spring organ touch to the piano, before the "tracker" touch became an accomplished fact.[41]

The Skinner console was also provided with an adjustable combination action which visibly affected the draw-knobs. It also had a standardized concave, radiating pedal board of thirty-two notes. Ernest was the first builder in America to make these two features standard equipment in his consoles.[42]

As is often the case with creative genius, Ernest Skinner frequently had to contend with those who were completely satisfied with the tried and true older ways and who doggedly refused to move forward. Like the romantic composers of the nineteenth century, Ernest found it increasingly necessary to take up his pen in defense of his new ideas. By 1913 he was emerging on the organ scene as a fluent and commanding writer as well as speaker, and articles and editorials expressing his viewpoints on organ building and music were appearing in organists' publications with increasing frequency. One example involves the combination action. Early in 1913 the console standardization committee of the American Guild of Organists recommended the adoption of the immovable stop combination action. Until about five years earlier Ernest believed the "dead" combinations to be the ideal system and had been building them for fifteen years, when he attended a meeting consisting mostly of Guild members who were unanimously opposed to the "dead" combination system. Then and there Ernest vowed he "would never build another instrument with non-moving stop knobs

...."[43] Thus, in an editorial published in the June 1913 issue of *The Diapason*, he went on record as being in opposition to the Guild's recent recommendation in favor of the "dead" combination action.

Ernest's editorial touched off a verbal battle which continued in the columns of *The Diapason* for months. He was said to have remarked, at the height of this controversy, "that he knew some 'ivory knobs' in the organ business that couldn't be moved with any kind of a combination action."[44] Eventually, Ernest Skinner won out on this issue, because virtually every organ builder is now able to furnish a combination action which visibly moves the stop controls.

FOOTNOTES

[1] T. Scott Buhrman, "Mr. Ernest M. Skinner's Record," *The American Organist*, 19, no. 4 (1936), p. 126.

[2] Ernest M. Skinner, "Fine Organ Tone Versus 'Ritualism'," *The Diapason*, August 1933, p. 21; *The Skinner Organ*, a brochure published by the Skinner Organ Company.

[3] This instrument (Opus 127), built in 1906, is probably the oldest playable Skinner in existence. A more detailed description of this organ can be found in Dorothy J. Holden, "The Tonal Evolution of the E. M. Skinner Organ, Part I," *The Diapason*, July 1977, pp. 4 & 5.

[4] Skinner, "Fine Organ Tone," p. 21.

[5] T. Scott Buhrman, "Ernest M. Skinner: Organ Builder," *The American Organist*, 8, no. 5 (May 1925), p. 182.

[6] *The Skinner Organ*, a brochure.

[7] Ernest M. Skinner, Letter to Alexander McCurdy, 3 June 1954.

[8] *The Skinner Organ*, a brochure.

[9] *Organ in the College of the City of New York*, Pamphlet published by the Ernest M. Skinner Organ Company (courtesy of Barbara Owen); E. A. Boadway, "The Skinner & Aeolian-Skinner Opus List," *The Boston Organ Club Newsletter*, July & August 1972, p. 3.

[10] Buhrman, "Ernest M. Skinner: Organ Builder," p. 183.

[11] In earlier Skinners, the 32' Bombarde was usually an extension of the Solo Tuba which was unified to play at 16', 8', and 4' pitches. Later on it was generally taken from an independent Pedal 16' Trombone, which was unified to 8' and, sometimes, 4' pitch.

[12] Boadway, p. 3.

[13] "Pitman-Chest Action," *The American Organist*, 19, no. 6 (1936), p. 199.

[14] Personal interview with Edward B. Gammons, 3 May 1976 (as told to him by Dr. Archibald T. Davison).

[15] Boadway, pp. 4 & 5.

[16] Elfrieda Kraege, "The Early Organs of the Fifth Avenue Presbyterian Church," *The Tracker*, XVIII, no. 2 (Winter 1974), pp. 8 & 9.

[17] Buhrman, "Ernest M. Skinner: Organ Builder," p. 183.

[18] Ernest M. Skinner, Editorial, *Stop, Open, and Reed*, 4, no. 1 (1927), p, 4.

[19] Ernest M. Skinner, Letter to Alexander McCurdy, 3 June 1954.

[20] Specification courtesy of Barbara Owen.

[21] Skinner, "Fine Organ Tone," p. 21.

[22] "Looking Back into the Past," *The Diapason*, January 1956, p. 22.

[23] Buhrman, "Ernest M. Skinner: Organ Builder," p. 183.

[24] "Inventions and Tonal Developments of Ernest M. Skinner," *The Diapason*, February 1946, p. 17.

²⁵Buhrman, "Ernest M. Skinner: Organ Builder," p. 183.

²⁶Specifications of the Hutchings organ at South Congregational Church, New Britain, Connecticut (courtesy of Barbara Owen); Homer D. Blanchard, "The Organ in the United States: A Study in Design, Part II," *The Tracker*, 25, no. 1 (Fall 1980), p. 40.

²⁷"Rebuild Grace Church Organ," *The Music Trades*, New York, 2 August 1902 (courtesy of E. A. Boadway); *Organ in the College of the City of New York*, Pamphlet published by the Ernest M. Skinner Organ Company (courtesy of Barbara Owen).

²⁸Buhman, "'Ernest M. Skinner: Organ Builder," p. 183; "Four Manual for Williams College," *The Diapason*, October 1912, p. 2.

²⁹Patent no. 1,169,687, *Specifications and Drawings of Patents*, 25 January 1916.

³⁰Buhrman, "Ernest M. Skinner; Organ Builder," pp. 182 & 183.

³¹Buhrman, "Ernest M. Skinner: Organ Builder," p. 183.

³²Trinity Lutheran Church, Detroit, Michigan (Opus 808, 1930).

³³Buhrman, "Ernest M. Skinner: Organ Builder," p. 183; Boadway, p. 5.

³⁴Buhrman, "Ernest M. Skinner: Organ Builder," p. 183; Boadway, p. 5.

³⁵Ernest M. Skinner, Letter to Mrs. Emmons Blaine, 13 February 1913, quoted in Morgan Simmons, "Fourth Presbyterian Church," *Music: The A.G.O.-R.C.C.O. Magazine*, 5, no. 2 (February 1971), p. 29.

³⁶Patent no. 1,076,069, *Specifications and Drawings of Patents*, 21 October 1913.

³⁷Ernest M. Skinner, *The Modern Organ*, 6th. ed. (New York: The H. W. Gray Co., Inc., 1945), p. 13.

³⁸Opus 467, 1925, formerly in the Baptist Temple, Charleston, West Virginia, now in the author's home.

³⁹Skinner, *The Modern Organ*, p. 48.

⁴⁰Ernest M. Skinner Organ Company advertisement, *The Diapason*, March 1915, p. 15; according to this ad, E. M. Skinner began using "tracker touch" in his instruments around the year 1911.

⁴¹Skinner, *The Modern Organ*, p. 13.

⁴²Ernest M. Skinner, "Mr. Skinner Writes of Console and Tone; Also Standardization," *The Diapason*, January 1933, p. 29; E. M. Skinner had built thirty note pedal boards up until around 1906, the organ at University of Virginia (Opus 127) probably being one of the last Skinners to have this pedal compass.

⁴³Ernest M. Skinner, "Visible as Against Dead Combinations," *The Diapason*, June 1913, p. 1.

⁴⁴William Harrison Barnes, *The Contemporary American Organ*, 3rd. ed. (New York: J. Fischer & Bros., 1937), p. 238.

CHAPTER 6

Personal Life
1906-1915

On 12 July 1906 Ernest Skinner's third child, Ruth Alden Skinner, was born, thus completing his family with two girls and one boy. His daughter Eugenia, then nearly ten years old, recalls Ernest's rushing up and down the street telling all his neighbors the good news.

Ernest adored his children and was a very affectionate father. He had an infinite stock of jokes and would tell them to his youngsters who called him "Papa." He almost never showed temper at his family, although he tended to get irritated over little things and did not display much patience. Ernest was a daydreamer and was often completely lost in his own world. He was on another plane of existence, although he was not aloof to what was going on around him. He seldom played with his children, and his daughter Ruth recalls:

> He was very fond of me. I can remember he'd pick me up, but wasn't the kind who would play with children. He really wasn't. And he wasn't around very much. He was on the road most of the time.[1]

When Ernest was out of town on business he and his wife Mabel constantly wrote love letters back and forth. According to Ruth Scott, they had a rare marriage and "really had something going." He apparently made her very happy, for even after years of marriage Mabel wrote Ernest love letters like a newly-wed bride. She felt his absence deeply. In one letter read to the author by Eugenia Shorrock,

Mabel pleads with Ernest, asking him why he cannot be home more because she misses him so much.

Mabel's frequent loneliness was somewhat alleviated by the company of her brother, Harved Hastings, and his family, who lived at 8 Evandale Terrace, directly across the street from the Skinner home. Mabel's brother bought this house after she and Ernest moved in at 7 Evandale Terrace so she would have someone to look after her while her husband was away on his long and seemingly endless business trips.

Since Ernest was seldom home, Mabel took most of the responsibility for engineering the family Christmas celebrations. Eugenia Shorrock recalls that when she was a little girl they had a big Christmas tree, approximately ten feet high, which reached to the ceiling of their home at 7 Evandale Terrace. This tree was decorated with tinsel, handmade popcorn balls and paper garlands and, in the early days, real candles.

The Skinners had a "Santa" who arrived in person laden with gifts (which were wrapped with brown paper and cord by Mabel who made most of her gifts to the family). On Christmas day, while everyone sat very quietly waiting for Santa, Mabel would ring up "Central" on the phone and ask the operator to inform Santa that the Skinners were ready for his visit. Presently, Santa would enter the upstairs window and come thumping down the stairs. He would go to the tree, pick up the bundles, and deliver them to each person. Then he would bow, say he would see them next year, thump up the steps, and depart "with the thundering of reindeer on the roof."

"Santa" was a neighbor at first, but later on when he was older and his appearance more suited the part, Ernest played this role. Eugenia, as a child who still believed in Santa, once found Santa's boots and whip upstairs in the bedroom. She related this discovery to her mother, who immediately called "Central" and asked the operator to tell Santa that he had left his belongings at their house. Shortly thereafter they heard "Santa" arrive, repeating all the sound effects of his Christmas visit. Later, when Eugenia went back upstairs, the boots and whip had vanished!

Mabel was a woman of many talents. Since she always had maids, as did her neighbors, she had ample time to engage in all kinds of crafts such as oil painting, water colors, china painting, and leather craft. She also took piano and French lessons. Mabel sometimes wrote her letters to Ernest in French, which would annoy him, since he could not understand that language.

Mabel's favorite pastime was oil painting, and her skill in this medium was such that she won a prize in an art contest. Her nephew Edward Hastings tells about his Aunt Mabel's paintings:

> Her real talent was as an artist. She was a most skilful painter, working largely in oils. This was her main way of passing the time when Ernest was on the road. Although some of her original things are pleasant enough, it was as a copyist that she came into her own. As far as I know she was largely self-taught, but her ability to reproduce the exact colors, the exact texture of other painters' work was quite miraculous . . .
>
> My mother *[Mabel's sister-in-law]* used to joke rather wryly about the fact that no one's pictures were safe from Mabel. If a friend or relative bought a picture he liked, Mabel was sure to ask to copy it— not once but often. As a result, it was simply impossible to have a picture that was yours only. Certain paintings (chiefly landscapes) are owned by almost every member of the family.[2]

Mabel Skinner never sold any of her paintings but used them as wedding gifts, Christmas presents, and the like. Ernest was very proud of her artistic ability.[3]

Having spent much of her girlhood on her father's sheep ranch in Montana, Mabel learned how to handle a gun at an early age and was an expert markswoman. Ruth Scott recalls her mother's and her father's respective skill in marksmanship:

> She could beat him with a gun, I can tell you that. I can remember them shooting out the window at a can on the beach at Savin Hill . . . He didn't stand a prayer with her on that.[4]

In those early days, before movies and radio, "taking pictures" was a popular form of family entertainment, thanks to Eastman-Kodak's invention of the easy-to-use box camera. Ernest and Mabel and their relatives and friends would amuse themselves by dressing up in various costumes and taking pictures of each other. However, the Skinners' interest in photography went considerably beyond the "you press the button, we do the rest" stage. Ernest and Mabel were avid photographers, and both owned sophisticated Kodak cameras which used large glass plate negatives. It was Mabel who developed most, if not all, of the many photos that she and Ernest took.

Mabel's favorite photographic subject matter was scenery and family. According to her daughter Ruth, she was forever taking pictures of the children until they never wanted to pose for another. For the most part Ernest's preferred subject matter was organs and scenery. He particularly loved to photograph the dramatic landscape at Yosemite National Park when on his frequent business trips to the west coast.

Although Ernest reportedly could not read a note of music he was capable of playing by ear, in spite of the limitations imposed by his unusually short and jointless little fingers.[5] According to those who knew Ernest in his later years, his playing was not particularly good when judged by the standards of today's professional musicians. One account, however, suggests that his ability to improvise was more than satisfactory to the ear of the average listener back in the first decade of this century. An unidentified newsclipping written early in 1905 describes an impromptu concert played by Ernest on New Year's Eve as 1904 drew to a close:

> The newspaper man who was accompanied by his wife and daughter . . . accepted Mr. Skinner's invitation to inspect the interior of Grace Church, that celebrated house of worship, where so many of New York's millionaires are regular attendants. Although it was then 10:30 at night, Mr. Skinner seemed to find no difficulty in securing a ready entrance through the fashionable rectory which adjoins, and he proceeded at once and with pardonable pride to show his willing visitors the magnificent organ he constructed about two years ago . . .
>
> Mr. Skinner, on being asked if he were an organist, requested the assistant organist of the church who was practicing, to allow him to use the organ, seated himself and proceeded to demonstrate that he was a thorough master. He played with a style and execution of technique far superior to the ordinary church organist. His selections coming to him by inspiration, included works of the old masters, celebrated masses, Te Deums, and just as the chimes of Trinity church heralded the entrance of the new year he concluded with a masterly rendition of "Parsifal."

In spite of his limited formal schooling, Ernest Skinner's education had not ended with his departure from school as a boy of fourteen. He was voracious reader and educated himself by reading the works of the great literary masters. Ernest would read Shakespeare by the hour. He had the entire set of these books which according to his nephew, Ned Hastings, were well worn. He was fond of Mark Twain's writings. He also enjoyed reading the Sherlock Holmes novels and the adventure stories of H. Rider Haggard. Among his favorite poets were Dante, Gabrielle Rossetti, and Christina Rossetti. His daughter Ruth recalls that Ernest loved words for their own sake and actually read the dictionary for his own amazement, thus acquiring a prodigious vocabulary.

Personal Life (1906-1915)   53

Being mechanically minded, Ernest was fascinated with the host of new devices which were being invented at a rapid pace during the late nineteenth and early twentieth centuries. He could not resist buying the latest new gadget that would appeal to him as soon as it came on the market, even when he could not really afford it. Often things were reclaimed because he couldn't keep up the payments.

Needless to say, Ernest always had the latest of musical devices. When the first Victrolas came out soon after 1901, he bought one, and the neighbors would come over to hear recordings of Enrico Caruso and the like on his marvelous "talking machine." He later bought one of the Orthophonic Victrolas when they went on the market in the mid-1920s.

The gadget of the decade was the automobile, though there were few paved roads. In those days, it was still too expensive and impractical for the average person to own one. Only those with money and a taste for adventure would venture to buy one of those new contraptions. Ernest was not wealthy, but he definitely had a love of adventure. Thus it was sometime early in the year 1907 that he came home with a brand new red Winton touring car. Eugenia Shorrock recalls that he arrived with his new car in the evening, when it was almost dark outside and the children were in bed. He had his youngsters dress and took the whole family out for their first ride that night. Ernest drove rather fast, as speeds went in those days. He must have been going all of fifteen miles per hour when Mabel said to him, "Ernest, you're driving too fast!"

At the turn of the century, typhoid fever was one of the leading causes of death. It came very close to claiming the life of Ernest Skinner while the most important part of his career still lay ahead. In a letter to Alexander McCurdy, 13 July 1954, Ernest writes:

> I never had but one illness that I remember that amounted to anything but that was awful. I had what is called walking typhoid and two relapses, all of which amounted to the fact that I had typoid fever for five months and incidently was reported DEAD . . .

Ernest's daughter Eugenia was a little girl at the time of his illness and can remember nurses being around in their home most of the time. The exact year that Ernest had typhoid fever is unknown, but some comments in a testimonial letter pertaining to the City College of New York Skinner give evidence that it may have been in the spring and summer of 1908. In this testimonial, dated 24 September 1908, Edwin H. Lemare devotes several paragraphs to praising the new organ at City College and then concludes with this line:

> I am sorry to hear that you have been so ill, and I sincerely hope that you may soon be fully restored to health, and able to continue a successful and artistic career, such as I am convinced is in front of you.[6]

Three years later, on 31 January 1912, Ernest Skinner's father, Washington Martin Skinner, died at the age of seventy-five. Soon after, Ernest's mother came to live with him and his family. Alice Francis Skinner, a severe lady then in her late sixties, was a strict and inflexible grandmother. According to Eugenia Shorrock she forbade her grandchildren to indulge in such worldly activities as card playing. Moreover, on Sunday, no one was allowed to read the "funnies" or chew gum. Alice Skinner would even refuse to accept a ride to church because she considered it wrong to travel in a car on the Sabbath. Her son Ernest, however, had no qualms about such "sinful" conduct and would drive alongside her in his car as she dutifully walked to church!

The Skinners did not have to endure the elder Mrs. Skinner's austerities for long, for she soon departed for California to join a religious sect which had its base there. Ernest continued to provide financial support for his mother, a responsibility which proved to be quite a burden for him as time went on. Every so often, Alice Skinner would be informed by her religious prophets that "the end of the world was near." She would then dispose of all her belongings, since there would be no need of worldly possessions when the "end" arrived. Predictably, the time of reckoning came and went, and nothing happened. Consequently, she would have to start all over again, replenishing the material necessities of life—with Ernest Skinner footing the bill.

Since Ernest's mother was now among the "redeemed," it was a great sorrow to her that her son had not also been "saved." In one letter, read to the author by Eugenia Shorrock, his mother wrote that she was praying for him to be "saved" so that he would go where she was going when "the end of the world came."

In the meantime, while Alice Skinner worried about her son's future in the next world, life went on for the rest of the Skinners in this world. Ernest's family was growing up fast and Eugenia and Richmond were now in their teens. The children were all developing their own distinctive personalities, each with a liberal share of their father's positive, optimistic outlook.

By 1914 Ernest's older daughter was emerging as a highly adventuresome and resourceful young lady. That summer, Eugenia distinguished herself by saving a companion from drowning while the two girls were swimming at Savin Hill Beach. An account of this rescue, originally appearing in the *Boston Post* on 11 August 1914, was reprinted in the September 1914 issue of *The Diapason*. Ernest Skinner undoubtedly was responsible for this account appearing in the latter publication for, in spite of the fact that he saw little of his children, he was exceedingly proud of their accomplishments. He wanted his youngsters to have every advantage he could afford to give them, and saw to it that they received all the education they wanted or needed. In 1914 Eugenia was attending the Lasell Seminary for Young Women. Within a few years, Richmond would be in the Massachusetts Institute of Technology, working toward a degree in engineering.[7]

In 1915 the Skinners bought a cottage at Alton Bay in New Hampshire. A large, two-story dwelling with a spacious front porch overlooking its own sandy beach on Lake Winnipesaukee, this was to be the family summer retreat from then on. Every year, Mabel and the children would spend most of the summer at Alton Bay and Ernest would join them for weekends or whenever he could get away from business concerns.

Ernest loved Alton Bay with a passion. He liked anything that pertained to nature and was fascinated with the schools of minnows which would come up and nibble at him in the crystal clear waters of Lake Winnipesaukee. He was very fond of animals, and dogs and cats were always a part of the Skinner household. Ernest's love of nature also included the appreciation of beautiful scenery. He enjoyed doing such things as taking the entire family to the top of Mount Washington, in New Hampshire, to watch a sunset.

Physically, Ernest was quite active and very strong. In old family photo albums made up by Mabel there are pictures of him at Alton Bay taking part in such activities as playing tug-of-war with a group of friends. In one photo Ernest is attired in a swim suit, his large biceps in evidence as he chops wood with an axe. When at home in Dorchester he would walk to work at the factory, a distance of about three-quarters of a mile.[8] On the other hand, Ernest was often content to sit and read in his spare time and was described by those who knew him well as being a "very relaxed fellow."[9]

In the recollections of Ruth Scott, her father was not a "Mr. Fixit," and could not repair anything around the house. When it came to doing household chores such as putting up screens, Ernest had a man who worked at the factory to come over to attend to those matters. Up at Alton Bay he may have cut the wood, but it was Mabel who built the fires.

One of Ernest's favorite outdoor pastimes was boating. According to

Eugenia Shorrock he acquired his first boat in 1912. This boat, a Naphtha launch, was berthed at the Savin Hill Yacht Club (of which he was a founding member) and "created quite a sensation in its day."[10] Later at Alton Bay, Ernest had to have the fastest boat on the lake. He was quite proud of a trophy cup won in a very early speed boat race, competing in what was probably one of the first speed boats in existence.

Ernest's love of speed also extended to his driving habits. He did a lot of driving and generally drove faster than he should. He could not bear to have anyone pass him on the road. Ned Hastings recalls that no one ever wanted to ride in the car with his Uncle Ernest because he drove too fast. One time, when they were at Alton Bay, the family decided to take the bus back home rather than risk riding with him. Ernest's car had just had new piston rings installed, and consequently could not be driven over thirty miles per hour for a certain period of time. So he wistfully asked if anyone wanted to ride with him, promising that he couldn't, and thus wouldn't go over thirty miles per hour. The family accepted his offer on the strength of his promise and, sure enough, Ernest never exceeded thirty miles per hour all the way home, right through stoplights and all!

Needless to say, Ernest acquired a reputation as a rather bad driver. Almost everyone who knew him has mentioned his driving "prowess." One former associate recalled that he would talk as he drove, driving all over the road because his mind was on what he was talking about instead of on his driving." It was inevitable that, sooner or later, he would become involved in an auto accident. On 30 December 1914, Ernest made headlines in Boston newspapers when he broke a rib in a collision of his car with a tree in Cambridge, Massachusetts. Fortunately, no one else was injured in the accident and, according to one report, Ernest "was able . . . to leave the hospital the following day and . . . made a rapid recovery."[12]

His driving habits may have been in part a manifestation of his forceful and argumentative personality, upon which many of his acquaintances remarked. In review of one of the many organists' conventions Ernest attended, often as a featured speaker, the critic comments: "He *[Ernest Skinner]* speaks like a Scot, though he is, I believe, a Yankee, with a certain pugnacity and joy in combat."[13] Ernest was the kind of man who, when he made up his mind on something, could not be budged.

According to one story, Ernest contracted to build an organ for a church in Omaha, Nebraska, the specification of which called for a 16' Double Trumpet, an 8' Trumpet, and a 4' Clarion in the Swell. When the organ was delivered, the Swell division had a 16′ English Horn, an 8′ Cornopean, and a 4′ Clarion! The organist objected, saying, "I don't want this English Horn!" Ernest replied, "Well, you'd better learn to like it!"[14]

Ralph Adams Cram, an authority on Gothic architecture and designer of some of this country's most outstanding academic and ecclesiastical buildings, was the architect of some of the edifices for which Ernest Skinner built organs. As is often the case when organ builder meets architect, Ernest and Cram did not always see eye to eye. In one of Cram's buildings, Ernest was alloted a space forty feet high but only *four* feet deep to install a big four-manual instrument. He was so furious with Dr. Cram that he said to him: "Cram, G__ d__ it! What do you want me to do?! *Paint* the organ on the wall?!!" This story was told to Edward B. Gammons by Dr. Cram who added the comment, "Oh, that man Skinner—he was impossible!"

There was no denying that Ernest Skinner could be absolutely maddening to those who opposed his viewpoints. However, for every one of those who found Ernest's obstinacy infuriating, there were just as many who "admired his tenacity of purpose . . ."[15] Indeed, Ernest was on of those rare individuals who really stuck to his convictions, no matter what, right up to the very end of his life.

FOOTNOTES

[1] Personal interview with Ruth Scott, 11 September 1974.
[2] Edward H. Hastings, Letter to Joseph Dzeda, 12 April 1972.
[3] Ernest M. Skinner, Letter to Alexander McCurdy, 28 June 1954.
[4] Personal interview with Ruth Scott, 11 September 1974.
[5] Helen Hulett Searl, "Wizard of the Pipes," *The Christian Science Monitor*, 5 June 1943, p. 6.
[6] *Organ in the College of the City of New York,* pamphlet published by the Ernest M. Skinner Organ Company (courtesy of Barbara Owen).
[7] "Richmond H. Skinner," *The Diapason,* July 1941, p.15.
[8] This was after the Ernest M. Skinner Company moved into a new factory in Dorchester in early 1914.
[9] Personal interview with George Scott, 11 September 1974.
[10] Letter received from Eugenia S. Shorrock, 20 April 1974.
[11] Personal interview with William Deveau, 3 May 1973.
[12] "Ernest M. Skinner Breaks Rib," *The Diapason,* February 1915, p. 10.
[13] "Convention Echos," *The Diapason,* October 1928, p. 39.
[14] Personal interview with Edward B. Gammons, 3 May 1976.
[15] Letter received from Harold Gleason, 14 March 1975.

CHAPTER 7

World War I and After: 1914-1919

BY 1914 INCREASED FACILITIES were necessary to handle Ernest Skinner's rapidly growing business. Early that year, the Ernest M. Skinner Company moved into a new factory building located at Crescent Avenue and Sydney Street in Dorchester, Massachusetts.[1] The Skinner firm had been settled into its new and larger quarters only about half a year when World War I broke out in Europe on 28 July 1914. However, the war had little immediate effect on the organ business in America, since the United States did not become directly involved for several more years. Between 1914 and 1917 the Skinner Company continued to build some large and important instruments.

One of the first noteworthy instruments to be constructed in the new Skinner factory in 1914 was the big four-manual organ for Finney Chapel, Oberlin College, Oberlin, Ohio.[2] In the April 1915 issue of *The Diapason* it was announced that Ernest Skinner had just been awarded contracts to build large four-manual instruments for New Old South Church, Boston, Massachusetts; Central Methodist Church, Detroit, Michigan; and Universalist Church, also in Detroit.[3]

Upon its completion, the Central Methodist Skinner was described in the December 1915 issue of *The Diapason* as being "one of the finest Skinner organs in the country." This account, which announced the dedication of the instrument on 9 November 1915, opined:

> In drawing up the specifications Mr. York *[then organist at Central Methodist]* had in mind an ideal organ for use in the church service.

This ideal has been realized by Mr. Skinner in producing an instrument whose massive and dignified tone, with the smooth and clear voicing of both flue and reed stops, makes it suitable for accompanying either the solo voice or the full congregation. In addition a number of stops of special tone color and orchestral effects have been included and these add largely to the value of the instrument as a recital organ.[4]

The Echo organ of the Central Methodist Skinner contained a Cor de Nuit and a Flute Celeste, the latter consisting of a second rank of Cor de Nuit pipes tuned slightly sharp. The Skinner Cor de Nuit is a capped metal flute of large scale with an almost pure fundamental tone. The use of the tremolo imparts a lovely, ethereal quality to a single Cor de Nuit rank. When this stop is paired with another identical rank, tuned sharp as a celeste, the result is at once hypnotic and incredibly mystical. A number of Skinner organs built during the mid-to-late 'teens had a single rank of Cor de Nuit pipes appearing in the Echo division. However, only two examples of a Skinner Cor de Nuit Celeste are known to the author, those being the one at Central Methodist Church, Detroit, and a "Night Horn" Celeste in the 1913 vintage Skinner at St. Thomas Church in New York City.

The larger Skinner organs built during the mid-teens contained a good representation of the many orchestral imitative stops which Ernest had developed since 1906. However, these stops were often included at the expense of the diapason chorus. The Great flue chorus now seldom went above the 4' Octave, and the Swell was often lacking a 4' Clarion.[5] Also, by this time, the diapasons tended to be somewhat bigger and heavier than before, and the chorus reeds were darker and less brilliant. At the same time, the mixtures, when present, were of larger scale and voiced to be louder and more assertive than those appearing in Skinner organs built around 1906.

In September 1916 the Ernest M. Skinner Company was awarded the contract to build an organ for the Municipal Auditorium of Portland, Oregon. According to an announcement in the October 1916 *Diapason,* the large four-manual, sixty-six stop instrument was predicted to be "one of the most notable organs on the Pacific coast." Ernest Skinner considered this instrument of such importance that he traveled to Portland and personally supervised its installation.[6]

Due to the rapid growth of the Skinner firm during the early and mid-'teens, Ernest Skinner found himself increasingly encumbered with sales and business concerns. This meant that there would be less time for him to spend in the voicing room creating new colors to incorporate in the tonal palette of the Skinner organ. Early in 1917 Ernest solved this problem by taking on William E. Zeuch as vice president of the firm. Mr. Zeuch had great ability as a salesman and was also an excellent organist. He was "to take an active part in the promotion of the sale" of Skinner organs and "devote his time principally to the business end of the firm, giving Mr. Skinner more time to devote himself to the artistic side."[7]

Among the more significant instruments built by the Skinner firm during the year 1917 were those for Carnegie Music Hall, Pittsburgh, Pennsylvania; and Brick Presbyterian Church and St. Bartholomew's Episcopal Church, New York City.[8] The Carnegie Music Hall Skinner contained two stops of particular interest. In the Swell division was a 4' Violette, a two rank string celeste. This is the first known instance of a 4' celeste being used in a Skinner organ. The Grosse Gedeckt also made its first known appearance in this instrument.[9] The Skinner brochure gives this description:

> The Grosse Gedeckt is very peculiar in its construction. The so called mouth of the pipe is about midway its length. The scale is large, but the amount of wind given it is somewhat limited, so that the tone is one of quiet fullness. It is very useful in large instruments, both to give body to a mass of tone, and also as a solo voice.

The author once had the opportunity to try out a Grosse Gedeckt in the Solo division of the Skinner in St. Joseph's Cathedral in Columbus, Ohio. When used with the tremolo for a solo melody, it had a most beautiful singing quality.

Meanwhile, Ernest completed the writing of a forty-eight page book, entitled *The Modern Organ,* in which he set forth some of his theories and opinions on the subject of organ building. A few years before, Ernest had built an organ for Appleton Chapel, Harvard University, where Dr. Archibald T. Davison was organist. Ernest and "Doc" Davison were close friends, but did not always agree when it came to tonal matters. Doc Davison, having studied with Widor in France, wanted Ernest to put French reeds in the organ at Appleton Chapel. Ernest agreed to do so, but his "French" reeds turned out to be more Willis English and Doc Davison objected, saying "This organ is not at all what I wanted." Consequently, when his book was published in 1917, Ernest dedicated it to Doc Davison out of spite![10]

In early 1917 the Ernest M. Skinner Company announced that it was "making a specialty of its house organs" and was "branching out in that field extensively."[11] During the 'teens and 1920s, residence organs were bought as status symbols by the wealthy, who had homes (and incomes) large enough to accommodate a pipe organ. Since most home-organ owners of that day were not organists, the Skinner residence organ, like other makes of residence organs, was equipped with a player mechanism which would play the organ by means of perforated rolls, much in the manner of the player piano.

On 25 September 1917, organist-composer Gordon Balch Nevin joined the Skinner staff to take "entire charge of the roll-cutting department." One of his most important duties was the arranging of musical scores for a rather complex and sophisticated player organ called the "Orchestrator," which had been invented by Ernest Skinner and "perfected after twenty years' work."[12]

This Orchestrator organ was made possible by some "new and useful Improvements in Automatic Musical Instruments" developed around the year 1915. These improvements enabled it to play an orchestral score with up to four independent voices, each sounding a different note simultaneously. According to E. M. Skinner,

> One of the objects of the invention is to secure the same musical effect as is produced by the several instruments of an orchestra. Ordinarily in an orchestra, each instrument produces a succession of single notes, and, to produce a chord, several instruments must be caused to speak simultaneously. For instance, to produce a chord of the key of c, the lower c may be sounded by a French horn, the e above by a clarinet, the g by an oboe, and the c above by a flute. Thus there is secured an independence of voices, which is not possible in an instrument operated by a single keyboard; for example, in a pipe organ, if the flute stop be drawn, all of the notes of the chord will sound a flute tone, and the same is true of any other stop. Hence one of the results which I desire to achieve by my invention is the independence of voices in a pipe organ, or other instrument containing groups of sounding devices, so that chords may be sounded in which each of the several notes is produced by the pipe or sounding device of only one of the different groups, and thus secure the effect of different instruments of an orchestra.[13]

The Orchestrator organ was apparently completed in 1917, the same year that the Skinner firm began to branch out more extensively into the house organ field.[14] This instrument was designed primarily as a display model for prospective home organ buyers.[15] It contained examples of most of the orchestral imitative stops which were available for inclusion in Skinner home organs. The October 1917 issue of *The Diapason* gives this description of the Orchestrator:

> The new instrument contains many of Mr. Skinner's inventions whereby the tones of the orchestral instruments are faithfully reproduced. In addition the instrument contains a full size concert grand piano, and it is possible to reproduce a concerto for piano with complete orchestral accompaniments.

At least one Skinner tonal development, the 16' Orchestral Bassoon, made its first appearance in the Orchestrator organ.[16] "The opening notes of Dukas' 'Sorcerer's Apprentice,' and Strauss' 'Thus Spake Zarathustra,'" both beginning "on the bottom note of the contra bassoon," served as inspiration for the development of the Skinner Orchestral Bassoon. After hearing these two works, Ernest "worked with a form of organ reed resembling closely the form of the bassoon and arrived at a satisfactory reproduction of the bassoon."[17] In the Skinner Company brochure, Ernest gives his description of the Bassoon's expressive capabilities:

> The Bassoon is the natural bass of the Oboe and English Horn. It is sometimes spoken of as the clown of the orchestra. It also may well typify the variety of purposes to which a somewhat inflexible musical sound will lend itself. There is an indescribable grotesqueness in the voice of the Bassoon. It is, in certain aspects, irresistibly ludicrous.
>
> On the other hand, there is about the Bassoon a certain level drone, a "bloodless indifference" that may suggest the inhuman, the terrifying or sinister. It is extraordinary that an apparently inexpressive tone will so perfectly voice such opposite extremes as the droll and the sinister.

The Orchestrator organ also contained what may possibly have been the first Skinner 4' Unda Maris.[18] This stop consisted of two sets of Aeoline pipes at 4' pitch, with one rank being tuned slightly flat to the unison. In regard to the 4' Unda Maris, the Skinner Company brochure states,

> It is a small voice. It contributes an effect similar to that which would be obtained if muted strings were playing, and other strings repeated the same an octave above. It is an effect that cannot be obtained by octave couplers. It is unfortunate that it belongs to that class of stops that only appear in organs of considerable size. It is a lovely touch, and belongs in significance with the effects produced in the orchestra by the great composers in their rarest moments.

The 4' Unda Maris was usually included in Swell divisions already equipped with at least two sets of celestes, a Voix Celeste and a Flute

Celeste. It is particularly well suited for use in combination with the Flute Celeste and makes an uncommonly lovely combination with the Flute Celeste and 8′ Unda Maris, when the latter is available.[19]

In a letter written to Alexander McCurdy on 11 June 1954, Ernest Skinner tells how the 4′ Unda Maris came into being:

> . . . the most beautiful possible combination of stops I have ever heard is my Flute Celeste of two ranks combined with a four Ft. two rank Unda Maris. I found this out by accident. I built an organ for a Catholic church in New York City and the Swell had a Flute Celeste and the Choir an eight Ft. Unda Maris.
>
> I just happened to have the swell coupled to great and the Choir to great at octaves and the two rank 8 Ft. plus the two rank 4 Ft. made the most beautiful sound I ever heard.

Also included in the Skinner Orchestrator organ was an Orchestral Flute, which was especially designed and voiced for use in residence organs.[20]

According to the October 1917 *Diapason,* a new building to house the roll-cutting department and a concert hall for the recently built Orchestrator organ was now under construction. It was not to be completed for another three years, for by mid-1917 this country was directly involved in World War I.

On 2 April 1917, after managing to avoid involvement in World War I for almost three years, the United States reluctantly entered the conflict. All Americans were, in one way or another, to be affected by the war, including Ernest Skinner and his family.

In June of that year, Ernest's daughter Eugenia graduated from the Lasell Seminary for Young Women. Now nearly twenty-one years old, she was at the age when most young women are seriously thinking about marriage. Ernest thought that William Zeuch, vice-president of his firm, would be a good husband for Eugenia. However, even though Zeuch was nice enough, he was so much older that he seemed like an "old fogy" to her. As it turned out, Zeuch played the organ for Eugenia's wedding instead, for she married another man, Ernest Shorrock, on 16 August 1917. Eugenia and her husband subsequently moved into a big house at 259 Savin Hill Avenue on the corner of Evandale Terrace, only a few doors away from her parents' home.[21]

In the fall of 1917, Ernest Skinner's adventuresome spirit along with the good fortune of having congenial friends led him to engage in an exciting new experience following the dedication of the Municipal Auditorium organ in Portland, Oregon. In those days, aviation was a relatively new mode of transportation and, not surprisingly, Ernest's imagination had been captivated by its possibilities. In "Organ Builder Soars Above Clouds" (*The Diapason,* December 1917, p. 6), Ernest admits to having entertained thoughts of buying a "flying machine" himself. However, he "hadn't the price, so remained on earth."

A long-time friend, J. B. Struble who lived in Oakland, California, also had a keen interest in flying and had recently bought a "hydroaeroplane." Following the Portland Auditorium organ dedication at which both Ernest and Mr. Struble were persent, Ernest accepted his friend's offer to take him on a flight. They crossed over the San Francisco Bay half a mile above the earth. Ernest was held spellbound by the scenery as viewed from above the clouds, and found the "whole experience was so gorgeously exhilarating that *[he]* forgot to be frightened." Naturally being an avid photographer, Ernest took his camera with him on the flight. One of his aerial photographs taken "at height of 5,000 feet . . . from airship above San Francisco Bay," appeared with his article in *The Diapason.*

According to his daughter Ruth, Ernest had not told his wife Mabel of his plans to take an airplane ride, knowing it would cause her to worry about him. Upon his return home, Mabel was rather "upset over his taking such a chance with his life."[22]

In 1918 World War I was to directly affect the Skinner family, for during that year Ernest's son Richmond enlisted in the armed forces, serving as a field artillery officer for the last six months of the war.[23] He did not see active combat and after the Armistice on 11 November 1918, returned to Boston and resumed his studies at the Massachusetts Institute of Technology.[24]

It was inevitable that America's involvement in World War I would affect the organ world. Wartime fuel shortages were responsible for the cancellation of organ recitals during the winter of 1918.[25] In that same year, organ construction was drastically reduced since the tin, lead, and zinc necessary for the fabrication of organ pipes was needed for military use.[26] Even in 1917 only fourteen organs were installed by the Skinner firm, and only one was installed by the firm during 1918.[27]

Even before the war began all was not well with the Ernest M. Skinner Organ Company. The firm had been repeatedly plagued with financial problems almost since the time it was established. Long before the United States entered the war there were signs that the company was once again in financial difficulty. Ernest, a man of high artistic principles, took a dim view of reducing quality to save on construction costs. Yet he did sacrifice quality in a few instances during the mid-teens, probably out of necessity. In at least one organ of that vintage, built in 1915 for the Church of Our Father Universalist Church (now First Unitarian-Universalist) Detroit, Michigan, Skinner resorted to building bass pipes out of sheet metal instead of the usual but more expensive zinc.[28] Also between 1912 and 1916, the Skinner Company did subcontracted work for M. Welte and Sons, Inc. of Poughkeepsie, New York. This subcontracted work consisted of seven two-manual organs and one three-manual organ. These instruments, some of which were equipped with a player attachment, were designed mainly as residence organs.[29] According to Joseph Dzeda they were identical in most respects to organs built under the Skinner name, but were somewhat cheapened in construction, having smaller magnets and the like.

By 1919 Ernest Skinner was at the point of bankruptcy. This may have been partly due to the interference of the war. Also, the construction of the new factory building for the Skinner firm probably put quite a dent in the company funds. On top of that, the 16th (Income Tax) Amendment was passed by the Federal Government in 1913, undoubtedly taking a bite out of any profits Ernest was able to realize, though above all, Ernest's driving ambition to build the "best organ ever" resulted in most of the recurring financial problems which beset his firm.

E. M. Skinner was undeniably one of the finest organ builders in the country. But as his long-time friend Dr. William H. Barnes put it, "the artistic attainments of Mr. Skinner greatly outranked his business ability."[30] Ernest's nephew Ned Hastings recalls:

> Ernest Skinner was always the organ builder first and the business man last. In fact he was the worst business man I know anything about. My father, who was a lawyer, was constantly engaged in various legal messes for Uncle Ernest. I was horrified to discover how many such difficulties there had been; these came to my attention when I was clearing out Dad's papers after his death . . . Apparently the chief problem lay in the fact that Ernest, in the interests of building the best organ possible, usually wound up spending more money on an organ than the contract had stipulated.[31]

Robert Baker, who knew Ernest Skinner as an old man, provides additional insight as to the way Ernest's mind worked when it came to business details.

> . . . extreme devotion to excellence, regardless of cost, may be one reason why Mr. Skinner never really was on firm financial ground.

He was, first of all, an artist, and always figured there would be a way found to add, uncontracted for, a 32′ stop, just because he felt it was needed. Only occasionally was he able to convince the church or college that this extra expense should be added to the contract, once the work was done![32]

In 1916 Ernest had made the acquaintance of Arthur Hudson Marks, a wealthy chemist and businessman who was the "active head" of the Goodyear Rubber Company, "in charge of all operations." In his autobiography, Mr. Marks tells of the events which led to his meeting with Ernest Skinner:

In 1914 I was pleased with a residence organ which I heard somewhere and got one for my home. I grew very fond of it. In 1915 I purchased an organ for my yacht. In 1916 I met Ernest Skinner and went to hear his work. It was conspicuously better than anything I had ever heard tonally and mechanically and there began instantly a friendship and a co-operation which has endured.[33]

One immediate result of the association of E. M. Skinner and A. H. Marks was that Marks ended up buying a Skinner residence organ for his home in Yorktown Heights, New York, around the year 1919.[34] Another outcome of this alliance was to have a far greater significance for the future of Ernest's foundering business. Marks had entered the Navy in 1917. When the war was over, he had "decided never to return to active business but to retain and enjoy *[his]* freedom after twenty-four years of heavy responsibility and hard work." As it turned out, Marks presently found himself once again up to his neck in business matters:

Skinner needed financial help and I helped him. But the needs of the Skinner Company were greater then either of us forsaw *[sic]*. We were both optimistic . . . I determined to study the business carefully to decide whether to liquidate it or refinance it . . .
This thorough study of the situation resulted in a reorganization of the business with ample capital, improvements in the factory and those safeguards of quality which were necessary.[35]

Thanks to Marks' financial assistance, the old Ernest M. Skinner Organ Company was given a new lease on life in 1919. The firm was now called the Skinner Organ Company and had an authorized capital stock of $250,000 of which $205,000 had been issued.[36] Arthur Hudson Marks, to whom Ernest had sold control of the company, was now its president with Ernest M. Skinner and William E. Zeuch both sharing the office of vice president.³⁷ The November 1919 *Diapason* had this to say regarding the artistic significance of the Skinner firm's reorganization:

> It is of special importance to the musical world in general, and to the lovers of organ music in particular, that under the new arrangement Mr. Skinner is enabled to devote practically his entire time to the development of the organ which he has made famous, without being handicapped with the details of business management.

FOOTNOTES

[1]"Skinner Factory is Ready," *The Diapason*, February 1914, p. 1.

[2]"Oberlin College Orders New Skinner," *The Diapason*, July 1914, p. 1. This instrument was rebuilt with extensive tonal changes in 1953.

[3]The organ installed in the Universalist Church (now First Unitarian-Universalist) was not entirely typical of the mid-teens Skinner, but is important due to the fact that it is the only large Skinner of its vintage without tonal changes or additions known to be extant (see Dorothy J. Holden, "The Tonal Evolution of the E. M. Skinner Organ, Part II," *The Diapason*, February 1978, p. 17, for specification and description of this instrument). The New Old South Church Skinner had been replaced by a new organ and the Central Methodist instrument had been rebuilt with extensive tonal revisions and additions.

[4]"Great Skinner Organ is Opened at Detroit," *The Diapason*, December 1915, p. 1.

[5]A few larger Skinner organs of that day did have a complete Great chorus which would include at least one Diapason (usually two Diapasons), a 4' Octave, a 2-2/3' Twelfth, a 2' Fifteenth, plus a Mixture of three or four ranks. Standard equipment for the average Skinner Swell included an 8' Diapason (or two), a 4' Octave, and a three rank Mixture of the Cornet type, plus chorus reeds at 16', 8', and (sometimes) 4' pitch.

[6]"Gala Days of Music at Portland, Oregon," *The Diapason*, October 1917, p. 1. This instrument is no longer extant.

[7]"William E. Zeuch Joins the Skinner Company," *The Diapason*, January 1917, p. 3; also a letter received from William H. Barnes, December 1974.

[8]E. A. Boadway, "The Skinner & Aeolian-Skinner Opus List," *The Boston Organ Club Newsletter*, July & August 1972. pp. 6 & 7; The St. Bartholomew's instrument incorporated some old pipe-work from the 1893 Hutchings organ, the installation of which had been supervised by E. M. Skinner.

[9]"Carnegie Music Hall Will Have New Organ," *The Diapason*, March 1917, p. 1; According to T. Scott Buhrman, this stop was introduced in the Skinner built for Second Congregational Church, Holyoke, Massachusetts in 1920, three years after the Carnegie Music Hall Skinner was built ("Ernest M. Skinner: Organ Builder," *The American Organist*, 8, no. 5 (May 1925), p. 183).

[10]Personal interview with Edward B. Gammons, 3 May 1976.

[11]"William E. Zeuch," p. 3.

[12]"Gordon Balch Nevin Joins Skinner Force," *The Diapason*, October 1917, p. 11.

[13]Patent no. 1,192,005, *Specifications and Drawings of Patents*, 25 July 1916.

[14]"Gordon Balch Nevin," p. 11.

[15]Skinner Organ Company Advertisement, *The Diapason*, November 1920, p. 23.

[16]Buhrman, p. 183.

[17]Ernest M. Skinner, "Ernest M. Skinner Recalls the Past on 85th. Birthday," *The Diapason*, March 1951, p. 4.

[18]This organ (Opus 290) was reinstalled in the Nardin Park Methodist Church (now Ebenezer A. M. E. Church), Detroit, Michigan, by the Aeolian-Skinner Company in the early 1940s, a diapason chorus being added by that firm soon after its installation. The 4' Unda Maris was retained in this instrument.

[19]In the Skinner organ, the 8' Unda Maris, like the 4' Unda Maris, is comprised of two ranks of Aeoline pipes. However, when both stops are included in a Swell division, the latter stop is not a duplicate of the former at 4' pitch. The 4' Unda Maris is very light and silvery in quality, while the 8' Unda Maris is scaled and voiced to be slightly louder and broader.

[20]"The Skinner Small Residence Organ," *Stop, Open, and Reed,* 1, no. 3 (July 1922), p. 12.

[21]Personal interview with Eugenia S. Shorrock, April 1973.

[22]Letter received from Ruth Scott, 25 May 1975.

[23]"R. H. Skinner," *The American Organist,* 17, no. 4 (April 1934), 177.

[24]"Richmond H. Skinner," *The Diapason,* July 1941, p. 15.

[25]"Trinity Concerts are Off," *The Diapason,* February 1918, p. 22.

[26]"Thirty Per Cent Cut in Organ Construction," *The Diapason,* May 1918, p. 1.

[27]Boadway, pp. 6 & 7.

[28]The sheet metal bass pipes in the First Unitarian Church organ are in the organ case and painted gold; all other bass pipes in this instrument are constructed of wood.

[29]Boadway, pp. 5 & 6.

[30]William H. Barnes, "Appreciation of Ernest M. Skinner Voiced by Barnes," *The Diapason,* December 1959, p. 39.

[31]Edward H. Hastings, Letter to Joseph Dzeda, 31 March 1966.

[32]Letter received from Robert Baker, 20 February 1976.

[33]Arthur Hudson Marks, "An Autobiography," *Stop, Open, and Reed,* 2, no. 1 (January 1924), 7.

[34]Boadway, p. 7.

[35]Marks, p. 7.

[36]"Skinner Company Starts in New Era," *The Diapason,* November 1919, p. 1.

[37]Letter received from Edward W. Flint, 10 April 1973; "Skinner Company Starts on New Era," p. 1.

CHAPTER 8

The Roaring Twenties

THE SKINNER Organ Company prospered in 1920. With A. H. Marks' financial backing and business know-how, the firm entered a new epoch in which its growth and prestige were to reach heights uncommon for an organ building establishment. By spring of that year it was necessary for the company to raise its capital stock from $205,000 to $250,000 to take care of its increased volume of business.[1] During 1920 the Skinner firm had approximately twenty-nine installations under way.[2] Some of the largest and most important of these installations were the organs built for Grove Park Inn, Asheville, North Carolina; Jordan Hall, New England Conservatory, Boston; Municipal Auditorium, St. Paul, Minnesota; Second Congregational Church, Holyoke, Massachusetts; and Kilbourn Hall, Eastman School of Music, Rochester, New York.[3]

The Grove Park Inn organ, which Ernest Skinner declared "was the best work he had produced up to then," contained his first Heckelphone stop.[4] Ernest described his Heckelphone as being "like an immense English horn with its richest development in the lower two octaves."[5] In his editorial appearing in the April 1921 *Diapason,* we learn of his inspiration for its creation:

> I heard a rare and beautiful voice in Richard Strauss' "Salome" one that was entirely new to me. Investigation disclosed its name and memory preserved its quality for ten years . . .

With the introduction of his Heckelphone, Ernest had essentially completed the creation of most of his orchestral imitative stops. However, his labor to improve the tonal resources of the Skinner organ was far from being finished.

The new studio building for the Skinner Organ Company was finally completed in 1920, and by November of that year the "Symphonic" (or "Orchestrator") organ was moved to its permanent location in the studio music room. Along with the organ, the roll-cutting department was moved across the street into the new building.[6]

The completion of the new studio was deemed an occasion for a party which was held on the evening of 12 April 1921 for the Skinner Company's employees and their families. This party was given "for the purpose of enabling those who make the Skinner organ to become acquainted with the player organ which the company is building." It was a gala occasion. Following a demonstration of the "Symphonic" player organ, refreshments were served in the main factory building, after which

> the entire party then returned to the music room, where the rugs and furniture had been taken out and dancing was enjoyed by all until a late hour . . .
> The affair not only fulfilled the purpose for which it was intended, but served to develop a spirit of friendliness among the workers, which makes for a better feeling in the days' work.[7]

The "get acquainted with the Symphonic organ" party was only the first of many social events to be held for the two hundred some employees of the Skinner Organ Company during the 1920s. Within a few years the employees had organized eight bowling teams and a company band.[8] This band performed under the direction of Ernest M. Skinner himself at the annual dinner and theater parties which were held for "the foremen, bowling teams and brass band of the Skinner factory."[9]

Ernest Skinner, whom the factory men called "E. M.," made a point of personally keeping in touch with every man who worked for him. According to John Stenberg, who did electrical work for Skinner in the 1920s, Ernest was the sort of employer who, when supervising organ installations, would take off his coat, roll up his sleeves, and pitch in to help the workers. He was kind to his employees and listened to their problems. The workers, in return, all loved him.

A staunch Republican, Ernest did not believe in unions. At one time, presumably during the 'teens when labor unrest was rampant, one of his employees attempted to organize a union in his factory. In a letter written to Barbara Owen on 16 April 1957, Ernest tells how he handled the situation when these unionized employees went on strike:

> I had a bench man working for me named Worley. He organized a union in my factory who demanded more wages which I refused as I was paying my men more than any other builder in Boston or near Boston. Well they went on a strike and Hastings called all the organ builders in Boston to a consultation and we agreed not to raise wages one cent and then Hastings went back home and gave his men what they went on strike for and so the rest of us had closed shops for five months, but when Worley came back and wanted to know if I wasn't sick of the strike, I told *[him]* I didn't have any strike. So he laughed and said he guessed I did, so I told him to go up and look for himself so he did and saw every single bench had a man working there. I had hired carpenters at the original wages and trained them to be organ builders and so every last striker except the Hastings men had to leave town to get work as organ builders. So that was that.

Apparently Ernest paid good wages during the 1920s, for he had no labor problems then, in spite of the fact that his workers were still not unionized.[10] The harmony that prevailed at the Skinner Organ Company during that decade was also undoubtedly due to the unusually good personal relationship which existed between the workers and their employer, Ernest M. Skinner.

Ernest Skinner was now undisputably the number one organ builder in the United States and had become a dominant influential figure on the organ scene. He had been elected president of the Organ Builders' Association of America in 1919 at its first annual convention and was now much in demand as a speaker at organists' conventions.[11] A review of one such convention during the 1920s stated that "Ernest Skinner always speaks with vigor and assurance, and always he is worth hearing."[12] It was also said of him that "his sincerity is so evident and his knowledge of his subject so profound that he can say sharp things without leaving a sting."[13]

Ernest's mere presence at an organists' convention commanded attention. With his full head of white hair and moustache set off by a very pink complexion and blue eyes, he made a most impressive and distinguished appearance. He always wore a white shirt and a vest with his suit. Ernest spoke with "clipped New England speech," and in normal conversation, had what has been described as a "soft mellow voice."[14] A touch of Goya Lily perfume, described by his daughter Engenia as having a "delicious lily smell," completed the image.

Even when Ernest was not a featured speaker at conventions he was generally the main attraction at such gatherings. He loved adulation and praise and being in the company of admirers, especially musicians.[15] In an article written many years later, William H. Barnes recalls:

> I remember well the national conventions of the Guild and of the old National Association of Organists of twenty-five or more years ago, when Mr. Skinner was the center of attention at all such gatherings. The younger and older organists all stood around him with bated breath, listening to his wit and wisdom. He furnished both with equal facility charm, and salty New England humour.[16]

According to Robert Baker,

> ... at the organist's conventions in the '20s Mr. Skinner cut the largest swath of anyone in attendance. He was always followed by a large retinue of admirers and friends, partly to share the spotlight, and partly to latch onto the latest supply of Skinner limericks which were seemingly inexhaustible ... .[17]

In a letter dated 17 March 1973, Wheeler Beckett, a close friend of Ernest Skinner for many years, relates:

> When I remember Ernest I always think of his sense of humor. His jests, his limericks about music ... One of his favorites was,
> There was a young fellow named Batch,
> Who was fond of the music of Bach (Batch),
> He said it's not fussy
> Like Brahms or Debussy,
> Sit down and I'll play you a snatch!
> Or this,
> There was a young singer named Hanna
> Who got caught in a flood in Montana,
> She floated away,
> Accompanied, they say,
> By her sister upon the piana.
> ... And he would recite these with a straight face—almost a frown— that made them seem funnier than ever.

Ernest carried with him a little black book which contained the catch lines to his humorous stories. Ned Hastings recalls that at family gatherings, his Uncle Ernest would often bring out his "little black book," thumb through it, and then start out by saying, "Did you hear the one ... ?" The family, of course, had heard them all many times, but they'd let him go ahead on the first one. However, on the second one, they'd say, we've heard it."

Few of the people who were eyewitnesses to Ernest Skinner's convention appearances during the 'teens and 1920s are still living. However, many of Ernest's humorous anecdotes and limericks are preserved in his personal correspondence. Letters written by him during his later years were particularly rich in examples of his brand of humor. One of his most often repeated verses was this one, quoted from a letter written by Ernest to Alexander McCurdy on 10 June 1954:

> A young theologian named Fiddle
> Declined to accept his degree
> He said, "it's all right to be Fiddle
> But not to be Fiddle D. D."

Ernest's anecdotes, like his limericks, frequently pertained to music, such as this:

> Once at a choir rehearsal in New Britain the Bass had a solo to sing and there was a very low note he had to sing. The Choir master accused the bass of singing flat. Bass said "impossible. It was all I could do to get down there that low."[18]

Or this:

> Did you ever hear of the lady who sang through her veil and strained her voice?

Some of Ernest's anecdotes could be a bit naughty:

> Did you hear of the lady who wrote asking husband to send check for $25.00. He replied, "didn't have $25. but was sending his check for 25 kisses." She replied thanking him for check for 25 kisses and said, milk man had cashed it for her that morning!!![19]

According to Ned Hastings, the following story was "one of the standards" in Ernest's repertoire and "he would make a great show of being sure no ladies were present."[20]

> A lady got a young fellow to mow her lawn and he was telling the boys about it afterwards. He said that "after the lawn was finished she invited him in to have something to eat. The last thing she brought on was a great big pumpkin pie. And she was awful nice to me. She sat on my lap and kissed me and said we were all alone and we could go the limit and by gosh I did; I ate the whole pie."[21]

Some of Ernest's humorous stories were mildly irreverent, such as this one which he told often:

> A tramp knocked at the back door of a house and asked for something to eat. The woman very grudgingly gave him a piece of bread, saying: "Now remember, I'm not giving this to you for your sake or for my sake, but for the Lord's sake." To which the tramp answered, "Then, madame, would you for Christ's sake put some butter on it."22

The moral fanaticism which attended American intervention in World War I culminated in the ratification of the 18th (or Prohibition) Amendment on 16 January 1920, making the consumption or sale of liquor, beer and wine illegal throughout the United States. This amendment turned out to be the joke of the decade, as moonshining and bootlegging thrived, and Americans continued to consume all the more alcoholic beverages in speakeasies and in the privacy of their homes.

According to his daughter Ruth, Ernest Skinner never drank until Prohibition. He then had the finest bootleg liquors available in his home, as he regarded Prohibition a violation of rights. Ruth recalls that "he mixed the lousiest drinks with the best of liquor." On one occasion during the 1920s, Ernest was entertaining some musicians in his home and his daughter Eugenia, now married, was present. She was very surprised to be handed a cocktail glass by her mother since the Skinners never had drinks in their home during the pre-Prohibition days, before Eugenia had married and left home.

Ernest did not conceal the fact that he relished this illegal pastime and openly showed his contempt for the Prohibition Amendment. In an account of a trip he made abroad during the mid-1920s he describes a dining experience in France and flagrantly comments:

> But I must and do say I did enjoy a pint of Sautern for 40 cents with my dinner. A delightful bouquet and delicate flavor, harmless and joyous after a busy day.23

During the 'teens, women persistently crusaded for the right to vote and finally won their cause in the year 1920. But this was only a part of the change which had taken place in the "fairer sex" over the previous decade. The younger generation of women now smoked cigarettes, drove automobiles, bobbed their hair, and generally "behaved in a manner that shocked [their] conservative elders."24

Ernest Skinner viewed this new breed of female with mixed feelings. He liked women to be ladies and had very definite opinions on this matter. Ernest hated to see women smoking cigarettes. He also generally disapproved of makeup and particularly disliked lipstick and red fingernails (which he disparagingly referred to as "bloody fingernails"). However, his wife Mabel surreptitiously used rouge and kept it hidden in her drawer.

Ernest was always a year or so behind times in his acceptance of new customs and fashion trends. During the mid-teens when Eugenia was going to college, she bought herself a swim suit which was rather daring for that time. It had short sleeves, a square neck, and short pants covered by a skirt with slits on the sides. Compared with today's swim attire it was exceedingly modest, but Ernest was furious at his daughter for buying this swim suit, as he thought it was indecent, "exposing" herself so much. Nevertheless, a year or so later he bought Mabel a much briefer one.

Ernest had an appreciation of good female figures and apparently made no attempt to conceal his enjoyment of looking at them. This annoyed Mabel, although she also had an excellent figure.

It undoubtedly took Ernest a while to get accustomed to the Emancipated Woman, but he soon grew to admire these ladies, especially as more and more of them were becoming accomplished professional musicians. Women were now breaking into the previously male-dominated organist's world, and a few of the more talented and determined of these female musicians were succeeding as recitalists.

The emergence of women into the organ recital field was due not only to the changing social climate, but also to the development and perfection of the electro-pneumatic action with its resultant lighter touch and ease of control. This enabled women to become virtuoso concert organists on a par with, or even surpassing, their male counterparts. Since Ernest had worked hard to improve the electro-pneumatic action and had succeeded in developing an action which was light and more responsive than that of any other organ builder of the day, it is not surprising that he took great personal pride in the increasing number of women organists who were becoming concert artists. As time went on, he did much to promote and encourage them. Several of these gifted and ambitious women recitalists, such as Georgia B. Easton, Edith Lang, and Charlotte Lockwood Garden, were among Ernest's wide circle of personal friends.

His admiration of talented women also extended into other creative fields. As previously mentioned, Ernest was very proud of his wife's ability as an artist. According to his daughter, Eugenia, he made the acquaintance of the famous actress Cornelia Otis Skinner (who was of no direct relation to Ernest Skinner and his family). But it was mainly musicians, male and female, who inspired Ernest's devotion and who constituted the majority of his friends.

Thanks to the new prosperity of the Skinner Organ Company and to the thriving economy of the 1920s, the Skinners were now enjoying a life of comparative affluence and Ernest could at last afford to have his wife occasionally accompany him while on business trips and installation jobs. The first account we have of Mabel being with him on one of these trips was when he was installing the organ at Grove Park Inn, Asheville, North Carolina. While working on this instrument Ernest made the acquaintance of a reserved gentleman named Calvin Coolidge. Later in life Ernest was to recall:

> Years ago my wife and I were staying at Grove Park Inn Ashville N. C. where I was placing an organ and where I had to pass Vice President elect who with Mrs. Coolidge were guests of the house. After I had passed Mr. Coolidge several times in going from the console to the Echo organ he got up from where he was sitting and came up to me and said, "How do you do, I'm from Massachusetts." I said "I know it, so am I." Mr. Coolidge said "I know it." I replied, "Mr. Coolidge if Geo. Washington had said some of the things you said during that Boston police strike they would have been quoted to this day." "What for instance," said Coolidge. I said, "Well there was a law forbidding police from unionizing and you replied 'You cannot arbitrate the law.'" "What else" said Mr. Coolidge. "You told them, 'Nobody anywhere, at any time, for any reason, has a right to strike against the public safety' and you called them 'deserters.'"
>
> Well perhaps you have heard that Mr. Coolidge was taciturn and non communicative, but every day I was there after that, Mr. Coolidge met me and told me of his various experiences and he was one of the most interesting conversationalists I ever knew.
>
> Mrs. Coolidge and Mrs. Skinner who was with me, used to sit and knit or crochet together and later when they [the Coolidges] were in the White House we wrote and congratulated them and they invited us to come and see them. I have always regretted that we did not accept this very friendly invitation.[25]

According to their daughter Ruth, Ernest and Mabel had been invited by the Coolidges to attend a reception at the White House. They turned down this invitation because Mabel did not want to go. Ruth could not recall the exact reason for her mother's reluctance, but she thought that Mabel felt uncomfortable about being around so much "top brass."

On several occasions, Ernest took both Mabel and Ruth (who, by this time, was the only child still at home) with him on extended business trips during the 1920s. Ruth recalled going with her father to California and to Florida while he was working on organ installations. Not all of their vacations during these years were busman's holidays, however.

Ernest and his family went "through the White Mountains every year," and even though they could now afford to do more traveling, the Skinners' favorite vacation spot was still their camp at Alton Bay.[26] According to Ruth Scott, they loved Alton Bay and did not have "any particular desire to go anywhere else."

By the early 1920s Ruth was old enough to go to college. Instead of following in her brother's and sister's footsteps, however, she decided to do extensive traveling, which included a trip to the Mediterranean with her mother. Ruth also studied dancing at the Theodore Kosloff School in Los Angeles and languages at the Berlitz School.

Ernest had a penchant for luxury and always had to buy the "best of everything." The only problem was, even though he was now earning a rather substantial income, he still spent more than he made. Ernest's improvidence was no doubt aggravated by the "buy now, pay later" consumer philosophy that, thanks to easy credit, became quite prevalent during the 1920s.[27] According to various accounts, Ernest was quite partial to Pierce-Arrow cars, the ultimate automobiles during the early part of this century. He also was very fond of painting and sculpture and "collected it in a small way." A favorite in Ernest's art collection was an Italian white Carrara marble sculpture of a nude woman, entitled *Aurora*. Not all members of the family shared his enthusiasm for *Aurora,* whom he displayed in a prominent place in his living room. Ned Hastings relates an interesting story of how his Uncle Ernest acquired one painting in his collection:

> On one of his trips, he *[Ernest]* visited a studio and saw a painting that he liked very much but could not afford. When he returned home some weeks later, he found that the artist had shipped it to him, hoping that he might be tempted to buy it . . . but Ernest felt he couldn't afford it and finally (rather belatedly) shipped it back to the painter. On his next birthday Mabel presented him with an absolutely perfect copy that she had made without his knowledge.[28]

Most of the presents Mabel gave to Ernest on Christmas, birthdays, and anniversaries were paintings and other handiwork that she had made herself. Ernest's gifts to Mabel were usually jewelry. He disliked imitations or costume jewelry and always bought the "real thing." Being a retiring person who seldom went out to formal affairs, Mabel rarely wore jewelry. She may have worn some of it when she and Ernest attended operas or special occasions.

Ernest had a "complete inability to keep a secret. With all the best intentions in the world, he always managed to spill them, even . . . his presents to his wife. It got to be a family joke."[29] Ruth Scott recalls that her father would "get so deep in thinking" that you could see the "wheels going around." Everything was "right out in the open, and he *never* could keep a secret . . . you never told him anything if you wanted it kept quiet."[30] Ruth can remember these two incidents:

One year Ernest bought Mabel a camera for her birthday and could hardly wait to give it to her. He made everyone in the family promise to keep it a secret from her. However, about a week before her birthday while he was reading the newspaper, Ernest punched the paper down and said, "Mabel—about that camera . . ."!

At the time Ruth was engaged to be married, her fiancé, George Scott, drove up with Ernest to visit her while she was staying at Alton Bay. On a curve near Somersworth, New Hampshire, the police were running a speed trap. According to Ruth, there were open fields on both sides of the road, with visibility up to a mile in either direction. Nevertheless, George passed on the curve and promptly was caught in the trap. He was a little embarrassed about this incident and did not want Ruth's mother to know about it. Some time after George's visit, the Skinner family departed for home in two cars, as was their custom, with Ernest driving one car and Mabel driving the other. As they approached the curve near Somersworth, Ernest pulled up by Mabel's car and waved her down saying "'Mabel, this is the curve where George got caught in that trap!"

Ernest's inability to keep a secret was related to his single-minded absorption in his own train of thought. Even in the midst of musicians, Ernest's thinking often went its own way. Ned Hastings tells of an incident when he was at Alton Bay with his Uncle Ernest and Aunt Mabel. Ernest and Wheeler Beckett were having a heated discussion about why all Pastoral symphonies (Beethoven's Sixth, etc.) were written in the key of F. In mid-discussion, Ernest turned to Beckett and asked, "Where can I get a good pair of suspenders?" Everyone in the room burst into laughter, much to the bewilderment of Ernest, who asked them in all seriousness, "What is so funny?"

Those golden days of the early 1920s came close to being seriously disrupted for the Skinner family when their Savin Hill home was nearly destroyed by fire while they were at Alton Bay for the summer. While their house was being painted, one of the painters was careless with a blowtorch and set the house on fire. In those days, the only telephone in Alton Bay was in the village store. Ruth can remember Mr. Wilson coming over from the store and taking her father aside to tell him that he had been informed by phone that the Skinners' Dorchester home was on fire. It was not known whether the firemen could extinguish the blaze in time to save the house. Ernest did not want Mabel to know about the fire until he knew the outcome of it and, needless to say, it was not easy for him to keep the fact from her. Ernest, a coffee connoisseur, had been in the process of making coffee when Mr. Wilson arrived with the news of the fire. He was putting eggshells in the coffee to settle it, and was so upset over the fire when he resumed his coffee-making, he put the yolks in the coffee and threw the shells on the floor. Later on, after he was informed that the fire was out and that half of the house was gone, Ernest told Mabel about it. Fortunately, the house and its furnishings were well insured. By the time the Skinners returned home at the end of the summer the house had been completely rebuilt and everything had been restored, right down to the pictures on the walls.

FOOTNOTES

[1]"Raises Capital to $250,000," *The Diapason*, April 1920, p. 13.
[2]E. A. Boadway, "The Skinner & Aeolian-Skinner Opus List," *The Boston Organ Club Newsletter,* July & August 1972, pp. 7 & 8.
[3]Skinner Organ Company advertisement, *The Diapason*, April 1920, p. 23; Boadway, pp. 7 & 8.
[4]"The Superb Four-Manual Skinner at Grove Park Inn," *The Diapason,* December 1927, p. 9; Ernest M. Skinner, "Features in Cleveland Organ," *The Diapason,* April 1921, p. 12.
[5]Skinner, "Cleveland Organ," p. 12.
[6]Skinner Organ Company advertisement, *The Diapason*, November 1920, p. 23.
[7]"Skinner Company Host to its Factory Staff," *The Diapason*, May 1921, p. 3.
[8]"Skinner Forces at Dinner," *The Diapason,* June 1926, p. 8.
[9]"Skinner Forces at Annual Dinner," *The Diapason,* May 1928, p. 35.
[10]Personal interview with John Stenberg, 7 May 1976.
[11]"Pittsburgh Sessions of N.A.O. are Inspiring . . . Organists and Builders Meet," *The Diapason,* September 1919, p. 6.
[12]"Convention Echos," *The Diapason,* October 1928, p.39.
[13]"Speaking of Mr. Skinner," *The Diapason,* April 1928, p. 30.
[14]Newsclipping from the scrapbook of Ernest M. Skinner, 1947; Newsclipping from the scrapbook of Mabel Hastings Skinner, presumably written in 1939.
[15]Personal interview with Eugenia S. Shorrock, 11 October 1972.
[16]William H. Barnes, "Appreciation of Ernest Skinner," *The Diapason,* December 1959, p. 39.
[17]Letter received from Robert Baker, 20 February 1976.
[18]Ernest M. Skinner, Letter to Alexander McCurdy, 10 June 1954.
[19]Ernest M. Skinner, Letter to Catharine Crozier, 25 February 1952.
[20]Letter received from Edward H. Hastings, 3 February 1973.
[21]Ernest M. Skinner, Letter to Alexander McCurdy dated "July 16, 1954 A.D."
[22]Letter received from Edward H. Hastings, 3 February 1973.
[23]Ernest M. Skinner, "A Trip Abroad," *Stop, Open, and Reed,* 3, no. 1 (1935), p. 32.
[24]Editors of Time-Life Books, *This Fabulous Century* (New York: Time-Life Books, 1969), II, p. 30.
[25]Ernest M. Skinner, Letter to Alexander McCurdy, 10 June 1954.
[26]Personal interview with Ruth Scott, 11 September 1974.
[27]Editors of Time-Life Books, *This Fabulous Century,* III, p. 99.
[28]Edward H. Hastings, Letter to Joseph F. Dzeda, 12 April 1972.
[29]Letter received from Ruth Scott, January 1973.
[30]Personal interview with Ruth Scott, 11 September 1974.

CHAPTER 9

An Impressive Year
1921

DURING 1921 the Skinner Organ Company installed fifty-one organs, nearly twice the total installed during 1920.[1] This was an impressive number of contracts considering that the company had built a total of only a few more than two hundred organs during its preceding twenty-year existence. It was the employment of mass production that, in part, enabled the Skinner Company to increase its number of installations so dramatically in such a short period of time. The windchests were standardized and consoles were available in stock models. However, the pipes were all custom made and voiced to suit each installation.[2]

Early in 1921 the Skinner firm took still another step which served greatly to increase its production capacity when it acquired the factory and business of the Steere Organ Company of Westfield, Massachusetts.[3] An announcement in the April 1921 issue of *The Diapason* proclaimed that "the addition of the Steere forces to the facilities of the Boston plant of the Skinner Company will make it possible to take care of the large amount of new work, orders for which have been received by the Skinner Company." According to a statement issued by Ernest Skinner, appearing in the May 1921 issue of *The American Organist,* the Steere Organ Company's plant would make "standard Skinner parts" under Skinner specification and inspection, and "the entire personnel of the Steere Company *[would continue]* with the Skinner Company under this arrangement, each member having substantially the same responsibilities as before."

The Skinner Company continued to have some of its instruments built at the Steere factory in Westfield for several years, but eventually phased out the Steere facilities, as the firm "found it more practical to do all the work . . . in Boston."[4] The absorption of the Steere Company had been A. H. Marks' idea.[5] Ernest Skinner apparently was not totally happy with Marks' decision. In a letter written to Harold Gleason on 1 March 1936, Ernest makes reference to the Skinner firm buying a Steere plant, building Steere organs in it, and putting the Skinner name-plate on them, clearly implying his disapproval of this practice. Evidently, what came out of the Steere factory did not meet Ernest's exacting standards of quality, tonal or otherwise, and therefore, to him, was not the true Skinner organ.

The Skinner installations in 1921 ranged from a small two-manual organ of nine ranks, built for St. Luke's Hospital Chapel in New York City, to the immense, five-manual, 143-stop organ built for the Municipal Auditorium in Cleveland, Ohio.[6] This was the era of the huge municipal organ. Although the Skinner Company built very few instruments for municipal auditoriums as compared to some organ builders, several of those few were very large and important installations.

One of the most noteworthy municipal auditorium organs built by the Skinner firm was the four-manual, eighty-four stop instrument installed in the Municipal Auditorium, St. Paul, Minnesota, in 1921.[7] The St. Paul Auditorium Skinner was "bought by the public through subscriptions . . . [and] pennies donated by school kids and the like."[8] The entire cost of the instrument was raised in an Organ Fund Campaign lasting from New Year's Day, 1920, to 10 March of that same year, culminating in the signing of the $62,000 contract by Ernest Skinner, who personally "visited St. Paul to look over the Auditorium in which the organ [was] to be placed."[9]

The St. Paul Auditorium Skinner, which was completed by September of 1921, contained virtually every tonal invention of Ernest Skinner in existence at that time, including the recently developed 4' Unda Maris and Heckelphone stops. It also had a String organ of six ranks playable on all manuals; a concert grand piano playable on the Great and Pedal keyboards; and even a Xylophone playable on the Great.[10]

Shortly before the dedication of the St. Paul Auditorium Skinner, the municipal organist, Chandler Goldthwaite, declared the organ to be "the best in the country, bar none." He further stated,

> Organs have a personality just the same as any artistic creation of man, and this organ has a pleasing one . . . It seems to lend itself to

musical passages that on other instruments are difficult. There is an eagerness about this organ that is not found on others, and because of this fact, visiting organists are going to discover that compositions may be played here that will be almost impossible on others.[11]

Elsewhere, Mr. Goldthwaite was quoted as saying that "this organ will soon become known to the musical fraternity as one that is to be loved."[12] And indeed Skinner organs were loved, not only by the organists who played them, but by the people who thronged to recitals held ot the municipal auditoriums with "standing room only" crowds. Large numbers of music lovers were often turned away at the doors because the mammoth auditoriums were already filled to capacity!

A series of four opening recitals was given on the St. Paul Auditorium Skinner by Mr. Goldthwaite on 29 and 30 September, and 1 and 2 October 1921. On the occasion of the first of these recitals it was reported that "8,000 or more persons . . . crowded into the Auditorium . . . to gain a first impression of the Auditorium's 'soul,' as the new municipal organ had been called."[13] All four concerts were attended by a total of more than 30,000 people, with "3,000 more who were unable to get in."[14] Ernest Skinner "wanted the people . . . to love the instrument," and his main purpose behind the design of the Skinner organ was to bring good music to the average person who, in those days, rarely had the opportunity to hear such music otherwise.[15]

Ernest's municipal auditorium installations were especially well suited for the rendition of orchestral transcriptions, and his intent was well carried out at the dedication series played at the St. Paul Auditorium. These programs consisted of a great proportion of operatic arias and orchestral transcriptions such as Wagner's "Fire Music" from *Die Walküre,* Handel's "Largo," Godard's "Berceuse" from *Jocelyn,* Sibelius' *Finlandia,* Wagner's "Liebestod" from *Tristan,* Sibelius' *Valse Triste,* and Dvořák's "Largo" from the *New World Symphony.*[16]

The $100,000 contract for the huge Skinner to be installed in the Cleveland Municipal Auditorium was signed in early 1921. Consisting of over 140 stops, this was the largest instrument to be built by the Skinner Organ Company to that time. According to the February 1921 issue of *The Diapason,*

> . . . Mr. Skinner was given an opportunity in the scheme of stops to cut loose without reservation in an effort to produce an instrument that will be one of the greatest ever constructed . . .
>
> The specification was prepared by Ernest M. Skinner in consultation with Edwin Arthur Kraft of Cleveland. It is along traditional lines—that is, the classic instrument plus the modern orchestral

color. Its diapason foundation is built up consistently on the scale of natural harmonics in just proportion for an ensemble of splendid richness and sonority, which is crowned by a mass of chorus reeds modeled after both the Willis or English types and the freer and more brilliant French school. The whole is to be adequately supported by a pedal of great power, depth and variety.

A Mason and Hamlin concert grand piano was incorporated in the Cleveland Auditorium Skinner, and its pedal division boasted no less than two 32' Bombardes! Two thirty horse-power motors and one five horse-power motor were required to provide wind for this immense instrument, with another five horse-power motor needed for the Echo organ![17]

On 10 September 1922 at 3:00 P.M., Edwin Arthur Kraft played the opening recital on the new Skinner organ at the Cleveland Municipal Auditorium. Quoting from a description of this opening concert, which was performed for an "audience of 20,000 Cleveland citizens," we read:

> Despite the oppressive heat the crowd which had been collecting since noon soon exceeded the capacity of the mammoth hall and long before the time set for the inaugural recital all seats were filled and more than 5,000 men, women and children were crowding the corridors of the colossal structure. The police which were out in large numbers were at first able to hold the crowd into a semblance of order, but soon gave up in despair as the eager mob swept all before it...
>
> Mr. Kraft chose a program well suited to show off the wonderful color, power and volume of the new Skinner instrument. Beginning with the National Anthem he gradually built a musical edifice that, crowned with five Wagnerian selections, brought his audience to such a pitch of enthusiasm that even the excessive heat failed to dampen it...
>
> Mr. Kraft's splendid program... began with the National Anthem, after which the grand march from "Aida" was played. This was a *[sic]* eye-opener and an ear-opener, pouring forth the most luscious and golden tones of the instrument. Six other numbers in the group were of a selection to demonstrate the resources of the organ, from the purling of Dethier's caprice, "The Brook," the majesty of Handel's "Largo," the orientalism of the Rimsky-Korsakoff's "Song of India" to Bartlett's "Toccata."
>
> The five closing numbers were compositions by Richard Wagner, closing with the startling "Ride of the Valkyries," which became truly startling as the huge stone structure seemed to vibrate to the manipulation of the keyboard."[18]

The municipal auditoriums had no monopoly on the full-house audiences which turned out to hear recitals on Ernest Skinner's creations. In May of 1922, Dr. William C. Carl, organist and director of music at First Presbyterian Church, New York City, displayed the new Skinner organ "with a series of interesting programs at the morning services each Sunday before congregations which . . . taxed the capacity of the historic church."[19] Later that same year, in mid-October, the large new Skinner organ at St. Luke's Church, Evanston, Illinois, was dedicated with a week-long series of recitals. "None of the recitals was attended by fewer than 1,000 people and the night of the service under the auspices of the Illinois chapter, A.G.O., hundreds stood in the aisles throughout the performance."[20]

By 1921, thirty-two colleges and universities either possessed or had placed orders for Skinner organs. These included some of the more prestigious schools, such as Harvard University, Yale University, Cornell University, Williams College, Rutgers College, Colgate University, Eastman School of Music, and Oberlin College. A few Skinner organs even found their way into high schools, such as those installed in McLain High School, Greenfield, Ohio (1915); East Side High School, Cincinnati, Ohio (1919); and Schenley High School, Pittsburgh, Pennsylvania (1924). The four-manual, forty-nine stop instrument for East Side High School was probably the largest installation of this type, and the three-manual, thirty-three rank Schenley High School Skinner was the most well-known and publicized.[21]

The Skinner Organ Company's great pride in its school and college installations can be seen in this statement pertaining to the educational value of a Skinner organ:

> A taste for good music and a just appreciation of a well rendered composition mark true culture.
>
> But fine music can only be properly rendered on a fine instrument and the standard by which musical quality is judged is only as high as one's educational concept of it. It is, therefore, a matter of great importance especially in the education of the younger generation that their first taste of good music should be of the highest quality, that their earliest standards should be high. Music on a mediocre instrument can never mold high ideals. The best is none too good for the forming thought.
>
> To equip a school or college with a Skinner Organ is like putting a Stradivarius in the hands of the youthful violinist. No greater inspiration could be given. So with the Skinner Organ in school *[sic]* and colleges! A veritable symphony orchestra on which and through which the musical tastes of hunderds of children, men and women

may be developed to a high point of artistic appreciation! The Skinner Organ will set the standard in more ways than one. Its precision of speech, its true color, its perfect rendition of orchestral tones and the great volume and variety make it an instrument upon which even the masters find nothing lacking for full musical expression.[22]

One of the Skinner Organ Company's largest college installations was the four-manual, ninety-four stop organ built for Kilbourn Hall at Eastman School of Music, Rochester, New York, in 1921.[23] This instrument incorporated such unusual features as "a crescendo pedal adjustable to three different crescendos," and "a coupler for reversing the order of the great and choir manuals" so it would be "the same as found in French organs, giving the opportunity for the player to perform French music more easily." It also had an orchestral string division which was "playable from any keyboard, at sixteen-, eight- or four-foot pitch," and which could be "coupled to the expression pedals of the manual on which it [was] drawn, or . . . placed on the choir or swell expression pedals." Tonally, the Kilbourn Hall Skinner was "built on sound lines, containing . . . the true foundation tones of the organ as a historic instrument, and the added tone colors of the modern organ."[24]

The Kilbourn Hall Skinner was designed by Harold Gleason, who had been appointed head of the organ department at the Eastman School of Music in 1919.[25] Mr. Gleason first met Ernest Skinner "in 1920 in connection with the organ for Kilbourn Hall," and was to assist Ernest in designing many of the instruments built by the Skinner firm during the 1920s.[26] In a letter dated 23 April 1977, Harold Gleason, who played the opening recital on this instrument, tells a little about the designing and building of the Kilbourn Hall Skinner:

> The Kilbourn Hall organ was designed by me, but after I had completed the specification I interviewed and discussed the specification with a number of the prominent organists of the time. These included Lynnwood Farnam, Samuel Baldwin, Charles Heinroth and others . . . I incorporated a few of their ideas . . .
> I got my ideas about the K. H. organ from reading Audsley and my experience with Farnam's Casavant in 1917-1918 at Emmanuel Church, Boston, where he had a complete complement of mutations and I had my lesson in it . . .
> As far as I know the K. H. organ was the first [Skinner] to have all the mutations . . .
> As I remember it the contract for K. H. was for $55,000 but Mr. Eastman put in a penalty clause and as the organ was late, as usual

with most organ builders, Mr. Skinner had to forfeit $5,000.00. He must have lost a considerable amount of money on that installation. The number of couplers, combination pistons, and various other controls far exceeded any organ of the time or even later . . .

The Solo organ had a complete set of the famous Skinner orchestral reeds which I don't believe any other Skinner organ had. In other words, I went "all out." I wanted everything on the organ I could think of. It is one of a kind.

The Orchestral Trumpet in the Choir was also a novelty on the Skinner or any other organ. I had quite a time getting it voiced the way I wanted. It seemed new to E. M.

During the year 1921, the Skinner Organ Company also built a three-manual organ of seventeen stops for the Eastman School of Music.[27] According to the company brochure, this instrument was designed for a studio, and probably was used for teaching purposes. George Eastman of Eastman-Kodak, and founder of Eastman School of Music, gave Ernest Skinner a "fine camera" for suggesting that the "practice organs be put up in the attic, thereby making the practice rooms quite roomy." However, Ernest never had a chance to use this camera, for it was stolen before he even got home with it.[28]

FOOTNOTES

[1] "1921 Skinner Installations," *Stop, Open, and Reed,* 1, no. 1 (January 1922), p. 6.
[2] Personal interview with George W. Collins, 7 May 1976.
[3] "Skinner and Steere Companies Combine," *The Diapason,* April 1921, p. 1.
[4] E. A. Boadway, "The Skinner & Aeolian-Skinner Opus List," *The Boston Organ Club Newsletter,* July & August 1972, p. 2; Ernest M. Skinner, Letter to Mr. John Van V. Elsworth, 9 March 1933 (courtesy of Henry Karl Baker).
[5] Personal interview with Alexander McCurdy, 7 October 1972.
[6] "1921 Skinner Installations," p. 6; "The Wise Selection of a Skinner Organ Was Made by these Educational Institutes," *Stop, Open, and Reed,* 1, no. 4 (December 1922), p. 6.
[7] "1921 Skinner Installations," p. 6.
[8] Karl Karlson, "Group Hopes it Can Break Spell on 'Sleeping' Skinner Organ," *St. Paul Dispatch,* 15 September 1973, p. 5.
[9] "St. Paul's Successful Organ Campaign," *The American Organist,* 3, no. 6 (1920), 215; "Skinner Will Build Organ For St. Paul," *The Diapason,* April 1920, p. 1.
[10] "St. Paul Out to Hear New Municipal Organ," *The Diapason,* October 1921, p. 1; "Skinner Will Build Organ For St. Paul," *The Diapason,* April 1920, p. 1.
[11] "St. Paul Out to Hear New Municipal Organ," p. 1.
[12] "What They Say About Recent Skinner Organs," *Stop, Open, and Reed,* 1, no. 1 (January 1922), p. 4.
[13] Wilbur Webster Judd, "The St. Paul Auditorium Organ," *St. Paul Pioneer-Press,* quoted in *Stop, Open, and Reed,* 1, no. 1 (January 1922), p. 7.
[14] "Thousands at St. Paul Hear New City Organ," *The Diapason,* November 1921, p. 3.
[15] Personal interviews with Edward B. Gammons, 1 and 3 May 1976.
[16] "Thousands at St. Paul Hear New City Organ," p. 3.
[17] "Skinner Wins Order For Cleveland Organ," *The Diapason,* February 1921, p. 1.

[18]"Twenty Thousand Hear Opening Recital . . ." *Stop, Open, and Reed,* 1, no. 4 (December 1922), p. 9.

[19]"Dr. Carl Presides at New Four Manual," *Stop, Open, and Reed,* 1, no. 3 (July 1922), p. 6.

[20]"The New Skinner Organ in St. Luke's," *Stop, Open, and Reed,* 1, no. 4 (December 1922), p. 11.

[21]"The Wise Selection of a Skinner Organ," p. 6; E. A. Boadway, "The Skinner & Aeolian-Skinner Opus List," *The Boston Organ Club Newsletter,* September 1972, p. 4; "Schenley High School Organ Being Built by the Skinner Co.," *The American Organist,* 7, no. 5 (1924), p. 296.

[22]"The Educational Value of a Skinner Organ," *Stop, Open and Reed,* 1, no. 4 (December 1922), p. 6.

[23]"1921 Skinner Installations," p. 6.

[24]"The Skinner Organ in Kilbourn Hall," *Stop, Open, and Reed,* 1, no. 3 (July 1922), p. 4.

[25]Letter received from Harold Gleason, 23 April 1977; "Four Well Known American Organists," *Stop, Open, and Reed,* 1, no. 3 (July 1922), p. 3.

[26]Letter received from Harold Gleason, 29 January 1974; Personal interview with Alexander McCurdy, 7 October 1972.

[27]"1921 Skinner Installations," p. 6.

[28]Ernest M. Skinner, Letter to Catharine Crozier, 25 February 1952.

CHAPTER 10

Theater and Residence Organs

WHEN EASTMAN-KODAK made motion picture photography practical for amateurs with the introduction of 16mm reversal film in the early 1920s, Ernest's weakness for the latest gadgets coupled with the general popularity of the "movies" made it inevitable that he should buy a movie camera. Ernest pursued his new photographic interest with typical enthusiasm, even taking his movie camera with him on a trip he made to England and France during the mid-1920s, shooting many movies in Paris and on his voyage home.[1] According to his nephew, Ned Hastings, Ernest would sometimes perform in home movies, no doubt taken by another member of the family with Ernest's camera, doing hilarious comedy routines. Ernest was a natural comedian, and his daughter Ruth recalls that he even walked something like the silent movie comic Charlie Chaplin—with his toes pointing out and throwing out his feet as he walked.

The Skinner firm also had a commercial interest in the movies. During the days of silent movies in the early part of this century, the theater organ came into use as a substitute for the orchestra employed by better theaters of the day to supply suitable musical accompaniment and sound effects for motion pictures. Owing to Ernest M. Skinner's consuming interest in reproducing orchestral imitative stops, the Skinner organ was virtually an imitation symphony orchestra by the mid-teens. By the early 1920s his larger instruments contained facsimiles of almost every orchestral instrument in existence. Thus, it is not surprising that the Skinner Organ Company became involved in the theater organ field. Their first instrument of this nature was the four-manual organ installed in Elmwood Theater, Buffalo, New York, in 1913.[2]

The earliest theater organs were basically Romantic church organs with traps (sound effects) added. According to William H. Barnes and Edward B. Gammons in *Two Centuries of American Organ Building,*

> The first complete theater organ was not really developed until about 1915. Theater organs of this period were characterized by well balanced, crisp orchestral sound, and generally reflected their origins in romantic church organ design. Some even had several straight ranks. Keen "pencil" strings, heavy, smoothtoned reeds, and several foundation sets were the basis of the specifications. Initially, the Tibia was considered a foundation stop and used little as a solo voice.
>
> Around 1921 the theater organ completely broke away from the church organ. Theater organs were more unified and included more solo stops. However, the Tibia was still only one of a collection of solo stops.
>
> In about 1926, the Tibia took over the theater organ tonal scheme completely. It was unified to the hilt and tremulated to the extreme. Voicing on all stops, with few exceptions, was less refined. Any attempt at ensemble was lost and the trend was to lushness and power rather than articulation . . .

The theater organ of the 1920s, as built by most organ companies, was a direct result of Robert Hope-Jones' influence. The Wurlitzer Organ Company, which acquired the Hope-Jones Organ Company and thus obtained "the most direct benefit of Hope-Jones' concepts," was the leading manufacturer of this type of instrument. Typical theater organs, as exemplified by the "Mighty Wurlitzer," had the following common characteristics: they were built on the unit organ principle; the pipework was made with exaggerated scaling and voiced on rather high wind pressures; the Hope-Jones Diaphone was used as a bass to diapasons at 16' and 32' pitch (The exceedingly prompt speech of the Diaphone was a great advantage to the 1920s theater organist for playing the lively jazz and rag-time selections which enjoyed great popularity during that decade.); independent mutations or mixtures were almost entirely absent; they had traps such as drums, cymbals, xylophones, bird calls, auto horns, etc.; almost without exception, they had the "horse-shoe" type of console with stop tabs.[3]

Judging by the success of the "Mighty Wurlitzer," most movie theater patrons and theater organists were apparently quite satisfied with this kind of instrument. Ernest Skinner definitely did not share their satisfaction and, in fact, detested the Wurlitzer Hope-Jones type of theater organ. In an article entitled "Cinema Music," which appeared in *The American Organist* in 1918 (vol. 1, p. 417), Ernest expresses his distaste for such organs in sarcastic terms as he describes a recent movie-going experience:

> The organist faced a rainbow of many colored devices known by various names: Flop Keys will do as well as any other. The tones of this organ were voiced as loud as possible. The first that struck my ear was a wood flute of vast proportions and it was subject to a tremolo of terrific effectiveness, accompanied by one of those bean blower strings on a fifteen-inch wind so stridently voiced that they tasted like copper, the kind you hear in the merry-go-round affair that makes you think the pipes must be screwed into the wind chest to keep them from blowing out. The whole sound a riot of immodest vulgarity that was an absolute shock to the sense and that made it impossible to fix your attention on the picture.
>
> This organ had traps.
>
> Once upon a time a man said to himself: I will make an organ imitate an orchestra; so he studied the orchestra, but all he could see was the traps, so he made organs having a few stops and many traps. This organ was built after this plan. It had dingdongs, sleigh bells, xylophones, and an epiglottis or something that sounded like that, and a pneuria that buzzed, and a tuba on many inches of wind and the effect of the full organ was most original. It put the picture entirely out of business. The whole thing was most carefully designed to create an appetite for vulgarity. I did not hear one single musical note at this performance or the slightest indication of the influence of good taste.

In "Organ Building as a Fine Art," which appeared in a 1925 issue of *Stop, Open, and Reed* (vol. 3, no. 1), Ernest provides his own definition of a unit organ and explains his reasons for being against the unit type of organ construction:

> The unit organ is built upon a principle which *substitutes octave couplers for pipes*. It therefore at the outset eliminates a large number of pipes with a consequent loss of variety ...
>
> ... each stop in the unit organ is made to draw in several pitches. The large number of registers, notwithstanding the small number of stops is caused by drawing the same stop, not only on all the manuals but in octaves, superoctaves, sub octaves, fifths, etc., making frequently an organ of seven or eight real stops and fifty or sixty registers.

Theater and Residence Organs 91

> In the classic organ, the backbone of the organ is of 8' pitch, the same as in any keyed instrument. The 16', 4' and 2' pitches are subsidiary and carefully voiced and proportioned so as not to distort the fundamental position of the sound as indicated on the printed page of a composition.
>
> In the unit organ, the 16', 4' and other pitches are borrowed from the 8' pitches. They are of the same strength and character. The voicer has no discretion whatever as to their strength of character; any possibility of artistic treatment does not exist; the design eliminated it at the outset. In the unit organ the 16', 4' and 2' and other pitches are greatly in excess of the fundamental 8' pitch. The very limited variety of normal pitch and color leaves nothing but octave couplers for variety and that is why all unit organs are all top and bottom. A distressing amount of sub growl or the sharp effect of the upper pitches is always moving the sound up or down an octave, from its indicated sound on the page of the music sheet. Inasmuch as the same colors are used on all the manuals there is no color independence. The substitution of octave couplers for new colors kills variety.

In the same article, Ernest offers his own theory for use of pipework with exaggerated scaling and tonal character in the unit type of theater organ:

> For some unknown reason the stops usually present in the theater unit organ seem to be selected for their antagonism to each other. Perhaps it is because they are so few in number that they are necessarily exaggerated in scale and tone in order to produce a forte.

Ernest Skinner had some very definite ideas on how a theater organ should be designed and built. Continuing in this same article, he gives a description of what he terms a "legitimate" organ as exemplified by the Skinner theater organ, along with his views of what a theater organ should be capable of doing:

> I hold that of all organs none is more demanding than one suitable for vitalizing pictures. Moving pictures reflect everything of life and are limited in scope only by the imagination of the producer. The organ should be able to reflect every shade of human emotion: love, anger, hate, sorrow, surprise, humor, ugliness, the sinister, and national idioms, to say nothing of dogs, chickens, horses, convulsions of nature, etc., dramatic qualities, fine shades of meaning, the military clang, etc . . .
>
> I am unable to convince myself that a colossal flute, an acid string,

a Vox Humana, a biting "Kinura" a tuba and a few traps can in any way cover the ground as outlined above. The unit organ touches the orchestra nowhere with an occasional exception in the strings.

The legitimate organ has a pianissimo in variety. The next step up is a variety of soft flutes and strings. Then the larger strings and flutes and a great variety of orchestral reproductions, Oboe, English Horn, Musette, French Horn, Clarinet, Bassoon, Harp and so on up to the larger, though *not* thick flutes and big strings, Tubas, soft and loud pedal reeds and Diapasons, *not* extended from the manuals.

All the foregoing voiced to work together or independently and a forte made up of many voices and not of two or three blatant ones. Every voice having neighbors in its own scale of dynamics and also in variety. All sounding as placed on the page and not an octave higher or lower as in the unit idea.

In some respects, the Skinner theater organ was not radically different from the same firm's church organ. The ranks were all straight with no unification, although many of the stops were borrowed, or made interchangeable, between manuals to a much greater extent than was customary in Skinner church or concert organs. Also, there was a greater proportion of orchestral imitative stops, particularly those of the string family. There was no chorus work to speak of, although Skinner usually did include a full complement of mutations up to the Septième for color effects. These mutations were separate and independent ranks rather than being taken from an 8' rank as was the case in most other makes of theater organs.

One of the largest and most complete theater organs built by the Skinner Organ Company was the four-manual instrument installed in the Capitol Theatre, Boston, Massachusetts, in 1922.[4] In the December 1922 edition of *Stop, Open, and Reed,* (vol. 1, no. 4), Ernest Skinner makes these comments pertaining to the Capitol Theatre organ:

> The great difficulty with the ordinary organ in a motion picture theater is the distressing drop in the musical atmosphere that occurs when the orchestra ceases and the organ takes up the story.
>
> The orchestra is full of virile tone color and beautiful qualities with which we are all familiar. Attempts to give the organ more of the characteristics of the orchestra have been ill judged. The result has been a noisy, coarse tone of very limited variety and a superabundance of so-called traps i.e. drums, sleigh bells, xylophones and other vaudeville specialties that are far removed from the fundamental characteristics of the orchestra with which it is intended to alternate or accompany.
>
> The organ in the Capitol Theatre is designed to be a substitute for the orchestra in the truest sense. It has all of the representative color

> present in the orchestra; strings of all qualities and strength of tone that will continue the orchestral strings so exactly that one cannot tell when the transition is made. The French Horn, English Horn, Clarinet, 'Cello, Oboe are all exactly duplicated in this organ. There is also a Musette, a humorous tone which is sometimes called the "Charlie Chaplin" of the orchestra.
>
> There are many lovely soft effects that . . . can hardly be approached by the orchestra.
>
> This organ also has the drums and other percussion effects above referred to but they are subsidiary as in the orchestra and do not dominate the instrument as customarily.
>
> The organ is fully shown on the screen whether it be sentimental, angry, sad, militant or merely scenic; in short its resources are as ample as those of the finest symphony orchestra.

It is evident from the preceding quotation that Ernest's ideal theater organ should as closely as possible resemble the symphony orchestra in its tonal character and flexibility and should do so to the extent that it is impossible to determine when one leaves off and the other begins.

Ernest Skinner also had very definite opinions about the movie music which was played on the theater organ. He was totally against the use of rag-time or any loud music that, in his opinion, distracted from the picture itself. He also disliked extemporization for movie background music because most movie theater organists apparently did not extemporize well enough to satisfy his demanding and critical ear. Ernest's own idea of appropriate movie music was the playing of "classics on some soft stops" while the picture was in progress.[5] The prompt-speaking Diaphone bass does not appear even in Ernest's largest theater organs. This, most likely, is no coincidence. He probably had no intention of hearing jazz or rag-time played on his instruments!

In "Cinema Music," Ernest has these comments regarding movie music:

> The Movie organist has great opportunity for the display of musicianship, for the use of a great variety of vital music, for the association of a particular action with a musical idea that is closely related to it, for deftness in modulation both by note and color suitable to change of scene or action in the picture, and, most important of all, for making the organ vitalize the picture, being at all times subsidiary, suggestive, never obtrusive or distracting.

Since the primary purpose of the theater organ was to serve as a substitute for the orchestra, the Skinner theater organ, which probably came the closest of any to simulating the sounds of the orchestra, should have been an outstanding success in this field. In spite of this fact, compared with many organ companies during the heyday of the theater organ, the Skinner Organ Company sold very few instruments to theaters. The total output of the firm in this category between 1913 and 1931 was only twelve instruments. The best known and most publicized of these were the four-manual organs installed in the Capitol Theatre, Boston, Massachusetts, in 1922 (described earlier), and the Colony Theatre, New York, New York, in 1924.[6]

One major reason for the small number of theater organ installations by the Skinner Organ Company was that they made an exceptionally high quality instrument, which naturally commanded a higher price than their competitors' product.[7] The other problem was that most movie-goers of that day were not "classically" oriented in their musical tastes and actually preferred the conventional unit organs that most theaters had. The Skinner theater organ, with its great refinement, no doubt sounded too much like a church organ to the public, as well as to movie theater organists and the theater managers, who had the say as to what kind of organ would be purchased for their theaters. In their minds, such an instrument just was not suitable for such a secular and profane function. Moreover, since Ernest Skinner was much opposed to the horse-shoe console with stop keys and insisted upon the consistent use of draw-knob consoles even for his theater organs, they also looked like church organs. In fact, those theater organists who were accustomed to playing Wurlitzers did not even know what to do with these instruments.[8]

The comparatively gentle and refined Skinner theater organ never really gained widespread acceptance. Meanwhile, the "Mighty Wurlitzer" reigned King of the movie organ scene throughout the 1920s, continuing in popularity even after the advent of the "talkies" in the late 1920s put an end to any real need for an organ to provide background music and sound effects for movies. It is ironic that Ernest Skinner's extraordinary success in building a truly orchestral theater organ was, for the most part, the very thing that was responsible for its commercial failure in the movie theater world.

The firm was more successful with residential organs. Between 1901 and 1931, the Skinner Organ Company built approximately eighty-one organs for private residences, this category constituting more than 9 percent of the firm's total output during that period.[9] A number of other builders were active in the home organ field and built a considerably greater number of residence organs than the Skinner firm. However, the Skinner residence organ, like the Skinner theater organ, was a refined and well-built instrument.

Theater and Residence Organs 95

Ernest Skinner, never content with the current level of excellence, was continuously working to improve the instruments built by his firm. As a result, the Skinner residence organ was completely redesigned sometime during the early 1920s. In the brochure *The Skinner Residence Organ,* published in 1927, we read:

> Skinner Residence Organs have been built for twenty years or more and until recently on about the same general principle as others. From time to time we had discovered improvements but were unable to use them because they did not fit the system.
>
> Finally, however, so many desirable improvements had accumulated that four years ago we decided to redesign the system, scrap the accumulation of master records which represented years of costly work and put the Skinner on a fresh foundation years ahead of the field. The new system, with double automatic expression, absolute freedom in orchestration, instantaneous and unlimited stop-changing and perfect flexibility in all functions, embodies all of our past experience in organ building, all of the improvements discovered in the past twenty years and in addition provides functional members in reserve for improvements that may come in future years. By this radical move, we severed at one stroke the encumbrances of the past and provided a system unlimited in musical possibilities.

The Skinner Organ Company had two separate libraries of rolls for their player organs, "a full automatic and a semi-automatic, playable on the same instrument by means of a two-way switch."[10] The Skinner Company provides this explanation of the terms "full-automatic" and "semi-automatic":

> "Full-automatic" means that you may place a roll of music in the instrument, start it and go away and leave it and listen to the performance of a noted organist who has recorded his interpretation of an orchestral selection for us by means of our recording machine. The selection will be rendered with all the subtle phrasing of hand playing by a master artist, and at the end the organ will stop itself and re-roll the roll.
>
> "Semi-automatic" means that you may place a roll of music in the organ and then sit at the console yourself, control the tempo, registration and expression by pulling out the different stops as desired, moving the tempo lever and opening or closing the expression shutters or swell boxes by means of foot pedals. This makes you feel as if you were really producing the music yourself . . .[11]

An exclusive feature of the Skinner residence organ was that their rolls were "all arranged for double expression, the melody and accompaniment being under separate control." Most of the rolls made for the Skinner organ were transcriptions of symphonic works, operatic selections, and old familiar songs. Many of these rolls, specifically the orchestral transcriptions, were prepared from orchestral scores by "distinguished musicians," with the tempo and phrasing being "the actual records of the work of fine organists."[12] In 1924, such pieces as Debussy's "Reverie," Wagner's *Tannhauser* Overture, Grieg's "Solveig's Song," Handel's "Air" from *Water Music,* and the Second Movement of Schubert's Unfinished Symphony were available on full automatic rolls. On semi-automatic rolls, one could buy Vierne's "Scherzetto"; Griffes' "The White Peacock"; Franck's "Andantino"; Von Suppé's "Poet and Peasant"; and "Scherzo," Prelude and Fugue, and "Noel and Variations" by Marcel Dupré.[13] We gain some idea of the cost of these rolls from a catalogue issued by the Skinner Organ Company during the late 1920s listing music available on rolls for Skinner automatic players which ranged "from Onward Christian Soldiers to Bach fugues and Yon's Sonata Cromatica." According to this catalogue, the least expensive of these rolls were $3.50 each, with "more at 4.00, 4.50, and 5.00." A Chopin Waltz was $9.00, Dickinson's "Reverie" was $6.50, Dukas' *Sorcerer's Apprentice* was $15.75, Dvorak's "New World" selection was $18.00, "Tannhauser Overture" was $15.75, and the Roger-Ducasse "Pastorale" was $12.00.[14]

Skinner residence organs differed from the firm's church organs in that they were "usually more orchestral in character, capable of rendering solemn pieces but especially equipped for light, melodious and orchestral music." Most of these instruments contained "the principal voices of the orchestra, the Strings, the Flutes, the Oboe, Clarinet, French Horn, English Horn, Bassoon, Flügel Horn, Piccolo, Violin, Vox Humana . . . voiced true to character with a refinement never accomplished elsewhere." The Aeolian Company, one of the Skinner Company's chief competitors in the residence organ field built a fine player, but its residence consoles were of unorthodox design. The Skinner residence organ, however, was "not only a self player but also a perfectly appointed recital organ with all the finest mechanical equipment for effective hand playing." The Skinner Company considered "an organ of forty stops" to be "a large and impressive installation, suitable for the largest residence and containing everything necessary for very distinguished effects, audible wherever desired in the house and in the adjacent gardens."[15] Probably the largest instrument to be actually built by this firm for a private home was the four-manual, thirty-eight stop organ installed in the Edwin Farnham Greene residence of Boston, Massachusetts in 1922.[16]

Theater and Residence Organs 97

The smallest home organ to be built by the Skinner Organ Company was the Skinner Small Residence Organ, a moderately priced two-manual instrument of ten stops, introduced around the year 1922. This organ was built as a unit for economy and ease of installation and it was 11' deep, and 9' high. It occupied "little more space than a good-sized closet," and could "be successfully introduced into almost any average-sized residence." It was designed to be played "full automatic" or "semi-automatic" by means of rolls and could also be played by hand. The Skinner Small Residence Organ, like its larger counterparts, was "equipped with double expression, i.e., two swell boxes—one for the solo and the other for the accompaniment." The Skinner firm regarded this instrument as representing "the last word in completeness for an organ of ten stops," and maintained:

> It will play anything that any organ will play and play it well; not merely a passable performance, but a highly effective and satisfactory one worthy of that of a conventional instrument of far greater dimensions and one altogether misleading and out of proportion to its number of stops.[17]

The most publicized residence organ by the Skinner firm was the three-manual, twenty-seven stop organ built for the Robert Law, Jr., residence, Port Chester, New York, in 1922.[18] This instrument represented "the latest Skinner work in voicing, expression and arrangement . . . coupled with a very favorable location and excellent acoustics." Upon completion, it was declared "to have created a new standard for residence organs."[19]

FOOTNOTES

[1] Ernest M. Skinner, "A Trip Abroad," *Stop, Open, and Reed*, 3, no. 1 (1925), p. 34.

[2] E. A. Boadway, "The Skinner & Aeolian-Skinner Opus List," *The Boston Organ Club Newsletter*, July & August 1972, p. 6.

[3] William H. Barnes & Edward B. Gammons, *Two Centuries of American Organ Building* (Melville, N.Y.: Belwin-Mills Publishing Corp., 1970), pp. 53 & 54.

[4] E. A. Boadway, "The Skinner & Aeolian-Skinner Opus List," *The Boston Organ Club Newsletter*, September 1972, p. 4.

[5] Ernest M. Skinner, "Cinema Music," *The American Organist*, 1 (1918), p. 418.

[6] E. A. Boadway, "The Skinner & Aeolian-Skinner Opus List," *The Boston Organ Club Newsletter*, July & August 1972, pp. 5 & 8; September 1972, pp. 4, 6–8; October 1972, p. 7; November 1972, p. 6. Fourteen theater organ opus numbers are listed between the years 1913–1931, but one (Opus 602) consisted only of additions to the Pedal division in an existing organ and another (Opus 755) was never installed.

[7] B. S. Moss, Letter dated 26 January 1922, quoted in *Stop, Open, and Reed*, 1, no. 2 (April 1922), p. 10.

[8] Personal interview with Edward B. Gammons, 3 May 1976.

[9] E. A. Boadway, "The Skinner & Aeolian-Skinner Opus List," *The Boston Organ Club Newsletter,* July & August 1972, pp. 4, 6–8; September 1972, pp. 4–8; October 1972, pp. 6 & 7; November 1972, pp. 3–6; December 1972, pp. 2–4. These figures take into account two of the instruments subcontracted for by Welte during the mid-teens, plus a *yacht* organ built for Col. E. A. Deeds of New York, New York, in 1929.

[10] Arthur Hudson Marks, "The Skinner Residence Organ," *Stop, Open, and Reed,* 3, no. 1 (1925), p. 13.

[11] "The Skinner Small Residence Organ," *Stop, Open, and Reed,* 1, no. 3 (July 1922), p. 11.

[12] Marks, pp. 13 & 15.

[13] "Additions to Skinner Organ Library," *Stop, Open, and Reed,* 2, no. 1 (January 1924), p. 21.

[14] "Skinner," *The American Organist,* 11, no. 7 (1928), p. 259.

[15] Marks, pp. 13 & 15.

[16] "1921 Skinner Installations," *Stop, Open, and Reed,* 1, no. 1 (January 1922), p. 6; Boadway, July & August 1972, p. 8.

[17] "The Skinner Small Residence Organ," pp. 11 & 12.

[18] "Recent Skinner Organ Installations," *Stop, Open, and Reed,* 1, no. 3 (July 1922), 2; Boadway, September 1972, p. 4.

[19] "The Law Organ," *Stop, Open, and Reed,* 2, no. 1 (January 1924), p. 2.

CHAPTER 11

The Skinner Reputation 1922-1924

DURING 1923 the Skinner Organ Company had ninety-two instruments under construction, nearly twice the number of organs installed during 1921. Among the most important of these installations were the organs built for St. Joseph's Cathedral, Columbus, Ohio; R. C. Ogden Auditorium, Hampton Institute, Hampton, Virginia; and Old Trinity Church, New York City. The Skinner at St. Joseph's Cathedral, a big four-manual organ, was situated in what was essentially an open position in the rear gallery of a highly reverberant edifice, rather than being bottled up in the usual organ chambers in an acoustically dead building, and was said to have been installed in a "perfect location." This organ possessed a full complement of strings and orchestral imitative reeds, a complete mixture and reed chorus, and a complete set of mutations in the Choir division. It was predicted that this instrument would "rank as one of the great organs of our country."[1]

The three-manual instrument built for the Ogden Auditorium at Hampton Institute was basically a duplexed orchestral organ, equipped with a semi-automatic self-player, and lacked any diapason chorus beyond an 8′ Diapason and a 4′ Octave. Nevertheless, its ceremonies of inauguration, extending over three days during April of 1923, were considered important enough to be attended by Ernest M. Skinner and Arthur Hudson Marks, as well as by the Governor of Virginia and Chief Justice Taft of the Supreme Court.[2]

At the dedication of the big four-manual Skinner organ at Old

Trinity Church in New York City on 10 March 1924, "the crush of people at the service was so great that the police had to keep hundreds from entering the edifice."!!³

For the second time in its twenty-some year history the Skinner Company installed an organ across the sea, this time a three-manual, thirty-two stop instrument for the Central Union Church in Honolulu, Hawaii. It was completed by mid-spring of 1924.⁴

Skinner organs "cost more to build than any others in the world," and yet, "in many cases, contracts were awarded without competitive bids, or consultation with other organ builders . . ."⁵ Over the years the reputation of the Skinner organ had been built upon its superb quality of workmanship and unequaled tonal beauty. In the early 1920s a new promotional campaign was undertaken by the Skinner Organ Company that would make the Skinner name a household word across the nation.

The first step in this promotional campaign was the publication of a periodical called *Stop, Open, and Reed* by the Skinner Organ Company. Its first issue, dated January 1922, featured an article by Ernest M. Skinner entitled "Shall the Swell Box Swallow the Organ Whole." It also contained various letters from "satisfied customers," and a number of reprinted newspaper reviews praising new Skinner organs.

Meanwhile, late in the year 1921, the Skinner Organ Company took out a ten-year lease for the fourth floor of the Cammeyer Building on Fifth Avenue in New York City.⁶ This was to be the New York studio and business headquarters of the Skinner firm. This new studio at 677 Fifth Avenue was in use by April of 1922, at which time the second issue of *Stop, Open, and Reed* was published, the publication department now having been moved from Boston to the New York studio.

During 1922 a three-manual organ with player attachment was installed in the Skinner Company's New York studio.⁷ This instrument consisted of forty ranks and was a comprehensive orchestral organ with an abundance of strings plus a 16' Bassoon, 8' Tuba, French Horn, English Horn, and Oboe. It also contained the more traditional voices including diapasons, a 4' Octave and a Solo Mixture in the Swell, plus a Nazard on the Great. It was cited as "an example of what a builder builds for himself when he buys his own product."⁸

In March of 1923 the first radio recital was broadcast from the Skinner Organ Company's New York City studio. "Arthur Hudson Marks was at the console at this experimental concert," which was presumably played from rolls.⁹

In the early days of radio the broadcasting of pipe organ tone left much to be desired. Because of this instrument's wide dynamic range, its volume tended to vary between "blasting" and inaudibility over the air. Also, certain tone colors did not come through as well as others. According to Mr. Marks,

> When a well-known station approached the Skinner Company, desiring to broadcast from the organ in the Fifth avenue studio, I refused to allow the Skinner organ or the name of the company to be connected with broadcasting on the ground that the results were not creditable to anyone concerned. I made a counter proposal that I would be glad to develop experimentally some ideas that I had formulated if the broadcaster would carry on similar development in the electrical aparatus. We finally agreed to carry on an experimental development in the studio of the Skinner Company in New York, the broadcaster to install and develop the best possible electrical outfit in the studio and the Skinner Company to carry on its own development at its own expense. It was further agreed that there should be no public broadcasting until such results had been achieved as to be satisfactory to me, and if, after exhausting our combined resources, the resulting quality was not satisfactory to me, we should abandon the attempt without public performance and each bear his own loss...[10]

Marks' own solution to the problem of broadcasting organ music

> ... involved a duplicate console in a room removed from the organ, picking up the tones by microphone and playing them back to the organist himself by radio, with a supplementary visible indicator of that rather troublesome element of dynamics so that the organist could see whether he was in danger of playing either too softly or too loudly.[11]

That first experimental broadcast by Marks apparently was moderately successful, for it was followed on succeeding Sunday nights with concerts played by organists Henry F. Seibert, W. A. Goldsworthy, G. H. Federlein, Lynnwood Farnam, William E. Zeuch, Chandler Goldthwaite, and Maurice Garabrant.[12]

By the fall of 1925 it was arranged that radio station WAGH of New York would broadcast an extensive series of weekly one-hour recitals played on the Skinner New York studio organ. These recitals, which were organized by Fay Leone Farote, who was also editor of the *Stop, Open and Reed* periodicals, were to run from 6 November of that fall to July of 1926, and included "a large number of distinguished organists ..."[13]

According to Harold Gleason, one of the organists who took part in these broadcasts, "the Skinner Co. had a room and bath *[at]* 677 Fifth Ave. where visiting organists and others could stay." Mr. Gleason stayed there on several occasions when he came to New York City from Rochester to play for broadcasts, and recalls that "the service of the room was free . . ."[14]

Ernest Skinner was very critical of the broadcasts from the Fifth Avenue studio because he felt that the radio of that day did not do the Skinner organ justice.[15] Even as late as 1927, Marks was to admit,

> At best organ music over the radio is still far from satisfactory and by no means a credit to the pipe organ. Let us hope at least for such improvement in the broadcasting train that the lovely quality of most of the stops may not be filtered out in the process. Now our most beautiful tones are robbed of their subtle quality, like a peach without it *[sic]* bloom.[16]

However, in spite of the limitations of radio in the 1920s, the broadcasts came across fairly well and were warmly received by the listeners. There were two main reasons for this: the artists—many of whom occupied positions at churches, colleges, or municipal auditoriums equipped with Skinner organs—avoided extremes in pitch or volume which might either be inaudible or "shatter" over the air; the other factor was the selection of music which would have wide appeal for audiences of that day.

> The old time songs are particularly well liked and called for most frequently. Handel's "Largo" is the greatest favorite, with the "Rosary" as either a vocal or instrumental number a close second. The well-known overtures, selections from the operas, light and simple melodies; these are most frequently requested. Nevin, Kinder, MacDowell and other such composers are much appreciated and although the organist may occasionally put in a heavier number by Bach or one of the other fine organ composers, it does not do, as yet at least, to include many of this character in the evening's entertainment, if you do not wish them to "tune off" to some other station broadcasting music more to their liking.

A "typical radio program" included "Lustspiel Overture," Keler Bela; "Reverie," Dickinson; "Legend," Federlein; "Prize Song" from *Die Meistersinger* by Wagner; "March of the Little Lead Soldiers," Gabriel Pierne; "Souvenir," Drdla; "Kamennoi Ostrow," Rubenstein; "Ballet Music" from *Faust* by Gounod; "Indian Summer," Victor Herbert; "Overture" to *Raymond,* Thomas; "Waltz in D Flat," Chopin; "Elsa's

Balcony Song" from Wagner's *Lohengrin;* "Onward Christian Soldiers"; and "Where the Dusk Gathers Deep" by Stebbins.[17]

The broadcasts from the Skinner Fifth Avenue studio reached radio listeners as far west as Kansas, as far south as the southern coast of Cuba, and as far north as Gravenhurst, 112 miles north of Toronto in Ontario, Canada. According to *Stop, Open, and Reed:*

> Reports from the southern coast of Cuba, from Florida, Louisiana, Iowa, Illinois, Kansas, Missouri, Minnesota, Wisconsin, Canada, say that the wonderful tone and color of the Skinner organ is plainly audible and that "it is by far the finest music so far put on the air." Letters from hospitals, clubs, rude huts in the mountains, schools, music academies, missions in the slums, camps in the far North, and residences far and near all bear witness to the beauty and grandeur of the Skinner Organ "on the air."[18]

The Skinner studio at 677 Fifth Avenue proved to be a most profitable acquisition for the Skinner Organ Company. By 1925, it was stated that "the Studio has not been an expense; it has paid for itself many times over."[19]

The Fifth Avenue studio, the radio broadcasts, and the company periodical *Stop, Open, and Reed* were not the only means the Skinner Company had for making new friends and holding on to the old. In a letter of 20 February 1976, Robert Baker writes:

> I can remember Dr. Noble's telling me that one way the Skinner reputation was established was due to having *twenty two* men on maintenance in New York City, all of whom were on duty on Sundays. The men in the key posts, such as Dickinson, Noble, Farrow, and Williams, never sat down to play Sunday services but that two Skinner men were there, without charge. Naturally, this made an impression!

Mr. Baker adds that ". . . the loyalty of the key New York organists in the twenties to Mr. Skinner was complete, and each vied with the other in feeling that *he* had the masterpiece in *his* church!"

Ernest Skinner himself frequently showed up at organ concerts when they were played upon his instruments. This was apt to occur in any part of the country where Ernest happened to be and he was just as likely to show up in an audience on the west coast as in New York City. When visiting any installation of his, if there were any complaint, Ernest would immediately take off his coat and fix the problem himself.[20] Organist Stanton A. Hyer relates a story told to him by Jesse

Crawford about an incident which occurred when, as a yet unknown young theater organist, Crawford was playing on the Skinner at the Alaska Theater in Seattle, Washington, "and was griping about an errant coupler to a theater visitor." This visitor, who was none other than E. M. Skinner, "removed his coat, took a screwdriver from his pocket and repaired the problem on the spot."[21]

The possession of a Skinner organ had become such a status symbol by the mid-twenties that the organist who was not fortunate enough to preside over one of these instruments envied those organists who had better luck. Edward Gammons relates a story about Albert Snow, who was organist at Emmanuel Church in Boston during the 1920s. Emmanuel Church had a Casavant double organ (Chancel and Gallery) which had been designed by Lynnwood Farnam when he was organist there during the 'teens. The Emmanuel Church Casavant had an unusual proportion of mixtures and mutations for that day and was a very comprehensive and complete instrument. However, this did not satisfy Mr. Snow, who would complain to Ned Gammons, "Oh God, Ned, it's terrible. Why, every church on Fifth Avenue has a Skinner, and I'm stuck with this Casavant!"[22]

The devotion and loyalty to Ernest Skinner of the organists who presided at Skinner organs was mutual. T. Scott Buhrman, in his biographical sketch of Ernest in *The American Organist* (8, no. 5, May 1925), stated that ". . . he is as proud of the organists who play Skinner organs as he is of the organs themselves; it's all one big Skinner Family to him." In fact, many of these organists were Ernest's close personal friends.

Geographically as well as in relationship, Dr. T. Tertius Noble, organist at St. Thomas Church, New York City, was one of Ernest Skinner's closest friends.[23] Dr. Noble had come to St. Thomas Church early in 1913, at the time the Skinner organ was nearing completion, and would remain there as organist until his retirement in 1943.[24]

This instrument, reportedly one of Ernest's favorite organs, was conveniently close to the Skinner Company's Fifth Avenue Studio. That, plus the unfailing generosity of Dr. Noble, made the St. Thomas Church instrument Ernest's showpiece for visiting organists and other musicians, and he took great pride in bringing them to hear and play that organ.[25] According to legend, Ernest used to watch from the window of the studio for Dr. Noble coming to work at St. Thomas Church in the morning. Upon Dr. Noble's arrival, Ernest would follow his friend into the church where he would enjoy listening to music played on the organ.[26]

Ernest was also close to New York organists Miles Farrow and

Clarence Dickinson.[27] Miles Farrow was organist at the Cathedral of St. John the Divine, New York City, from 1909 when the Cathedral's Skinner organ was under construction until his retirement in 1931. In spite of being largely a self-taught musician, Farrow was an expert with choirs of men and boys and was author of a book on the subject of training boys' voices.[28] Clarence Dickinson came to Brick Presbyterian Church, New York City, in 1909, ten years before the completion of this church's large Skinner organ. He served as organist and choirmaster at Brick Church for over half a century, retiring in 1960. During those fifty years Dickinson distinguished himself as a teacher and composer, founded the School of Sacred Music of the Union Theological Seminary in 1928, and was one of the founders of the American Guild of Organists.[29]

The legendary concert organist Lynnwood Farnam was a good friend of Ernest Skinner.[30] Late in life, Ernest recalled

> Farnam had a prodigious technique and was a very great organist but however great the technical necessities in performing a work he hardly moved except hands and feet, far removed from Virgil Fox in console manner.[31]

After serving as organist at Emmanuel Church in Boston and, briefly in the 'teens, Fifth Avenue Presbyterian Church, New York City, Lynnwood Farnam came in 1920 to the Church of the Holy Communion, New York City, remaining there as organist until his death ten years later.[32] At the Church of the Holy Communion Farnam presided over a four-manual Skinner which had been installed in 1910.[33] He played the dedication recitals on many Skinner organs which were installed during the 1920s, including those at Rockefeller Chapel of the University of Chicago and the Toledo Museum of Art.[34] According to *The American Organist* (vol. 14, no. 1, 1931, p. 27), Farnam recorded Jepson's "Pantomime," Roger-Ducasse's "Pastoral," and Stoughton's "The Enchanted Forest," on rolls for the Skinner Organ Company on 29 July 1925.

In a letter to Alexander McCurdy of 10 June 1954, Ernest writes of visiting Lynnwood Farnam "in St. Luke's hospital a few days before he died" and listening to Farnam tell of the program he was planning for the opening recital on one of Ernest's greatest instruments—the organ at Washington National Cathedral. This instrument would not be constructed until several years later. Ernest "knew *[Farnam]* was going to die but *[Farnam]* had no idea of it."

Another famous musician who was one of Ernest's friends was

Leopold Stokowski, conductor of the Philadelphia Orchestra from 1912 to 1938. Between 1905 and 1908 he was the music director at St. Bartholomew's Church, New York City, which had the 1893 Hutchings organ containing Ernest Skinner's first electric action.[35] Stokowski was a great admirer of Ernest's work and considered the Skinner organ at St. Thomas Church, New York City, to be "the most magnificent instrument he had played in America."[36]

According to Ernest's daughter Eugenia Shorrock, Edwin Arthur Kraft was a special friend. Mr. Kraft assumed the post as organist and choirmaster at Trinity Cathedral, Cleveland, Ohio, in 1907, the same year that the Church's Skinner organ was completed and dedicated. He remained there for over fifty-one years. Mr. Kraft played dedication recitals for many of Ernest Skinner's new organs, the most notable of which were the Skinners at St. Joseph's Cathedral, Columbus, Ohio, and the Cleveland Municipal Auditorium. Kraft felt that the Cleveland Auditorium Skinner, "through no fault of the organ builder, was badly placed," and considered it "useless for organ recitals for that reason." As a result, in the early 1930s, he led the Northern Ohio Chapter of the A.G.O. in an unsuccessful campaign to persuade the city of Cleveland to "spend $20,000 to relocate and save this magnificent instrument." Mrs. Kraft, an accomplished singer and voice teacher, was also a musician in her own right. Ernest often stayed overnight at the Krafts' home and enjoyed their hospitality when in Cleveland on business trips.[37]

Ernest was fond of Eric De Lamarter, who was organist at Fourth Presbyterian Church in Chicago. De Lamarter was appointed organist and director there in 1914, at the time its large four-manual Skinner was completed, and played the opening recital on the instrument. He served as organist at that church for twenty-two years.[38]

One of Ernest's favorite organists was Chandler Goldthwaite. Mr. Goldthwaite was, for a short time, municipal organist at St. Paul, Minnesota. He was also "associated with the Skinner Organ Co. in connection with the enlargement of its residence organ library and other astistic and musical developments," such as the radio broadcasts from its New York studio.[39]

Palmer Christian served as concert organist at the prestigious Grove Park Inn, Asheville, North Carolina, for two years following the installation of its Skinner in 1920. He left Grove Park Inn in 1922 to serve briefly as associate organist to Eric De Lamarter at Fourth Presbyterian Church of Chicago. He subsequently was appointed to a prominent position at University of Michigan, where he later would be instrumental in designing one of Ernest Skinner's most famous organs.[40]

Wheeler Beckett, whose friendship with Ernest spanned forty years, "was a great admirer of his work."[41] The two men shared the common middle name of *Martin* and were in fact fourth cousins. However, neither of them knew of this relationship during Ernest's lifetime. It was discovered by Eugenia Shorrock, after her father's death, while she was doing research on the Skinner family geneology. Mr. Beckett had a summer home at Ragged Isle on Lake Winnipesaukee, and Ernest saw him frequently during the summer when he was at the Skinners' Alton Bay camp. Ernest was very fond of chess and often played it with Mr. and Mrs. Beckett when he visited with them. Mr. Beckett is a symphony orchestra conductor, organist, and composer, so, naturally, one of their favorite pastimes was discussing music.

The friendship between Ernest and his financial benefactor Arthur Hudson Marks continued to flourish during the early 1920s. Though there was sometimes a conflict of interest between the two men, as Ernest's son Richmond Skinner put it, Marks "had the business experience and he was interested in making money . . . my father was interested in building organs that would have a tone he would be proud of."[42] According to his daughter Ruth, Ernest could not manage money or keep track of where it went. She recalled that Marks and the Skinner Company "brass" became peeved at him because he never could account for his money on business trips.

Ernest also tended to forget tools and often had to "make do" on the job.[43] Ned Gammons tells this story about what happened when Ernest returned from one trip he made in connection with a big new contract. Upon Ernest's return to the factory, A. Perry Martin, the company's chief drafting engineer and Ernest's cousin, asked, "Well now, have you got the dimensions just right?" Whereupon Ernest pulled out a sketch marked 4—5—etc. Mr. Martin commented, "Well, Mr. Skinner, this can't be feet." Ernest then exclaimed, "Oh G__ d__, no! Those are the lengths of my umbrella and—I lost the d__ umbrella!"[44]

After three years of study at the Massachusetts Institute of Technology, Ernest's son Richmond had gone to the California Institute of Technology where he graduated with "high honors" in 1923.[45] Ernest looked forward to having Richmond join him in the organ business upon graduation from college. However, things did not work out quite as Ernest and his son had planned. According to Richmond Skinner, this is what happened:

> In 1923, I graduated from California Tech., after having been to M.I.T.. My father and I had always expected that I would go into business with him. The school-mates of mine were already starting out there at that time at fifty dollars a week. I was about to get

married. My father said that Mr. Marks had kindly offered to pay me thirty-five dollars a week if I would come and work with him. So, thinking that I was writing to my father, and *[to]* which I addressed it and sent it, I said that all my school-mates were making fifty dollars a week when they were starting on their jobs, and here I would have to support a wife on thirty-five dollars a week. Was that the best they could do? My father very foolishly took the letter to Mr. Marks, and Mr. Marks said "I've had enough of the Skinners. That man will never work for us." So, I was not allowed to work for the Ernest Skinner Organ Company because of the letter my father showed Mr. Marks, which I think . . . would be a natural letter.[46]

Ernest's wish to build organs with his son was not to be realized for another decade. Meanwhile, Richmond, who had studied engineering in college, went on to a distinguished career in that field, with his most outstanding achievement being "in charge of all inspection on the $56,000,000 Conowingo Dam in Maryland."[47]

In spite of the fact that Ernest Skinner and Arthur Hudson Marks had their differences of opinion, Ernest still appreciated having "someone else . . . in charge of the Department of Worries."[48] This, along with Marks' substantial financial backing, would enable Ernest to soar to even greater heights in his artistic accomplishments within the next few years. His work was to take on a new dimension the very next year.

FOOTNOTES

[1]"Recent Skinner Installations," *Stop, Open, and Reed,* 2, no. 1 (January 1924), 15. See also "The St. Joseph's Cathedral Organ," pp. 2 & 3; "Skinner Organ in Ogden Hall, Hampton Institute, Hampton, Va.," p. 20; and "The New Skinner Organ for 'Old Trinity'," p. 25. The St. Joseph's organ is no longer extant.

[2]"Skinner Organ in Ogden Hall," p. 20.

[3]"Famous Old Church Welcomes New Organ," *The Diapason,* April 1924, p. 1.

[4]"New Honolulu Organ is Opened by Carruth," *The Diapason,* September 1924, p. 3.

[5]"Recent Skinner Installations," p. 14.

[6]"Skinner Co. Leases Space," *The Diapason,* October 1921, p. 20.

[7]E. A. Boadway, "The Skinner & Aeolian-Skinner Opus List," *The Boston Organ Club Newsletter,* July & August 1972, p. 8.

[8]"Organ Stoplists," *The American Organist,* 10, no. 8 (1927), p. 200.

[9]"Broadcasting the Skinner Organ," *Stop, Open, and Reed,* 2, no. 1 (January 1924), pp. 9 & 10.

[10]Arthur Hudson Marks, quoted in "Patent for New Way of Transmitting Organ Music by Radio . . ." *Stop, Open, and Reed,* 4, no. 1 (1927), p. 24.

[11]"Arthur Hudson Marks *[Obituary],*" *The American Organist,* 22, no. 6 (1939), p. 197.

[12]"Broadcasting the Skinner Organ," p. 10.

[13]F. L. Farote, Letter to Harold Gleason, 27 October 1925.

[14]Letter received from Harold Gleason, 7 April 1976.

[15]Personal interview with Alexander McCurdy, 7 October 1972.

[16]"Patent for New Way of Transmitting Organ Music," p. 25.
[17]"Broadcasing the Skinner Organ," pp. 9 & 10. See also "A Typical Radio Program," *Stop, Open, and Reed*, 2, no. 1 (January 1924), p. 13.
[18]"Broadcasting the Skinner Organ," p. 9.
[19]T. Scott Buhrman, "Ernest M. Skinner: Organ Builder," *The American Organist*, 8, no. 5 (May 1925), p. 179.
[20]Personal interview with Alexander McCurdy, 7 October 1972.
[21]Letter received from Stanton A. Hyer, 14 April 1978.
[22]Personal interview with Edward B. Gammons, 3 May 1976.
[23]Personal interview with Alexander McCurdy, 7 October 1972.
[24]"T. Tertius Noble Stays in America," *The Diapason*, February 1913, p. 3; "Hymn Society Honors Noble," *The Diapason*, June 1943, p. 11.
[25]Ernest M. Skinner, "Interesting Light on Life and Work of Sigfried Karg-Elert," *The Diapason*, December 1933, p. 24.
[26]Personal interview with Joseph F. Dzeda, Fall 1967.
[27]Personal interview with Alexander McCurdy, 7 October 1972.
[28]"Dr. Miles Farrow, Former N. Y. Cathedral Organist, Dies," *The Diapason*, August 1953, p. 2.
[29]George L. Knight, "Clarence Dickinson: A Retrospect," *The Diapason*, October 1969, p. 16; "Dean of Church Musicians Retires From Brick Church," *The Diapason*, August 1960, p. 21; "Nunc Dimittis," *The Diapason*, September 1969, p. 21.
[30]Personal interview with Alexander McCurdy, 7 October 1972.
[31]Ernest M. Skinner, Letter to Alexander McCurdy, 15 June 1954.
[32]Jeanne Rizzo, "Lynnwood Farnam," *The Diapason*, December 1974, pp. 3 & 4.
[33]Boadway, p. 4.
[34]Rizzo, p. 5.
[35]"Stokowski, Leopold," *Music Lover's Encyclopedia*, 1954 ed., p. 420.
[36]R. P. Elliot, Letter to Ernest M. Skinner, 19 September 1927 (courtesy of Henry Karl Baker).
[37]This information on Kraft was gleaned from: "Stoplists," *The American Organists*, 40, no. 12 (December 1957), p. 406; "Edwin Arthur Kraft Who Retires After 51 Years," *The Diapason*, July 1959, p. 1; "The St. Joseph's Cathedral Organ," p. 2; "Twenty Thousand Hear Opening Recita By Kraft . . ." *Stop, Open, and Reed*, 1, no. 4 (December 1922), p. 9; Edwin Arthur Kraft, "S.O.S. Organists," *The American Organist*, 15, no. 4 (April 1932), p. 249; "Marie Simmelink Kraft Takes Cleveland Position," *The Diapason*, May 1949, p. 32; and Ernest M. Skinner, Letter to Harold Gleason, 1 March 1936.
[38]Sources for information about Delamarter include: Personal interview with Edward H. Hastings, 12 October 1972; "Eric Delamarter Chosen," *The Diapason*, May 1914, p. 2; "Chicago Organ is Finished," *The Diapason*, June 1914, p. 1; "Fourth Church Post to Barrett Spach," *The Diapason*, March 1936, p. 7.
[39]Sources include personal interview with Ruth Scott, 12 October 1972; "Chandler Goldthwaite Dies After Nine Years' Illness," *The Diapason*, June 1946, p. 1; and "Goldthwaite Goes Abroad. Organist Will Be Associate With Skinner Company," *The Diapason*, June 1923, p. 3.
[40]"News and Notes," *The American Organist*, 5, no. 9 (September 1922), p. 410; "News Record and Notes," *The American Organist*, 7, no. 1 (January 1924), p. 55.
[41]Letters received from Wheeler Beckett, 23 July 1973 and 17 March 1973.
[42]Telephone interview with Richmond H. Skinner, 15 September 1977.
[43]Personal interview with Barbara Owen, 12 May 1976.
[44]Personal interview with Edward B. Gammons, 3 May 1976.
[45]"R. H. Skinner," *The American Organist*, 17, no. 4 (April 1934), 177; "Richmond H. Skinner," *The Diapason*, July 1941, p. 15.
[46]Telephone interview with Richmond H. Skinner, 15 September 1977.
[47]"R. H. Skinner," p. 177.
[48]Buhrman, p. 183.

CHAPTER 12

The New Skinner Organ 1924-1926

IN EARLY 1924 Ernest Skinner, for the second time in his life, embarked on a voyage to England and France. This second journey abroad took place during what, in recent years, has been considered by many to have been an all-time low point in American organ building history.

The romantic organ, as it had been developed in France and England by Cavaillé-Coll and "Father" Henry Willis during the mid to late nineteenth century, while orchestral in the sense that it had weight and warmth, was still built on sound tonal principles. These instruments possessed the essential classic diapason (or principal) chorus consisting of a proper harmonic build-up, complete with mixtures and reed choruses. When the romantic organ migrated to America, builders became so enamored of making the organ into a "symphony orchestra" that they did so at the expense of the diapason chorus. As a result, by the 1920s the average organ was unlikely to have anything over 4' pitch, with the exception of perhaps a 2' Piccolo, or a Dolce Cornet (if any compound stop was present at all). The abundant 8' stops, particularly the diapasons and flutes, tended to be dull, hooty and lacking in adequate harmonic development.

Ernest Skinner has generally been credited (or blamed) for this conversion of the American organ into an imitation symphony orchestra because of the many orchestral reeds and other imitative stops which he developed during the two decades following the founding of his own company in 1901. In a sense, this prevailing belief about

The New Skinner Organ (1924-1926) 111

Ernest's role in creating and popularizing this type of instrument is justified, for he did very definitely set out to build what he termed a symphonic organ. But his intent went far beyond this, for his ultimate ideal was an instrument on which all music—organ, piano, orchestral, operatic arias, etc.—could be played with sensitivity, warmth, and an infinite variety of color which would surpass the symphony orchestra.

Notwithstanding his brief association with Robert Hope-Jones, Ernest's organs never completely degenerated into the muddy, lifeless type of instrument that so many other American builders were turning out during the 'teens and 1920s. In his book *The Modern Organ*, originally published in 1917, Ernest states on page ten:

> In planning specifications for an effective organ, the Swell-organ should be provided with a full equipment of chorus reeds of 16 foot, 8 foot, and 4 foot pitch, a good Diapason 4 foot Octave and mixture.

This foundation appeared quite consistently in Ernest's larger instruments. In a few instances he even had a complete diapason chorus up to a Twelfth, Fifteenth, and mixture in the Great division. The four-manual organs he built for Finney Memorial Chapel at Oberlin College in Oberlin, Ohio in 1914, and New Old South Church in Boston in 1915, both had complete Great choruses, as described above.[1]

During the early 1920s, Ernest frequently included mutations such as the 2-$2/3'$ Nazard, 1-$3/5'$ Tierce, and 1-$1/7'$ Septième in larger installations. The organ built in 1918 for Brick Presbyterian Church, New York City, contained a 2-$2/3'$ Nazard in the Choir division and is the first Skinner known to have any stops of this classification.[2] The organ built in 1921 for Kilbourn Hall, Eastman School of Music, would appear to have been the first Skinner equipped with a complete set of mutations up to the 1-$1/7'$ Septième.[3] Some of the other Skinner organs of the early 1920s which contained a full complement of mutations were those built for Second Congregational Church, Holyoke, Massachusetts, 1921; Cleveland Public Auditorium, Cleveland, Ohio, 1921; Capitol Theatre, Boston, 1922; St. Joseph's Roman Catholic Cathedral, Columbus, Ohio, 1923; and Colony Theatre, New York City, 1924.[4] Mutations were included in the Skinner organ for the purpose of "lending delicate tints to such stops as the choir Concert Flute, Dulciana, etc."[5]

It may well have been Ernest Skinner's quest for the ideal organ which prompted him to return to England and France. A fairly detailed description of this second trip appears in Ernest's article entitled "A Trip Abroad" in *Stop, Open, and Reed* (3, no. 1, January

1925, 30–34). According to this account, he departed on 1 March 1924 with England as his first destination. The day after his arrival he went to the Willis factory where he met with Henry Willis III, grandson of "Father" Willis and now head of the company. When Ernest first had gone to England a quarter of a century earlier, he had been primarily interested in the "Father" Willis high pressure reeds. Now, in 1924, his attention was directed to the Willis diapason chorus and to the boldly scaled and voiced mixtures which topped off these superbly designed choruses.

Ernest Skinner stayed in England fifteen days, during which he saw and heard a number of fine organs, most of them built by the Willis firm. The first organ he saw was a new Willis at an unnamed church on Westminster Bridge Road. This instrument was demonstrated by organist Reginald Goss-Custard during that visit. Ernest was much impressed with the "fine and brilliant" ensemble of that instrument. Another important instrument he saw during his stay in England was the partly completed Willis organ in Westminster Cathedral. Here, he took special note of the ensemble build-up on the Great division, particularly the five-rank Chorus Mixture which he told Mr. Willis "paid me for my trip to England." Ernest recalls:

> The effect of this Chorus Mixture gave me a real thrill. It came through the entire Great, including the big Reeds, with a splendid tang which gave a most satisfactory quality to the full Great.[6]

As a result of these experiences, Ernest made an arrangement with Henry Willis to obtain scaling of some of Willis' mixtures and fluework in exchange for blueprints of the Skinner combination action.[7]

Ernest also visited St. Bartholomew's Church at Armley near Leeds, York Minster, St. Mary's Church in Bristol, and St. Paul's Cathedral. He was impressed with the Great Mixture at St. Bartholomew's, "voiced throughout and scaled as Diapason pipes," but thought English diapasons, in general, were too small.[8]

The remainder of Ernest's trip abroad was spent in Paris, France. Here, with the assistance of organist Joseph Bonnet, Ernest gained first hand knowledge of French mutations on the organ at St. Eustache. He also met with organist Marcel Dupré, who spent many hours in familiarizing Ernest with the historical foundation for mutation work as found in the French organ.

Ernest Skinner's return from this journey marked the beginning of a new era for the Skinner organ and a turning point for the organ in America. A new, brilliant, English "Willis type" mixture, accompanied

The New Skinner Organ (1924-1926) 113

by new life and buoyancy in the entire diapason chorus from 8′ pitch up, was incorporated thereafter in all larger Skinner organs. Even smaller two- and three-manual instruments (which, due to the preferences of many organists of that day, did not always have mixtures) were characterized by a clarity, brightness, and blending capacity that organs of similar size and composition did not have earlier.

The first Willis mixture to appear in a Skinner organ was introduced with the instrument built for the Church of the Ascension, Pittsburgh, Pennsylvania.[9] This organ was already under construction at the time Ernest made his eventful journey abroad in early 1924, the Willis mixture evidently being added after his return home.[10] Also among the first instruments to reflect the Willis influence in their upperwork was the Skinner built for Carnegie Free Library, North Side (also known as Carnegie Hall, North Side), Pittsburgh, Pennsylvania.[11] This instrument, likewise, was under construction before Ernest's trip abroad.[12] In *Stop, Open, and Reed* (3, no. 1, 1925, 35), Pittsburgh City Organist Caspar P. Koch, in a glowing testimonial, speaks of the "extraordinary ensemble effects made possible by the installation of the five-rank French Cornet in the Swell, the four-rank English Mixture in the Great, and the complete set of mutation registers in the choir." Mr. Koch continues:

> Dulness has given way to brilliancy, stodginess to life and buoyancy.
> To you, Mr. Skinner, is due the credit for having, through your personal interest and attention, made this new type of concert organ a reality.

The earliest existing Skinner organ known to contain the Willis mixture is the four-manual, sixty-eight rank instrument installed at Jefferson Avenue Presbyterian Church, Detroit, in 1925.[13] The contract for the Jefferson Avenue Presbyterian Church (J.A.P.C.) Skinner was signed in early spring of 1924, probably making it one of the first larger instruments to be designed and built by the firm after Ernest Skinner had returned from his second trip abroad.[14] The installation, final finishing and tuning of this organ were completed by late March of 1926.[15] Its opening recital, played on 8 April by Palmer Christian, professor of organ at the University of Michigan, was provided free of charge by the Skinner Organ Company.[16]

The J.A.P.C. Skinner, one of the most complete church organs built during the mid-1920s, contains an abundance of strings and orchestral imitative reeds. It also contains what is believed to have been the first

Flute Triangulaire, a fairly bright wood flute which, as its name suggests, is constructed with three sides rather than the usual four.[17] However, it is the diapason chorus which clearly distinguishes this instrument from its predecessors. Every component of the chorus is clean and rich in harmonic development right on up to the Fifteenth in the Great and the five-rank Mixture in the Swell. The Swell Mixture, unlike most mixtures incorporated in American organs prior to 1924, contains no tierce. The octave-sounding ranks of this mixture are of diapason scale and voicing, but the quint-sounding ranks are somewhat smaller in scale, thus making the latter less conspicuous. The mixture adds brilliance, without being shrill, and serves to enrich the harmonic texture of the ensemble rather than emphasizing the higher pitches. This mixture is remarkable in that it can be used with the Swell 8' Second Diapason and 4' Octave alone without being at all overpowering, and still, with the Swell box open, is capable of topping off full organ, minus the Solo Tubas.[18]

Some authorities have criticized Ernest Skinner's work during this era because he continued to use big, relatively high pressure diapasons which had the narrow, high-cut mouths. His critics felt that these diapasons did not blend with the more brilliant upperwork he now used.[19] Yet, in spite of their bigness, Skinner diapasons of the mid-1920s were sufficiently bright that they did indeed blend well with the rest of the chorus. The main effect of these diapasons on the ensemble was to give it a full, rich tone.

The mid-1920s Skinner organ, as exemplified by the J.A.P.C. instrument, is well suited for the performance of romantic and contemporary organ music, as well as for orchestral transcriptions. However, it is its capacity for the effective playing of Bach and other contrapuntal music that distinctly sets the Skinner organ of this vintage apart from all other organs built in this country during the first quarter of the twentieth century. Even with the predominance of 8' tone, the diapason chorus is clean enough for every voice of a Bach fugue to be clearly discerned by the listener. In addition, the warm brilliance charcterizing the ensemble lends a rich glow to the lean textures of contrapuntal music. The mid-1920s Skinner marked a return to clarity of ensemble in American organs. With its capacity for the satisfactory interpretation of all types of music (classic, romantic, contemporary, etc.), the "new" Skinner organ now came very close to approaching Ernest Skinner's ideal of an all-purpose organ.

During the three years following E. M. Skinner's second trip to England and France, thirty of the more than 170 organs installed by the Skinner Organ Company contained replicas of Willis mixtures, with many more containing "Willis type" mixtures based on the Willis models and designed by Ernest Skinner. The more notable of these installations were those built for Temple Emanu-El, San Francisco; the Auditorium at University of Florida, Gainesville; Scottish Rite Cathedral, Detroit; Trinity Episcopal Church, Boston; Henry H. Stambaugh Auditorium, Youngstown, Ohio; and the Toledo Museum of Art, Toledo, Ohio.[20] The Temple Emanu-El organ contained a tonal novelty in the form of a Shofar stop in the Echo organ, possibly the only one of its kind to appear in Skinner organs.[21]

Ernest Skinner's English Horn stop had now been incorporated in his largest instruments for fifteen years. In the meantime, he had decided that it needed improvement. He saw "the way around a corner [he] could not turn until lately."[22] With the help of his pipemaker, he finally succeeded in developing an English Horn that not only was a more authentic reproduction of its orchestral prototype, but also was "sound as to pitch."[23] One of the earliest examples of this improved type of English Horn is in the Solo division of the Skinner built in 1925 for the Scottish Rite Cathedral in the Masonic Temple of Detroit, Michigan.

Anyone who has played or heard a large and comprehensive Skinner built during the 'teens or early 1920s is probably familiar with the tendency of the 32' Bombarde to be slow in speaking and to continue vibrating for several seconds after the note has been released (a phenomenon sometimes referred to as a "death rattle"). It has been maintained by some organists that the slow release of these 32' reeds creates somewhat of an illusion of reverberation in acoustically dead buildings, and the most devoted of "Skinnerphiles" generally love the Skinner 32' Bombardes just as they are, "death rattle" and all! However, many organists, especially those who demand a very clean and clear pedal bass for the playing of contrapuntal music, dislike this idiosyncrasy intensely. Around 1901, about three years after Ernest made his first trip to England, the Willis firm of London devised a pneumatic starter for 32' reeds which facilitated a prompt attack and release when a note was played. Following his second visit to England Ernest began using his own adaptation of the Willis pneumatic starter on the 32' reeds.[24] According to one source, Ernest did not especially like to use these devices, for he believed that proper treatment of the reed would insure a sufficiently quick attack without the starters, although he was not averse to using them in unusual accoustical situations where an abnormally large amount of reverberation existed.[25] Ernest himself was not at all disturbed by the slow release of his 32' reeds and has been quoted as responding to criticism of their slow starting with the remark, "Yes, but think how long they hang on after the note is released."[26] It is quite likely that the complaints of organists may have induced him to employ the pneumatic starter in his instruments, in spite of his own personal preferences. As in the case of his recently improved English Horn, the first known use of a pneumatic starter on a Skinner 32' reed was on the 32' Bombarde in the organ at the Scottish Rite Cathedral in Detroit.

Even though Ernest Skinner's primary attention over the preceding twenty-some years had been devoted to the improvement of the tonal resources of the Skinner organ, his mechanical genius was still much in evidence during the mid-1920s. Prior to 1925 Ernest incorporated a melody-coupler "for playing the octave of the top note of any chord."[27] It is possible that this feature was based in principle on a similar device used by Hilborne Roosevelt in the instrument he built for the Church of the Holy Communion, New York City, in 1872, since this Roosevelt organ was replaced by a Skinner organ in 1910. The earliest Skinner known to be equipped with this invention was the instrument completed 1925 for Church of the Holy Trinity, Brooklyn, New York. The only other Skinner organ known to contain this device is the instrument installed in St. Paul's Episcopal Church, Rochester, New York, in 1927.[28]

Early in the 1920s Ernest's ingenuity was called upon for a project which did not directly involve the King of Instruments. The Skinner Organ Company "installed for Walter F. Starbuck, in the music room of his home at Waltham, Mass., a pedal board of thirty-two keys connected with a Steinway upright piano, for practicing and teachning purposes . . ." This apparatus, designed by Ernest Skinner, functioned by means of a vacuum-operated tubular-pneumatic action. The mechanism for this pedal board was "believed to be unique" and was the only one constructed by the Skinner firm.[29]

In 1926, the Skinner Company built a rather unusual organ for Holy Trinity Episcopal Cathedral in Havana, Cuba. According to the June 1926 issue of *The Diapason,*

> Designing an organ for a church in Cuba did not present much of a problem for the Skinner Organ Company. But how to keep the organ from being eaten alive offered a more baffling conundrum. The problem has been met and overcome, however, according to word from the Boston factory.
>
> The organ in question is being built for Holy Trinity Cathedral at Havana. The enemy who had to be vanquished to prevent the destruction of the instrument was the wood louse, called in Cuba "comejan," which gets into all soft woods and eats them away. As

The New Skinner Organ (1924-1926)   117

sugar pine is a very soft wood, it was decided that it would be folly to build a fine organ for installation in Cuba merely to prepare a feast for wood lice.

Consequently before Holy Trinity Cathedral purchased the organ the authorities sent some working samples of Cuban cedar and Cuban mahogany to the factory of the Skinner Company for experiments. These experiments proved that an organ could be built entirely of Cuban mahogany, both as to chests and wood pipes. After the report on these tests the contract for the organ was placed with the proviso that it be built of Cuban mahogany, to be shipped direct to the factory of the Skinner Company from Cuba for this purpose.

In early 1926, Ernest had extended business in California and took his wife and youngest daughter there with him for the winter. According to the February 1926 issue of *The Diapason,* Ernest Skinner and his family were staying in "an apartment near the Ambassador Hotel" in Los Angeles. In a letter written to Harold Gleason on 3 February 1926, Ernest remarks:

Diapason says I'm out here for the winter. Trying to make a Plutocrat out of me. I've been so busy with clients I haven't had time to gaze at the scenery.

Ernest Skinner, who was said to have been a very good salesman, undoubtedly spent much of that winter in California pursuing new contracts.[30] He may also have been following up on the approximately eleven Skinner installations which had been completed in that state in recent years, making sure his customers were satisfied and remedying any problems that had developed in these new organs. The most significant of these installations were the large four-manual instruments built for the Palace of the Legion of Honor, San Francisco, and Temple Emanu-El, also in San Francisco.[31]

Even though Ernest was preoccupied with business matters during his stay in California, he still managed to find some time for more pleasurable activities, both en route to his destination and during his sojourn there.

One of the stops Ernest made on his way to the West Coast was at Muncie, Indiana. In "A Trip Abroad at Home," appearing in *Stop, Open, and Reed* (4, no. 1, 1927), he comments that "this stop was for business reasons, but we had the remarkable good fortune to hear the Russian Symphony Choir . . ." This chorus was renowned for its basso profundos, which Ernest referred to as "human bombardes." He was much impressed with the entire concert, which provided him with an evening of "unbounded delight." Ruth Scott recalls that they stayed at the home of William Ball, manufacturer of Ball Mason Jars, where her father had recently installed a residence organ. It was the Balls who took the Skinners to hear the Russian chorus. According to Ruth, the entire chorus was entertained at the Ball residence after the concert.

The Skinners also visited the Grand Canyon, where Ernest and his daughter, Ruth undertook the adventure of riding to the bottom of the canyon by mule. Ernest, of course, took his motion picture camera along to capture the "grandeur of the scenery."[32]

While in California, Ernest spent much of his leisure time satisfying his insatiable hunger for beautiful music. In "A Trip Abroad at Home," Ernest tells of the musical treats provided by his organist friends and their wives and also reveals the extent to which music was a necessary part of his life:

> Mr. Marsh, at the University of Redlands . . . played some of his organ compositions for me, one of which suggested a touch of Richard Strauss. Then I had, as always when in the west, some pleasant hours with Dr. Mixell who, with Mrs. Mixell played a duet for organ and piano by Dr. Mixell—a very beautiful work which ought to be better known.
>
> Then there is Warren D. Allen, who made a worn out Guilmant composition sound new and colorful. A fine musician who is well and favorably known in the east. He is organist at Stanford University. Mrs. Allen sang Strauss songs for me to Mr. Allen's accompaniment on the piano. If I am grateful for anything in this world it is for a good fortune in the choice of friends who seem so willing to make music for me of the kind that sticks in the memory, and which, when you are fed up with business and fatigue, you can call up and live over again when you have turned in for the night in some lonely hotel room, away from everybody and everything that you care about, or perhaps on a railway train crossing the desert in quest of the next big contract.

Ernest also went to the Bohemian Club, where he was captivated by the music of a young organist and composer named Wheeler Beckett. Mr. Beckett was to become one of his closest friends, and would remain so for the rest of Ernest's life.

Ernest Skinner's stay in California would not have been complete without a side trip to his beloved Yosemite Valley. "A Trip Abroad at Home" is profusely illustrated with his own photographs, most of which were taken at Yosemite. In his estimation, there was no other "spot in the world of such overwhelming beauty."

FOOTNOTES

[1]"Oberlin College Orders a Skinner," *The Diapason,* July 1914, p. 1; "Skinner Building Three Large Organs," *The Diapason,* April 1915, p. 2.

[2]"Brick Church, New York," *The American Organist,* 1, no. 11 (November 1918), p. 563.

[3]Letter received from Harold Gleason, 23 April 1977.

[4]"Organ of 84 Stops for Holyoke Church," *The Diapason,* January 1921, p. 1; Specification of Cleveland Auditorium Skinner, courtesy of Joseph F. Dzeda; "The Capitol Theatre Organ, Boston, Mass.," *Stop, Open, and Reed,* 1, no. 4 (December 1922, p. 15; "Specification of Skinner in St. Joseph's Cathedral," *Stop, Open, and Reed,* 2, no. 1 (January 1924), p. 16; "The Skinner Organ in Colony Theatre, New York City," *Stop, Open and Reed,* 3, no. 1 (1925), p. 7.

[5]*The Skinner Organ,* brochure published by the Skinner Organ Company, p. 27.

[6]Ernest M. Skinner, "A Trip Abroad," *Stop, Open, and Reed,* 3, no. 1 (1925), p. 30.

[7]Aubrey Thompson-Allen, "Information Given/Part III," *Music: The A.G.O. Magazine,* 6 (January 1972), p. 33.

[8]Skinner, "A Trip Abroad," p. 30.

[9]Daniel Phillipi, Letter to the Skinner Organ Company, 27 October 1924, quoted in *Stop, Open, and Reed,* 3, no. 1 (1925), p. 37. Note: This was an actual replica of a Willis mixture.

[10]E. A. Boadway, "The Skinner and Aeolian-Skinner Opus List," *The Boston Organ Club Newsletter,* September 1972, p. 5.

[11]Caspar P. Koch, Letter to Ernest M. Skinner, 11 April 1925, Quoted in *Stop, Open, and Reed,* 3, no. 1 (1925), p. 35. Note: This was not an actual replica of a Willis mixture, as in the case of the Church of the Ascension, but a mixture of E. M. Skinner's design, based on the Willis model. This instrument and the one at the Church of the Ascension are no longer extant.

[12]Boadway, p. 6.

[13]This is an actual replica of a Willis mixture.

[14]*The Detroit Presbyterian,* 10 April 1924 (Newsclipping from scrapbook in the Archives of Jefferson Avenue Presbyterian Church).

[15]Unsigned carbon copy of letter to Mr. John R. Russel, 24 March 1926.

[16]Church bulletin, Jefferson Avenue Presbyterian Church, 4 April 1926 (Easter Sunday).

[17]While searching through J.A.P.C. records and correspondence, the author found some type-written notes describing the J.A.P.C. Skinner, presumably used by the pastor, Dr. Samuel Forrer, for an illustrative talk about the organ at a demonstration-concert given by William E. Zeuch on 3 May 1926. These notes make mention of the "New type Flute Triangulaire" which appears in the Swell division of this instrument. Further research would tend to strongly indicate that this was the first Skinner installation to include this stop.

[18]For a more detailed description of this instrument, see Dorothy J. Holden, "The Tonal Evolution of the E. M. Skinner Organ, Part IV," *The Diapason,* March 1979, p. 13.

[19]Edward W. Flint, *The Newberry Memorial Organ at Yale University* (New Haven: Yale University Press, 1930), p. 54.

[20]E. A. Broadway, "The Skinner and Aeolian-Skinner Opus List," *The Boston Organ Club Newsletter,* September 1972, pp. 5, 7 & 8, and October 1972, pp. 6 & 7 *List of Mixtures of the Skinner Organ Company,* furnished by William Bunch.

[21]"Example in Placing Organ Successfully," *The Diapason,* May 1926, p. 3.

[22]Ernest M. Skinner, Editorial, *Stop, Open, and Reed,* 4, no. 1 (1927), p. 4.

[23]Ernest M. Skinner, "Ernest M. Skinner on Fine Organ Tone Versus 'Ritualism'," *The Diapason,* August 1933, p. 21.

[24]"Pneumatic Reed-Control," *The American Organist,* 22, no. 2 (1939), 54 & 55.

[25]Personal interview with Sydney F. Eaton, 30 April 1973.

[26] William Harrison Barnes, *The Contemporary American Organ,* 3rd. ed. (New York: J. Fischer & Bro., 1937), p. 63.

[27] T. Scott Buhrman, "Mr. Ernest M. Skinner's Record," *The American Organist,* 19, no. 4 (1936), p. 126.

[28] Orpha Ochse, *The History of the Organ in the United States* (Bloomington & London: Indiana University Press, 1975), p. 266; E. A. Boadway, "The Skinner and Aeolian-Skinner Opus List," *The Boston Organ Club Newsletter,* July & August 1972, p. 4, September 1972, p. 8, and November 1972, p. 3.

[29] "Novel Piano Pedal Board," *The Diapason,* January 1923, p. 19.

[30] Letter received from Harold Gleason, January 1974.

[31] "New Skinner Organs That Have Been Completed and Installed During the Past Two Years," *Stop, Open, and Reed,* 3, no. 1 (1925), p. 41.

[32] Ernest M. Skinner, "A Trip Abroad at Home," *Stop, Open, and Reed,* 4, no. (1927), p. 16.

CHAPTER 13

G. Donald Harrison Joins The Skinner Firm, 1927–1929

THE YEAR 1927 began well for Ernest M. Skinner and his company. According to the January 1927 issue of *The Diapason*, six large Skinners and many smaller ones were then under construction. This report stated that "both the Boston and Westfield plants are running full time," and that "Mr. Skinner is working overtime superintending the finishing of these instruments." Some of the more important work to be done by the Skinner Organ Company during that year included the enlargement of the 1917 Skinner at St. Bartholomew's Church, New York City, plus the construction of new organs for the Music Hall at Lake Erie College, Painesville, Ohio; Hill Auditorium, University of Michigan, Ann Arbor; Warner Hall, Oberlin Conservatory of Music, Oberlin, Ohio; and Idlewild Presbyterian Church, Memphis, Tennessee.[1]

In spite of the new bouyancy and brilliance in the Skinner ensemble, which was the result of Ernest Skinner's second visit to England and France in 1924, he was not to remain satisfied with its sound for long. During the years following World War I more and more young organ students were traveling to Europe, where they were exposed to an abundance of early organ music and the crisp, clean, and silvery sonorities of European organs. These students returned with a keen interest in the performance of the music of Johann Sebastian Bach and other early composers, along with the conviction that this music should be performed on instruments that closely approximated the type of organ for which it had been composed. To their ears, the lush and massive tone of the Skinner organ, even with its increased brilliance and clarity, was not suitable for the authentic interpretation of Bach, and a demand arose for a classic ensemble which more closely resembled that in the organ of Bach's day. As a result of the demands of these young organists, Ernest now evidently felt that the Skinner ensemble still had room for improvement.

By early 1927, Ernest began what was to be "twelve months hard work at running down every possibility of improvement" in his chorus work.[2] Apparently, in his quest for an ensemble that would meet the approval of this new generation of organists, Ernest became aware that his knowledge concerning the design of a traditional diapason chorus was still inadequate. He turned to England once again for assistance in tonal matters.

In July of 1927, G. Donald Harrison, a director of the Willis firm in England, joined the Skinner staff, taking the position of assistant general manager.[3] In his *Diapason* article entitled "G. Donald Harrison" (January 1928, p. 2), Ernest Skinner introduces Donald Harrison to the American organ world and gives a brief sketch of his background prior to coming to the United States:

> He was born April 21, 1889, at Huddersfield, Yorkshire, England; he is a graduate of Dulwich College, near London. In 1912 he passed the qualifying examination of the Chartered Institute of Patent Agents and joined his father's firm. In 1914 he did some work as patent attorney for Henry Willis...
>
> Mr. Harrison studied organ with Arthur Pearson, and also played cornet in [the] Dulwich military band. All his spare time in boyhood days he studied the organ, and on leaving college he tried to get into the Lewis firm, but Mr. Lewis discouraged the idea, saying: "There is no money in it." "I therefore took my second love, engineering, until I met Henry Willis just before the war," says Mr. Harrison.
>
> He acted as assistant to Willis and studied voicing methods, afterward becoming a director of the Willis firm. He had made a special study of ensemble and mixtures, more especially as related to the conspicuous examples of Father Willis, Cavaillé-Coll and Schulze...

Ernest Skinner first met G. Donald Harrison "on the occasion of *[his]* visit to the factory of Henry Willis in 1924," at which time Harrison and Henry Willis III took Ernest on a tour of various Willis installations.[4] Ernest's son Richmond Skinner relates:

> My father went to England and he visited the main organ maker *[Willis]* there, and he *[Willis]* had a man who knew the city *[London]*

G. Donald Harrison Joins the Skinner Firm (1927-1929)

because he maintained the organs. That was Donald Harrison. Donald Harrison acted as a guide and escorted my father around the city to see the organs. He made himself attractive to my father—and my father brought him over the the United States.[5]

In his article "G. Donald Harrison," Ernest describes his meeting with Don Harrison and relates his own version of the events leading up to Harrison's joining the Skinner Organ Company:

> I had with me at that time a set of blueprints of various mechanisms, which I thought might be regarded, in some measure, as an exchange for time given to me in showing the Willis work. I explained them at some length to Mr. Willis, but received the impression at the moment that he was not especially intrigued by them, which, I afterward became aware, was but a characteristic reserve. Mr. Willis was called away for a few moments, whereupon Mr. Harrison seized the opportunity to tell me not to take Mr. Willis' aloofness to heart, that he was more interested than he seemed. A sense of humor had, however, carried me along well enough, as I had nothing to sell, but the occasion gave me an illuminating viewpoint toward Harrison.
>
> My previous meetings with "Father Willis" and his son, whom I met at Liverpool thirty years or so ago, at the time the St. George's Hall organ was being rebuilt, had left me with a sense of obligation toward the House of Willis; so I invited Mr. Willis to America, saying such a visit would save him twenty years of experimentation and expense in the development of electrical mechanism and chest design, as there was nothing, as far as I knew, but tracker-pneumatic and tubular work in vogue in England, and France was, and is, in a hopeless state of antiquated stagnation on mechanical questions.
>
> The business outlook was such that Mr. Willis could see no prospect of such a visit, so I said to Harrison from the open window of a train, as I was leaving: "You come."
>
> As it happened, Mr. Willis and Mr. Harrison both came, but Mr. Willis came first, and Mr. Harrison later.
>
> Mr. Harrison decided, after looking us over, that he would like to carry on in America...

Prior to G. Donald Harrison's arrival in America, Henry Willis made several "short annual visits as consultant to the ... Skinner Organ Co. in 1924, 1925, and 1926 ..."[6] During the first of these three visits, which took place in the fall of 1924, Willis was immediately impressed with the mechanical equipment of the American organ. However, with respect to their tonal character, he had the following comments:

> Tonally, I must confess, I was disappointed on the whole with the effect of organs in the States. The pernicious teaching of Hope Jones would seem to have had a deplorable effect upon tone production which is only now being overcome; I refer to the productions of massive foundation tone with feeble upper work and very often no mutation or mixture work at all, the result being instruments representing a mere collection of stops without any true ensemble...
>
> Mutation and mixture work have been under a cloud from which I trust they will be rescued; an incorrect order of arrangement and power of the harmonies is only too frequently met with. There is every sign of a renaissance in this branch of Organ Builders Art and I most sincerely trust that in the near future fine mutation and mixture work following the best European traditions will be found in the best American organs. On this point I have had the pleasure of many interesting discussions with Mr. Skinner, both in England and America, and I look forward to the future with confidence.[7]

According to Henry Willis, following his third visit to the Skinner factory in 1926,

> It became obvious that if progress was to be effectively made it was necessary for one with the right technical knowledge and ability to be appointed to carry on the good work. On my recommendation Don Harrison joined the Skinner Organ Co. in 1927 . . .[8]

Arthur Hudson Marks, along with the stockholders at the Skinner Company, was very much in favor of bringing Harrison into the firm.[9] Marks had his own very practical reasons for encouraging this. Ernest Skinner was now over sixty years old, and Marks realized that eventually Ernest "would need to have a successor."[10] He undoubtedly saw business potential in having Harrison's knowledge of the "classic" ensemble, in view of the younger organists' changing tastes.

Donald Harrison, likewise, had his own reasons for joining the Skinner Company. One purpose was to "straighten out the organ in America."[11] But his chief reason for joining the firm was a practical one. The story of what prompted Harrison to leave the Willis firm was told to Joseph F. Dzeda, curator of organs at Yale University, by his predecessor, Aubrey Thompson-Allen, who worked for Willis at the time Harrison left for the United States. Shortly before that time, the wife of Henry Willis III was expecting a child. Harrison knew that if it was a boy, the son would inherit the business, leaving Harrison with no chance of rising any higher in the Willis firm. However, if the child was a girl, Harrison would eventually succeed Willis III as head of the business. According to Dzeda, "Aubrey told me that Harrison told him, 'the sex of this child will determine whether or not I stay in England—if its a boy, I'm off to America!'"[12] As it turned out, "Henry Willis IV, heir to the eminent family of organ builders, arrived January 19th" of 1927.[13]

When G. Donald Harrison joined the Skinner organization in 1927, Ernest Skinner "welcomed Mr. Harrison with open arms," and the two men quickly became good friends.[14] Their respective personalities were at once very different and yet complementary. In contrast to Ernest's warm, outgoing and aggressive nature, Don Harrison was, in the words of Ned Gammons, "one of the most shy individuals that I have ever known."[15] T. Scott Buhrman gives this description of the appearance and character of Don Harrison:

> In person Mr. Harrison is six feet tall and a little over, about the correct weight, slightly sandy and somewhat curly hair, is mild-mannered and soft-spoken, with much of the English manner . . . in his speaking. He has force of character but doesn't carry it on the surface. He won't try to out-talk anybody. In a crowd it will be the others who do the talking. We might call him the world's worst salesman; he just can't talk loud and fast enough. He's an English gentleman, not an American go-getter. You'd like him even if you didn't approve his ideas; he gives you the right to have ideas too.[16]

According to Eugenia Shorrock, Harrison was a frequent visitor to the Skinner camp at Alton Bay. One year (probably 1928), Don Harrison along with his wife, Dora, and their two sons rented the cottage next to the Skinners for the summer.

It was within a half year after Harrison's arrival in the United States that Ernest Skinner wrote his article "G. Donald Harrison" appearing in the January 1928 issue of *The Diapason* for the purpose of introducing his "friend and co-worker" to its readers. In this essay, Ernest remarks on the Skinner firm's "great good fortune" in having Don Harrison as a member of the staff. He also praises Harrison's experience and knowledge and expresses his faith and confidence in him:

> He is a modern by temperament and inclination. His musical taste is of the highest order. His experience as an artist brought him into intimate contact with all the recent great work of Mr. Willis, including Dunedin, Westminster and Liverpool Cathedrals, of which the last-named is regarded as the greatest example of the art of organ building anywhere.

> Mr. Harrison is fully acquainted with the great French masterpieces and has, in short, that wide knowledge of the art and its historical foundation without which no work of distinction can be created. Mr. Harrison is destined to be a great figure in the art of organ building in America...
>
> ... Mr. Harrison had the most profound knowledge of tonal architecture, commonly described as "specifications," of anyone I ever met. My confidence in his judgment stands at 100 per cent, which is somewhat better than I rate my own, to be perfectly frank about it.
>
> I welcome with relief one with whom I can, in the fullest confidence, share the responsibility of bringing to a state of perfection such great undertakings as we are carrying out at the present time.

As 1927 drew to a close, it proved to have been a highly productive year for the Skinner Organ Company. A first-page article in the January 1928 issue of *The Diapason* reported that

> ... contracts in 1927 exceeded those for 1926. As the demands of production and experimental work have increased, the Skinner Company is completing two new voicing rooms, which will give a total of eleven voicing rooms, in addition to Mr. Skinner's own experimental room.

This report also stated that the Skinner staff had been "strengthened materially" during the year, and that G. Donald Harrison, who had been secured as assistant general manager, was "working in close cooperation with Mr. Skinner on artistic development work."

The greater part of Ernest Skinner's time and effort was now being devoted to research with respect to the composition and voicing of mixtures. In the April 1928 issue of *The Diapason,* Ernest tells how he approached this project:

> A vast number of experimental tryouts were made with respect to scales, treatment of pipes, composition of mixtures and tonalities of various ranks of mixtures to enable us to arrive at a particular timbre. Special voicing machines were made to enable us to voice entire 5-rank mixtures with opportunity for giving each rank a precise effect upon the whole. We even went so far as to give an acoustical treatment to the voicing room in which certain of the stops, especially mixtures, were voiced in order to avoid the misleading effect of an over-resonance.

Continuing in this account, Ernest states that,

... the twelve months' hard work at running down every possibility of improvement is already reflected in recent organs. Notable examples are speaking for themselves in Warner Hall, Oberlin College, and in St. John's Church, Washington, both of which have very fine ensembles, due to the treatment of mixtures and upper work, and especially of the chorus reeds.[17]

The well developed ensembles featured in the organs at St. John's Church, Washington D. C., and Warner Hall, Oberlin College, were only a preview of what was yet to come. A large organ was now being completed by the Skinner Organ Company for Hill Auditorium at University of Michigan in Ann Arbor. According to a Skinner Company advertisement, which appeared in the April 1928 issue of *The Diapason* "the 'Renaissance of Mixtures' [*reached*] a culmination in this organ."

In a letter dated 23 April 1974, Dr. Alle D. Zuidema, Director of Music Emeritus at Jefferson Avenue Presbyterian Church in Detroit, writes that "the U. of M. Skinner organ was bought because of Palmer Christian's delight in playing the J.A.P.C. dedication program." The specification of the U. of M. Skinner was drawn up "by Ernest M. Skinner in consultation with Palmer Christian," with "valuable suggestions by G. Donald Harrison."[18] According to Ernest Skinner, "the original scheme was modified from time to time to get the benefit of our research."[19] The construction of the U. of M. Skinner had already been well under way by the end of the summer of 1927, at which time Mr. Christian went to "the Skinner offices in New York" to confer "with the Skinner officials on the finishing of the new organ for his department of the school of music of the University of Michigan."[20] Since this was shortly after Donald Harrison joined the Skinner firm, it is quite likely that some changes were then made in the tonal scheme of this instrument at his suggestion.

As the U. of M. Skinner was nearing completion, Ernest Skinner made these comments relating to its tonal design:

> An especial emphasis is made in this instance on account of the extraordinary opportunity afforded for a summation of the art of organ building, from classic tradition to the equally permanent contributions of the present time. There are in this organ, some fine reproductions of the best English and French reeds and mixtures, which (to say the least) have not suffered under the American technique, together with a wealth of orchestral color which is peculiar to the American builder ...

> This organ is an organ builder's creation. It was developed, criticized, built and set up by organ builders exclusively...
>
> Inasmuch as the mutation ranks and all the upper work are independent ranks, we had something to say about how they should be scaled and voiced. We will, accordingly, get a *character* and sound of many voices not possible with octave couplers. Perhaps I don't know how to voice an octave coupler! Of one thing I am certain: I am looking for one of the finest ensembles in the world, *with no octave couplers.*[21]

The U. of M. Skinner also contained a completely new voice, the Solo Flauto Mirabilis, as well as a revised version of the Great Erzähler, which had been appearing in Skinner organs for well over twenty years. Ernest gives the following descriptions of these two recent developments:

> The great erzahler, now so widely copied in its original form, has taken on a new form, and is again an exclusively Skinner voice, and a very beautiful one.
>
> The solo flauto mirabilis is a new voice in the organ, in point of fact, the result of a desire and tiresome search for a big voice of orchestral character, as far removed from the hooting tibia and ensemble destroying philomelas as possible. We have all heard stops of great power and other stops of great beauty, but I believe this is the first very big organ voice that is at the same time beautiful in quality. The flauto mirabilis is both, and particularly rich in blending qualities. It is also agreeably obedient to the tremolo, which makes it a most unusual solo voice. Its power places it naturally in the solo division.

The U. of M. Skinner was formally dedicated on 15 May 1928 "before an audience which filled every seat of the 5,000 in the Hill Auditorium on the campus at Ann Arbor." The recital was played by Palmer Christian and guest organist Eric De Lamarter of Fourth Presbyterian Church, Chicago, who performed a well-rounded and varied program of music by Bach, Karg-Elert, Gigout, Franck, Widor, Saint-Saëns, Alexander Russell, De Lamarter, Debussy, and Vierne.

> In the audience were invited guests, including organists from various cities in Michigan and from other parts of the country. A number of these were guests of Mr. and Mrs. Christian at an informal reception, together with Regent Clements, Mr. Skinner and Messrs. Donald Harrison and William E. Zeuch of the Skinner Organ Company, at the Michigan Union after the recital...

G. Donald Harrison Joins the Skinner Firm (1927-1929)

> May 16 marked the opening of the University of Michigan May festival, an annual event . . . In the initial program, for which the Hill Auditorium again was packed, the organ was the central attraction and the concert was put down as the event dedicating the instrument.[23]

Abram Ray Tyler, columnist for *The American Organist,* attended both opening concerts, sitting next to the builder of that monumental masterpiece in Hill Auditorium during the May sixteenth concert. Mr. Tyler relates:

> It was my privilege to sit and talk with Mr. Skinner on Wednesday evening, and his modesty and appreciation of the fine demonstration Mr. Christian was giving of his great work was refreshing and a great privilege. Mr. Skinner is truly a great artist and man, and says he can "do even better" in his next great work. May he live long![24]

Praise of the new Skinner organ at Hill Auditorium continued long after its dedication was over. *The American Organist,* 11, no. 7 (1928), which contained Mr. Tyler's complimentary remarks, also printed the following news item:

> Skinner is being deluged with compliments on the new organ Mr. Palmer Christian has at Ann Arbor, University of Michigan. It is an instrument of unusual proportions, and unusual acclaim. Mr. Skinner in the building of this ensemble has again wrought a masterpiece.

Years later, toward the end of his life, Ernest was to state in a letter written to Alexander McCurdy on 19 June 1954 that he considered the instrument he built for Hill Auditorium, Ann Arbor, to be one of his "very best organs."

During the remainder of 1928, that extraordinary year, two large and comprehensive instruments were completed for the Princeton University Chapel in Princeton, New Jersey, and the Rockefeller Memorial Chapel at University of Chicago.[25]

The organ built for the Princeton University Chapel was another landmark installation for the Skinner Company. The 32' Contrafagotto, developed by Ernest Skinner, was first used in this organ. G. Donald Harrison tells how it came about:

> Dr. Alexander Russell was very anxious that a 32' Violone be included in the specification, but unfortunately there was no room in

the chambers for such a rank. As a substitute Mr. Skinner devised the 32' Contrafagotto, which we were able to mitre down to a height of but 12'.[26]

The contract for the Princeton University organ was signed late in June of 1927, at which time the tonal scheme was drawn up by Ernest Skinner in consultation with Charles M. Courboin and Princeton University organist Alexander Russell.[27] Shortly after the original specification was drawn up,

> Mr. Donald Harrison arrived in this country; and as a result of a discussion between him and Dr. Russell and Dr. Courboin, the original specification was somewhat modified . . . the construction of the organ did not begin until after that conference . . .

At the time the Princeton University Skinner was finished and opened, ". . . it was generally understood . . . that Mr. Harrison was largely responsible for decisions as to scaling and voicing, and also took part in the final regulation of the instrument . . ."[28] According to Ralph Downes, who presided at the Princeton University Skinner for seven years, that organ "was the first large Skinner instrument to bear the imprint of Mr. Harrison's personality, evident in the very English-sounding diapason choruses, and reed choruses, which were a compromise between American and English practice."[29]

Probably the single most noticeable influence of Donald Harrison's ideas in the Princeton University Skinner was in the tonal quality of the diapasons. Until then, the Skinner diapason had been characterized by weight, warmth, and a prominent octave harmonic.[30] The diapasons in the Princeton University Skinner, unlike their predecessors, displayed a more distinct quint harmonic, and were described as being "pungent . . . incisive," and "downright *clean*."[31]

The Princeton University Chapel Skinner was played for the first time by Dr. Alexander Russell on Memorial Day of 1928 when the new chapel was dedicated.

> The instrument . . . was not entirely finished for the dedication, but Dr. Russell was able to use about two-thirds of it . . .
> On baccalaureate Sunday afternoon, June 17 . . . the organ was inaugurated with a recital by Charles M. Courboin. The audience, some 2,500 people, gathered from all points of the compass, including cities as far distant as Philadelphia, New York, New Brunswick, Trenton and Atlantic City, besides throngs of commencement visitors, old graduates and underclassmen.[31]

The Skinner Organ Company was immensely proud of the Princeton University Chapel organ. On 13 October of that year, in conjunction with the National Association of Organists, the firm sponsored an informal demonstration of their latest masterpiece, staging

> one of the most impressive affairs ever put on by an organ building firm. Special trains were chartered from New York City to Princeton and special "Skinner party" cars were attached to trains running from Philadelphia.

The music for this demonstration concert was played by organists Chandler Goldthwaite, Charles M. Courboin, Lynnwood Farnam, Rollo Maitland, Fernando Germani, and Ralph W. Downes. "Following the recital the 350 guests adjourned to Princeton Inn, where a splendid dinner was served."[32] After the dinner, which was provided by the Skinner Company, "the special trains chartered by Mr. Skinner for the occasion carried the guests back to Philadelphia and New York . . ."[34]

A few weeks later, on the first of November, the Skinner organ in Rockefeller Memorial Chapel, University of Chicago, was dedicated with a recital played by Lynnwood Farnam "in the presence of a congregation of more than 2,500 people."[35] The tonal scheme of the organ, as it "was finally built, was prepared by Mr. Skinner himself . . ."[36] The instrument contained a total of 126 stops. In addition to the very complete chancel organ, it also incorporated an antiphonal to the gallery organ, with its own two-manual console, "designed chiefly for the accompaniment of the gallery choir."[37]

William H. Barnes praised the tonal design of the Skinner organs completed during the preceding year for University of Michigan, Princeton University, and University of Chicago with these comments in *The American Organist:*

> The most remarkable fact to be noted about all three of these great university organs is that they mark a distinct step forward in tonal design and in ensemble from organs of this size that have been built in this country heretofore . . .
>
> Perhaps the most note-worthy change that has taken place in the Skinner ensemble is that, with the greater emphasis on Diapason Chorus and brilliant Reed Chorus that now exists, the Solo Tuba now assumes its proper place and importance in the ensemble, naturally and artistically as a crowning touch. The same lovely and sympathetic quality of tone remains, that formerly charcterized the solo reeds, strings, and flutes of the Skinner Organ, to which has been added the extreme brilliancy and clarity of the finest examples of the English organ . . .[38]

In this same article, Dr. Barnes gives credit, in part, to the "very valuable assistance" of Donald Harrison, who by then had been with the Skinner Company for well over a year. Nevertheless, a few months later, referring to the very complete three-manual Skinner installed in Our Lady of Mount Carmel Church (Roman Catholic), Chicago, Illinois, in early 1929, Dr. Barnes gives Ernest Skinner credit for his insistence on building moderate sized three-manual instruments with complete tonal schemes over the "past few years," and states that "when left to his own devices, Mr. Skinner does build up an ensemble that has a proper Diapason Chorus and a Reed Chorus."[39]

Not all of the notable organs built by the Skinner Organ Company in 1928 were large ones, and not all were installed in the United States. During that year, a three-manual instrument with player was installed in the Chateau de Cande, Monts, France.[40] In a letter dated 30 January 1977, Mr. J. R. Knott gives a description of this instrument:

> From French sources, I have got certain details of the organ, which now stands derelict, and is the property of "Department de l'Indre & Loire." There are 3 manuals and pedal. Solo (top) Swell (center) and Great (bottom). There is a player mechanism as well, and has the curious title "Limonaire." There are 80 drawstops, but the pipework is extended up and down, duplexed and borrowed, and boils down to basic ranks for Diapason, String tone, Flute tone, Vox *[Humana],* Horn, Cornopean, Tuba, Clarinet, Harp, Celesta, Chimes, Tympani, Bass Drum.

The Chateau de Cande was the residence of Charles E. Bedaux, "President of the Washington Lafayette Institute and founder of many corporations bearing his name . . ."[39] The Chateau de Cande organ, the first European installation by the Skinner firm, was given considerable publicity in magazine advertisements at the time it was under construction and following its completion in mid-1929. Within a decade, the Chateau was to make international headlines when the marriage of the former King Edward VIII to Mrs. Wallis Simpson took place there in June of 1937.[42] Organist Marcel Dupré played the Skinner organ for the wedding ceremony.[43]

M. Dupré, who was organist at St. Sulpice in Paris, played the opening recital on the Chateau de Cande Skinner. Dupré was a great admirer and close friend of Ernest Skinner. Shortly after this concert, in a letter dated 27 August 1929, Dupré wrote:

> Gentlemen:
> I need not tell you what a joy it was to me when I found myself sitting before one of your organs and this one is really a most

delightful instrument. It just suits the room in every way. It has great variety and I like the beautiful tone of it. It was possible to get the most wonderful effects in colour with just that small number of stops. The recital was a tremendous success and I know the quality of the organ made a great impression on the audience.

Yours sincerely
(signed) Marcel Dupré[44]

In "A Trip Abroad," *(Stop, Open, and Reed, 3, no. 1, 1925, 32),* Ernest Skinner wrote of his friend:

M. Marcel Dupré is a vitally alive musical personality. His interest in the ancient organs is great but he is equally interested in the modern organ. He does not glorify the past to the disparagement of the present. Our American Orchestral Color has received the entire approval and indorsement of M. Marcel Dupré. He leaves no room for doubt in his admiration for it. His use of it will make a further contribution to organ literature unless I am very much mistaken.

Marcel Dupré was evidently an advocate of electric action and valued Ernest's opinions, as evidenced by an excerpt from his letter to Ernest Skinner, 8 April 1926, written shortly after Dupré was appointed Professor of Organ at the Paris Conservatory:

The building of the music-room started yesterday and I hope it will be ready in August at which moment the organ I have just purchased will be put up there. That organ is Guilmant's organ which has remained in his house at Meudon ever since his death. It is a very fine Cavaill'-Coll *[sic]*, 3 manuals, 28 stops. You may think that such an instrument is not in harmony with my ideas about the electric organ, but in present circumstances, I think it was a wise thing for me to get that organ at once. I should have had to wait for years before I could have got the organ of my dreams considering that Convers is just starting the building of electric organs, and with my new life, I was in great need of a real organ for my students. The organ is still in Guilmant's house and will remain there till my music-room is completed, but I can use it for myself and my pupils for now. I played the whole afternoon there yesterday and it is really a fine organ, with a beautiful tone. I should like you to see and hear it to have your advice.[45]

During the 1920s, Marcel Dupré came to the United States on five different occasions, playing his first recitals here in November of 1921, his last American concerts of that decade being performed in October of 1929. On his 1929 concert tour, he recorded his "improvisation on Adeste Fidelis," on an organ roll for the Skinner Organ Company, and also played a recital on the recently completed Skinner instrument at Princeton University.[46] In a letter written to Ernest Skinner on 13 December 1929, shortly after his return from this concert tour, Dupré recalls his "delightful" visit with Ernest and praises the Princeton organ:

> What a wonderful memory that day we spent with you in Boston has left upon our minds! Hours simply flew away but they were most delightful and not to be forgotten. It was good to have a long talk with you on our one topic: organs, and to feel once more that mutual interest and understanding that means so much to me. It was such a thrill to play on your wonderful organs again and to open my tour with a recital on that recent masterpiece of yours, the Princeton organ.
> Let me, once more, express all my profound admiration for your great art.

Another great French organist who was an ardent admirer of Ernest Skinner's work was Louis Vierne, organist at Notre Dame Cathedral of Paris. Vierne made an extensive concert tour of the United States in early 1927, at which time he was a guest in the Skinner home.[47] Following this tour, M. Vierne wrote Ernest the following letter:

> Dear Mr. Skinner
> During the long trip that I made all over North America I had the occasion, unlimited times, to play your instruments. I wish, then, to express the profound admiration and also the joy I have experienced each time that I encountered an organ of your firm. Let me name only the most important—Williams College, Williamstown, Mass.; Trinity Church in Boston; High School in Hollywood; St. Thomas', New York City; St. John's at Los Angeles and many others still.
> Everywhere I have found the greatest mechanical perfection of your consoles and the alluring and rational perfection of your combination actions—finally, the variety, the distinction and the power of the sonority.
> These artistic instruments do you great honor and justify fully the reputation of your work which has come to me even in Europe. I wish, then, to assure you that on return to my country I shall make an attempt to express publicly my opinion that you are the greatest builder of this time.
> Believe then, dear Mr. Skinner, in my feeling of great admiration and in my entire devotion.
> L. Vierne[48]

M. Vierne was also quoted as saying, upon hearing one of Ernest Skinner's instruments, "If I had had an organ like that when I was a young man, it would have changed the whole character of my compositions."[49]

Ernest was also close to Joseph Bonnet, organist at St. Eustache in Paris.[50] Bonnet had made many concert tours in America, his first one taking place in 1917. Also, for a time, he taught at the Eastman School of Music in Rochester.[51] According to Harold Gleason, Ernest Skinner "offered to *give* one of his consoles to St. Eustache" during the 1920s, while Bonnet was organist there. "Bonnet wanted it but the church authorities said no!"[52]

In 1929, the Skinner Organ Company built what was probably the smallest instrument ever made by that firm. This was a one-manual, four-rank replica of a Roosevelt parlor organ for Thomas Edison's Menlo Park laboratory which had been moved to Greenfield Village in Dearborn, Michigan. This instrument was made with tracker action.[53] Ernest Skinner himself took charge of the installation of this organ. While on this job, he became acquainted with Henry Ford, who master-minded and financed the creation of Greenfield Village. In 1944, Ernest reminisced:

> ... Henry Ford ... had me replace a small one-manual organ that was missing from the Edison laboratory, which he moved from Orange, N. J., to his museum area at Greenfield, Mich. He moved this laboratory with all its shelves, fixtures and every known chemical, all contained in jars and bottles, on said shelves. Photographs of the laboratory of an earlier time showed a small one-manual organ which he wanted replaced. Its character was determined by the photograph.
>
> I remembered that when the X-ray came out Edison immediately started an investigation to develop what we now know as the fluoroscope and I happened to recall the name of the chemical which brought success to Mr. Edison's efforts—namely tungstate of calcium. I hunted around some and found the identical jar from which success came one day when Mr. Ford was there, which seemed to interest him very much, and then he asked me to go over and see his dance pavilion, where he had a four-piece orchestra on call at any hour, day or night. This consisted of a cembalo, a 'cello, a viola and a violin. Mr. Ford asked me to name an old-fashioned dance; so I suggested "Turkey in the Straw," and Mr. Ford said "that goes this way" and he danced the old step that went with it and then said, "Now you try it." I managed to accomplish this not too involved step, after which he asked me for another. So I named "Money Musk" and again Mr. Ford said "that goes this way; now you try it," which I did,

getting in an extra kick to amuse the orchestra when Mr. Ford wasn't looking. Since that time I have justly claimed that Henry Ford was my dancing instructor.[54]

By this time, Ernest was now sixty-three years old, but it was obvious from the above experience that it was a very young and exuberant sixty-three. A year later, he was among the guests at a meeting of the Bohemian Club in Detroit, Michigan, which featured music composed and performed by Detroit area organists. After the program, it was said that Ernest Skinner "danced like a youngster of 19."[55] Ernest's daughter Eugenia Shorrock, recalls that he was "always full of fun, clowning like a little kid." He would try anything and never seemed to get hurt, even as an old man.

FOOTNOTES

[1] "Big Addition to Organ at St. Bartholomew's," *The Diapason*, August 1927, p. 8; "Painesville, Ohio Lake Erie College," *The American Organist*, 18, no. 8 (August 1935), p. 308; "Michigan University to Have Large Organ," *The Diapason*, September 1927, p. 1; "New Oberlin Organ to Be Skinner Work," *The Diapason*, October 1927, p. 2; "Skinner Four-Manual For Memphis Church," *The Diapason*, March 1927, p. 4.

[2] Ernest M. Skinner, "Mr. Skinner Writes of His Latest Work, and Other Matters," *The Diapason*, April 1928, p. 35.

[3] T. Scott Buhrman, "Clarity and its Development," *The American Organist*, 20, no. 2 (1937), p. 47; Ernest M. Skinner, "G. Donald Harrison," *The Diapason*, January 1928, p. 2; "Year is Good for Skinner," *The Diapason*, January 1928, p. 1. According to a letter written by E. M. Skinner on 7 October 1955 to the rector of St. Thomas Church, N.Y.C., Harrison "was formerly in charge of sending out men on maintenance work for Willis . . ."

[4] Skinner, "G. Donald Harrison," p. 2; Ernest M. Skinner, "A Trip Abroad," *Stop, Open, and Reed*, 3, no. 1 (1925), p. 30.

[5] Telephone interview with Richmond H. Skinner, 15 September 1977.

[6] Henry Willis, "A Footnote by Henry Willis," *Musical Opinion*, no. 947 (August 1956), p. 673.

[7] Henry Willis, "My First American Visit," *Stop, Open and Reed*, 3, no. 1 (1925), 27 & 29.

[8] Willis, "A Footnote," p. 673.

[9] Personal interview with Alexander McCurdy, 7 October 1972.

[10] Letter received from William H. Barnes, 13 August 1974.

[11] Personal interview with Edward B. Gammons, 3 May 1976.

[12] Letter received from Joseph F. Dzeda, 5 June 1975.

[13] "With the Builders," *The American Organist*, 10, no. 2 (February 1927), p. 45.

[14] Letter received from William H. Barnes, 13 August 1974.

[15] Personal interview with Edward B. Gammons, 3 May 1976.

[16] Buhrman, p. 47.

[17] Skinner, "Mr. Skinner Writes of His Latest Work," p. 35.

[18] Skinner Organ Company advertisement, *The Diapason*, April 1928, p. 28.

[19] Skinner, "Mr. Skinner Writes of His Latest Work," p. 35.

[20] "News Brevities," *The American Organist*, 10, no. 10 (October 1927), p. 263.

[21] Skinner, "Mr. Skinner Writes of His Latest Work," p. 35.

[22]Ibid.
[23]"Michigan Dedicates Its Great New Organ," *The Diapason,* June 1928, pp. 1 & 2.
[24]Abram Ray Tyler, "Detroit," *The American Organist,* 11, no. 7 (1928), 262.
[25]"Princeton Dedicates Beautiful Chapel," *The Diapason,* July 1928, p. 4; "Chicago University Opens Great Organ," *The Diapason,* December 1928, p. 1.
[26]T. Scott Buhrman, "A Comparison," *The American Organist,* 15, no. 10 (October 1932), p. 610.
[27]"Princeton Will Have Large Skinner Work," *The Diapason,* July 1927, p. 1; William H. Barnes, "University Organs," *The American Organist,* 12, no. 1 (1929), p. 22.
[28]William K. Covell, "Donald Harrison's Work in America," *Organ Quarterly,* 24 (1944–1945), p. 139.
[29]Ralph Downes, "The Baroque Organ," *Organ Quarterly,* 23 (1943–1944), p. 140.
[30]Ernest M. Skinner, "Fine Organ Tone Versus 'Ritualism'," *The Diapason,* August 1933, p. 21.
[31]"Organists as Guests Hear Princeton Organ," *The Diapason,* November 1928, p. 2.
[32]"Princeton Dedicates Beautiful Chapel," p 4.
[33]"Organists as Guests," pp. 1 & 2.
[34]"Skinner," *The American Organist,* 11, no. 12 (December 1928), p. 572.
[35]"Chicago University Opens Great Organ," p. 1.
[36]"University Organs, F. Barnes, p. 22.
[37]"Chicago University Opens Great Organ," p. 1.
[38]University Organs, Barnes, p. 22.
[39]William H. Barnes, "The Organ," *The American Organist,* 12, no. 5 (1929), p. 287.
[40]E. A. Boadway, "The Skinner and Aeolian-Skinner Opus List," *The Boston Organ Club Newsletter,* November 1972, p. 5.
[41]Skinner Organ Company advertisement, *The Diapason,* June 1928, pp. 30 & 31.
[42]Ralph G. Martin "Did Edward Mourn Vanished Power?" *The Detroit Free Press,* Saturday, 1 March 1975, p. 14 C.
[43]Letter received from J. R. Knott, 30 January 1977.
[44]Marcel Dupré, Testimonial in Skinner Organ Company advertisement, *The Diapason,* October 1929, p. 7.
[45]Courtesy of Henry Karl Baker.
[46]Rollin Smith, "Dupré in the Twenties" (courtesy of Paul W. Townsend); Marcel Dupré, Letter to Ernest M. Skinner, 13 December 1929 (courtesy of Henry Karl Baker).
[47]"Vierne to make U. S. Tour," *The Diapason,* August 1926, p. 1; "Vierne to Sail in January," *The Diapason,* October 1926, p. 1; Advertisement for Vierne's first U. S. tour, *The Diapason,* October 1926, p. 11; Personal interview with Ruth Scott, 10 October 1972.
[48]Ernest M. Skinner & Son Company advertisement, *The Diapason,* December 1943, p. 15.
[49]Ernest M. Skinner & Son Company advertisement, *The Diapason,* April 1937, p. 27.
[50]Personal interview with Alexander McCurdy, 7 October 1972.
[51]"Joseph Bonnet Dead; End Career in Canada," *The Diapason,* September 1944, p. 1.
[52]Letter received from Harold Gleason, 22 February 1974.
[53]E. A. Boadway, "The Skinner and Aeolian-Skinner Opus List," *The Boston Organ Club Newsletter,* July & August 1972, p. 2. The only other Skinner organ known to have mechanical action was the instrument in the Cathedral in Tokyo, Japan, built in 1906 ("Pitman-Chest Action," *The American Organist,* 19, no. 6, [1936], 199).
[54]Ernest M. Skinner, "Mr. Skinner Traces Rise of Organ Playing to Highest Pinnacle," *The Diapason,* November 1944 p. 11.
[55]Abram Ray Tyler, "Detroit," *The American Organist,* 13, no. 6 (1930), 372.

CHAPTER 14

Tensions Build at Skinner Organ Company 1929–1930

IN EARLY 1929, it was reported that "by the most fortuitous circumstances Mr. Harrison and Mr. Skinner work together in the most cordial fashion, each fittingly admiring the knowledge and ability of the other, and the resulting team of organ builders would be hard to beat anywhere in the world."[1] Indeed, Ernest Skinner was fully willing to share with Don Harrison the credit for the huge success of his recent college installations, and he felt bad when others did not give Harrison the credit due him, as evidenced by a letter written to Harrison by Ernest on 23 November 1929:

> Dear Don:
>
> I feel some embarrassment when Marcel handed me that testimonial so personal to myself regarding the Princeton organ, and I can imagine you may not have been without some feeling of being left out of it, so I want to say right here that I hold your contribution to the quality of that great instrument to be such that my opinion of you as an artist publicly and privately expressed, is more than justified.
>
> Cordially, and with great admiration,
>
> (signed) Ernest M. Skinner[2]

Approximately sixty-three organs were completed by the Skinner Organ Company during 1929.[3] By far the largest and most impressive of these installations was the rebuilding and enlargement of the organ in Woolsey Hall, Yale University. The original organ in Woolsey Hall was built in 1902–03 as opus 1,469 by the Hutchings-Votey Organ Company, and mechanically improved and almost doubled in size by the Steere Organ Company in 1916 as opus 682. This instrument was now being completely reconstructed and greatly enlarged by the Skinner firm to a total of 12,573 pipes, 175 speaking stops, and 196 ranks of pipes, making it "the largest Skinner Organ ever built."[4] The old pipework was "being entirely revoiced on revised wind pressures so as to form an integral part of the new ensemble," and the completed instrument was to be played from a new Skinner console. The specification of the Woolsey Hall organ was drawn up by Harry B. Jepson, professor of organ at Yale University, "in consultation with the builders."[5] According to Edward W. Flint, who assisted in the tonal finishing of this instrument, "Harrison and Skinner collaborated on the work at Woolsey Hall."[6]

The contract for the Woolsey Hall organ was signed early in the summer of 1928.[7] Edward Flint recalls:

> As usual the Skinner Co. was behind schedule. The work was to have been done during the summer but did not break until September. Jepson had to teach the entire year on a crippled instrument.[8]

The Skinner rebuild of the Woolsey Hall organ was finally completed by the fall of 1929. On 6 December of that year, Professor Harry Jepson played the dedication recital "before an invitation audience that almost filled the vast auditorium of Woolsey Hall." This concert was preceded by a complimentary dinner given by the Skinner Organ Company to distinguished members of the organ profession such as Alexander McCurdy, Edward Shippen Barnes, Lynnwood Farnam, Seth Bingham, and many others.[9]

The completion of the Woolsey Hall instrument turned out to be somewhat of a bittersweet triumph for Ernest Skinner. Ernest and Professor Harry Jepson did not always get along too well. According to Edward Flint, "Skinner objected strongly to the 3-rank celestes" which Jepson insisted upon.[10] It is not known whether this was their major disagreement, but whatever the reason may have been, Jepson ended up telling Ernest to "stay away and let Mr. Harrison finish the organ" at Woolsey Hall.[11]

In the fall of 1929, the stock market crash brought on the worst economic depression in the history of the United States. However, business did not seem to suffer any immediate decline at the Skinner Organ Company. According to an advertisement in the March 1930 issue of *The Diapason,* no less than seventeen new contracts were received by the firm between 1 January and 15 February of 1930, with more than half of these contracts being for fair-sized four manual instruments.

At this time only one thing threatened to seriously disrupt the apparent continuing prosperity of the Skinner Organ Company. In early 1930,

> . . . Organ Workers' Union No. 9 joined the Building Trades Council and by strikes and threats of strikes brought pressure . . . upon organ manufacturers who were having organs installed by non-union men.

The matter was settled by 7 April of that year when,

> Reversing a decision of the Federal District Court, the United States Circuit Court of Appeals in New York . . . granted an injunction to the Rudolph Wurlitzer Company, the Estey Organ Company, the Aeolian Company and the Skinner Company restraining Jacob Fischer, president of the Piano, Organ and Musical Workers' International Union of America, from causing strikes or walkouts in buildings wherein non-union-built organs are being installed or any organs are being installed by non-union labor.[12]

During 1930, a Celestial Organ was installed in the dome of St. Bartholomew's Episcopal Church in New York City.[13] This new section was added to the existing three-manual and pedal Chancel Organ and four-manual and pedal Gallery Organ, both of which were built by the Skinner Organ Company. All of this was controlled by a five-manual console, the fifth manual being for the latest addition. The January 1931 issue of *The Diapason* contains this description of the Celestial Organ:

> This new department consists of a diapason and reed chorus with an echo section and an independent pedal organ, voiced on pressures varying from 6 to 25 inches. The chest and pipes are situated in the top of the dome above the ornamental screen, sixty-six feet above the level of the church floor, and occupy one half of the space available. The other half is covered with hard plaster and forms an enormous resonance chamber. This resonance chamber has greatly improved the general acoustics of the church, which were inclined to be dead, and at the same time gives life and vigor to the powerful stops of the new section and a delightful mystery to the softer voices.
>
> The full power of the celestial organ is just sufficient to form a fitting climax to the chancel and west end organs and, being situated

about midway between the two, binds them together. The wonderful acoustics of the dome enable the sound waves from the celestial organ to flood the church so that it is difficult for the listener to locate the position of this section, with the result that it is possible to play a solo on one of the stops of the celestial organ and accompany it on the chancel organ, or vice versa, without the listener being conscious of the fact that the two sections are widely separated.

Among the more notable new organs installed by the Skinner Company in 1930 were the four-manual instruments built for the American Academy of Arts and Letters, New York City; Temple Methodist Episcopal Church, San Francisco; National City Christian Church, Washington, D.C.; Severance Hall and Church of the Covenant, Cleveland, Ohio; and the Cathedral Church of Our Lady, Queen of the Holy Rosary, Toledo, Ohio.[14] During the same year a three-manual, twenty-one rank Skinner organ was installed in the Chapel of Walter Reed General Hospital in Washington, D.C., a distinction that very few hospitals can claim.[15] Not only was this instrument played for weekly Protestant and Catholic worship services for the patients, but it was also used for monthly musical events, which included organ recitals.[16]

The Skinner built for Severance Hall, home of the Cleveland Orchestra, was an unusually comprehensive instrument of eighty-nine speaking stops. This organ was somewhat at a disadvantage acoustically, due to poor placement. Nevertheless, following the dedication recital given by Palmer Christian on 6 March 1931, *The Diapason* had these remarks pertaining to the Severance Hall Skinner:

> The tone of the instrument is characterized by great beauty of individual solo registers. The ensemble is of the English type, with great prominence of chorus reeds and brilliant mixtures. These features were sufficiently outstanding to cause comment from the musical critics, one calling it a present-day "fashion" in organ design.[17]

Two of the largest and most complete church organs installed by the Skinner Organ Company in 1930 were those built for the Church of the Covenant, Cleveland and the Cathedral Church of Our Lady, Queen of the Holy Rosary (now called Rosary Cathedral) in Toledo. Both of these instruments were designed personally by Ernest M. Skinner. The Church of the Covenant Skinner, which contained ninety stops and six divisions (Great, Swell, Choir, Solo, Antiphonal, and Pedal), was rebuilt and tonally altered in 1957.[18] However, the seventy-three stop (seventy-five rank) Rosary Cathedral Skinner, which is very similar to the Church of the Covenant Skinner, is still in its original tonal design in 1983.

The Rosary Cathedral Skinner contains most of the lovely solo stops and soft effects which had characterized the Skinner organ for some fifteen or twenty years, such as the English Horn, French Horn, 8' Corno di Bassetto, Orchestral Flute, Orchestral Oboe, Flute Celeste Kleine Erzähler and Kleine Celeste, as well as more recently developed voices such as the Flauto Mirabilis, a 16' Corno di Bassetto, and a 32' Fagotto. According to a description of the Rosary Cathedral Skinner, presumably written by Ernest Skinner at the time it was dedicated in June of 1931, an 8' Harmonic Flute of a new scale was used for the first time in this organ.[19] It also has the very complete diapason and reed choruses that were, by the early 1930s, fairly standard in larger Skinner organs.

The Rededication Program has this to say about the chorus-work of the Rosary Cathedral instrument:

> The Diapason section is carried through very completely in its buildup by the Harmonic intervals, Octave, 12th, 15th, 17th and 19th, 21st, 22nd, 26th and 29th, above which the 16', 8' and 4' chorus reeds stand as a culminating power of the Great organ division.
>
> The Swell organ also has a fine Diapason build-up in its 8' Diapason, 4' Octave, Flautino and Mixture composed of a 15th, 19th, 22nd, 26th and 29th. Again as in the case of the Great, capped by the chorus reeds of 16', 8' and 4' pitch . . .
>
> The Choir organ is unusually complete. It has a 16', 8' and 4' soft family, of Gamba 16' and 8', and Gemshorn of 4' pitch, of a power suitable for their association together . . . The Nazard, being the second Harmonic of the stops of 8' pitch, is of a power and character to make it useful in forming what may be termed synthetic tones, in which a large, well designed organ is so rich. The Carillon of three ranks of the 12th, 17th and 22nd intervals is peculiar to Skinner organs. It is very piquant and colorful.

In addition to the above described chorus-work, there is also a four rank mixture topping off an "augmented" Pedal diapason chorus.

The Skinner ensemble of the early 1930s bore a strong resemblance to the Willis English sound, as it also did in the mid-1920s. However, at this point, a hint of Cavaillé-Coll French flavor was becoming more evident. The former was, of course, the direct result of Ernest's acquaintance with the Willis family and their work and, later, his association with Don Harrison. This new French flavor may have been,

Tensions Build at Skinner Organ Company (1929-1930)   143

in part, due to Harrison's influence. It also owed its presence, to a great extent, to the assistance of Ernest's friends, Joseph Bonnet and Marcel Dupré. The mid-1920s had seen the emergence of clarity and brilliance in the Skinner organ. Now, in the early 1930s, the Skinner ensemble was clearer and more brilliant than ever, but still without any suggestion of being forced or harsh sounding. It also had the added quality of a certain amount of *transparency*. It was this type of organ which Ernest Skinner was to build for the rest of his career.

By 1930, however, a growing number of younger organists were developing a preference for G. Donald Harrison's concepts of tonal design over those of Ernest Skinner. Three incidents occurring during 1929 and 1930 forcibly brought this fact to Ernest's attention. The first incident took place when the Woolsey Hall organ rebuild was being completed, when Ernest was told by Professor Harry Jepson to let Harrison finish the organ.

The second incident occurred toward the end of 1929 in connection with the organ built by the Skinner firm for Royce Hall at the University of California at Los Angeles. In a letter dated 29 January 1974, Harold Gleason, who was consultant for the designing of this instrument, writes: "In 1929 when I was consultant for the organ in Royce Hall at U.C.L.A., I was much impressed with the ideas of Mr. Harrison and asked that he take charge of the building of the organ."

According to Robert L. Tusler,

> Harold Gleason was a close friend of Ernest Skinner and worked with him frequently, yet for this instrument the ideas and goals of Skinner's young associate were more in keeping with the sounds the designer hoped to achieve. The result was that the Royce Hall organ was probably G. Donald Harrison's first major instrument in the U.S. for which he was totally responsible for scaling, wind pressures, and voicing. To my knowledge, the final and determining voice in all previous instruments on which G. Donald worked, was that of E. M. Skinner.[20]

Ernest naturally was hurt by this turn of events. Nevertheless, he took it graciously. Mr. Gleason recalls:

> when I designed the large organ in Royce Hall at U.C.L.A., I know that E. M. was hurt that I should have chosen D. H. to be the tonal man. However, I was surprised and grateful that E. M. never once complained to me that I had let him down after our many years of working together.[21]

In 1930 Harvard University contracted with Ernest Skinner to make tonal revisions in the 1912 Skinner organ in Appleton Chapel. Ernest apparently did not deliver what the authorities at Harvard University had in mind. Upon completion of the work, they held out $3,000 of the $10,000 payment because they were not satisfied with the finished organ. Subsequently, A. H. Marks assigned G. Donald Harrison to "straighten" things out at Appleton Chapel—against Don Harrison's wishes![22]

Ernest was by nature a warm and generous man, but he was also a sensitive artist who firmly believed in his own tonal concepts. Therefore, it was not surprising that, by 1930, the friendship which existed between Ernest Skinner and Don Harrison had cooled markedly. Before long, tensions grew until a full-fledged battle erupted between the two men. According to Ned Gammons, Don Harrison "tried not to make trouble with Ernest." Mr. Gammons continues: "You couldn't help but love *[Ernest]* . . . Don Harrison loved him as a person—even though they might disagree—and it was the changing pace of the times that spoiled it . . ."[23]

Arthur Hudson Marks, who has been described by former Skinner people as being a very "hard-nosed" businessman who had little regard for people's feelings, may have deliberately caused the dissension between Ernest Skinner and Don Harrison, with the object of forcing Ernest into retirement.[24] From a purely business standpoint, Marks had just cause for such a move. In a letter written in December of 1974, William H. Barnes states:

> Around 1929, after Don Harrison had been there two years, Mr. Marks decided that the future of the Skinner Co. lay with Mr. Harrison, and *not* with Mr. Skinner. It appeared that many organists preferred the organs that Don Harrison was building to those of Mr. Skinner.

In addition to the growing preference among organists for Don Harrison's tonal designs, there was another more urgent factor which undoubtedly led Marks to favor Harrison.

In spite of the impressive number of large and prestigious contracts received by the Skinner Organ Company in early 1930, its business was clearly showing the effects of the economic depression by the end of that year. During the entire year only thirty-five organs were installed by the firm, as contrasted with the sixty-three instruments installed during the previous year, 1929.[25] Its production had dropped by nearly one-half in *one* year!

Ernest Skinner's supreme goal as an organ builder was to build the most beautiful instrument possible, regardless of cost. According to Harold Gleason, "E. M. was always losing money and Marks being a business man was no doubt hopeful that D. H. *[Don Harrison]* could get them out of the red."[26] Ernest's son, Col. Richmond Skinner, relates that "Marks was falling in inclination to telling Harrison to save money in the construction of the organ." As a result, various steps were taken at this time to cut expenses. The extraordinarily fast and efficient double primary key action of Ernest's design was discarded in favor of the less efficient but more economical-to-produce single primary action. Likewise, Ernest's reliable and durable wood-capped magnets, which he had used successfully for over thirty years, were replaced by cheaper bakelite-capped magnets. As Col. Skinner stated it, ". . . anything *[Harrison]* could do which would save money would be opposed to what my father wanted to do, which was to build beauty . . . that's why they were fighting." Col. Skinner continues:

> Now, there's another thing, a characteristic in which my father was wrong. My father never grew up with the company. He started out by going to every man who worked for him, personally—he would go to his desk every day, find out what he was doing, and talk with him. Well, now, my father in a big factory is going around on his rounds and he sees something that he has never authorized—"What are you doing here? Why are you doing it?" "Well, because Mr. Harrison told me to." So, then he'd go and fight with Harrison about changing the things from the way they were. And this is what caused the fights—partly my father's traits and the attempt to reduce costs.[27]

FOOTNOTES

[1]William H. Barnes, "University Organs," *The American Organist,* 12, no. 1 (1929), p. 22.

[2]Ernest M. Skinner, Letter to G. Donald Harrison, 23 November 1929, (courtesy of Barbara Owen).

[3]E. A. Boadway, "The Skinner and Aeolian-Skinner Opus Lists," *The Boston Organ Club Newsletter,* November 1972, pp. 5 & 6, and December 1972, p. 2.

[4]Specification of Woolsey Hall Skinner, Yale University (courtesy of Joseph F. Dzeda); "Skinner Opening in Yale," *The American Organist,* 13, no. 1 (1930), p. 40.

[5]"New Scheme of Stops of Great Yale Organ," *The Diapason,* November 1928, p. 3.

[6]Edward W. Flint, Letter to Joseph F. Dzeda, 29 May 1970.

[7]"New Scheme of Stops," p. 3.

[8]Letter to Joseph F. Dzeda, 29 May 1970.

[9]"Skinner Opening in Yale," p. 40.

[10]Letter to Joseph F. Dzeda, 29 May 1970.

[11]Personal interview with Edward B. Gammons, 3 May 1976.

[12]"Organ Union is Enjoined," *The Diapason,* May 1930, p. 2.
[13]Boadway, December 1972, p. 3.
[14]Boadway, December 1972, pp. 2 & 3; "Cleveland Orchestra Will Have a Skinner," *The Diapason,* February 1930, p. 1.
[15]"Organ For Medical Center," *The Diapason,* June 1930, p. 1.
[16]"Army Medical Center Organ . . ." *The American Organist,* 15, no. 7 (1932), p. 439.
[17]"Organ is Dedicated in Severance Hall," *The Diapason,* April 1931, p. 6.
[18]"Large Skinner For Cleveland Church," *The Diapason,* October 1930, p. 1; Boadway, December 1972, p. 3.
[19]"Description of the New Organ in the Queen of the Holy Rosary Cathedral," *New Cathedral Festival* (Rededication Program), June 1931 (courtesy of Hugh L. Murray).
[20]"A Concert Organ For Royce Hall, U.C.L.A.," *The Diapason,* April 1972, p. 7.
[21]Letter received from Harold Gleason, 7 April 1976.
[22]Telephone interview with Edward B. Gammons, 1 May 1976; Personnal interview with Edward B. Gammons, 3 May 1976.
[23]Personal interview with Edward B. Gammons, 3 May 1976.
[24]Letter received from Barbara Owen, 2 May 1975.
[25]Boadway, November 1972, pp. 5 & 6, and December 1972, pp. 2–4.
[26]Letter received from Harold Gleason, 7 April 1976.
[27]Telephone interview with Richmond H. Skinner, 15 September 1977.

CHAPTER 15

Serlo Hall and the Five-Year Contract, 1929-1932

THE ROMANTIC STYLE of organ building, brought to its ultimate state of development by Ernest Skinner, was originally introduced to America with the importing of the big Walcker organ, installed in the old Boston Music Hall in 1863. This instrument was now to be associated with Ernest and his career in a far more direct way. The Walcker organ had been removed from the Boston Music Hall in 1884 to make room for a growing Boston Symphony Orchestra. In 1897, after being in storage for thirteen years, this instrument was bought by Edward F. Searles of Methuen, Massachusetts, and subsequently was installed in a large hall especially designed and built by Mr. Searles to accommodate it. Adjacent to this hall, known as Serlo Hall, was a building which housed the Methuen Organ Company, founded by Mr. Searles around 1890.[1] After Mr. Searles' death in 1920, Serlo Hall and the adjoining organ factory "supposedly remained closed and unused until . . . 1929."[2] It was at that time that Ernest Skinner purchased Serlo Hall along with the old Music Hall organ and the organ factory.

According to an announcement of this sale which appeared in an unidentified Lawrence, Massachusetts, newspaper, the purchase price of Serlo Hall and the factory was reported to have been "in excess of $200,000."[3] Although this property was in Ernest Skinner's name as early as 1929, his ownership of it was not made known to the organ world until early 1931.[4]

By now the situation for Ernest at the Skinner Organ Company had reached the point of no return. In a letter to W. K. Kellogg dated 26 September 1941, Ernest writes that "about 1930 things began to get so uncomfortable" for him that he "traded *[his]* stock in the Skinner company" for Serlo Hall and its adjoining organ factory.

Ernest had something very definite in mind when he bought this property. It was his intent that, at long last, he and his son Richmond would go into business together, using the facilities of the Methuen Organ Company for their new firm, the Ernest M. Skinner & Son Organ Company. However, a few years prior to 1930, Ernest had moved into a large and expensive house on Beacon Street in the Chestnut Hill section of Boston, and now was carrying the additional burden of a huge mortgage on Serlo Hall.[5] On top of that, the country was in a serious economic depression. Needless to say, Ernest's family was not particularly enthusiastic about his plans to undertake such a risky venture. Richmond Skinner recalls:

> ... my father, wanting more and more to have me in business with him, he saw Serlo Hall in Methuen, Massachusetts, which had the old Boston Music Hall Organ. He, without telling me anything about it, bought it. And then he came to me and said, "Let's go in business together." Whereupon my mother came to me and said, "Richmond, your father cannot afford at this time to leave the Skinner Organ Company. Please don't let him."[6]

Presently, A. H. Marks was informed of Ernest's purchase of Serlo Hall and his plans to go into business with his son. Ernest Skinner relates:

> When Marks found this out there was a great reversal of behavior. Much repentence was expressed and I was told that if I would remain where I was their attitude would be satisfactory and that if I left the stock of the company would not be worth over $5.00 a share. I was, therefore, talked out of my plans to leave and signed a contract with them for five years more.[7]

This five-year contract between Ernest Skinner and Marks was signed in January of 1931.[8] From Richmond Skinner, who was present at the signing of this agreement, we learn more of its details:

> So, my father had announced to Marks and the Company that he was leaving. And they asked him to meet with *[Marks]* and the board of directors. And he asked me to go along as his lawyer. So, he had a meeting, and Mr. Marks' offer was five thousand dollars a year for

Serlo Hall and the Five-Year Contract (1929-1932) 149

five years. He wouldn't have to do a thing—he didn't have to enter the doors. He was not forbidden to enter the doors, but he didn't have to. He could do whatever he wanted. All that Marks asked him for was that he keep his name connected and associated with the Skinner Organ Company because the stock was at that time selling about thirty-six dollars a share . . . So my father talked it over with me, and I went and talked with Mr. Marks, and they came to that agreement.[9]

Thus it was that Ernest Skinner was obliged to remain associated with the Skinner Organ Company for another five years. During that period of time, his son was to be in charge of the organ factory connected with Serlo Hall. According to Col. Skinner,

> But in the meantime, he had this Serlo Organ [Hall] which had connected with it a three story wood factory . . . So, I agreed with Mr. Marks that I would maintain that building by rebuilding organs, accepting no contracts for new organs, for the period of five years. My father agreed that he would not promote the sales of any organs to the Ernest M. Skinner & Son Organ Company for that period of time . . .
> . . . I, myself, with a few workmen, did some rebuilding under that name of Methuen Organ Company. We couldn't use the Ernest M. Skinner & Son [name] until the five years were up. But we did a number [of rebuilds] with the Methuen Organ Company. So, Mr. Skinner was not on any of these projects, other than what he did by chance. He might say "go see my son," or something.[10]

Ernest and his family moved to the large house at 130 Beacon Street, Chestnut Hill, in 1928, after living in their relatively modest home on Savin Hill for thirty-three years. Ernest had always wanted a house big enough for an organ. Now that he finally had a house that was sufficiently roomy, he could not afford the organ. Nevertheless, with the acquisition of Serlo Hall, he finally got his wish, in a way, for a "house organ" of his own so he could have guest musicians and entertain. At the time his purchase of Serlo Hall and the organ factory became known to the public, Ernest made the following statements pertaining to Serlo Hall and the old Boston Music Hall organ:

> I entered Serlo Hall for the first time less than two years ago. It made an unforgettable impression upon me. Its fate seemed uncertain; there were rumors that the organ was to be sold or destroyed. This seemed to me nothing short of vandalism—almost sacrilege. It was only through a miracle of unforseen circumstances that I became

> the owner of Serlo Hall. Now that it is mine, I want to make some additions to the organ to bring it up to date, and then make it a shrine for the lovers of organ music, a meeting place if possible for the A.G.O., for the N.A.O., and perhaps other musical organizations. This will be carrying out Mr. Searles' original ideal and at the same time save this great monument from destruction.
>
> I also have in mind some concerts in which music for organ and piano may be given. The opportunity for doing something that is based upon the ideal and not upon financial considerations seems to find a fitting setting in Serlo Hall.[11]

Under Ernest's ownership, Serlo Hall indeed became somewhat of a musical shrine for a brief spell. During the next several years, the Serlo Hall organ was played in concert by a succession of visiting organists. It can be truthfully stated that the presentation of these recitals was very definitely "based upon the ideal" rather than "upon financial considerations." According to his daughter, Ruth, Ernest never sold tickets for these musical events, but paid for them himself.

One of the famous recitalists to make his appearance at Serlo Hall during the early to mid-1930s was E. Power Biggs. Biggs, then a young man who had recently graduated from the Royal Academy of Music in London, had come to the United States in 1930 to make his home in Cambridge, Massachusetts.[12] At that time Mr. Biggs and Ernest Skinner were friends. However, by 1937 Biggs was to become allied with G. Donald Harrison in an effort to recreate a "baroque" organ similar to those built in the day of J. S. Bach.[13] Within one decade Biggs would emerge as the leading exponent of the classic revival in organ building, pushing it to an extreme that G. Donald Harrison had never dreamed of when he came to America in 1927.

Another up and coming young organist who gave concerts at Serlo Hall was Alexander McCurdy. Mr. McCurdy recalls the occasion of his first meeting with Ernest Skinner:

> No one is more kind and helpful to young people than Mr. Skinner. I first met him in 1921 at the Bohemian Club Grove in California. Mr. Skinner received me cordially; and no word or action served to remind me that he was already famous while I was only a youngster with a local reputation.[14]

In the December 1931 issue of *The Diapason,* we read that Alexander McCurdy played a program "on the great organ at Serlo Hall, Methuen, Mass.," on the evening of 5 November 1931.

>The recital was followed by a social half-hour which gave Mr. McCurdy an opportunity to meet visiting organists and friends. Guild members from Boston and surrounding towns were present as guests of Ernest M. Skinner, owner of Serlo Hall and its famous organ, and it was just short of a capacity attendance.[15]

The following year on 22 June 1932, Mr. McCurdy played another recital at Serlo Hall, "by courtesy of Mr. Ernest M. Skinner," as part of the American Guild of Organists' eleventh General Convention which was being held in Boston.[16]

Also among the visitors to Serlo Hall was Ernest's nephew, Edward (Ned) Hastings, who, long after, remembered the pleasure of playing on that "mighty old instrument."[17] Ned, then in high school, was the only member of the family who showed any real interest in becoming a musician. Ernest personally financed two years of organ lessons for his nephew with Francis Snow, then organist at Trinity Church of Boston.

One of the most memorable events to take place in Serlo Hall occurred on Christmas Eve in 1932. Between the hours of six and seven that Sunday evening, a special musical program using the old Boston Music Hall organ was broadcast by a Boston radio station. This was an occasion of historic significance, for it was the first time that this great instrument was ever heard over the air by radio audiences.[18] According to one newspaper account, this program "was broadcast through station WBZ and the National Broadcasting Company over its entire network and by short wave length to France and Germany." This program began with the rendition of "Adeste Fideles" by organist Lloyd Del Castillo, with William E. Zeuch continuing the program and directing the choir.[19]

It is interesting to note the prominent part in this program taken by Mr. Zeuch, a vice president in the Skinner firm, even though Ernest Skinner's relations with the Skinner Company officials at this time must have been rather uneasy, at best. However, it is possible that his conflicts with company brass did not extend to Bill Zeuch, for, as his daughter Ruth recalled, Ernest "liked his brand of music."[20] At any rate, whatever hard feelings there may have been were apparently put aside for the moment.

The Skinners' stately house at 130 Beacon Street was spacious, making it ideal for entertaining the many guests whom Ernest invited to his home. According to his daughter Ruth, most of his visitors were either relatives or musicians. Anyone who could play music was in "rarefied air" in Ernest's estimation, and he took them all to his heart with open arms.[21]

Not long after they moved to 130 Beacon Street, the Skinners entertained the entire Russian Symphonic Choir, whom they had heard a few years earlier while they were staying at the William Ball residence in Muncie, Indiana. The Russian director of the chorus could not speak English and Ernest could not speak Russian, but this proved to be no obstacle to communication between musician and music lover. The two men spent the entire evening conversing by musical terms and sign language![22]

One of the most distinguished musicians to stay as a houseguest at 130 Beacon Street was the renowned German organist and composer Sigfrid Karg-Elert, who came to America on a recital tour in early 1932.[23] Ernest Skinner relates:

> I had the very great honor of a personal visit from him at my home, where his accounts of various adventures he met in this country were so delightfully humorous and entertaining that he kept the guests whom I had invited to meet him convulsed. He was a born comedian, with an exquisite sense of the ridiculous. Dr. and Mrs. Carl McKinley acted as interpreters on this occasion.[24]

Karg-Elert's concert tour was not particularly successful, and he was the target of much criticism. Ernest, however, was devoted to Karg-Elert and staunchly defended this artist's playing and his music. Ernest wrote in *The American Organist:*

> I feel that the way he was criticized because he did not play the organ as we play it was very unfortunate. Quite obviously he tried to find German effects on the American organ. Also he labored under conditions of noise and interruption and insufficient opportunity for practice. Later on when he becomes an immortal, as I feel sure he is destined to become, I believe the hastily spoken criticisms will be regretted.[25]

Ernest Skinner's editorial would seem to have been almost prophetic, in a way. At the time of his visit to America, Karg-Elert was not in the best of health. "He was afflicted with Bright's disease, angina pectoris and a blood pressure of 240 . . ."[26] Following his return to Germany, Karg-Elert took to his bed, writing Ernest, " 'I hear the fluttering of the wings of the angel of death.' He died shortly afterward."[27]

Karg-Elert did return from his U.S. tour visit with at least one happy memory to brighten his last months, thanks to Ernest M. Skinner. In his article on the life and work of Sigfrid Karg-Elert, appearing in the December 1933 issue of *The Diapason,* Ernest recalls:

Serlo Hall and the Five-Year Contract (1929-1932)   153

> I could not bear that Dr. Karg-Elert should return to Germany without some ideas of the way his music was performed by our American organists and so I arranged for him to be present at St. Thomas' Church in New York City, where Charlotte Lockwood, Andrew Tietjen and Paul Calloway came to meet him and to play some of his compositions. This was made possible through the always generous, always friendly Dr. T. Tertius Noble. I do not recall just which of the three young organists played Karg-Elert's "O Gott, Du Frommer Gott," which was dedicated to his mother. I do remember that it was most beautifully registered and played in a way that left no room for improvement, and that Karg-Elert was deeply moved by it. His only comment was: "Meine liebe Mutter!" The "Soul of the Lake" followed, played by Charlotte Lockwood. Those who have heard this composition as she plays it will know what she did with it. At the conclusion of this piece Dr. Noble asked Karg-Elert what he thought of it. He replied: "It is better than it is." Paul Calloway followed with "Jerusalem, Thou City Built on High," an extraordinary virtuoso piece, both as to composition and performance. Andrew Tietjen played, I believe, his chorale prelude "In dulci Jubilo." I need not say that Karg-Elert expressed himself in deep gratitude for what these three young American organists did for him. I have reason to know that he remembered it, and I am sure that they will not forget the hour when they entertained Karg-Elert with his own music.

With the steady stream of musician guests who came and went at the Skinner home, one is led to wonder how Ernest's wife Mabel coped with this frequent disruption of domestic life. A revealing story is told by Ernest's nephew, Ned Hastings, relating to Karg-Elert's stay at 130 Beacon Street:

> I remember once when Ernest was reminiscing about the time that Karg-Elert spent a week in their Brookline home, telling stories about the great composer and his idiosyncrasies. Mabel sat by listening quietly. When Ernest was through with his chronicle, her quiet voice took up the tale: "Yes, it was interesting to have a celebrity of this sort as a guest. I had just bought a new rug for the bedroom he used. He spent the week smoking in bed and tossing the butts on the floor. When he left the rug was full of holes." This was not said in anger—simply as a matter of fact footnote to her husband's account . . .[28]

Although Mabel was gracious to Ernest's guests, it was no doubt a strain on her. With Ernest away from home so much of the time, she surely must have had mixed feelings about having to share the little time her husband did spend at home with the endless parade of his friends. Also, Mabel was not in the best of health, and all this company must have been quite taxing for her limited strength and energy. Mabel's frail health was partly caused by worrying about the lack of money, for it was she who had to stay home and meet the bill collectors, in her husband's altogether too frequent absence. Due to his complete inability to manage money, Ernest was always in debt. Ruth Scott recalls that this "was very much of a trial" for her mother.

Ernest did not intend to make life difficult for his family. He was concerned about his wife and children and loved them dearly. Nevertheless, in the words of his daughter Ruth,

> . . . he was a terribly intense person . . . If he made up his mind he wanted something, he had to have it, that was all—just like that Serlo Hall in Methuen . . . He had to have that, but he couldn't pay for it—but he got a big boot out of it while he had it, there was no doubt about that.[29]

Ruth tells this story about her father, illustrating what she termed his "single-minded nature: Ernest liked his paper on time. If it did not come when it was expected, he would impatiently pace the floor with his hands behind his back, muttering, "When is that darn newspaper going to get here," until it came. Once the paper finally did arrive, he would go to the door and get it, open it and look it over—then he would lay it down and resume his pacing as though it had never come, again muttering "When is that darn newspaper going to get here," as he paced, so ingrained in his mind was this thought!

By now all three of Ernest's and Mabel's children had left home. In 1929, Ruth had married George Scott, a former neighbor and a boyhood playmate of her brother Richmond when they were young children living on Savin Hill. The whole family would still gather for Christmas at 130 Beacon Street, where they would enjoy a sumptuous dinner prepared by Mabel. In spite of her poor health it was Mabel who held the family together and who provided the stability that her impractical husband had great need of, especially during the trying years of the early 1930s. Ned Hastings recalls:

> All the time I knew her (and for many years before that) Mabel was in very delicate health. She had to lie down a lot, had to husband her strength. But she was far from inactive. Her family—children and grandchildren—looked to her as the center of their lives.[30]

Mabel was a flexible and understanding wife. When Ernest would be difficult, she could simply laugh it off and say, "Oh, Ernest!!" and he'd usually end up laughing, too. Mabel bent with her husband's whims and was the one who "made the marriage."[31]

FOOTNOTES

[1]Edward W. Flint, *The Great Organ in the Methuen Memorial Music Hall* (Methuen: Methuen Memorial Music Hall Inc., 1954), pp. 1 & 3.

[2]Letter received from Robert Reich, 27 June 1975.

[3]Undated item from Lawrence, Massachusetts, newspaper in the Everett Truette Scrapbooks (unpublished collection in the Boston Public Library).

[4]Letter received from Robert Reich, 2 August 1975; "Boston Music Hall Organ Shrine Center," *The Diapason*, March 1931, p. 4.

[5]Ernest M. Skinner, Letter to W. K. Kellogg, 26 September 1941 (courtesy of Henry Karl Baker); Personal interview with Ruth Scott, 11 September 1974.

[6]Telephone interview with Richmond H. Skinner, 15 September 1977.

[7]Ernest M. Skinner, Letter to W. K. Kellogg, 26 September 1941 (courtesy of Henry Karl Baker).

[8]Ernest M. Skinner, Letter to Arthur Hudson Marks, 31 May 1932 (courtest of Henry Karl Baker).

[9]Telephone interview with Richmond H. Skinner, 15 September 1977.

[10]Telephone interview with Richmond H. Skinner, 15 September 1977.

[11]Undated item from Lawrence, Massachusetts, newspaper, found in the Everett Truette Scrapbooks (unpublished collection in the Boston Public Library).

[12]"E. Power Biggs," *The Diapason*, June 1943, p. 13.

[13]William Harrison Barnes, *The Contemporary American Organ,* 3rd. ed. (New York: J. Fischer & Bro., 1937), pp. 164–166.

[14]Alexander McCurdy, "An Organ Builder's Opinions," *Etude,* 72, no. 10 (October 1954), p. 64.

[15]"Alexander McCurdy at Organ in Serlo Hall," *The Diapason,* December 1931, p. 3.

[16]Program for Recital of Alexander McCurdy Jr., 22 June 1932, found in the Everett Truette Scrapbooks (unpublished collection in the Boston Public Library).

[17]Edward H. Hastings, Letter to Joseph F. Dzeda, 31 March 1966.

[18]"Builders of the Future," Article from unidentified newspaper, found in the scrapbook of Mabel Hastings Skinner.

[19]"Serlo Organ Program Broadcasts Through WBZ," Article from unidentified newspaper, found in the Everett Truette Scrapbook (unpublished collection in the Boston Public Library).

[20]Personal interview with Ruth Scott, 11 September 1974.

[21]Personal interview with Eugenia S. Shorrock, April 1973.

[22]Personal interview with Ruth Scott, 10 October 1972.

[23]"Sigfrid Karg-Elert Arrives in U. S. Jan. 4," *The Diapason,* January 1932, p. 3.

[24]Ernest M. Skinner, "Interesting Light on the Life and Work of Sigfried Karg-Elert," *The Diapason*, December 1933, p. 24.

[25]Ernest M. Skinner, *The American Organist,* March 1932, p. 175.

[26]Skinner, "Karg-Elert," p. 24.

[27]Ernest M. Skinner, "Mr. Skinner Traces Rise of Organ Playing to Highest Pinnacle," *The Diapason,* November 1944, p. 11. Karg-Elert died on 9 April 1933.

[28]Edward H. Hastings, Letter to Joseph F. Dzeda, 12 April 1972.

[29]Personal interview with Ruth Scott, 11 September 1974.

[30]Edward H. Hastings, Letter to Joseph F. Dzeda, 12 April 1972.

[31]Personal interview with Dick Hastings, 12 October 1972.

CHAPTER 16

The Aeolian-Skinner Organ Company 1932-1933

B Y THE END of 1931, the depression was having a very pronounced effect on the organ business, and it was reported that there was a drop of 51.2 percent in the number of organs produced by American organ builders during that year as compared with the number built during 1929.[1] Although a report issued by George Catlin, treasurer of the Skinner Organ Company, proclaimed that their firm was "among the last to be affected, and among the least," it was, nevertheless, markedly affected by the state of the economy.[2] According to the "Skinner and Aeolian-Skinner Opus List," which was published in the *Boston Organ Club Newsletter* in 1972, the number of Skinner installations during 1931 was even below what it had been in 1930, with only twenty-seven organs being installed during that entire year, as compared with the thirty-five installed in 1930. The firm was now producing less than half the number of organs that it did in 1929, before the stock market crash.

Another organ building firm, the pipe organ division of the Aeolian Company, was hit even harder by the depression. This firm specialized in residence organs, which accounted for approximately 80 percent of its business.[3] Because of the depressed economy, home organs were increasingly becoming a luxury few could afford. By the end of 1931 the home organ business was not good, and it was said that the Aeolian Company was on its way out.[4]

In January of 1932 it was announced that a merger of the Skinner Organ Company and the pipe organ division of the Aeolian Company had been approved by the stockholders of the two firms, becoming effective as of 2 January that year. The name of this new organization was the Aeolian-Skinner Organ Company, Inc. Arthur Hudson Marks was its president, and the vice presidents were W. H. Alfring (president of the Aeolian Company), Ernest M. Skinner (vice president of the Skinner Organ Company), George L. Catlin (general manager and treasurer of the Skinner Organ Company), and Frank Taft (managing director of the pipe organ department of the Aeolian Company). It was planned to discontinue the pipe organ department of the Aeolian Company's plant at Garwood, New Jersey, and combine the facilities of both companies in the Boston plant of the Skinner Company. The newly-formed Aeolian-Skinner Company would "continue to maintain the present Skinner studio at 677 Fifth Avenue, New York, and *[would]* also take over and operate the Aeolian organ studio in the Aeolian building" at 689 Fifth Avenue, New York.[5]

Along with the announcement of the Aeolian-Skinner merger appearing in the January 1932 issue of *The Diapason* is a letter from Arthur Hudson Marks, Ernest M. Skinner, and Frank Taft, setting forth the objects of their newly consolidated firm. In this letter we read:

> We are all happy and enthusiastic about this alliance and we earnestly hope to do a good job and to hold the respect and confidence of our good friends all over the country.
>
> In the first place, we wish to state emphatically that this is not a step in the direction of big business, trusts or monopolies. On the contrary, we are firm in the opinion, which we have often expressed in your columns, that the field for the highest quality is limited; that artistic merit and big business do not get on well together. This move may rather be regarded as an alliance to preserve the prestige of the Skinner and Aeolian names and to better meet the onslaughts of commercialism . . .
>
> What seems more natural than a union of these two organizations, which, for a generation, have been moving with the same ideals toward the same goal and which so well supplement one another? Under one management and under one roof, so to speak, are gathered the long-established prestige and good will of the Skinner and Aeolian names in both public and private work. All of the resources, developments, inventions and experience of each will be at the disposal of the other.
>
> From such a consolidation we hope for artistic and mechanical improvements, together with greater financial strength. We see the possibility of many economies in the normal operations of buying, building and selling, and these economies should ultimately benefit our clients.

> The new company will be financially independent, standing on its own feet, with ample liquid assets, its properties free of encumbrances, and its total liabilities will be little or nothing.
>
> The greatest care will be taken to see that there is no destruction in either Aeolian or Skinner organs of a single element which has contributed to their individuality and to their position in public esteem. All of these details which are common factors will be under consolidated management.

Although vice president, general manager and treasurer George L. Catlin was quoted in the January 1932 issue of *The Diapason* as saying that "both companies involved in the merger are in such sound and healthy condition financially, with ample accumulation of liquid reserves and surplus, that the new organization will not require any financing other than is already available," many established authorities in the organ world seem to think that the main reason for the Aeolian-Skinner merger was financial. However, William H. Barnes states that "Skinner acquired the organ department of the Aeolian Company for one purpose only, to get their library of organ recordings for the Aeolian player."[6] Another statement, made by Ernest's son Richmond Skinner, would tend to support Dr. Barnes's viewpoint:

> The two companies did not merge. The Skinner Organ Company bought the player, and only the player, from Aeolian ... They did not merge as a company. They just bought the player rights at that time from Aeolian, and at that time changed the name.[7]

By mid-1932 it appeared that the consolidation of the Aeolian and Skinner organ companies was proving beneficial, artistically and commercially, for all concerned. According to the August 1932 issue of *The American Organist,* "the value of contracts for university and church organs awarded to the Aeolian-Skinner Organ Co. during the first five months of 1932 was 78% greater than during the previous five-month period," taking into account the business figures for "both the Aeolian and the Skinner companies as they existed independently prior to the merger..." Also, in April of that year, "the Company added 10% to its employees in the Boston factory."[8]

Among the organs listed as under construction in the above report were: Hershey Auditorium, Hershey, Pensylvania; East Liberty Presbyterian Church, Pittsburgh, Pennsylvania; University of Minnesota, Minneapolis; St. Mary the Virgin, New York City; and Girard College, Philadelphia.

Ernest Skinner designed several large and important organs which were installed and completed during the year following the Aeolian-Skinner merger. One of these was the Skinner in First Congregational Church of Los Angeles, completed by spring of 1932, which Ernest designed in consultation with Dr. William H. Barnes.[9] The instrument installed in Hershey Auditorium is believed also to have been designed by him. One of the larger organs installed that year was a very comprehensive instrument of more than one hundred stops which was built for Girard College in Philadelphia.[10] According to Alexander McCurdy, "the Girard College organ . . . was finished by E. M. himself, at the request of Harry Banks *[then organist at Girard College]*. Harry did not like the work of G. Donald Harrison too much."[11] Also during this period, Ernest and Don Harrison collaborated in the design of the big four-manual organ which was under construction for East Liberty Presbyterian Church of Pittsburgh.[12]

In the "Skinner and Aeolian-Skinner Opus List," published in *The Boston Organ Club Newsletter* in 1972, a three-manual "experimental" organ "with player attachment" was listed as having been installed in Boston during 1932. This may have been an elaborate orchestrator organ designed by Ernest Skinner to produce seven separate tone colors at once. Played by rolls, it was to be the ultimate for reproducing orchestral transcriptions. A fascinating story about the conception of this "orchestrator" is told by Ernest's friend Wheeler Beckett. Mr. Beckett writes:

> He once interested himself in making organ rolls that would produce not three separate tone colors but *seven*. His love of the symphony orchestra prompted him to feel that with seven independent colors, say strings, double reeds, single reeds, flute quality, high brass, low brass, horns,—he could do justice to the scores of the great composers. He was impressed, in his imagination, by the beauty which was potential in such a scheme. But he could not work out the complicated blue print that would result in the perforations (holes in the roll) that would permit seven independent voices to sound. He told me this story.
>
> He was sleeping in the lower berth of a Pullman car when something awakened him. The curtains were shut, the shade was down, the train was going along at a good clip. And of course the aisle of the car was dark. Yet, above his head, on the shiny surface of the upper berth was a curious chart made of lines of light, many fine lines crossing each other in a complex way. He studied it for a while, peeked out the window to see if the light could come from the outside but all was dark and the train speeded along. It puzzled him and as he put it to me "it was the darndest thing you ever saw." He looked at it so long that he finally memorized it. Then it suddenly dawned on

him what it was. It was the blue print of the seven independent voices!

The next morning he reproduced it on paper and would have proceeded to make organ rolls that would produce seven independent voices, but just about this time developments in other reproducing media were made and I think the cost of putting such rolls on the market deterred him.

As for the experience itself he would ask us "what was it?" Of course our answer was simply that we did not know any more than he did. Was it a projection of his sub-conscious? Or a mystic answer to his problem, an occult manifestation? He was broad in his thinking, not carried away by mysticism but willing to admit that such an experience bordered upon the unknown world of the Mind, of which we get, as he did, occasional glimpses.[13]

During 1931 and early 1932 a new spirit of cooperation seemed to exist among Ernest Skinner, A. H. Marks, and Donald Harrison. This apparent cooperation was not to last long, however. More and more organists were asking for Don Harrison to design their new organs. One of these instruments was the organ built for Trinity College Chapel, Hartford, Connecticut, in 1931. Harrison was quoted as saying that the Trinity College organ "was the real starting-point" in his work.[14]

The Great, Swell, and Solo divisions of the Trinity College Chapel instrument were typical of recent Skinner installations, but the Choir was "quite a departure from the usual Skinner practice." This division was on low wind pressure with a chorus type Trompette on 5" wind; a four rank Sesquialtera (15-17-19-22); and a "miniature" chorus consisting of an 8' Spitzfloete, a 4' Gemshorn, a 2-2/3' Nazard, and a 2' Piccolo. A 16' Spitzfloete replaced the usual Skinner 16' Gamba or Dulciana, making a total of three "tapered" stops in the Choir. In the Pedal division, a "fairly small-scaled metal 32' Bombarde" replaced the large-scaled wood Bombarde which Ernest Skinner favored.[15]

Shortly afterward, Harrison designed the tonal schemes of organs built for the new chapel at Harvard University; Northrop Memorial Auditorium, University of Minnesota, Minneapolis; and the Church of St. Mary the Virgin, Episcopal, New York City, all of which were installed in 1932.[16] Of these three instruments, the tonal scheme of the organ at St. Mary the Virgin Church was the most radically different from anything Ernest had ever designed. Among many other points of departure from previous tonal schemes, this instrument had a Positif in place of the Choir division and the Solo organ was replaced by a Bombarde division. Raymond Nold, who along with Harrison was responsible for the design of the instrument, stated that the St. Mary the Virgin organ marked "a return to the principles of the classic organ, the organ of the Thomas-Kirche and the older French and German Builders." This description of the tonal character of the St. Mary the Virgin organ is provided by Mr. Nold:

> Classic influence is noted in the emphasis on ensemble, in the more complete rounding out of the several tonal divisions of the organ ... The building up of a satisfactory ensemble has involved the employment of bright-toned Diapason work, for blend with orchestral instruments and voices as well as for ensemble, the curbing of the 8' Diapason tone and the enormous strengthening of the upperwork, the transparent, golden toned French reeds, rather than the more opaque modern reeds, and the substitution of a metal Principal, with a completely developed chorus, for the all but universal open-wood Diapason, with its objectionable boom and heavy tread, as the main Pedal rank.
>
> An interesting detail ... is the Flute Conique in the Swell Organ ... In the Pedal Organ a Flute Ouverte, with its clear and beautiful tone, replaces the more usual and commonplace Bourdon. It may be added that there are no stopped 16' ranks in the instrument.

Shortly after the dedication of the St. Mary the Virgin organ, T. Scott Buhrman remarked,

> ... this is not a German organ, it's not a French organ, it's not an English organ. Very well then, it must either be a Chinese organ or an American organ, and since the Chinese do not have organs, it must be American.[17]

The St. Mary the Virgin organ was, in fact, the first one to be called an "American Classic" organ, and it was with this instrument that Harrison officially started the "Classic Revival," as most organists recognize it.[18] At that time, this organ was rather controversial, arousing "some hostile criticism" and being "the subject of many a warm discussion."[19] Ernest Skinner did not care much for it. In a letter dated 10 April 1972, Paul Townsend recalls sitting next to Mr. Skinner at a recital given "twenty-five or thirty years ago" on the "then new" Aeolian-Skinner organ in St. Mary the Virgin Church. According to Mr. Townsend, who described the organ as having "many mixtures and over-brilliant upper work ... the poor man proceeded, *in self defense,* to put his fingers in his ears." Ernest strongly disapproved of the new type of reeds which Harrison had been using in recent installations. In late spring of 1932, he made a report to Marks concerning the type of reeds Harrison was using, stating that "they were bad musically, that they were causing criticism," and requesting that the firm instead use Trumpet reeds of his own design "which were not only without the disagreeable characteristics of the Harrison Trumpets, but were brilliant and musical in character."[20]

Ernest's criticism of Harrison's reeds prompted Marks to write Ernest a letter in reply, setting certain limits on his authority in the company regarding tonal matters, as well as urging him to cut down on his travel expenses, which Marks apparently considered excessive. In this letter, dated 27 May 1932, Mr. Marks writes:

> My dear Ernest:
> I have received your long letters re remote control and re the Nold matter. I regret your attitude and cannot agree with you.
>
> I am particularly sorry that you persist in the patently erroneous idea that no one but yourself ever has contributed or ever can contribute to the success of the Company. The postscript on your last letter clearly indicates the existence in your mind of this idea. It is not shared by your associates or by the Board of Directors. Every one is willing to give you generous credit for your achievements. You should be equally generous with numerous others in the organization who have contributed largely to our success.
>
> I have earnestly endeavored to arrange your status so as to make you as comfortable as possible, consistent with the best interests of the Company. I am afraid some points remain to be cleared up in order to avoid confusion.
>
> I wish to remind you of the existence of the Technical Control Committee, of which you are Chairman, also of your contract with the Company. Please leave the Minnesota and the Church of St. Mary the Virgin organs entirely to Harrison. If, in their design, there is anything which appears wrong, you may lay it before the Technical Control Committee.
>
> In future you are to specify scaling and voicing on jobs which you sell. Harrison shall do the same on his. Others will be decided by myself in case of any disagreement.
>
> The Technical Control Committee is to be made an active and useful body.
>
> Our travelling expenses are too heavy. Too many people are spending the money of the Company without any business like control. Unnecessary trips have been made and, at times, two men have made trips which might have been consolidated into one. I know of no other corporation more lax than ourselves in allowing representatives to incur travelling expenses at will and with no attempt at coordination.
>
> As an example of abuses in respect to travelling expenses, I can see

no justification for hotel bills in New York when there is bed and bath available at the studio.

This is all in the effort to promote the best interests of our stockholders and to avoid friction. If you feel that I am wrong, I will be glad to call a special meeting of the Board so that we can have them investigate all matters thoroughly and make a decision. I am hoping, however, to have your generous and wholehearted cooperation.

Yours sincerely,
(signed) Arthur H. Marks
President[21]

Ernest was indignant over Marks' orders and wrote him three very heated letters dated 31 May, 3 June, and 6 June of 1932, defending his actions which had displeased Marks. In his letter of 31 May, Ernest writes:

> There is much in yours of May 27th that I anticipated. Generally speaking, I never expected you to take my side of any question, so I will go into details a little bit more.
>
> The reeds Harrison specifies in all his organs are neither Willis nor Skinner reeds. They belong to a period before the advent of the Willis reed, about 75 years ago. They are thin and unmusical and are far removed from the quality that made the Skinner name as they can possibly be. The Diapasons are also of an ancient variety. Why can't Harrison sell Skinner organs? The public think they are going to get Skinner organs when they come to us, and the Skinner quality. What do you want to knock it down for?
>
> I utterly refuse to accept your fifth paragraph. It is agreed that I am head of the technical end of the organization and until the directors meet to vote that I am not, I intend to be the head of it, for the simple reason that that is where the business comes from. Otherwise, why did you say that the Skinner stock would not be worth $5.00 a share if I left the Company? You said this last January at our meeting. I looked over the letter that you referred to and I don't see anywhere in it that I said anything about that I was responsible for the success of the Company. I have a very definite idea that I am responsible for the artistic success of it for the simple reason that the name was at the top of the heap before I ever met you. Riding down from Yorktown one day, you said you were going to have the credit of making a financial success of the business and I was going to have the credit for the artistic success. What's the matter with sticking to that? . . . I think it is an outrage that another man is invited into this organization after all the years I have worked somewhere and put on a par with me and allowed to thrust

his ideas into the thing in spite of my wishes, when my wishes are based wholly on preserving the name for the quality that I produced. I took Harrison in this organization with open arms and gave him 50-50 in the factory and with my friends, and gave him the best show I know how to do, and there was no trouble until he started in on the idea that he didn't need me any more, so that the last two or three years I might as well not have existed as far as having any connection with jobs that he was particularly interested in.

Now with regard to the Technical Control Committee, you can't sit in and talk about things for an hour and a half and make correct decisions. Most of these points require intense concentration in the light of all the experience that can be brought to bear on it, and the only function the Technical Control Committee can have is to dilute my experience and opinions, which happen to be the best in this country if results mean anything....

I don't know what you mean by two men going on a job when one could serve. I went up to Danbury to help Hardy at his request. I went to Binghamton at Kingsbury's request. I go to Philadelphia at Cliff White's request. We signed all these jobs. I think all three will tell you that I was of substantial assistance.

About sleeping in the Studio, the last times but one that I went to the Studio, the rooms were filled and I had to go down to the Hotel at an ungodly hour when I was tired enough to drop, besides which the bed that I slept in the last time I stayed there but one tilted so far front that I was very uncomfortable. I understand that has been fixed, but there is a multigraph machine overhead that starts at a very early hour in the morning and makes any sleep out of the question.[22]

A few days later, on 3 June, Ernest writes:

> Now inasmuch as the public think I am back of the Skinner quality (except for such impressions to the contrary as is created by competitors) and the letterhead says I am Technical Director gives the same impression. I am the Technical Director and I do not propose that the title is of tissue paper and that you may say lay off this or that I give it to Harrison. Your letter of May 27th, paragraphs 5 and 6, tend to largely nullify the letterhead and the public impression, which puts me in the position of a stool pigeon, a cat's paw, a figurehead to attract business, which position I decline to accept. If you do not wish me to be Technical Director and to have pretty much the final word that made the Skinner reputation, you can call a meeting of the Board of Directors and vote me out, and take my name off the stationary, and make a public announcement to that effect.

Further on in the same letter, Ernest continues:

Why do you want Harrison to keep on, as he will, using his own Trumpets, which are neither Willis, Skinner nor anything else but Harrison, belonging to a vintage of 75 years ago, before anybody knew anything about reeds. I ask you again, why don't you tell him to use *[my Trumpets]* and end the trouble, instead of writing me that he shall scale his own organs? When he goes out to sell organs, does he go out to sell Harrison organs? Can't he sell Skinner organs? He uses the Skinner name, the Skinner prestige, and the Skinner backing. If he can't sell Skinner organs, he has no business in the organization.

When these reeds first appeared, owing to criticisms of our ensemble, I backed them as much as anybody, hoping to eliminate the criticism of the Bach fans. I overlooked the fact that the public liked the Skinner organ as it was, and it has cost us considerable business. When people have criticized those reeds to me, I said, "Well, we are trying to give you what you want. They make for clarity and for brilliance, etc." I defended them. If we persist in making them in the future, I cannot defend them. I will be forced to say that I do not like them any better than you do. "Well why do you put them in?" "I don't put them in. Harrison puts them in." "Well, what do you let him for?" "I have no voice in the matter"—an inevitable conversation if we continue to put out these reeds.

If you propose to interfere with me in the church organ game, either personally or with a Technical Control Committee, I shall have to find some way to get out of an intolerable position. I am under such a strain financially that I am unable to sleep, and I am not going to stand a lot of business worries and wrangling with Harrison or you on top of that. My prestige and influence ought to lead you to stand back of me and assist me in every way possible. The thing that stands in the way of it is your determination never to admit that I am right whether you think so or not. If you think I am claiming too much for my prestige, etc., I will refer you to your remark at the time of our blow-up in January, 1931. You said that if I left the Company, the stock would not be worth $5.00 a share. If you do not think the tone of this letter is characteristic of me, I wish to say that I took it laying down for ten years with the result that the more I took, the worse it got, so I am calling a spade a spade and hope that the conditions will improve. My prestige and influence are factors entirely outside of the contract between us, but I do not propose that they shall be brushed aside thereby putting me in the position of an ordinary employee with a contract. Nothing gets me into a row quicker than resistance to attacks on the quality that I have built up, and which I propose to defend regardless of consequences.

Competitors say I am eliminated and offer as evidence the change in our quality of tone for which I am in part responsible. All our

> salesmen are put to denying this while you at the same time do your damdest to make it true. You also studiously do everything in your power to make the worst possible feeling between Harrison and myself as your paragraph 5 in letter of May 27th.
>
> Your treatment of me previous to January, 1931, didn't work so you talked me into a contract which I was idiot enough to sign and now you are starting in again where you left off. I am sick and disgusted with the whole business and I am going to find a way out of it. I am going to get the consideration which my name and prestige entitle me. I would not live under the conditions implied in your last communication for the next three and one half years under any circumstances. I don't propose to live my remaining years in a stew. I am going to have relief. I hereby give you fair warning.[23]

Ernest was becoming painfully aware that he was, in fact, little more than a "figurehead," with almost no real authority in the company which he had established thirty-one years ago. His realization of this becomes quite evident as we read from his third and final letter written to Marks on 6 June:

> I have yours of May 27th. and I follow your train of thought quite easily.
>
> Of course, by putting E. M. on the stationary as Technical Director, we give to the public the impression that the Skinner quality will go on as usual. Then, not so public we can give Harrison all his sales to run and all the rest except Skinner's as we fancy, and maybe Skinner's later, and then we will have the Technical Control Committee put over everything else we like and Skinner will have to be satisfied with his title because he is under contract and can't help himself, or it may be that he is too dumb to see through the scheme, though it is pretty thin I'll admit.
>
> When E. M. reported criticism of the Harrison reeds, I might have said let's talk it over and fix it up, but the authority of the President must be preserved regardless, so I wrote and said Harrison is to scale all his sales instead of only those called for by contract. I suppose this will increase tension between them but I always take the opposition and I must do so at all hazards.
>
> E. M. ought to be satisfied with his title of Technical Director. He is a little man, very excitable and jealous. We will wear him out sooner or later. I don't know a damn thing about remote control but whatever E. M. says about it—"I don't agree with him."
>
> You can do as you like A. H. but I suggest that if you will let the man who made the quality stay in command of the quality, I will resign as Vice President and Technical Director—the title is nothing I want to substance. You won't believe in a thousand years that there

is no small motive in my composition. I want to build the finest organs in the world and you elect to stop me if you can. You don't like me. I am sixty-five and I have no time to waste in wrangling and foolish opposition or in a stew about something of which you are generally the cause.

Ernest ends the letter with this statement:

> You don't want harmony—you promote discord. You are responsible for all the trouble I ever had with Harrison. We got along perfectly before you put him up to going over my head . . . [24]

Ernest Skinner's friendship with Henry Willis III continued in the fall of 1932, notwithstanding the enmity which now prevailed between Ernest and Willis' former associate, Don Harrison. The two men regularly corresponded with each other, exchanging ideas and opinions on tonal and mechanical matters. A letter to Willis dated 20 October 1932 is totally devoted to Ernest's comments about the specification for a new organ Willis was installing in Sheffield City Hall. Only one brief line betrays Ernest's unhappy and desperate situation at the Aeolian-Skinner firm during this time. Stated directly and without elaboration, Ernest asks Willis, "Do you want a partner?" Ernest obviously received no positive response to this request, for we hear no more about the matter.

The differences between the tonal ideas of Ernest Skinner and G. Donald Harrison were so basic that Ernest, accustomed to being his own boss for so many years, could never become reconciled to promoting, or even accepting, the younger man's concepts. The most elementary difference was that Harrison was mainly interested in music which was specifically written for the organ, while Ernest loved music in general. Harrison's musical affinities stemmed from his experience as an organist in the Church of England. As a student at Dulwich College in London, he occasionally played Evensong services. Through this experience he acquired a great love of the Anglican service and its hymns. As a result, Harrison conceived of the organ in liturgical terms and wanted a chorus which was very clear and brilliant. On the other hand, Ernest thought of the organ primarily in orchestral terms and wanted his instruments "to be very smooth and very round and full . . ."[25] According to Ernest's son, Col. Richmond Skinner,

> The Harrison theory was that you will build up harmonics by a lot of mixtures. My father's claim is that they don't produce body. He wanted body by pipes of full length. He wanted mixtures to add, but not to fill out.[26]

Some of the disagreement between Skinner and Harrison stemmed from their respective ideas of what type of organ was best suited for interpreting the music of J. S. Bach. Harrison favored an instrument which more closely resembled the type of organ built in Bach's day. Ernest had other opinions on this matter. Col. Skinner recalls:

> Mr. Harrison formed an alliance with Biggs, the Harvard College organist, and they promoted the Bach music. My father, by studying the writings of Bach, always claimed that Bach's music wouldn't be what it is if he had had an organ of the modern kind, that Bach played the way he did because that's all he had to work with . . . he [Bach] was complaining bitterly all the time about it. And here, Harrison and Biggs were promoting what Bach didn't like. And my father was trying to maintain that, had Bach been alive to choose, he would have chosen a modern organ. So, there was a difference of opinion.[27]

There was one other source of friction between the two men. Don Harrison had a broad knowledge of specifications and tonal design, or "architecture." He also had a very keen ear. When finishing an organ, Harrison would sit at the keyboard, with his voicer up in the organ chamber, working over details for days that would "stretch on into weeks."[28] The rub was, however, that Harrison was not actually a voicer himself, while Ernest Skinner was highly skilled and experienced in this art.[29]

Since Ernest failed in persuading Arthur Hudson Marks to restore his former authority in the company or to accept his tonal concepts over those of Harrison, there remained only one way to fight back—in the editorial pages of organists' magazines. Between November of 1932 and August of 1933, a number of lengthy entries written by Ernest Skinner appeared in the pages of *The Diapason*. In these writings, he criticized the growing fondness of organists for the highly academic contrapuntal music of early composers, particularly that of J. S. Bach, along with their attendant preference for a "classic" organ which stressed ensemble to the exclusion of orchestral imitative stops. He also defended his ideas on organ building and music against the now frequent attacks by such young upstarts as Senator Emerson Richards and others who embraced the new classic ideal with unbounded enthusiasm.

Following criticism by Senator Richards at a National Association of Organists' convention in Rochester, New York, Ernest defended the use of orchestral color and "full-toned" diapasons in his instruments and denounced the current trend of advocating a return to the organ of Bach's day with these words:

The mixture, twelfth and fifteenth, however useful in the ensemble, are of no use in a response after prayer or to reflect devotion in a communion service, in which place the flute celeste is eminently suitable. The English horn lends dramatic atmosphere and contributes artistic flavor to the service in obbligato figures, which are outside any possible use of the harmonic group.

If we are going to discard the developments made possible by the advent of the electro-pneumatic action and the increased pressures which it made possible, let us make a job of it and throw out the swell-box and the Willis trumpets, and go back to two and one-half and three-inch wind, and the beardless, slow-speaking dulcianas and keraulophones common to the time.

Organ voices are subject to the same laws as human voices. A good tone is the result of the harmonious and coordinated structural elements which produce it. If a singer forces his voice we do not consider that it is richer in harmonics. We say it is forced, hard and unmusical. So if we put an ancient diapason with a wide, low mouth designed for two and one-half or three-inch wind on a wind of five inches or over we must either knock the wind off at the toe, thereby developing windiness, or the pipe is overblown. This latter is often done, and the result is the hard, unmusical quality that is supposed to blend with mixtures and to be rich in harmonics. The wide mouth was necessary to develop power with a low pressure, but the power available in Bach's time is not sufficient for the present.

The statement current on both sides of the Atlantic that the full-toned diapason will not blend with upper work is absurd. The treatment to produce a blend is simple. The first requisite of an organ is to accompany the choir. The diapasons in St. Thomas' Church, New York, are on six-inch pressure. The octave harmonic is very highly developed, which gives them a rich singing quality ideal for accompanying voices. The mouths are cut up to a point where the wind sheet is flexible and is entirely subject to the command of the sound-wave within the pipe. They are not phonons. The lips are thickened with leather to remove mechanical noises and to enrich the tone. A thickening with metal would do as well, but it is not so convenient to manipulate. To say that these diapasons will not blend with mixtures is absurd. They do blend with mixtures. This organ did not get a national reputation and more on sophistry. It speaks for itself. Its first requirement is as a background for voices, as are other organs of like build and purpose.

Quality of diapason tone should be determined by scale and not by a low, wide mouth if harmonic development is desired. Putting a pipe under stress by abnormal conditions of forcing will not develop harmonics. It develops stridency and a hardness that is foreign to use with voices, having nothing in common with them.

I do not see the point in making a fetish of ensemble and setting it against solo or orchestral voices. It is another vogue of the moment, making the usual mistake of glorifying the past to the disparagement of the present. When we say modern orchestral voices must be thrown out and a return made to the time when transcriptions were taboo because the organ was cold and unresponsive, we undo everything that has been done to give the organ an increased vocabulary, warmth, and make it a really responsive instrument.

Bach looked forward, not backward. He wanted a good tremolo and was the first to put percussion into the organ. If he were here now he would save me the trouble of writing this screed. I have just examined the specifications of an organ which "fulfilled the highest expectations," which Bach played for his own pleasure and for his friends. It is destitute of real strings and of reeds that present ears could tolerate. Of thirty-eight manual stops twenty are above 4-ft. pitch. It may be all right for a fugue, but how would Bach's "O Lord, Have Mercy upon Me" sound on it—a deeply devotional, poetic piece of writing which found complete and perfect expression as played by Andrew Tietjen on the kleine erzahler, unda maris, English horn and pedal dulciana, if I remember correctly, at St. Thomas' Church at the A.G.O. convention of 1931? Bach had none of these stops. Why not have the perfect diapason ensemble and the highly musical warm-toned modern contributions as well?

Ernest followed the above comment, printed in the November 1932 issue of *The Diapason,* with the remark: "P.S.—Bach had no telephone."

Two months later, in the January 1933 issue of the same publication, Ernest reviewed his accomplishments in the development and standardization of the Skinner console. He then continued as follows:

Well, as time passed, so far as I was able, I made the organs bearing my name responsive and sympathetic. I am learning now that I am all wrong; that the traditional ensemble is missing; that the singing diapasons will not blend with mixtures; that the flute celeste and English horn represent a debauch of departure from the traditional. All this may be true—it depends on who is doing the talking and, according to my opinion, how musical he is. All persons are not given ears to hear. At all events, the tone of the Skinner organ as represented at Ann Arbor, St. Thomas', New York; the Methodist Temple, San Francisco; the Cathedral of St. John the Divine, New York, and at the National Cathedral in Washington, and about 700 others has been voiced by a music-lover, however lacking in tradition. They seem to have made a name for me and to have brought me many friends. I like my crowd. The traditional organ *sans* orchestral modern voices bores me stiff, along with the majority of music-lovers. Until harmonic development and the classic ensemble become reconciled to the principles of good tone production that gives us the poetic, the artistic and the emotional qualities that appeal to me, I shall continue to live in the present, with an eye to the future, and let the past take care of itself. The past is all right for a foundation, but who wants to live in the basement?

In a third article printed in the February 1933 issue of *The Diapason,* Ernest fended off accusations that he was against J. S. Bach by stating his ideas on how the music of that composer could be heard to best advantage (this topic will be covered in more detail in a later chapter). He then advocated recital programs which included music of Bach *and* transcriptions so that organ recitals would have appeal for the public and not just for organists.

In the last of these articles, appearing in the August 1933 issue of *The Diapason,* Ernest had this to say about the newly emerging "scholarly" organists:

> Now with regard to the development of the organist: Some become ministers of music, or missionaries; they are interested in the people in the pews—the public. And the term "public" does not imply the gum-chewing public. I mean the decent people who attend divine worship, the organ recital, the opera, oratorio and symphony concerts. They are not professional musicians, nor will they ever become so, as listeners. But they are people of refinement and culture to whom the minister of music may well give his best.
>
> Now there is also developed in the music school what may be termed the scholarly type. He has absorbed and has been absorbed by the highly technical side of his art, the so-called academic music, counterpoint, the fugue, etc. He is without the spirit of the missionary, which burns to give. He is not a minister of music. This lack of interest in the public is sometimes accompanied by more or less contempt or a feeling of superiority toward those who do not share his interest in the cerebral, literate, dry, technical type of composition of which a large part of organ literature is composed. The vox humana, the chimes, the flute celeste and the harp are not included in organ specifications with which he has anything to do. Likewise the French horn is an undesirable voice. The traditional organ as made in France, England and Germany has none of the modern voices distinguishing the American organ except the French horn, which I gave to an English builder.

Ernest followed the above remarks with a summary of his tonal developments and ended with these comments:

> The organ as I first heard it, and as I occasionally see surviving examples, was a shrill, cold affair, inexpressive to the last degree—hardly a musical instrument. The organ of today is devotional, churchly, vital and filled with tonal charm.
>
> Compositions are written calling for erzahler, celeste and most of the orchestral voices I have contributed. I may have been on the wrong track all these years, but I have been royally supported by the people I wanted to please, and that includes ministers of music who give to the public and make tradition, as represented by the finest churches in America.
>
> I cannot see the wisdom of making a fetish of ensemble at the sacrifice of the charming voices so much loved by the public, especially when funds are sufficient for both. Instead of going back to the primitive we should go ahead and develop refinements that they never thought of. Why haunt the cemetery?

Ernest's defense of his tonal ideas also found expression in the pages of *The American Organist*. In December of 1932, his article entitled "Thoughts on the Organ Pipe" appeared and was obviously aimed at G. Donald Harrison and the officials of the Aeolian-Skinner firm, although no names were mentioned. Ernest made the following statements which bear the essential message he intended to convey:

> While all questions of shape, size, proportions, pressures, etc., are important, the fact remains that however exactly these details are tabulated, recorded or carried out by various voicers, no two results will be precisely alike, nor need they, in point of fact, be necessarily similar. Voicing is as much a personal art as painting or playing the piano, and one of the greatest factors in the production of tone is the personal taste, or shall we say, the ear of the voicer. So, obviously, it is not possible for one builder to duplicate the tone of another . . .
>
> A technic, however fine, is of no value without the musical taste to direct it. The same holds good with the piano player. May I again suggest the futility of any claim of one builder to produce the tone of another, which leads us in natural sequence to point out the fact that specifications guarantee about as much, as to the quality of an organ, as a beautiful composition guarantees a beautiful performance . . .

The unspoken but clearly implied message in the above statements: G. Donald Harrison may have extraordinary technical knowledge, but without me, Aeolian-Skinner cannot build the true Skinner organ.

Ernest Skinner had come to the realization that the firm he had founded never again would build the Skinner organ as he had conceived and developed it. Therefore, sometime around 1932, Ernest began work on his second book, which was to be called *The Composition of the Organ*. This book was to be a greatly expanded version of his first one, *The Modern Organ,* published in 1917, and would contain detailed explanations of his tonal and mechanical developments.[30] The main hope that Ernest had in writing this second book was to assure that his knowledge of the art of organ building would not die with him.[31] This project was to occupy much of his attention for the remainder of his life.

Little is known about what Ernest Skinner was doing during the year following his second major blow-up with A. H. Marks in May of 1932. We do know of the many printed letters and articles he wrote during that period. No doubt he was working hard on writing his book *The Composition of the Organ*. Also, Ernest was probably spending a fair amount of time working on the Girard College organ, which was nearing completion by the spring of 1933.[32] Other than that he was mainly a salesman for the Aeolian-Skinner Company, and little else, at the time.

In June of 1933 Ernest was in California on business, presumably for the specific purpose of closing the contract with Grace Cathedral, San Francisco, for the building and installation of a large four manual instrument. The contract for the Grace Cathedral organ was signed on 10 June of that year.[33] It specified that G. Donald Harrison "was to personally supervise the construction and installation of the instrument . . ."[34] Naturally, Ernest was not at all happy with this arrangement and apparently tried to get the Harrison stipulation removed at the time the contract was signed.[35]

A. H. Marks sent Ernest an "urgent message" requesting him to return to New York. Marks had expected Ernest to be back by the fifteenth of June, and when Ernest did not return until the twenty-first, Marks was furious. Marks thereupon went to the Board of Directors at Aeolian-Skinner and, after discussing the situation with them, wrote Ernest a very dictatorial letter calling him down for "apparently" trying to waive the Harrison stipulation at Grace Cathedral and wasting time and money, as well as accusing him of "possibly aiding and abetting a competitor" when he stopped over in Chicago on his way back. In this letter of 14 July 1933, Marks went on to issue a series of orders which severely restricted Ernest's activities:

> Unless otherwise directed, in writing, from time to time by George Catlin or myself, you are to remain in Boston or at your summer camp in New Hampshire or, if desired by you and agreed to by Mr. Catlin or myself, elsewhere.

> You are to come to the factory or elsewhere, for consultation or other service when—*but only when*—directed by Mr. Catlin or myself. You are to travel in the service of the Company when directed by Mr. Catlin and myself and not otherwise.
>
> You are to incur no expenses chargeable to the Company except in connection with such approved services.
>
> You are to write no letters to clients or prospective clients except as directed and with correct copies in the usual files. All letters received by you pertaining to the business of the Company are to be handed to Mr. Catlin.
>
> The directors feel that your frequent association with competitors leads to disclosures and remarks of such nature as to aid and abet competitors. You are directed to cease contact and communication with competitors.
>
> It is reported that you are writing a book. The Company feels entitled to see that anything you write for publication in books or otherwise is in furtherance of the best interests and good will of the Company and that such writings are not injurious to such interests; therefore you are directed not to allow any of your writings to be published without my approval in writing so long as your service contract is in force.

Marks follows this series of orders with these threats:

> You are advised that a violation of these directions may result in serious damage to the interests of your employer and that you will be held responsible for such damages.
>
> You are also reminded that the obligation of the Company to pay your salary ceases upon commission by you of any material breach of your contract with it.

Marks closes this letter by stating:

> In case this is not clear to you, you may make an appointment with me and come to New York for a discussion. Kindly do not write any letters on the subject and please regard these instructions as effective now.[36]

In the meantime, on 19 June 1933, G. Donald Harrison received an honorary degree of Master of Arts at Trinity College, Hartford, Connecticut, where, two years earlier the first organ of his own exclusive design had been installed.[37] This, no doubt, was a bitter pill for Ernest Skinner to swallow, who had not gone beyond ninth grade in his formal education, and who, after being a leader in the organ world for several decades, had yet to receive any kind of honorary degree. According to his daughter Ruth, Ernest's lack of formal education bothered him. In a letter written late in life to his friend Alexander McCurdy, Ernest reveals that he was indeed quite hurt because he had never received an honorary degree, in spite of the many contributions he had made to the development of the American organ.[38]

Harrison's honorary degree was made public in the July 1933 issue of *The Diapason*. A month later, another announcement of considerable interest to the organ world appeared in this publication. It proclaimed that G. Donald Harrison was the "newly-appointed Technical Director and Chief of the Aeolian-Skinner Staff."[39]

The month after the announcement of Harrison's promotion appeared, William E. Zeuch published "An Appreciation of the Work of G. Donald Harrison" in *The American Organist*. In this article, Zeuch summarizes the development and perfection of the Skinner organ prior to 1925, as conceived by Ernest M. Skinner, and explains its "deficiencies" which led to the import of Don Harrison. He then cites the developments and improvements in the "tonal architecture" of the Skinner organ since Harrison became associated with the Skinner Company, mentioning specific landmark installations exhibiting the increasing influence of Harrison in their design. After an exposition of Harrison's background and his ideals as an "organ architect," Zeuch has these comments:

> Fundamentally it has been a process of development along lines demanded by the organ playing and buying public. Mr. Harrison has augmented and enhanced the beauty of the typical Skinner Organ with his own ideas, giving it the flavor of old world Cathedrals. That these tonal effects are based on close study of foreign masterpieces does not alter the fact that they are new to our ears. Furthermore, the individualistic quality of his tonal architecture makes the final product intrinsically original. It is not change so much as progress, perfecting the old, introducing new blood.[40]

Even with the changing times Ernest Skinner still had many friends, and the above article was probably written to justify Ernest's demotion in the Company and, possibly, to prepare the public for his eventual departure from the firm. Ernest, the victim of a society which increasingly was placing high value on youth and change for its own sake, was now officially relieved of his meaningless title of "Technical Director."

FOOTNOTES

[1]"Build 917 Organs in 1931, Census Reveals," *The Diapason*, December 1932, p. 1.
[2]"Skinner and Aeolian Companies to Merge," *The Diapason*, January 1932, p. 1.
[3]"Skinner and Aeolian," p. 1.
[4]Letter received from Harold Gleason, 29 January 1974; Personal interview with George W. Collins, 7 May 1976.
[5]"Skinner and Aeolian," pp. 1 & 2.
[6]Letter received from William H. Barnes, 13 August 1974.
[7]Telephone interview with Richmond H. Skinner, 15 September 1977.
[8]"Up 78%, Aeolian-Skinner Company Reports Excellent Condition," *The American Organist*, 15, no. 8 (August 1932), p. 494.
[9]William H. Barnes, "The Organ," *The American Organist*, 15, no. 5 (May 1932), pp. 282-284.
[10]"Skinner Organ for Girard College," *The Diapason*, October 1931, p. 1.
[11]Letter received from Alexander McCurdy, 24 April 1974.
[12]Letter received from Joseph F. Dzeda, 31 October 1967.
[13]Letter received from Wheeler Beckett, 17 March 1973.
[14]T. Scott Buhrman, "Clarity and its Development," *The American Organist*, 20, no. 2 (1937), p. 50.
[15]William H. Barnes, "Trinity College," *The American Organist*, 16, no. 7 (July 1933), pp. 364-365.
[16]"Large Organ Designed for Harvard Chapel," *The Diapason*, May 1932, p. 1; Arthur Hudson Marks, Letter to Ernest M. Skinner, 27 May 1932 (courtesy of Henry Karl Baker); T. Scott Buhrman, "The St. Mary Festivities," *The American Organist*, 16, no. 2 (February 1933), p. 98; E. A. Boadway, "The Skinner and Aeolian-Skinner Opus List," *The Boston Organ Club Newsletter*, December 1972, p. 4.
[17]Buhrman, "St. Mary," pp. 98-99.
[18]Emerson Richards, "An American-Classic Organ Arrives," *The American Organist*, 26, no. 5 (May 1943), p. 105.
[19]Ralph Downes, "The Baroque Organ," *Organ Quarterly*, 23 (1943-1944), 140; Herbert D. Bruening, "Inveterate Recital Goer Remembers Five Decades," *The Diapason*, December 1959, p. 47.
[20]Ernest M. Skinner, Letter to Arthur Hudson Marks, 3 June 1932 (courtesy of Henry Karl Baker).
[21]Arthur H. Marks, Letter to Ernest M. Skinner, 27 May 1932 (courtesy of Henry Karl Baker).
[22]Ernest M. Skinner, Letter to Arthur H. Marks, 31 May 1932 (courtesy of Henry Karl Baker).
[23]Ernest M. Skinner, Letter to Arthur H. Marks, 3 June 1932 (courtesy of Henry Karl Baker).
[24]Ernest M. Skinner, Letter to Arthur H. Marks, 6 June 1932 (courtesy of Henry Karl Baker).
[25]Personal interview with Edward B. Gammons, 3 May 1976.
[26]Telephone interview with Richmond H. Skinner, 15 September 1977.
[27]Telephone interview with Richmond H. Skinner, 15 September 1977.
[28]Buhrman, "Clarity," p. 49.
[29]Ernest M. Skinner, Letter to Alexander McCurdy, 11 June 1954.
[30]"E. M. Skinner is Guest of Guild in New York," *The Diapason*, November 1942, p. 2; Edward H. Hastings, Letter to Joseph F. Dzeda, 15 July 1965.
[31]Ernest M. Skinner, Letter to Alexander McCurdy, 26 May 1954.
[32]"Large Organ Opened at Girard College," *The Diapason*, June 1933, p. 3.
[33]Arthur Hudson Marks, Letter to Ernest M. Skinner, 14 July 1933 (courtesy of Henry Karl Baker).
[34]Ralph B. Valentine, "An Answer for Mr. Ditewig," *The American Organist*, 49, no. 5 (May 1966), p. 3.

35Marks, Letter to Skinner, 14 July 1933.
36Marks, Letter to Ernest M. Skinner, 14 July 1933 (courtesy of Henry Karl Baker).
37"G. Donald Harrison," *The Diapason,* July 1933, p. 13.
38Ernest M. Skinner, Letter to Alexander McCurdy, 2 August 1954.
39"G. Donald Harrison, Newly-appointed Technical Director and Chief of the Aeolian-Skinner Staff," *The Diapason,* August 1933, p. 5.
40William E. Zeuch, "An Appreciation of the Work of G. Donald Harrison," *The American Organist,* 16, no. 9 (September 1933), p. 439.

CHAPTER 17

A New Start
1933—1938

ERNEST'S LEADERSHIP in the organ world was already on the wane by mid-1933, when G. Donald Harrison was appointed Technical Director of the Aeolian-Skinner firm. The entire 1933 volume of *The American Organist* gave evidence of an increasing preference among organists for more Germanic ideals in organ building, along with a growing worship of the "pure and spiritual" music of J. S. Bach, plus a new disdain for transcriptions, tone poems, or any music which relied on "fancy effects." This was a new generation of organists and they were revolting against what they considered the excessive sentimentalism of the older generation of organists who had revered Ernest Skinner and his work.

By this time, not only were the new Aeolian-Skinner organs being built according to the tonal concepts of G. Donald Harrison and his followers, but Harrison had begun to rebuild Ernest Skinner's instruments to conform with his own ideas. The first of these was the 1929 reconstruction of the large Skinner organ in the Old First Presbyterian Church of New York City, which originally had been built in 1920. This rebuild involved "a number of important additions to the instrument, a new console and revoicing of some of the stops . . ."[1] The second known Harrison rebuild of one of Ernest's instruments was that of the Skinner installed in Town Hall, New York City, in 1923. By 1935, this organ had been "completely overhauled and renovated by the Aeolian-Skinner Organ Co. under the personal direction of G. Donald Harrison." This work included the revoicing of three sets of reeds and the "replacing *[of]* the old English Horn with a new one."[2]

Another organ builder by the name of Walter Holtkamp was now emerging on the organ scene as a leader in the "classic revival." His ideas on organ design were even more revolutionary and extreme to American ears than those of Don Harrison. Ironically, the attention of the organ world was first drawn to Mr. Holtkamp by a nine rank Rückpositiv division which he added to the 1922 Skinner organ in the Cleveland Museum of Art in the year 1933.[3]

Ernest Skinner apparently was no longer in demand as a speaker at organists' conventions, his last known engagement in this capacity having taken place in May of 1932 at the Pennsylvania National Association of Organists' Convention in Philadelphia.[4] In fact, most organists, young and old, now avoided Ernest's company at organists' gatherings for fear of being considered "old fashioned." To add to his isolation, Ernest was now becoming somewhat hard of hearing. In a letter dated 20 February 1976, Robert Baker tells this humorous and touching story of an incident which took place at an organists' convention during the 1930s:

> . . . when Harrison took over the Skinner company, the old man found himself a pariah, and his former admirers shunned him, lest they be guilty of being thought "old fashioned." So, it transpired that at the Boston Convention in the 30's, Mr. Skinner found himself standing *alone* and both hurt and bewildered in the lobby of the Copley-Plaza. Walter Holtkamp, who told me this story, saw him standing there, and said to himself, "Now, this is a perfect shame!! There stands one of the greatest figures in the art of organ-building, and all those sissies are afraid to go up to speak to him, for fear they might lose face amongst their peers!" So Walter sauntered over, saying "Mr. Skinner, I am Walter Holtkamp from Cleveland, and I just want to thank you for all you have meant and done for the art of organ-building through your splendid career." Mr. Skinner, by that time a bit hard of hearing, and a bit slower on the uptake by then, got only one thing out of this, and that was the word, "Cleveland." So he responded, "Cleveland! Say, you know, I have one of my best organs out there in the Art Museum, and some damn fool has come along and just ruined it."

Although Ernest's hearing was now becoming somewhat impaired, he still retained his acute tonal sensitivity, which was to stay with him throughout the remainder of his career.[5] Ernest's apparent lack of awareness at that Boston convention may well have been due to preoccupation as much as deafness and old age. It has been said by some who were close to him that the treatment given Ernest by the officials at Aeolian-Skinner affected his emotional state so deeply that it actually impaired his health. According to one account he came close to having a nervous breakdown, at one point.[6]

During the entire year of 1933 there were no reports of Ernest's activities in any of the major organists' magazines. After mid-1933, no articles by Ernest Skinner appeared in any of these publications, with the exception of his article on the life and work of Sigfrid Karg-Elert, published in the December 1933 issue of *The Diapason*. This undoubtedly had to do with A. H. Marks' command in his letter of 14 July 1933, requiring Ernest to submit anything he wrote to Marks' approval before allowing it to be published. Apparently, most of what Ernest had to say in writing at this time did not meet with Marks' approval.

Ernest's literary silence continued through 1934. In April of that year, however, an interesting article by his son Richmond entitled "Facts and Fancies" was published in *The American Organist*. The younger Mr. Skinner was introduced to the readers of this publication with a brief biographical sketch which stated that he was owner and manager of the Methuen Organ Company and that "his present activities with the M. O. C. have occupied his time for the past three years." In his article Richmond Skinner objected to the current overemphasis on brilliance and clarity at the sacrifice of color and diapason tone in the organ, expressing a viewpoint not unlike that of his father.

Meanwhile, in the year 1934, the Aeolian-Skinner Company relocated and rebuilt the C. H. K. Curtis Aeolian residence organ, installing it in Christ Episcopal Church, Philadelphia, Pennsylvania. Ernest Skinner, who wrote descriptive program notes for the dedication of this instrument on 29 May 1935, was apparently in charge of this work, and a number of tonal revisions were made according, one would assume, to his own design.[7] It is very likely that he was given this project at the request of the donor, the daughter of C. H. K. Curtis. This was probably the last installation supervised by Ernest while he was associated with the Aeolian-Skinner Organ Company.

During his two and one-half years of enforced silence, between mid-1933 and January of 1936, Ernest evidently spent much of his time working on his book, *The Composition of the Organ*. By early 1936 it was announced in *The American Organist* that his "second book, virtually completed in manuscript, is now being prepared for publication."[8] Ernest's silent years had at last come to an end.

In January of 1936, Ernest Skinner's five year contract with the Aeolian-Skinner Organ Company expired, and he was now free to build organs in partnership with his son Richmond at their factory in Methuen. Ernest was president and treasurer of their firm, now called the Ernest M. Skinner & Son Company, and Richmond was its vice-

A New Start (1933-1938) 181

president and secretary.⁹ The opening of their factory under this new name was made public in the February issues of both *The Diapason* and *The American Organist*. The announcement which appeared in *The American Organist* read as follows:

> The Ernest M. Skinner & Son Company announce that Ernest M. Skinner is established at Methuen, Massachusetts, where organ building, as exemplified by the instruments at the Cathedral of St. John the Divine, St. Thomas and St. Bartholomew's churches, New York City, and similar examples elsewhere, will be continued.
>
> The traditional ensemble, enhanced by Mr. Skinner's orchestral and other tonal inventions, combining to make the classic American organ, will insure the character of these instruments. Their beautiful tone and *uncompromising fidelity to quality* are acknowledged by American and foreign artists alike.¹⁰

By this time, Ernest and his wife Mabel had moved to a smaller and less expensive home at 78 Beacon Street, Chestnut Hill.¹¹ It was well that they had, because the Ernest M. Skinner & Son Company was beset by many difficulties during its first year of operation. On 1 March 1936, Ernest wrote Harold Gleason:

> I seem to have a lot of prospects but nothing signed up yet. I have only been loose for a couple of months anyhow. I dug up a lot of prospects and have sent out schemes for most of them.

He also asks Mr. Gleason, "When are you going to send for me professionally, I shall starve if I cannot get professional occasionally." Further on in this letter, Ernest laments the eternal conflict between financial considerations and artistic achievements:

> Do you ever stop to think . . . how much the need to make a living delays advance in art and science. If I could devote all my time to development of the organ I would make something so much finer than I have ever done that you wouldn't believe it. But no; I have to plug to support myself and half a dozen others. So I only build 'em pretty good.

Ernest's problems with the Aeolian-Skinner Company did not end with the termination of his contract with them. In the above letter to Harold Gleason, Ernest also writes:

> Well the Aeolian S. Co. are trying to stop my naming the hall at Methuen, Skinner Organ Hall. They say it may lead people to think I build Skinner organs up there. I have built Skinner organs for 35

years but if I build exactly the same thing as I always have I cannot call it a Skinner organ but they can buy a Steere plant and build Steere organs in it and put the Skinner name plate on it and it is all right. Or they can build anything as far away from the Skinner Organ as possible and call it a Skinner organ but that is not misleading the public. Well old man if they do not keep their hands off me we are going to do some publicity work. It will eminate at Skinner Organ Hall and we shall all have a merry time of it.[12]

A series of ads for the Ernest M. Skinner & Son Organ Company appeared in *The American Organist* throughout 1936. During the middle part of that year these ads featured "Skinnergrams." These Skinnergrams were slogans which were, without any doubt, aimed at the Aeolian-Skinner Company. The first of these Skinnergrams, appearing in the May issue of this publication, was: "If traditions are so respectable—make some." The following month, we read: "Don't mistake a hearse for the bandwagon." A few months later, in the September issue of *The American Organist,* the Aeolian-Skinner Organ Company declares in its ad.: "St. Mark's Church, Philadelphia, Pa. selects a S K I N N E R" (the last word printed in huge letters!). In April of the next year, that firm, in the same publication, advertises "A Real Skinner at Low Cost."

However, this battle of the ads ceased when Ernest found out that the editor of *The American Organist* had been complying with a request of the Aeolian-Skinner Company to show them all of the advertising copy for the Ernest M. Skinner & Son Company before publishing it. Upon discovering this, Ernest never sent them "another word . . . for advertising copy."[13]

Ernest was harassed by the officials at Aeolian-Skinner in still another way. In his letter to organ builder Wallace Kimball, dated 4 February 1937, we read:

> Now there is only one other thing I must tell you which is not quite so pleasant. Your letter to me was directed to 677 Fifth Ave., New York City, from which place it was forwarded to me at 78 Beacon St., my home. But here is the point—your letter was opened in the New York office and read as all my personal mail has been treated for years in spite of my violent protests . . . A letter to me from Caspar Koch, marked personal in letters one inch high, was opened in the Boston office, read and forwarded to me. Next time this happens, I am going to make a public notice of it. In the meantime, if you will direct mail to me at 234 Broadway, Methuen, Mass., it will reach me without being inspected on the way.

These tactics pursued by Aeolian-Skinner undoubtedly hurt Ernest's business prospects. Another obstacle faced by Ernest was his advanced age, for he was seventy years old by the time he re-established in Methuen. Joseph Dzeda tells the following story, which presumably took place at about this time:

> ... Skinner put in a bid to build a new organ for some church, but his contract was turned down. Skinner was furious when he heard that it was not won by anyone else, and demanded to meet the organ committee immediately. They assembled, trembling and frightened, and Skinner addressed them: "Gentlemen: I presume you have not given this contract to me on account of my age." Whereupon he stripped off his shirt, revealing enormous biceps which he flexed for their startled eyes. As if this weren't enough, it is reputed that at that moment he then proceeded to do handsprings across the room before them. Skinner was awarded the contract by a sheepish organ committee.[14]

In spite of all the problems Ernest had to contend with, his firm had begun work on at least eight projects by the end of 1936. These ranged from repairs and minor additions to several complete new organs, one a three-manual instrument of forty-seven stops. A list of work "in process," appearing in the December 1936 issue of *The American Organist,* included a two-manual, seventeen stop organ for First Methodist Church, Reading, Massachusetts; a two-manual, sixteen stop organ for Bethany Congregational Church, Foxboro, Massachusetts; and a three-manual, forty-seven stop organ for First Church of Northampton, Northampton, Massachusetts.

Ernest Skinner was not lacking in help at his Methuen factory. He had approximately thirty-four men in his employment. Many of these men had worked with him at the old Skinner Organ Company in Dorchester and were experienced and highly skilled workers. It was fortunate that Ernest had a good supply of well-qualified help, for the monumental project which was now under way at Methuen would demand all the skill and manpower he could summon.

In February of 1937, only a little over a year after the opening of Ernest Skinner's Methuen factory was made known to the public, it was announced in *The Diapason* and *The American Organist* that he had received the contract for a 114 stop organ to be built for the Washington National Cathedral in Washington, D.C. According to the announcement which appeared in *The American Organist,* this contract was awarded to the Ernest M. Skinner & Son Company with "no competition."

In the following month *The Diapason* announced that "work is under way at the factory of the Ernest M. Skinner & Son Company in Methuen, Mass., on the great organ of 114 stops for the Washington Cathedral...." This account continued as follows:

> In view of the fame of the cathedral and the size of the instrument the entire organ fraternity is interested in what this instrument will be ... At the request of *The Diapason* Mr. Skinner has ... sent in various details concerning the design. He writes that "the principal characteristic of the organ is to be an ensemble of light and medium tone, unforced and of high musical significance."
>
> The organ is to be installed in an elevated position on each side of the great choir. This position offers great opportunity for developing affects by the placement of the various divisions, which it is proposed to utilize to the utmost. The scheme provides adequate brilliance and diapason tone of great breadth and richness. The swell organ is exceptionally well equipped in the 4-ft register. The reeds of the trumpet family are to be on adequate pressures to obtain authority and brilliance.
>
> "The organ is to be very rich in the orchestral flavors that have found such favor in the past," Mr. Skinner writes. "The swell 4-ft. harmonic flute is of an entirely new design developed in 1936."
>
> The seven-rank mixture in the solo division will be a cymbale of new design given to Mr. Skinner by the late Dr. Sigfrid Karg-Elert and extends throughout the seventy-three note compass. The choir orchestral bassoon, it is stated, is of entirely new design developed in 1936 and Mr. Skinner says it is much more like its orchestral prototype than anything previously developed. This should prove a very useful tint in the gamut of orchestral voices in this instrument. The solo strings likewise are to be of an entirely new design and of great richness and breadth. The solo tuba mirabilis will not be subject to the solo-to-great coupler, but will draw by separate knob on the great manual.
>
> There is also to be a register provided in the great organ group which transfers to the great any solo heavy pressure reed that may be drawn on the solo excepting the tuba mirabilis. This was devised by Palmer Christian, who makes great use of it at Ann Arbor. Mr. Skinner's high-speed electro-pneumatic action will be employed throughout.
>
> The muted string ensembles on three manuals will consist of four ranks of 8-ft. flauto dolce pipes and one 4-ft. rank. Some of these pipes will be located on one side of the great choir at one end and the remainder at the other end, on the other side. This is expected to produce an effect of tonality without a location, but present everywhere, and with an effect of mysticism.[15]

Ernest Skinner had already signed the contract for the Great Organ in Washington Cathedral when he was still with the old Skinner organization in Dorchester.[16] According to Richmond Skinner, his father "knew that the Charter of the National Episcopalcy [sic] of Washington, D.C. said the big organ for the Cathedral must be built by Ernest M. Skinner personally."[17] So, once Ernest's contract with Aeolian-Skinner had expired, he and his son began work on this instrument. Two and one-half years were to pass after the opening of the Methuen factory before the Washington Cathedral organ would be completed.

While the Washington Cathedral organ was under construction, Ernest acquired a number of other new contracts for work which was begun and carried on at this time. The first of these was a new three-manual organ of over thirty sets of pipes for the First Presbyterian Church of Newburgh, New York, completed during 1937. This instrument was dedicated on 5 December 1937 with a recital by Ernest's long-time friend, T. Tertius Noble. According to the January 1938 issue of *The Diapason,*

> ... it was a big day for the organ and a successful one, both the instrument and the performance of Dr. Noble arousing marked enthusiasm among the people of the church and the music-lovers of Newburgh and vicinity.[18]

In March of 1938 The Ernest M. Skinner & Son Company had the following "work in process and on hand": completion of a new two-manual organ for Holy Trinity Church, Pawling, New York; construction of a new two-manual organ for Lakewood Mortuary Chapel, Minneapolis, Minnesota; a new three-manual console and electric action for First Parish Church, Concord, Massachusetts; the revoicing and modernization of orchestral reeds for Plymouth Church, Minneapolis, Minnesota; the rebuild of an existing four-manual instrument for the new chapel at Mount Holyoke College, South Hadley, Massachusetts; the rebuilding and reinstallation of the "very large" four-manual Skinner at Brick Presbyterian Church, New York City, in a new building; the rebuilding and moving of the large four-manual Skinner in Trinity Church, Boston, Massachusetts, to the chancel; and the construction of the two-manual Edgar Priest Memorial Organ for the Chapel of St. Joseph of Arimethea, National Cathedral, Washington, D.C.[17]

By July of that year these projects were among the "recent additions to the clientele of the Ernest M. Skinner & Son Company, Inc.": the addition of nine new stops to the organ at Unitarian Church, Dedham, Massachusetts; extensive repairs on the organ at St. Stephen's Church, Providence, Rhode Island, where Ernest's father, Washington Martin Skinner, had been choirmaster about sixty years earlier; a new four-manual, fifty-one stop organ for St. John's Evangelical Lutheran Church, Allentown, Pennsylvania; a new two-manual, thirteen stop organ for an un-named installation in Rhode Island; and the installation of a new electric action in a practice organ for Dr. T. Tertius Noble at St. Thomas Church, New York City. Also among the new contracts received at this time was the reinstallation of the temporary two-manual organ, formerly in the Great Choir of the Washington National Cathedral, in the Lasell Junior College, Auburndale, Massachusetts. A Choir organ was to be added, making it an instrument of three manuals and twenty-eight stops.[20] Ernest originally intended to incorporate eighteen stops from this temporary instrument in the new organ which was now under construction for the Cathedral, "but structural complications ... changed this plan."[21]

By March of 1938 the tonal resources of the Washington Cathedral organ had been expanded from the original scheme of 114 stops to a total of 120 stops.[22] By April of that year it was reported in *The Diapason* that this instrument was now "approaching completion," and that the regulation and tuning were "being done by Richmond H. Skinner." On 6 September 1938, "Ernest M. Skinner ... supervised last-minute finishing touches to the organ in the Great Choir of Washington Cathedral."[23]

The new Skinner organ was first heard in concert on 30 October 1938. We have the following account of this event, as reported by Glenn Dillard Gunn in the *Washington Herald:*

> Mr. Skinner was present and spent the first hour defining the artistic ideals which he has sought to embody in this instrument and discussing the technical means by which they have been attained. During this time, Robert G. Barrow, organist of the Cathedral, improvised to order, illustrated various stops and combinations as Mr. Skinner called for them.
>
> While Mr. Barrow was playing the too brief program, which supplemented Mr. Skinner's talk, the builder, quite forgetful of his numerous audience, walked up and down the chancel, completely absorbed in this magnificent creature of his own imagining. He felt, I fancy, much as old maestro Antonio Stradivari felt when he held the complete "Betts" violin in his hands.

Mr. Gunn continues with his own impression of this newly created masterpiece of Ernest Skinner:

Unforced beauty of tone has been the goal sought in every stop and every choir in the whole imposing set of 125 stops. It is not too much to say that it has been attained. Though practicing caution in the use of superlatives I nevertheless find it necessary to describe the Cathedral organ as the greatest instrument I have heard in Europe or America, and, by some unkind trick of fate, I have earned the unenviable reputation of being no friend of the organ.

This is an instrument of a varied capacity to match its unique beauty. It represents, as I am quite aware, the only school in the organ world which, to escape technical description, I would call the unbrilliant ideal. The instrument, of course, has enormous power, and certain of the solo stops, notably the one counterfeiting the orchestral trumpet, are starting [sic] brilliant. The ensemble, however, escapes that overemphasis of mixtures which has produced the characteristic organ tone of the past and to which many cling.[24]

Mr. Robert Barrow, the Cathedral organist and choirmaster, had these words in praise of the magnificent new instrument at his command:

The Great Organ recently completed at Washington Cathedral is, in my opinion, the greatest instrument as yet produced in this country, and one of the really great organs of the world. It is a truly musical instrument, capable of presenting the whole field of organ literature, and not designed for a particular, narrow portion of that literature. All its many voices are musical and lovely, yet this beauty of individual stops does not in any way preclude an effective ensemble which is clear and brilliant beyond description. This is, indeed, an organ designed by a musician, for musicians.[25]

The Washington Cathedral Skinner was formally dedicated on 10 November 1938.

Robert G. Barrow . . . played the recital which constituted the major portion of the service, choosing a program designed to exhibit the resources of the instrument, in which the exquisite, refined, even restrained, blending of the voicing was noted. Mr. Barrow's facile technique, delicate and accurate sense of color values and lucid program notes served to heighten the enjoyment of the large, distinguished and highly artistic audience, who had eagerly awaited this event. The program, selected with rare good taste and obviously taking into account the sacredness of the surroundings and the occasion, opened with the Mendelssohn Sonata 6, on the chorale "Our Father, Which Art in Heaven," followed by three Bach chorale preludes—"Das alte Jahr vergangen ist," "Alle Menschen mussen sterben" and "Ich ruf' Dir, Herr Jesu Christ"; Intermezzo from

Symphony 6, Widor; "A Legend," Barrow; "Landscape in the Mist," from "Seven Pastels from the Lake of Constance," Karg-Elert, and the Scherzo and Finale from Vierne's Third Symphony. Mr. Barrow's own "A Legend" is a new work written especially for the occasion . . .[26]

The day following the dedication concert, this complimentary review appeared in the *Washington Herald:*

> Three thousand music-lovers attended the dedication of the great organ at the Washington Cathedral last night. They heard one of the greatest instruments in the world today in so far as its capacities, ordinary and unusual, could be demonstrated in a program of less than an hour's duration, and left with the conviction that they had touched another world of sound and beauty so vast that its possibilities exceed finite imagination.[27]

As to how the master builder himself felt about his monumental creation at Washington Cathedral, we read this statement which appeared in an Ernest M. Skinner & Son Company advertisement upon completion of the instrument:

> Desiring the future to be as kind to the present as we have been to the past, we have, we believe, created a masterpeice. The completed organ in the National Cathedral at Washington will stand as a supreme example of the art of organ building for the next century.[28]

FOOTNOTES

[1]"Big Work Completed in New York Church," *The Diapason,* December 1929, p. 3.
[2]"New York," *The American Organist,* 18, no. 11 (November 1935), p. 433.
[3]"The Rückpositiv Reappears," *The American Organist,* 16, no. 12 (December 1933), p. 597.
[4]"Events Forecast," *The American Organist,* 15, no. 5 (May 1932), p. 314.
[5]Unidentified newsclipping, dated 1947, from the scrapbook of Ernest M. Skinner.
[6]Personal interview with Sydney F. Eaton, 30 April 1973.
[7]Ernest M. Skinner, Program for the dedication of the C. H. K. Curtis Memorial Organ, 29 May 1935 (courtesy of Barbara Owen); E. A. Boadway, "The Skinner and Aeolian-Skinner Opus List," *The Boston Organ Club Newsletter,* January 1973, p. 5.
[8]T. Scott Buhrman, "Mr. Ernest M. Skinner's Record," *The American Organist,* 19, no. 4 (1936), p. 126.
[9]Telephone interview with Richmond H. Skinner, 15 September 1977.
[10]Ernest M. Skinner & Son Company advertisement, *The American Organist,* 19, no. 2 (February 1936), 65.
[11]Skinner, Ernest M., *Who's Who in America,* vol. 19, (1936).
[12]Ernest M. Skinner, Letter to Harold Gleason, 1 March 1936.
[13]Ernest M. Skinner, Letter to Alexander McCurdy, 16 July 1954.
[14]Letter received from Joseph F. Dzeda, 19 October 1976. In regard to Ernest allegedly

A New Start (1933-1938)   189

doing handsprings before the organ committee, Mr. Dzeda comments parenthetically in this same letter, "That is the part which seems a bit *too* much to believe, but that is what I was told."

[15]"Washington Organ's Design is Announced," *The Diapason,* March 1937, p. 1.

[16]Personal interview with William Deveau, 3 May 1973.

[17]Telephone interview with Richmond H. Skinner, 15 September 1977.

[18]"Organ at Newburgh Opened by Dr. Noble," *The Diapason,* January 1938, p. 1.

[19]Ernest M. Skinner & Son Company advertisement, *The Diapason,* March 1938, p. 14.

[20]Ernest M. Skinner & Son Company advertisement, *The Diapason,* July 1938, p. 9.

[21]"Washington Organ's Design," p. 1; Ernest M. Skinner & Son Company advertisement, *The Diapason,* February 1938, p. 21.

[22]Ernest M. Skinner & Son Company advertisement, *The Diapason,* March 1938, p. 14.

[23]"The Organs at Washington Cathedral" (courtesy of Barbara Owen).

[24]Glenn Dillard Gunn, *The Washington Herald,* quoted in "Builders of the Future" (name and date of source unknown), newsclipping in the scrapbook of Mabel Hastings Skinner.

[25]Ernest M. Skinner & Son Company advertisement, *The Diapason,* November 1938, p. 7.

[26]"Great Organ Opened in Capital Cathedral," *The Diapason,* December 1938, p. 1.

[27]*Washington Herald,* 11 November 1938, quoted in "Great Organ Opened in Capital Cathedral," p. 1.

[28]Ernest M. Skinner & Son Company advertisement, *The Diapason,* October 1938, p. 18.

CHAPTER 18

Problems and More Problems
1938-1941

ERNEST SKINNER'S mother, Alice, became ninety-four on 30 August 1938. By then, her correspondence with Ernest had dwindled to almost nothing.[1] A Miss Jennie Anderson was now caring for her and wrote Ernest in the summer of 1938, informing him of his mother's failing health, apparently against her wishes.[2]

Ernest sent Miss Anderson a reply on 5 July 1938, expressing his gratitude to her for informing him of his mother's condition and for caring for her. In this letter he reveals his concern for his mother's welfare and his regret that he cannot do more for her, owing to the distance between them. She had been living in Pasadena, California, for twenty-five years. Along with the letter to Miss Anderson, Ernest enclosed a brief note to his mother plus her monthly support check.

By mid-September of 1938 his mother's condition apparently had further deteriorated, as evidenced by this letter to Ernest written by Miss Anderson on 15 September 1938:

> Dear Mr. Skinner:—
> I am sorry to have to write for the check. Please send in my name for your mother can not endorse it any longer. Am sure you do not realize her condition for now it is almost impossible to reason with her for the mind is weak and unbalanced. Her first impulse is to rebel against any thing like dressing, undressing, a bath or going to bed or almost any thing you want her to do and she has to be cared for as a very small child is and I have to know when and what her needs are night and day.
> She likes and eats her usual meals without any objections so far.

A month later, on 15 October 1938, Ernest's mother died in the night.³ It was really a blessing, since she was no longer completely in her right mind nor able to care for herself. It also must have been somewhat of a relief to Ernest, who had been supporting his mother and her fanatical religious interests for many years. Characteristically, in a letter dated 14 November 1938, Ernest tells Miss Anderson that she may "keep such of *[his]* mother's effects as *[she would]* care for," in repayment for looking after her during her last months.

The following spring Ernest's former financial benefactor, Arthur Hudson Marks, died suddenly at the age of sixty-five, after having been retired from Aeolian-Skinner as president for a very brief time.⁴ A year later, on 2 April 1940, at a meeting held at the factory in Boston, the stockholders elected G. Donald Harrison president of the Aeolian-Skinner Organ Company.⁵

Meanwhile, the classic ideal as exemplified by the organs built by Harrison since 1931 was rapidly gaining general acceptance among organists, leaving Ernest Skinner, a highly progressive individual in his own generation, to be considered a reactionary in a world of rapidly changing ideas and tastes. By 1940 Ernest was engaged in a controversy with an ardent classic organ advocate by the name of William King Covell in the editorial columns of *The Diapason,* with Ernest still staunchly defending the use of orchestral imitative voices in the organ.

Although Ernest seemed more than a trifle dogmatic in his opinions to the young "purists," he was not totally unwilling to meet the changing tastes of the times at least part way. Every organ of his design, from his earliest years as an organ builder until the 1940s, bore the unmistakable imprint of his personality.

There was, however, a very pronounced difference in the tonal character of his instruments built during the 30s and 40s over what it was until the 1920s. In a testimonial written in early 1942 by William Anderson, organist and choirmaster of St. John's Episcopal Church, Stamford, Connecticut, we read:

> Recently you completed some changes in our organ which you built for us in 1918. It is surprising how little you found it necessary to do in order to raise the brilliance. Rightly, a start was made with the pedal organ in making it more definite through the addition of metal Diapasons, 16', 8' and 4'. Also an 8' Tuba, 4' Clarion, crowned by a glorious 5-rank Mixture.
>
> On the Swell manual more "bite" was achieved by adding a second 4' Principal and 4' Clarion. With the revoicing of the Cornopean into a keen Trumpet and the addition of a fine four-rank Mixture, an amazing change was wrought. It is no longer necessary to use the

Coupler Sw. to Gt. 4' in order to get brilliance. The delightful Mixture of the Swell is not only telling in full organ, but is so beautifully voiced that it can be used in many ingenious ways with the softer stops, particularly the Oboe. You have obviously enhanced the character of Mixture work in consonance with other tonal developments.

Observing this work with us has given me an insight into the new instruments you are now building and how you have adapted your art to present-day demands. These are: more definite pedal, lighter quality Diapasons, greater prominence to 4' tone, more brilliant reeds and transparent Mixtures on all manuals and pedal.[6]

For this reason, even in the midst of a classic revival which denounced orchestral color in organs as unnecessary, Ernest still had a substantial number of friends and admirers. Following the completion of his magnum opus, at Washington National Cathedral, Ernest had no shortage of customers.

In 1939 the Ernest M. Skinner & Son Company relocated the existing four-manual Skinner in the Cathedral of St. John the Divine, installing a temporary organ to serve while the main organ was being moved.[7] Also that year the organ at St. George's School, Newport, Rhode Island, was rebuilt with additions by the firm.[8]

Work for 1940 included rebuilding and adding to the organ in St. Paul's Church, Albany, New York; a new three-manual instrument for Seventh United Presbyterian Church, Philadelphia; completion of the enlargement and rebuilding of the four-manual Skinner at Brick Presbyterian Church, New York City; and tower chimes and a new four-manual, seventy-two rank organ for First Baptist Church, Jackson, Mississippi. The Jackson organ, considered to be "one of the oustanding organs of the South," was dedicated in concert on 26 November 1940.[9] According to the January 1941 issue of *The Diapason*, "the governor of Mississippi and his wife were among the 2,000 who heard the recital," which was played by Thomas H. Webber of Memphis, Tennessee. Mr. Webber, a friend of Ernest Skinner, was organist at Idlewild Presbyterian Church in Memphis.[10]

On 10 December 1940, the dedication recital for the rebuilt and enlarged Skinner organ, now relocated in the new building of Brick Presbyterian Church at Park Avenue and Ninety-first Street, New York City, was played by Dr. Clarence Dickinson.[11] The January 1941 issue of *The Diapason* remarked that the full organ of this instrument was "brilliant and clear, each tonal family and section blending as it did in the finest organs of fifty years ago."

An advertisement for the Ernest M. Skinner & Son Company,

appearing in the March 1941 issue of *The Diapason* stated: "The Original Skinner Quality Still in Demand!" This was followed by a list of "recent installations and work in process." According to this list, the firm had fourteen jobs under way. These ranged from minor additions for existing organs to a new organ of four manuals.

The most significant work done by Ernest Skinner during 1941 was the installation of a new four-manual instrument in St. Martin's Church, New York City, and the rebuilding of the organ at First Methodist Church, Wilkes-Barre, Pennsylvania. The St. Martin's Church Skinner was dedicated in recital on 27 April 1941 "before a congregation of more than 2,000 people."[12] The First Methodist Church, Wilkes-Barre rebuild, dedicated on 26 February 1942, involved the installation of a new four-manual console, new reservoirs, and extensive tonal revisions and additions.[13]

One 1941 installation, that of an organ built for St. John's Church, Washington, D.C., proved to be a rather bad experience for Ernest Skinner. This instrument was to be a "baroque" organ with tin pipes, cone tuning (which Ernest had abandoned by then), low wind pressures, and slider chests. According to one account, Ernest signed the contract without reading the fine print. He tried to back out when he discovered that he would have to build a classically voiced instrument on low wind pressures. However, the church insisted that Ernest go through with it, and the result apparently was not very successful. William Deveau, who worked with Ernest on this installation, recalls that it was a "nightmare." The windchests (which had been bought second-hand by the organist at St. John's Church) leaked, causing runs between channels. Ernest refused to have his name put on this instrument.[14]

The difficulties encountered by Ernest Skinner on the St. John's installation were not the only problems which beseiged him. An unidentified newsclipping from the year 1940 reported:

> Officials of the Skinner Organ factory on Broadway *[in Methuen]* complained to police Monday evening that boys are stealing excelsior and wood from storage sheds, and setting fires in a field adjacent to ... Serlo organ hall.

In December of 1940, on his way home from the dedication of the big organ recently installed in First Baptist Church, Jackson, Mississippi, Ernest Skinner and his friend Ernest Douglas were involved in a serious automobile accident. This account of the accident appeared in the January 1941 issue of *The Diapason:*

Ernest M. Skinner, the organ builder, and Ernest Douglas, prominent American organist, whose home is in Los Angeles, were severely injured in an automobile accident in Connecticut in December. For a time it was not expected that Mr. Douglas would recover, but latest reports indicate that he is making good progress and is believed to be out of danger. Mr. Skinner was less critically injured, but is still confined to his home. He expects to be back at his factory in Methuen, Mass., after the holidays.

Mr. Skinner and Mr. Douglas were returning from Jackson, Miss., where they had gone for the dedication of the large four-manual organ which Mr. Skinner had just finished installing in the First Baptist Church. About twelve miles east of New Haven, Conn., in a driving snowstorm which made the roads very slippery, a bus skidded into Mr. Skinner's car head-on. Mr. Douglas suffered a brain concussion, a broken leg, a broken hip, a broken nose, a broken wrist and internal injuries. Mr. Skinner's injuries consisted of a broken bone in his right foot, badly bruised knees and lacerations on the forehead.

The car was demolished and it seemed almost a miracle that anyone could come out of the wreck alive.

By February of 1941 *The Diapason* reported that Mr. Douglas was "making rapid strides toward recovery," and was expected to "be able to leave the hospital in about three weeks." It also stated that Mr. Skinner was "back at his factory in Methuen, Mass., and suffered no permanent injuries in the accident."

Debt also continued to plague Ernest. He was such a perfectionist that he would go so far as to throw out an entire rank of pipes and start all over again if not completely satisfied with them. Bill Deveau could recall Ernest sending one set of pipes back to the melting pot not once, but two or three times! Because of this passion for perfection, Ernest was still unable to make ends meet, in spite of the many new contracts he had received over the preceding few years. By mid-1941 the money situation was so bad that he was forced to beg for financial assistance. On 26 September 1941 Ernest wrote a long letter to Mr. W. K. Kellogg, beginning it with this statement:

> I am writing you this letter in the belief that you are interested in the organ generally. I would not write you as I am going to for purely personal reasons.

Ernest continues with four paragraphs summarizing the history, problems, and accomplishments of his career as an organ builder, following these with a bid for much needed financial help:

Problems and More Problems (1938-1941) 195

I am loaded to the hilt with business but my capital is too small. I have also been working in my spare time on a book which I am calling the Composition of the Organ—the same being an attempt to crystalize my developments so that they will not be lost to future generations. My son is with me and he inherits his father's love for the work, but the going is very difficult with insufficient capital. I have a man who wants to come in with me who would normally have about $20,000. available but his money is in Canada and can not be had at present, so my only alternative is in writing a man like yourself whom I regard as having an interest in the work outside of a speculative one. I don't suppose anything I am suggesting would be of sufficient magnitude to interest you in a purely commercial way.

If I could sell $10,000. worth of stock I would have all I need to carry on to good advantage. I could easily pay an 8% dividend. I am not only writing to you but am writing to one for whom I built an organ in Winston-Salem who is a large figure in the tobacco world. I am also writing to another man in Memphis, Tenn.

I am still active and in perfect health. If it occurs to you that I may be too far along in years to be very active, I have to say that in the last twenty-nine months I have traveled 125,000 miles in my automobile. I do all my traveling by auto, which I could not do if I was in a condition of instability as regards my health.

If you could buy as much as $3,000. worth of stock it would be an enormous help to me and when the war is over and my friend comes in with his $20,000., I will be able to pay it back if you so desire. I suppose it would be trite to say that I would greatly appreciate anything you are willing to do in the direction I suggest, but such is the case nevertheless. Every particle of machinery in the plant is paid for. I have a crew of first-class men who are very loyal to me and my kind of work. My only handicap is insufficient capital which the Aeolian-Skinner Company helped to bring about as far as they could.[15]

Ernest's eloquent plea for help was to no avail, as evidenced by the following letter, dated 29 September 1941, from Mr. Kellogg:

Dear Mr. Skinner:
 I have yours of September 26th.
 It seems too bad that a man of your experience and ability should have been crowded out of the old company. Several years ago I suspected that something was happening to you but I did not know exactly what it was.
 With reference to an investment or financial help, I haved retired from business activities and resigned as Chairman of the Board of the Kellogg Company some time ago. I have had wretched health for several years, although just at the present time I am feeling better.

> After four operations I lost the sight of one eye and have a cataract on the other. When away from home I am accompanied by a nurse. Some years ago I gave to the W. K. Kellogg Foundation more than 90% of my estate. No strings of any sort were tied to the contribution and I receive no benefits of any sort from the Foundation. I have rounded up my business affairs and have things in shape for the inevitable. Under the circumstances I do not think that it would be wise for me to make such an investment as proposed.
> Very truly yours,
> (signed) W. K. Kellogg[16]

In the midst of these problems, Ernest Skinner saw the culmination of his entire career as an organ builder with the dedication of his masterpiece, the Great Organ at Washington National Cathedral. Two and one half years later, in June of 1941, at an A.G.O. national convention in Washington, D.C., Ernest was to have the ultimate musical experience of his entire life. In *The Diapason* (November 1944) Ernest writes:

> The culminating point in my recital experience was at a Guild convention in Washington, D.C., where Catharine Crozier played the Sowerby Symphony on the organ in the National Cathedral. There were 600 members of the A.G.O. present, who sat in the great choir. The friends around me at that moment were practically speechless. I have never in my life seen an audience more profoundly moved than at the conclusion of this recital.

We learn more details of this musical event in a review which appeared in the July 1941 issue of *The Diapason:*

> The afternoon recital was one of those events which will stand out as a high point in the history of conventions of organists. Miss Catherine Crozier of Rochester, N.Y., was at the console of the great new organ in the Washington Cathedral, built by Ernest M. Skinner & Son. Miss Crozier, the only woman recitalist of the 1941 convention, gave a performance that aroused enthusiasm. Though young in years, she has attained a place in the front rank for her generation— a budding generation that has produced much prodigious talent in the form of virtuoso players. The new organ is an outstanding instrument and ranks as one of the great works of a noted figure in American organ construction and design of this age . . .
> The program was right up *[to]* the minute—Sowerby's Symphony in G major, a work of colossal proportions and in all its three movements a fine example of what our moderns are producing today;

the Pastorale of Roger-Ducasse, and Karg-Elert's Symphonic Chorale, "Ach bleib' mit Deiner Gnade." Miss Crozier played with the authority and punch of a veteran recitalist and with meticulous perfection of detail. In the Sowerby work she overcame all the technical difficulties without a quiver and Karg-Elert's impressive work, based on one of the most beautiful of the German chorales, was tastefully registrated. As for the organ, its powerful but smooth ensemble and fine solo effects were equally admirable.

Shortly after this convention, on 16 July 1941, Ernest wrote Catharine Crozier:

> I had for a long time lived in the hope that I might hear a program on the great Cathedral organ entirely outside the conventional program that I have been hearing for the last fifty years. This is to say that the Sowerby Symphony brought me a full confirmation of my belief in what the great Cathedral organ was capable of.

Ernest Skinner's experience at the 1941 A.G.O. National Convention was, in a sense, a supreme reward for all the long years he had spent, not only in laboring to improve and perfect the organ as a flexible and expressive musical medium, but also in a tireless effort to bring about higher standards in organ music and its performance. To a great extent, the improved standards in the latter were an outgrowth of improvement in the former. Again, in the November 1944 issue of *The Diapason,* Ernest recalls:

> When I was a youngster recital programs consisted of such works as Batiste's Communion in G and the Thiele Variations, and when pages were turned the right hand held the final chord on the turned page and sometimes two pages were turned and one turned back in a leisurely manner, with the right hand chord sostenuto with the most matter of fact unconcern, *sans* embarrassment. There were no feminine recitalists that I can recall. The organ mechanism of that period was too tough and weighty and for the same reason there were no organ recitals remotely comparable to those of today. With the advent of the tubular action, shortly followed by the electro-pneumatic action, the perfect touch with its enormous speed and sympathetic response came into being . . .
>
> The American organist, masculine and feminine, has capitalized *[on]* the perfect mechanism of the American organ to such an extent that in my opinion he or she outclasses the foreign artists completely . . . And now that there is no factor of physical strength involved and perfection in response is present, the music possible on the modern

organ is authentically of such a character that a high-class music critic of a daily paper is moved to say that the tonal resources of a modern organ surpass those of a symphony orchestra!

Some of the improvement in the quality of organ music and of its performance can be attributed to Ernest's own continuing personal interest in the work of young composers and musicians. He was a devoted supporter of American musicians and composers. His special concern for the promotion of American composers is revealed in this quotation from an article by Helen Hulett Searl, entitled "Wizard of the Pipes," which appeared in *The Christian Science Monitor* on 5 June 1943:

> Once in San Francisco he was invited out to the Bohemian Grove to hear an opera called "Rajvara," composed by one of the members of the society, a curly-headed youth named Wheeler Beckett. Anticipating a boring evening listening to trite phrases and melodies, Mr. Skinner was thrilled by the freshness and beauty of the music. "If that man were a foreigner," he said indignantly, "he would be rated one of the foremost composers of the day. But because he is a plain American, few people have heard his lovely music." Mr. Skinner feels strongly on the preference given by Americans to foreign music and foreign performers. Not that he has any prejudice against foreign artists, but he thinks equally talented Americans should be given a fair show.

Ernest Skinner had some very definite opinions regarding the performance of organ recital music, including that of J. S. Bach. As early as 1911, long before Bach's music became popular with American organists, he had this to say about its interpretation:

> The organ has outgrown the player. Imagine a vaudeville actor trying to interpret Shakespeare and you have a picture of the average organist who attempts to play compositions of John Sebastian Bach. Bach is only begun when you have him on your fingers. His music has to be developed and colored. A great artist is needed to do him justice. The reason why he is not liked by the public is because he is so badly played. We assume that dignity and dulness are the same thing. The French organist Lemaire makes Bach the most interesting composer he puts into his programs.[17]

Many years later, in 1941, Ernest elaborates on his opinion that the rich and varied tonal resources of the modern Skinner organ will enhance the music of Bach:

> I believe Bach has more enemies posing as friends than any other composer who ever lived. He was in a ceaseless search for color. He was the first to put chimes in an organ, which he did in two instances of record. He had a 32-ft. untersatz (wood diapason) in his pedal organ. We in our day throw away magnificent examples from existing organs in our efforts to sterilize—I mean clarify—the organ. Here we are in our time with a marvelous mechanical equipment and a tonal splendor having no parallel anywhere in the world—strings, orchestral color, resonant diapasons of a richness never known before our day, a pedal foundation from the 32-ft. depth to the mixtures that put an orchestra to shame. In point of fact, no orchestra in breadth and splendor can approach the modern big organ forte.
>
> Every improvement that has been made in the organ has been fought and frowned upon. I remember that there was a kick that the keys of a coupled manual didn't drop when an electric or tubular coupler was in action. They kicked at the electric swell pedal because they loved the sympathetic response of half a cord of lumber in the swell shutters. This attitude is nothing new. Silbermann preferred the old untempered scale, which prohibited freedom in modulation and rendered certain keys useless. He violently opposed Bach's desire for the equal temperament. I am expecting any day now to hear someone come out for the unequal temperament just as Silbermann did it. The only true method of tuning! Why should the music of Bach, of all people, be denied the advantage of beautiful tone colors? . . .
>
> We say that the earlier music of the baroque period should be played upon an organ of that period. Well, there was nothing else on which to play it at that time. How would the people of the baroque period prefer to hear it if they were alive today? I state unequivocally that beauty of tone will enhance the music of *any* period . . .[18]

Still later, in the May 1946 issue of *The Diapason,* Ernest gives a specific example illustrating his idea of how Bach's contrapuntal music can be heard to best advantage by the use of orchestral color in the organ:

> The contrapuntal music of Bach is ideally suited to the modern organ, vastly more so than the organ of Bach's own time. The Bach organ was practically limited to pitch contrasts, as it was without color in the modern acceptance of the term. I suggest for those who have an organ of modern tonal resources that Bach trios and fugues be played, each voice on a separate manual, the manuals to be set up each with a single voice, as English horn, clarinet, bassoon, orchestral oboe or voix celestes and 4-ft. flute in combination. On occasion

one voice may be played by manual to pedal coupler in three-voice compositions. Expression boxes set to balance dynamics.

I believe with these modern voices, employed to give individual character to each voice, the wonderful independence of Bach contrapuntal writing would be emphasized sufficiently to excite interest on the part of the hearers who are not interested where the similarity of voice parts develops lack of understanding.

When it came right down to it, Ernest himself did not especially care for the highly academic major organ works of Bach, but personally preferred this composer's chorale preludes and other less cerebral music.[19] He believed that this "more easily understood" music of Bach should more often be played, and maintained that "mediocre organists and the dullest music of J. S. B. placed first on the program *were* directly responsible for the dislike of Bach's music by the general public." From a psychological standpoint, Ernest Skinner considered the opening number on a recital program as being the "worst possible position for *any* composition, and especially so for one by Bach."[20] Ernest explains his reasons for this opinion in the following quotation:

> A work of majestic proportions, particularly a contrapuntal work, will not "blot out the varied interests left behind." On the contrary, the varied interests left behind, together with cold feet, laying off overcoats and wraps, people coming late, opening and closing doors, and what not, will blot out said *[piece of]* "imposing majestic proportions as an opening number" about 90 per cent. Opening with a contrapuntal piece, *sans* emotional or poetic quality, will let the average audience down to a point that will take half the recital to restore, if ever . . .

In this same issue, Ernest continues with his ideas on how to make organ recitals have interest and appeal for the music-loving public who are not organists:

> My idea of a recital is that those who enter jaded may leave refreshed, and any program not built on that idea is badly arranged. I once had the running of five recitals given in Boston at the Old South Church. These were all given by outstanding organists, all of whom were glad to cooperate with my ideas as to the programs. There was a Bach number on every one, placed at the head of the second section. The programs opened with a stirring, buoyant piece, having no flavor of gloom, minor keys or extended length. Guilmant's Fugue in D major served in one instance. Will it be sufficient to say that 1,200 people attended the first recital, and 2,500 the last

one, and numbers turned away? The organ had the traditional ensemble and a good equipment of orchestral color. Yes, the programs contained transcriptions . . .[21]

Further, in the May 1946 issue of *The Diapason,* Ernest Skinner gives the program played for the dedication of his organ in the First Methodist Church, Wilkes-Barre, Pennsylvania, in February of 1942, as an illustration of the type of recital program which he found to be successful:

Concert Prelude and Fugue, Faulkes; Chorale Preludes, "From the Depths of My Heart," Karg-Elert, and "Lord, Hear the Voice of My Complaint," Bach; Toccata on "From Heaven on High," Edmunson; Elegie, Peeters; "In dulci Jubilo," Karg-Elert; "The Hen," Rameau; Largo, Handel; Etude in A minor, Chopin; Theme and Variations, Thiele; "Ave Maria," Schubert; Intermezzo, Bonnet; "The Bells of St. Anne de Beaupre," Russell; Finale, Sixth Symphony, Vierne.

Ernest continues with these comments about the above recital program sequence:

The Faulkes Concert Prelude and Fugue is ideally in the organ idiom of sustained chords, easy to listen to and in a major key. The following numbers were selected for their sequence of mood and character in the development of a musical atmosphere. The Largo and "Ave Maria" were, of course, by way of interesting those who enjoy the more familiar music. The Chopin Etude is a brilliant piano piece which is not for the limited technique. When played on a modern organ, by one with a brilliant technique, it is a marvelous exhibit of virtuosity which completely out-classes its effect as a piano piece. This Etude contributes several elements to the character of an organ recital—novelty, surprise, an exhibition of technical accomplishment and an increased respect for the artist and for the organ. The Etude should be played on a gamba celeste and 4-ft. flute or voix celeste and 4-ft. flute, both hands on the same manual, as per piano, and with an 8-ft. pizzicato pedal, coupled to manual. It makes a stimulating contrast to the preceding Handel Largo.

Organist-composer Richard Purvis tells of a personal experience illustrating Ernest Skinner's attitude toward organ registration, that is, the choice of stops for a given piece of music. Once, when Purvis was giving a recital at Washington Cathedral, Ernest drove all the way down there for no other reason than to hear his concert. While Purvis was practicing for this concert, Ernest sat next to the console telling him how to play his music (Understandably, this made Mr. Purvis rather nervous!).

Ernest told him, "The trouble with most organists is that they don't know how to *listen!*" What Ernest meant by this is that organists should use the registration that sounds right to the ear, and not try to slavishly copy registration indicated on the music, regardless of the type of organ the music is being played on. Purvis added, "Of course, he was right."[22]

In regard to the use of transcriptions for organ recitals, Ernest Skinner states:

> Early in my career as an organ builder I advocated and loved to hear transcriptions of orchestral and operatic music on the organ, not because they were transcriptions, but because they were good music.[23]

The Skinner organ, with its abundance of orchestral imitative stops, was particularly suitable for the satisfying rendition of transcriptions. So fond of orchestral transcriptions was Ernest Skinner that in 1929, when he was still with the Skinner Organ Company, he sponsored a contest offering $100 for the best organ arrangement of the "Overture" to *Prince Igor* by Borodin. Ernest intended that "the award should be made for the arrangement giving the most comprehensive and complete arrangement rather than for a simpler one which might be more suitable for a small organ." The purpose behind this contest was "to add a worthwhile piece to recital programs."[24]

In remarks appearing in the March 1942 issue of *The Diapason,* Ernest gives the following lengthy argument in support of transcriptions for the organ:

> I hear in certain orchestral works harmonies that never once in my life have I heard in "legitimate organ music"—works, for example, by Mahler, Delius, Ravel and Chopin. The only relief from a lifetime of classic platitudes that I have heard on the organ one thousand times are Karg-Elert, Sowerby, De Lamarter, Wheeler Beckett, and Vierne. Until colorful writers discover the modern organ, the only way it can sound for what it is is through transcriptions. Have you ever heard objections to transcriptions except with regard to the organ? Answer NO . . .
>
> Have you ever read the "Rubaiyat of Omar Khayyam"? Well, it was originally written in Persian. Did you read it in Persian? Well, you read and enjoyed a transcription, or translation, if you prefer. Now in a literary transcription great changes must be made. For example:

Problems and More Problems (1938-1941) 203

There was a door to which I found no Key.
There was a veil through which I might not see.
Some little talk awhile of Me and Thee.
There was—and then no more of Thee and Me.

In English "key" rhymes with "see," "thee" and "me," four words, each of which has a definite meaning. Do they rhyme in the original Persian? Definitely no. So Fitzgerald must necessarily in translation rewrite the actual sense of the lines, which he did in point of fact. This is unnecessary in a musical transcription. Music is just as definitely a language as the spoken word and may be translated from one language to another with perfect justice to its meaning. The Bible, originally in Hebrew, has been translated into many languages, but the cult who hates the public and would make a golden calf of the organ says "no" to transcriptions. Why not be logical and object to translations?

Musical compositions in large form frequently appear arranged for piano, as, for example, I have a piano score of Richard Strauss' "Rosenkavalier," an opera of brilliant and sparkling orchestral character, transcribed for piano. A modern organ would interpret most of this score in wonderful fashion. Strauss' "Death and Transfiguration" and "Till Eulenspiegel" are arranged for organ and can be performed effectively on a modern organ. They cannot be heard otherwise more than once or twice in a lifetime by the average music-lover.

It is a very good idea to have a wholesome respect for the organ, but when such respect works to make the king of instruments an insufferable bore and to drive people away from it, we must transcribe respect into some other term.

If you say Strauss' "Don Quixote" is not church music, it may also be said: Neither is Bach's "Fuge a la Gigue" or the G minor Fugue. They are both recital music. The recital is not an exhibit of the organ; it is an entertainment, and its first objective should be entertainment, and a 100 per cent regard for the audience.

Ernest continues this argument, with a somewhat different approach, in a letter written to Catharine Crozier about 1943:

A musical composition is a picture: an idea, an inspiration. The basic character of the picture is present, however it is done. An orchestra does it in one way, a Skinner organ in another. It is not necessary for either one to try to imitate the other. The sermon on the mount can be spoken in any language.

Supposing you were present at a recital and heard something entirely new, that you were extremely excited about and went out and bought it and added it to your programs. Would it spoil it for you to learn later that it was a transcription?

There is comparatively little literature for the modern organ. You know to be classical you must play the old music as it was played on the old organs for which it was written. If you play it on the modern organ and employ the modern resources of the present day organs you are transcribing it for the modern organ. There is to me more difference between the Bach organ and the Washington cathedral organ than there is between the orchestra and the Skinner organ . . .

Now you are missing one great fundamental which is often overlooked except by me. i.e. how many people attending the average organ recital ever hear an orchestra? And is it not true therefore that some beautiful music is never heard if not heard on the organ, if written for orchestra? How about that? Do you ever play Handel's Largo? An operatic piece. Well some others will be accepted too if given opportunity. A painting is a transcription, as is a statue. You accept them without question. Why the inhibitions against the most authentic of all the arts. A picture, a statue, represent something else. Music is not only the thing itself but intensifies our appreciation of everything.[25]

In the 5 June 1943 *Christian Science Monitor,* Helen Hulett Searl writes:

Not a musician in the sense of being a composer or performer, Mr. Skinner has a consuming love of music and will go back again and again to hear some particular bit that pleases him. He went to every performance of "Jack and the Beanstalk," given by the Juilliard School of Music, because he so enjoyed a waltz number played by a student pianist.

Miss Searl also remarks that Ernest Skinner, who by this time was in his mid-seventies, "still thinks nothing of traveling several hundred miles to hear good music," and quotes him as saying that his "whole life has been given up to music."[26]

Ernest's love of music was the motivating force behind his lifelong efforts to improve the organ and its literature. Moreover, for him, music was a necessity of life. Ned Gammons relates it in these words:

If you take it and put it into one phrase . . . and I'll quote this from Dr. *[Archibald T.]* Davison—he said, "He suffered from an unrequited love of music." He just never could have enough. Now, this is what Ernest really meant.

Mr. Gammons recalls one of the more humorous manifestations of Ernest's unrequited love:

... even in that car of his ... he always had a portable phonograph in it ... I'd be riding with him in that big Lincoln and he'd be going about fifty miles an hour, and he'd have something going on—it might be an overture or something—it was a regular wind-up phonograph. But, you know, he'd almost drive somebody off the road *[while he was changing records]* and he'd yell out, "Come on, you G -d rummy, you!"[27]

By now Ernest's musical gadgetry included a 1940 vintage disc recorder. He also had a "sizeable record collection" which, according to his nephew Ned Hastings, "was surprisingly catholic but showed his great favorites clearly." In a letter written to the author on 10 July 1972, Mr. Hastings recalls:

I think he bought every record of Richard Strauss that came out in the 78-rpm days. *Salome* and *Rosenkavalier* were his special favorites. He loved Wagner and owned a great deal of that. Among the favorites of his later years were Wolf-Ferrari's *Serenade for Strings* and Mahler's *Fourth*. Not too long before his death he acquired Mahler's *Ninth* also. At the other end of the scale, he loved Gilbert and Sullivan and owned all the original D'Oyly Carte recordings.

Ernest was so captivated by the beauty of Mahler's Fourth Symphony that, in the July 1946 issue of *The Diapason,* he had the following comments in one of his ads:

Instead of a usual word with respect to the Skinner organ in this issue of The Diapason, I want to suggest to lovers of recorded music Mahler's Fourth Symphony, issued by the Columbia Recording Corporation.

The vocal part at the conclusion of this symphony contributes to its unusual beauty.

The Columbia Record Company was so pleased with Ernest's unsolicited praise of their new recording of Mahler's Fourth Symphony that they sent him a free record of Mahler's Fifth Symphony, recorded by the same conductor, with the hope that he would also give it some free advertising. He played the record once and did not like it—much to the disappointment of Columbia records![28]

We learn a little more about Ernest's musical preferences in another letter written by Ned Hastings to Joseph Dzeda on 15 July 1965:

His musical tastes were primarily romantic, as one might guess from his organs. His greatest loves were Richard Strauss *(Salome* in particular) and Wagner, especially *Parsifal*. He could find nothing of interest in Beethoven or Mozart, but liked a good deal of Brahms and was devoted to Mahler . . . One of his great loves was a cantata by Wolf-Ferrari entitled *La Vita Nuova*. He spent a good deal of time trying to interest Charles Munch in doing it with the BSO. Other favorite works were Loeffler's *Pagan Poem* and *Partita for Violin and Piano*, various compositions by Holst, and the Scarlatti-Tommasini *Good Humored Ladies* ballet score.

Even though he did not care much for the music of Beethoven, Ernest did own a recording of one work by that composer, a bassoon concerto. He bought it for the simple reason that he liked the bassoon.[29]

Ernest had recordings of Elgar's *Dream of Gerontius* and considered it to be "the best thing that has come out of England, musically speaking."[30] He liked the "impressionism of Delius."[31] He was also fond of the music of Debussy. Ned Hastings writes:

> Among his records which I now have are 78's of *Pelleas and Melisande* and an early LP of Sayao doing *The Blessed Damoiselle* with the Philadelphia Orchestra and Ormandy. He had obviously played the latter a lot for it is horribly scratched.[32]

As evidenced by his writings, Ernest had very definite preferences when it came to music written for the organ. Returning to Ned Hastings's letter of 10 July 1972, we read:

> As for organ composers, he loved the Romantics—Karg-Elert, Vierne, early Dupre, the Purvis chorale preludes on Protestant hymn tunes. He also admired much of Bach—though not the trio Sonatas which he disliked intensely. The Fugue a la Gigue was one of his pets; also the O God, Be Merciful chorale prelude with the broken-chord accompaniment. One of his great pets—and now one of mine—was the almost totally unknown Concert Prelude and Fugue in G by William Faulkes . . . Ernest particularly treasured the Karg-Elert Fugue, Kanzone, and Epilogue for organ, violin, and ladies' voices. He was constantly trying to get organists interested in this lovely piece.

A number of organ compositions were dedicated to Ernest Skinner. Among these, Ernest's favorites were Vierne's "Clair de Lune," from Pieces de Fantasie; Karg-Elert's "Partita Retrospettiva"; and Ned Hastings' "Noel in Olden Style." Regarding the third of these, Ned says, "I rather think that his fondness for the latter was based on family grounds, for it is an imitation of d'Aquin and is definitely *not* romantic."[33]

FOOTNOTES

[1] Ernest M. Skinner, Letter to Alice F. Skinner, 5 July 1938 (courtesy of Henry Karl Baker).

[2] Ernest M. Skinner, Letter to Miss Jennie Anderson, 5 July 1938 (courtesy of Henry Karl Baker).

[3] "Alice F. Skinner, Church Founder, dies at 94" (name and date of source unknown), newsclipping in the scrapbook of Mabel Hastings Skinner.

[4] "Arthur Hudson Marks Taken Off Suddenly," *The Diapason,* June 1939, p. 1.

[5] "G. Donald Harrison Heads Organ Concern," *The Diapason,* May 1940, p. 1.

[6] William Anderson, Testimonial written in early 1942, quoted in Ernest M. Skinner & Son Company advertisement, *The Diapason,* March 1942, p. 15.

[7] Personal interview with William Deveau, 3 May 1973; Ernest M. Skinner & Son Company advertisement, *The Diapason,* December 1940, p. 17.

[8] Ernest M. Skinner, "The Slider Chest," *The American Organist,* 22, no. 6 (1939), p. 205.

[9] Ernest M. Skinner & Son Company advertisement, *The Diapason,* September 1940, p. 13; Ernest M. Skinner & Son Company advertisement, *The Diapason,* March 1941, p. 15; "Large Organ is Dedicated in Jackson, Miss. Church," *The Diapason,* January 1941, p. 2; "Dickinson Opens New Brick Church's Organ," *The Diapason,* January 1941, p. 4; "Large Four-Manual for Jackson, Miss.," *The Diapason,* February 1940, p. 2.

[10] Personal interview with Edward H. Hastings, 12 October 1972.

[11] "Brick Church's Organ," p. 4.

[12] "Four-Manual Placed in St. Martin's New York," *The Diapason,* June 1941, p. 4.

[13] First Methodist Church, Wilkes-Barre, Pa., Organ Dedication Recital Program, 26 February 1942 (courtesy of Barbara Owen); "Wilkes-Barre Organ Will Be Remodeled," *The Diapason,* March 1941, p. 1.

[14] Personal interview with William Deveau, 3 May 1973; Personal interview with Robert Hawksley, 14 January 1972.

[15] Ernest M. Skinner, Letter to W. K. Kellogg, 26 September 1941 (courtesy of Henry Karl Baker).

[16] W. K. Kellogg, Letter to Ernest M. Skinner, 29 September 1941 (courtesy of Henry Karl Baker).

[17] "Organ Builder and Player Meet," *The Christian Science Monitor,* 1 August 1911, p. 5.

[18] Ernest M. Skinner, "Modern Organ Ahead as Compared with Old," *The Diapason,* November 1941, p. 22.

[19] Ernest M. Skinner, "Programs That Will Not Bore," *The Diapason,* February 1933, p. 17.

[20] Ernest M. Skinner, "Recitals That Will Make Organ Popular," *The Diapason,* February 1946, p. 30.

[21] Skinner, "Programs," p. 17.

[22] Personal interview with Richard Purvis, 6 October 1974.

[23] Skinner, "Recitals," p. 30.

[24] Ernest M. Skinner, "Details of Mr. Skinner's Offer," *The Diapason,* October 1929, p. 31.

[25] Ernest M. Skinner, Letter to Catharine Crozier, undated (courtesy of Harold Gleason).

[26] Helen Hewlett Searl, "Wizard of the Pipes," *The Christian Science Monitor,* 5 June 1943, pp. 6 & 14.

[27] Personal interview with Edward B. Gammons, 3 May 1976.

[28] Personal interview with Edward H. Hastings, 12 October 1972.

[29] Personal interview with Edward H. Hastings, 12 October 1972.

[30] Ernest M. Skinner, Letter to Charlotte Lockwood, 27 September 1932 (courtesy of Henry Karl Baker).

[31] Skinner, "Programs," p. 17.

[32] Ned Hastings, Letter to author, received 2 June 1975.

[33] Edward H. Hastings, Letter to Joseph Dzeda, 15 July 1965.

CHAPTER 19

World War II: The Fire And After, 1941-1947

BY 1941 WORLD WAR II had been raging on in Europe for two years. The United States, not yet directly involved in the war, had meanwhile become a refuge for the many immigrants who fled from the tyranny of Nazism. Among those refugees was Ernest Skinner's old friend Joseph Bonnet who, along with his family, came to America in 1940 after being "virtually driven from his native land by the invading forces of Hitler..."[1] Also among those who were driven to the shores of this country by the Nazis was Albert Einstein, who left Germany shortly after the establishment of the Hitler regime in 1933. As well as being a brilliant physicist, Einstein also loved music and played the violin and the piano.[2] He was a professor at Princeton University, where one of Ernest Skinner's more important instruments had been installed in the late 1920s, and it was inevitable that these two great men should eventually meet. Ernest became acquainted with Einstein at a recital given by Charles Courboin in the Princeton Chapel and "was introduced to him at that time by Mrs. Grover Cleveland who changed seats along with several others in order to hear better."[3]

Whereas Einstein was a scientist whose hobby was music, Ernest, whose vocation was intimately concerned with music, had an interest in the physical sciences. One of Ernest's pet theories along this line had to do with the reason the needle of a compass always points North. He attributed the phenomenon to "static electricity developed by wind friction *[polarizing]* the earth..."[4] Ernest and Einstein, at one point, had a lengthy correspondence over this theory.[5]

The United States entered World War II in December of 1941, after the Japanese surprise attack on Pearl Harbor. By July of 1942 the organ building industry, which only in recent years had begun to recover from the great 1930s depression, was ordered by the U.S. Government to convert to defense work.[6] Richmond Skinner tells how the Ernest M. Skinner & Son Organ Company was affected by World War II:

> In 1941, at least in the early part of '42, the government said no more organs may be built. They used nothing but critical materials. The zinc and the tin and the lead and all those things were needed in the war. The only thing allowed was rebuilding organs. At that moment, the government sent me an invitation to become an officer in chemical warfare service. And my father and I talked it over, and we decided that would be the better thing for me to do during the restricted period . . .
> I tried to get some military work for our factory in Methuen, but I didn't know the red tape necessary, at that time, to get to the right person . . . So, we never got any work that way. That's why I went in the Army.[7]

In the meantime, organ builders were allowed critical materials to finish contracts signed prior to U.S. involvement in the war and to take care of repair and maintenance jobs while plans for converting the industry to defense work were being formed.[8]

During the spring of 1942 Ernest Skinner completed the installation of a large and complete Solo division built for the organ at the John Hayes Hammond Museum in Gloucester, Massachusetts. This new division consisted of seventeen stops and included a Kleine Erzähler and Kleine Erzähler Celeste and a four rank Cornet, in addition to the more usual Skinner Solo stops. Ernest also made some of the Great Diapasons for this instrument. The John Hayes Hammond Museum organ, which was designed for the "rendition of classical organ music and the performance of orchestral transcriptions," was the brain child of the inventor, John Hayes Hammond, and had been under construction for over twenty years.[9] Mr. Hammond (who, incidentally, had no connection with the Hammond electronic organ) and Ernest Skinner were friends and had much in common. Both men were inventors, and Mr. Hammond, who was very much in favor of including orchestral imitative stops in the organ along with the more traditional voices, had devised his own sophisticated mechanism for orchestrating transcriptions on organ rolls.

In that same year, a small two-manual Skinner organ was installed in St. Peter's Episcopal Church, Beverly, Massachusetts. This was the last completely new instrument to be built by the Ernest M. Skinner & Son Organ Company of Metheun, Massachusetts.[10]

In April of 1942 *The Diapason* announced,

> The Ernest M. Skinner & Son Company has been commissioned to make extensive additions to the organ in the historic Bruton Parish Church, Williamsburg, Va., the restored eighteenth century capitol of the old Virginia colony. At the same time the instrument has been redesigned according to plans made in consultation with Dr. David McK. Williams of St. Bartholemew's Church, New York, and Mrs. Iona Burrows Jones, organist of the Bruton Parish Church. The three-manual of twenty-five speaking stops is being enlarged into one of some forty ranks of pipes. The Samuel Green eighteenth century organ, which is playable from the console of the modern instrument, will be kept intact.[11]

The acquisition of the Bruton Parish Church contract must have provided Ernest Skinner with an extra measure of satisfaction, for the instrument which he was to redesign and enlarge had been rebuilt and enlarged by G. Donald Harrison only a few years earlier.[12] However, any sense of triumph he felt over this fact was to be shortlived. He began the work at Bruton Parish Church on 6 August 1942. Two months later, on 1 October of that year, he went bankrupt. The Bruton Parish Church rebuild was completed by Ernest Skinner in March of 1943, with the total payments for work done running about $5,500 over the original contracted price of $11,130.00, the insurance company paying the bill after the bankruptcy.

According to William Francis Vollmer, who assumed the post of organist at Bruton Parish Church in January of 1944, the year after the rebuild was completed,

> The wonderful gent, Ernest M., was caught up with the circumstances of the times; namely the war years and its inflationary period. He was also over extended in work commitments . . .[14]

Mr. I. L. Jones, who was treasurer of Bruton Parish Church at the time of the Skinner bankruptcy, provides us with some revealing comments about the character of Ernest Skinner and the unfortunate situation which led to his bankruptcy:

> Mr. Skinner was a very fine man as well as *the best organ man in the country* at that time. He also was the rare person who *considered*

> *quality of the work performed above financial considerations* which is probably *why he went bankrupt.* We are sure that our job did *not* put him [into] bankruptcy rather he admitted that he had had higher costs than the contract prices on ours and a number of jobs before ours. He therefore used the first $5,500. that we paid him to finish up a prior job (as he had done for the job before that and the one before that.) He might have gotten jobs after ours and used the down payment money to finish up our job but the war was now on and he apparently could not get any more jobs at that time. He was honest in every way except that his costs overextended his contract prices, costs were rising because of war time inflation and scarcities and they overwhelmed him. He was the only one we could find to do a quality job such as ours was on an old organ.[15]

It would appear that during these difficult war years Ernest supplemented his perpetually inadequate income by doing such things as giving lectures. This was evidenced by an item in *The American Organist* (25, no. 8, August 1942, 231), which announced that, among the courses offered for the coming fall season by the Guilmant Organ School in New York City, Ernest M. Skinner was to lecture on *The Physical Properties of Pipes*.

On 11 October 1942, shortly after Ernest went bankrupt, he received a letter from his good friend Ernest Douglas, who wrote:

> Dear Ernest; I was pleased to hear from you once more, but sorry to learn that the business is so rotten . . .
> Why not come out there and do repair work? Stanley and his two helpers are so busy that they can't take care of my organs; there is lacking men who know the business . . .
> Why not think of bringing Mrs. Skinner West and start again?

Ernest did not take his friend's suggestion to re-establish in California as an organ maintenance man, and it was unfortunate that he did not do so. He might have thus escaped the calamity that, within a year, was to befall the Ernest M. Skinner & Son Organ Company.

Shortly after Ernest went bankrupt in 1942, the Essex Savings Bank, which held the mortgage for Serlo Hall and the organ factory, took over that property.[16] On 17 June 1943, Ernest Skinner's Methuen factory burned to the ground. A report of the fire appeared in the July 1943 issue of *The Diapason:*

> The factory operated by the Ernest M. Skinner & Son Company in Methuen, Mass., for a number of years, was destroyed by fire June

> 17. The origin of the spectacular blaze has not been established. The three-story wooden structure was razed, only the frame front remaining.
>
> Serlo Organ Hall, adjacent to the factory and nationally famous because it houses the great organ that originally stood in the Boston Music Hall, being later acquired by Ernest M. Skinner, was saved from the flames by a fire wall . . .

The loss of his factory in Methuen was a severe blow to Ernest Skinner, but it did not hold him down for long. Soon afterwards he acquired a shop on the third floor of the Lyceum Building in Reading, Massachusetts.[17] From this shop at 199 Haven Street, Ernest and the four workers who remained with him during the war kept the business going by rebuilding organs. Meanwhile, his son Richmond was "writing home from the Philippines since the invasion of Leyte where he was one of the first men ashore."[18]

In 1944 Ernest went to Grace Covenant Presbyterian Church in Richmond, Virginia, to make repairs on an organ he had installed there many years before. This instrument had been damaged by water due to leaks in the roof. A report of his work at Grace Covenant Church, appearing in the *Richmond News Leader* of 27 November 1944, had this poetic description of the veteran organ builder, who was now seventy-eight years old:

> He sat there in the fused light from the stained-glass windows, fingering the organ keys, his white hair, like fine silk, falling on his neck. A modern composition of Haydn in a European cathedral was Ernest Skinner, master organ builder, sitting at the console which bears his name in the Grace Covenant Church.

In "Wizard of the Pipes," *(The Christian Science Monitor,* 5 June 1943), Helen Hulett Searl comments:

> . . . Ernest M. Skinner reminds you somewhat of Lloyd George in looks. His blue eyes, sharp and lively, reflect the indomitable spirit that would fight any day in defense of his ideas.

Ernest particularly liked the profile photo of himself which appeared with the above article because in it he did indeed resemble the British statesman, Lloyd George. According to his daughter Eugenia, he was quite proud of the fact.

Miss Searl's article in *The Christian Science Monitor* was a highly complimentary biographical sketch of Ernest Skinner. Three years later, after the war was over, Ernest offered the Mother Church in Boston a gift of one of his Flute Celeste stops out of gratitude for this article. His gift was graciously accepted by the church and acknowledged with this warm letter, dated 26 March 1946, from the Corresponding Secretary of the Christian Science Board of Directors at the First Church of Christ, Scientist, Boston, Massachusetts:

> Dear Mr. Skinner:
> Mrs. Ruth Barrett Arno has informed us of your offer of a Flute Celeste organ stop, to be added to the organ in The Mother Church. We are pleased to accept your gift and do so with much appreciation.
> Accomplishments such as yours are welcome subjects for articles in The Christian Science Monitor, and the one which appeared in the Magazine Section about you and your work was widely read and appreciated.
> Please be assured of our kindest regards.
> Sincerely yours,
> THE CHRISTIAN SCIENCE BOARD OF DIRECTORS
> (signed) Rose V. Sweetland

In 1945 Ernest Skinner was engaged to rebuild his famous instrument at St. Thomas Church, New York City. Fairly extensive tonal changes were included in the revised tonal scheme which was drawn up by Dr. T. Frederick H. Candlyn, successor to Dr. T. Tertius Noble as organist and choirmaster at St. Thomas Church.[19] The July 1945 issue of *The Diapason* announced these proposed tonal changes:

> The great trumpet and clarion are to be revoiced on Willis lines. A new mixture will be added and the twelfth will be changed to a two-rank mixture. The wald flöte is exchanged for a principal, 4 ft., and a new flute, 8 ft., will replace the present flute. A gemshorn, 8 ft., will be installed in place of the philomela. On the swell the double trumpet and clarion will be revoiced as Cavaillé-Coll reeds, the oboe will be replaced by a flügel horn from the solo and the claribel flute, 8 ft., will be replaced by a geigen, 4 ft.
> The whole choir will be increased in tone and two mutation stops (tierce and septieme) will be added. The piccolo will become a nazard.
> On the solo a new enclosed orchestral trumpet will be added. The fagotto, 16 ft., will be made available on the pedal and revoiced. Two flutes of 8-ft. pitch on the echo organ will be exchanged for a diapason, 8 ft., and a principal, 4 ft., in order to support congregational singing.
> The pedal bourdon is eliminated in favor of a gemshorn, playable at 16, 8 and 4 ft., while the great diapason 16 ft., is to be made available on the pedal at 16 and 8 ft.

A number of mechanical improvements in the console were also listed in the above announcement.

In addition to rebuilding organs Ernest had another interesting project under way during the war years. With the assistance of Carl Bassett, one of the few men who were working with him at this time, Ernest Skinner developed an instrument called the Clinic Organ. We find this description of the Clinic Organ in an advertisement appearing in the February 1946 issue of *The Diapason:*

> This organ is for hospital use. It is portable, being supported on casters. It has a 42-note keyboard weighing less than ten pounds and connected by 20 feet of flexible cable, thereby permitting a patient to play it while in a recumbent position. This organ can be moved comfortably through a six-foot door. Its two ranks of pipes are commonly known as the Kleiner Erzähler.

According to Carl Bassett, the Erzähler and Erzähler Celeste were enclosed in a glass box. A button, or lever, under the keyboard (which had adjustable touch) provided control of expression by opening and closing the lid, or top, of the glass box.[20]

One of these Clinic Organs was especially designed and built for use at Walter Reed Hospital during World War II.[21] Another was "being used by Musical Guidance in Boston, under the direction of E. Flagler Fultz," at this time. The Sigma Alpha Iota National Music Fraternity had recently "established an International Music Fund, whose first aim *[was]* to give aid to the hospitalized armed forces of our country."[22] When Kathleen Davison, National President of this organization, wrote Ernest Skinner for information about the Clinic Organ, Ernest replied 19 June 1945, telling about the conception of the Clinic Organ and further describing this instrument:

> My dear Mrs. Davison:
> I am, as you understand, the manufacturer of the clinic-organ. Mr. Fultz gave a lecture to the Choir Directing Guild at which I was present, and we got talking the matter over, with the result that I designed this organ which seems to be very much appreciated. The instrument has a little 3-octave and 5 note keyboard—Low A to D¹— 41 notes which can be placed on the bed where the patient can amuse and find entertainment in playing it.
> One of these organs is now in use in the Hospital of the Good Samaritan in Boston, or perhaps I should say, Brookline. Another is in the residence in Pawling, New York, of Mrs. John Dutcher, and I have another one in stock of precisely three octaves. The instrument

is entirely new, but there seems to be substantial demand developing for it . . .

There had been plans to make about one hundred Clinic Organs.

Only six were actually built, for the war ended shortly thereafter and there was no longer any real demand for these instruments.[23]

As World War II was drawing to a close in the Pacific, Ernest Skinner's handiwork was bringing emotional and spiritual relief from the ravages of war as far away as Hawaii. In the July 1945 issue of *The Diapason,* we read:

> R. Kenneth Holt, whose good work in bringing organ music to the people of Hawaii has been the subject of attention in *The Diapason* is shown in this picture at the large Skinner organ in the Central Union Church of Honolulu. His programs have drawn large congregations within the shadow of Pearl Harbor and have not been interrupted by the war in the Pacific.

According to the March 1943 issue of this publication, these recitals, which apparently continued throughout the war, were played by the light of the moon, with the programs being printed on dark blue paper with white ink, since war-time black-outs prevented the use of lights at night.

World War II came to an end on 14 August 1945, and American organ builders were allowed to resume building new organs. By September of that year Ernest Skinner announced in his ad:

> Church organs built by Ernest M. Skinner & Son are again available. Those who have been awaiting the war's end may now arrange for the classic American organ by communicating with its builders.

A few months later, in December of 1945, his ad read as follows:

> Lieutenant Colonel Richmond H. Skinner, who tone-regulated and tuned the great organ at the National Cathedral in Washington, has returned from his military activities in the Pacific, notably at Leyte and Lingayen, for which he was awarded the Legion of Merit.
> Upon his release from the army he will resume his activities in the building of Skinner Organs . . .[24]

However, things did not work out as Ernest Skinner had planned. Col. Richmond Skinner tells what happened upon his release from the Army:

> ... when I came out, in '46, my father had been president and treasurer, and I had been vice-president and secretary. I had done the outside work, and he had done the factory work. When I came out, he asked me to come back with him. I said, "If you will allow me to be treasurer, I will do so." I had around $15,000 for my work in the Army to put in the factory—and he wanted me to—and I said, "If you will allow me to be treasurer." And he said no, he wouldn't do that. So I said, "Well, then, there's no further partnership."

Col. Skinner continues:

> ... I'll tell you how good a businessman he was, and this is why I wouldn't go back in. It came time to get some new machinery to do a little enlarging. And I went to the bank, and said, "We have some treasury stock. I'd like to leave it as collateral on a loan." The banker said: "Why, Mr. Skinner, don't you know that when your father paid $50,000 for that building, he also assumed a $50,000 mortgage?" And I said "No, I did not." My father's stock went down from about a quarter million dollars to nothing. So, he had no money and we had a $50,000 mortgage that I hadn't known about for five years. So, I said that I wouldn't go back unless I could be treasurer. And that's why I did not return after the Army even though I loved it. So, I went into the flying business. I ran an airline.[25]

Early the following year Ernest received this letter, dated 2 February 1946, from W. J. Cushing of the Arkansas Organ Company:

> Dear. Mr. Skinner:
> Our compliments to you sir, whom we esteem as one of the very few who have stuck to principal and quality thru all the throes and ups and downs of organ construction. Certainly you have no peer in the field of artistic organ performance.
> We as service men over a period of forty years from our father down to us boys, can truthfully say we never seen any evidence of poor workmanship or material in a Skinner Organ.
> It might interest you to know that one of the outstanding organists of Arkansas Mr. Kenneth R. Osborne, Dean of Music at the University of Arkansas, is another of your ardent boosters of the Skinner organs.
> We are interested in representing the Ernest M. Skinner organs in Arkansas. There will be a few large organs ordered in Arkansas within the next year or two and we would like to make them Ernest M. Skinner organs. We maintain the largest repair shop in the state and by far the largest service staff of qualified workmen.
> We will appreciate your consideration of representation and will

assure you that your ideals and policies will be fulfilled to the best of our ability.

                              Sincerely yours,
                           (signed) W. J. Cushing
                            Arkansas Organ Co.

The author has not found any evidence that Ernest Skinner accepted this offer by the Arkansas Organ Company. It is quite likely that Ernest may not have been able to handle the building of complete new instruments due to lack of adequate facilities and help, combined with post-war material shortages.

Even though war-time restrictions on the use of tin for organs were somewhat eased by early 1946, the availability of this material was yet limited by the government to

> secondary tin taken from inventories of organ builders or acquired from old organs . . .
>
> Before an approach to normal can be achieved it will be necessary to lessen the restrictions so that the organ builders may buy tin in the market, since inventories in the majority of factories indicate only small supplies on hand. And the situation will have to improve so that there will be a sufficient supply of the metal in the market. The shortage of tin and of lumber has been the handicap since the close of the war that has held up what promises to be a great revival of organ construction.[26]

During the years immediately following World War II, Ernest Skinner's work consisted mainly of repairing and rebuilding existing organs. He had several projects of this nature under way in 1946, the largest being the rebuilding of the 1902 Hutchings chancel organ at Trinity Church, Boston. The March 1946 issue of *The Diapason* describes this work:

> Besides doing a complete releathering job Mr. Skinner is installing a new French trumpet and a clarion mixture, both on the great. The swell is to have a new small-scale French trumpet, also a new cymbal mixture, the choir a new grave mixture and a new piccolo, and the pedal a new five-rank mixture and a 32-ft. bourdon, all to be finished before Easter.

That same year Ernest rebuilt, revoiced and modernized a three-manual Hook & Hastings organ at the First Presbyterian Church of Englewood, New Jersey. Tonal changes in this instrument included a new diapason chorus with a five-rank mixture, a new 8′ Principal Flute, and a new Erzähler in the Great; a new Flauto Dolce and Flute Celeste, a 4′ Principal, a three-rank Mixture, and a Cor d'Amour in the Swell; a new Unda Maris, a 2-2/3′ Nazard, and a French Horn in the Choir; and a new 16′ Gemshorn, a five-rank Mixture, and a 32′ Fagotto in the Pedal. The rebuilt instrument was dedicated on 20 October 1946.[27]

All through his career Ernest had difficulty in meeting the deadlines specified in contracts. Now, after repeated financial set-backs plus lingering post-war material shortages and lack of manpower, he was farther behind schedule than ever. One of his 1946 rebuilds, which involved the installation of a new console and the addition of a new Mixture and Trombone at St. Matthew's Church, Worcester, Massachusetts, was to have been completed by 15 April of that year. However, by 28 October 1946, the church was still waiting for Ernest to install the Mixture and the Trombone.[28]

A new organ which Ernest Skinner installed in Mount Calvary Lutheran Church, Charlotte, North Carolina, during the year 1947 took four years to complete.[29] According to a letter written on 4 June 1947 by the pastor of this church, the organ was originally due to be delivered on 1 July 1946. It had not yet been delivered at the time this letter was written.[30]

In February of 1947 it was announced in *The Diapason* that Ernest M. Skinner had joined the Schantz Organ Company of Orrville, Ohio, as technical director. This announcement stated,

> The combination of Mr. Skinner's talents and lifelong experience and an organization known for many years for its conservatism and high business principles is expected to result in an important contribution to post-war organ building.

John A. Schantz tells about Ernest's association with the Schantz Company:

> Mr. Skinner was associated with our firm for approximately two years, from January 1947 through 1948. Our original aim was to acquire some of the excellent features of the Skinner organ that would up-grade our own product. For example, at that time we had no capture-type combination action and assumed he could furnish us drawings, data, etc. from his experience. Through the association, we hired his former head pipe maker for many years, Jack Cook, to set up our pipe shop . . .
> We actually gained far more in the way of Skinner expertise (pipe

scales, methods, etc.) from Jack Cook than we did from his former employer. It soon developed that Mr. Skinner was not a detail man. Rather he painted with a broad sweep . . . He was a superb front man and more than a modicum of his success was undoubtedly due to his flamboyant behavior . . .

He made only one trip to Orrville and maintained his residence in the Boston area. His principal contribution to our firm was in writing our advertisements in those two years. This was his only function as "Technical Director". He would mail us the ad copy a few days in advance of the deadline. He did not provide any of the drawings we had expected and we soon found that he had little to contribute that would have changed our product to advantage.

The termination of his association with us was friendly and mutually understood to have served its limited purposes to both of us.

In fairness to Mr. Skinner, it should be remembered that he was probably in his 80s during this period.[31]

The author has good reason to believe that Ernest Skinner did in fact possess knowledge of the technical details of his art. During the two years he was associated with the Schantz firm, his book, *The Composition of the Organ,* had not yet been published. It is more than likely that he did not wish to divulge all his organ building secrets prior to the publication of his book.

FOOTNOTES

[1]"Joseph Bonnet," *The Diapason,* September 1954, p. 20, reprinted from *The Diapason,* September, 1944.
[2]Ernst G. Straus, "Einstein, Albert," *Encyclopedia Americana,* 1966 ed.
[3]Ernest M. Skinner, Letter to Alexander McCurdy, 7 June 1954.
[4]Ernest M. Skinner, Letter to Alexander McCurdy, 2 August 1954.
[5]Personal interview with Edward H. Hastings, 12 October 1972.
[6]"Organ Building Stops July 31 by War Order," *The Diapason,* July 1942, p. 1.
[7]Telephone interview with Richmond H. Skinner, 15 September 1977.
[8]"Finish Organ Orders; Change to War Work," *The Diapason,* April 1942, p. 1.
[9]"Great Organ Built in Course of 20 Years," *The Diapason,* April 1942, p. 2.
[10]Personal interview with Sydney F. Eaton, 30 April 1973.
[11]"Bruton Parish Church Will Add to its Organ," *The Diapason,* April 1942, p. 13.
[12]"Bruton Parish Church," *The American Organist,* 22, no. 10 (1939), p. 336.
[13]Letter received from I. L. Jones, 20 June 1975.
[14]Letter received from William Francis Vollmer, 6 August 1974.
[15]Letter received from I. L. Jones, 20 June 1975.
[16]"Ernest M. Skinner Factory in Methuen, Mass., Burned," *The Diapason,* July 1943, p. 1; James H. Eaton, Letter to Ernest M. Skinner & Son Co., 24 November 1942 (courtesy of Henry Karl Baker).
[17]Letter received from Eugenia S. Shorrock, 16 May 1975; This building was razed some years ago to make room for a new and modern brick structure which houses a bank and other businesses.

[18]"Organ Builder Retains Youth by Love of Music," *Richmond News Leader,* 27 November 1944.
[19]"To Rebuild St. Thomas' Organ in New York," *The Diapason,* July 1945, p. 5; "Dr. T. Frederick H. Candlyn," *The Diapason,* July 1954, p. 17.
[20]Personal interview with Carl Bassett, July 1967.
[21]Personal interview with Sydney F. Eaton, 30 April 1973.
[22]Kathleen Davison, Letter to Ernest M. Skinner, 5 June 1945 (courtesy of Henry Karl Baker).
[23]Interviews with Eaton and Bassett.
[24]Ernest M. Skinner & Son Company advertisements, *The Diapason,* September 1945, p. 16, and December 1945, p. 17.
[25]Telephone interview with Richmond H. Skinner, 15 September 1977.
[26]"New Order Permits Use of Tin in Organs," *The Diapason,* January 1946, p. 1.
[27]"Englewood, N. J. Organ Work of E. M. Skinner," *The Diapason,* December 1946, p. 1.
[28]John V. McKenzie, Letters to Ernest M. Skinner, 6 April 1946 and 28 October 1946 (courtesy of Henry Karl Baker).
[29]Unidentified newsclipping from the year 1947, found in the scrapbook of Ernest M. Skinner.
[30]Leslie F. Frerking, Letter to Ernest M. Skinner, 4 June 1947 (courtesy of Henry Karl Baker).
[31]John A. Schantz, Letter to author, received 16 October 1974.

CHAPTER 20

Last Years In Business
1947-1949

ERNEST SKINNER'S love for his camp at Alton Bay remained undiminished in his later years. He continued to spend his summer leisure time at Lake Winnipesaukee where, even though he was now in his eighties, he still enjoyed boating. Ernest's ancient speed boat, however, did not fare as well as its owner. Many times, when he cruised over to Ragged Isle to see his friend Wheeler Beckett, his cantankerous old craft would conk out, leaving him stranded on the island and making it necessary to phone the Coast Guard for assistance. He also went canoeing during those years, once even going alone to Ragged Isle in this manner (probably when he could not coax his old speed boat to run!). According to Eugenia Shorrock, her father, then a white-haired old man, was something to behold as he furiously paddled away—almost standing up—in his canoe.

Even at his advanced age Ernest exuded vitality and made quite an imposing appearance, regardless of what he was doing or how he was dressed. He was just as uninhibited and lacking in self-consciousness as ever. He did not especially concern himself about the way he looked, at least when he was at leisure, as long as he was comfortable. Eugenia Shorrock recalls her father showing up in front of the Shorrocks' Alton Bay gift shop dressed in blue-striped swim trunks, leather slippers (the kind with elastic sides), dark stockings with elastic garters, a linen summer weight suit coat, and a straw hat. Ernest often dressed in this manner at his Camp, which was several miles from the Shorrocks' store, and had come into town by canoe in this attire on that particular occasion. Nevertheless, Eugenia and her daughter Dorothy were rather startled by his appearance.

By 1947 Ernest and Mabel were no longer able to keep up a house by themselves. Mabel, always frail, was becoming more so with advancing years and Ernest could no longer afford to hire a maid to help her with the housework. By now, the cost of maintaining their house at 78 Beacon Street had undoubtedly increased far beyond what Ernest's meager income could cover. At this time Eugenia Shorrock bought a house at 30 Prospect Street in Reading, a suburb of Boston, so that her parents could move in with her and her family.

Ernest and Mabel moved to 30 Prospect Street in mid-year 1947. They now had a comfortable home provided for them and Ernest could at last retire and look back with pride and satisfaction on his long and distinguished career as an organ builder. So it seemed that this was to be the beginning of their golden years. There would be time to relax—time to enjoy life and each other's company. But Ernest would not rest. According to Eugenia, her father *promised* to retire when he and Mabel came to live with her. Nevertheless, Ernest continued to go on the road.

Even though Ernest continued to work in the organ business after moving in with his daughter, he still could not make ends meet because of his complete lack of good judgment and common sense with regard to money, plus his penchant for photography and musical gadgets—both rather expensive hobbies. By this time Ernest owned a wire recorder and wanted a tape recorder. Shortly after moving to 30 Prospect Street Ernest sold the knick-knacks on his grand piano to get money to buy a color camera.

Eugenia recalls that her father went on a "mattress kick" after moving in with her. When staying overnight at the homes of friends and customers Ernest would take a liking to the mattress he slept on and, deciding that it was the "best ever," would have to buy one like it for himself. Once, he ordered a new mattress only to have the wrong one delivered. He immediately jumped in his car and drove all the way to New York City to be sure of getting the mattress he wanted. Upon finding the right one, he wrote his initials, E. M. S., *on the mattress* and had it delivered to his home. After he returned to Reading, he discovered that he could have obtained the same mattress at the factory, only a mile away from home, and saved himself a trip to New York. While Ernest was on this "mattress kick," he would drive to work in New York City and return home in the same day just so he could sleep in his own bed.

Once again, Ernest Skinner's old dream of having his own home organ began to reassert itself. He wanted to add on a music room to the house at 30 Prospect Street, install an organ in it and entertain his friends. The music room was to have been built onto the south side of the house, where there was (and still is, as of this writing) a vacant lot. Ernest actually went so far as to have an architect draw up plans for the addition, but abandoned the idea when he found that it would cost him five thousand dollars.

The first two years of residency at 30 Prospect Street brought about little change in the life-style of Ernest M. Skinner, in spite of his family's attempts to persuade him to retire. He continued to drive all over the country supervising work on organs, some jobs being as far away as Kansas City, Missouri. According to an unidentified newsclipping written in 1947, when Ernest was finishing the installation of the organ at Mount Calvary Lutheran Church, Charlotte, North Carolina, he was "ostensibly retired at 81." However, this same article also stated that the next organ he would be installing was in Iowa! Ernest now wore a hearing aid, but still could pick out flaws in organ tone that few people could detect.[1]

The following year, on 24 May 1948, Ernest Skinner was the special guest of honor at the American Guild of Organists' annual dinner meeting, held in New York City. The July 1948 issue of *The Diapason* gave the following report of this occasion:

> Ernest M. Skinner, the guest of honor, was introduced by Mr. Elmer, who read a letter of greeting from Dr. Noble containing praise and thanks for knowing an "artist" whose work will live to the end of time. He then presented to Mr. Skinner a package which proved to be a scroll from the American Guild of Organists, inscribed as follows:
>
> "We, the undersigned officers, councillors and members of the American Guild of Organists, wish to record our high esteem and sincere affection *[for]* our fellow member, Ernest M. Skinner, whose friendship and jovial personality hold an enduring place in our professional relations. For many years in all his work he has distinguished himself by ever placing art as his chief goal and we are happy to honor him as an artist whose achievements will leave lasting impressions on the art of organ building.
>
> "Our warmest personal greetings are hereby extended to our honored friend with continuing good wishes."
>
> Mr. Skinner accepted with heartfelt thanks and recalled the first Guild meeting in 1896, at which there were in attendance as many organ builders as organists. Reading from a prepared list, he named many organists, past and present, and recalled anecdotes connected with them. Following some pertinent comments on the inclusion of

American composers on recital programs, Mr. Skinner said he couldn't recall any improvement that hasn't met with initial resistance, and as an organ builder his theory has always been that "if it makes music it's worth while."

In 1949 Ernest traveled to Kansas City to make repairs on the large Skinner organ at Grand Avenue Methodist Temple, originally designed and built by him in 1912. According to an article which appeared in the *Kansas City Star* on 8 July 1949, Ernest was to remain in Kansas City on this job for "several days before continuing to Charles City, Ia., where he will fulfill another contract." This article also stated that he was soon going back to Taunton, Massachusetts, to repair the one-hundred-year-old organ at the Unitarian Church where his father was once tenor singer and where, as a young boy, he saw his first pipe organ. In addition to repairing the old "Hooke" organ at the Unitarian Church in Taunton, Ernest also installed "several new stops."[2]

In July of 1949 Albert Schweitzer, the world-famous theologian, doctor, missionary, organist, and Bach authority, made his first visit to the United States.[3] Schweitzer's opinions on organ building, as expressed in his writings, have been taken out of context as proof that he advocated a return to the baroque organ of Bach's day. Dr. Schweitzer's ideal organ, however, was embodied in the romantic instruments built by the great nineteenth century organ builder, Aristide Cavaillé-Coll. In his book, *Out of My Life and Thought,* Schweitzer states:

> While to me the monumental organs of the eighteenth century, as they were perfected later by Cavaillé-Col *[sic]* and others, are the ideal so far as tone is concerned, music historians in Germany have been trying lately to go back to the organ of Bach's day. That, however, is not the ideal organ, but its forerunner only. It lacks the element of majesty, which is part of the organ's essential nature. Art has absolute ideals, not archaistic ones. We may say of it: "When that which is perfect is come, that which is in part shall be done away."[4]

It is a little-known fact that Albert Schweitzer was a friend and admirer of Ernest Skinner. Until 1949 the two men had enjoyed a "corresponding friendship" but had never actually met.[5] After arriving in the United States, Dr. Schweitzer wrote Ernest the following letter dated 16 July 1949 from New York City:

> Dear Mr. Skinner:
> Mr. Nies-Berger has already telephoned you that I should very much like to visit you in Boston where I shall be on the 19th. of July

at 9:30 A.M. at the Beacon Press on Beacon Street and where if you wish to meet me we will be able to fix the hour when I shall be able to visit with you one of your organs in Boston. But also I shall not be able to stop more than one day. But I am very interested to see with you one of the organs that you have created. I was also a friend of Widor and of Vierne.

Albert Schweitzer

On the day that Ernest Skinner and Albert Schweitzer spent together in Boston, Dr. Schweitzer gave Ernest a book entitled *The Africa of Albert Schweitzer*. Eugenia Shorrock, who translated the above letter into English from the original French, gives the following translation of the inscription which Dr. Schweitzer wrote on the title page of this book:

> To Ernest Skinner, the manufacturer of organs venerated by my master Widor and by me, on the day when I have had the pleasure of making his acquaintance in Boston.
> (signed) Albert Schweitzer
> (signed) Helene Schweitzer

It is not known which one of Ernest's instruments Schweitzer saw and heard when they met in Boston. We do know that prior to their meeting, Dr. Schweitzer had already made the acquaintance of at least one of Ernest's great masterpieces, that being the organ installed in Rockefeller Chapel, Chicago in 1927. Before coming to Boston, Dr. Schweitzer went "to accept the degree of doctor of laws from the University of Chicago." At that time,

> ... he delighted a small company with his informal performance from memory of works of Bach on the Rockefeller Chapel organ, and it seemed that this gave him even greater pleasure than the more formal entertainments.[6]

Francois Paradis, a French Canadian by birth and a voicer at the Aeolian-Skinner Organ Company during the late 1940s, was asked by company officials to be their interpreter for Albert Schweitzer while he was in Boston, since Schweitzer could speak fluent French but no English. While he was trying out a G. Donald Harrison organ, in Harrison's presence, Schweitzer commented to Francois in French, "Nobody will ever surpass Monsieur Skinner!"[7]

In a letter dated 16 May 1975, Eugenia Shorrock remarks: "At this point *[at the time of their meeting]* I note that Papa and Schweitzer resembled each other in appearance." Francois Paradis, who first met

Ernest Skinner during the late 1940s, described Ernest as having snow-white hair and a very pink complexion and said that he stood straight and tall. Francois also recalled that Ernest had a hearty handshake and that he still wore glasses only for reading. Aubrey Thompson-Allen, who also worked for Aeolian-Skinner at that time, saw Ernest Skinner at the "castle-like" residence of John Hayes Hammond in 1950 and remembered Ernest as being "a very old man by then but in full possession of his faculties."[8] All in all, Ernest, now in his mid-eighties, was carrying his advanced age exceedingly well. Nevertheless, in 1949, finally complying with the wishes of his family, he gave up building and repairing organs and sold the business to his foreman, Carl Bassett.[9] Ernest Skinner was now completely retired from his work as an organ builder after sixty-three years of devotion to that art.

FOOTNOTES

[1] Unidentified newsclipping from the year 1947, found in the scrapbook of Ernest M. Skinner.

[2] "Ernest M. Skinner and Our Organ," *First Parish Church News,* February 1961, p. 2 (courtesy of Eugenia S. Shorrock).

[3] "America in Tribute to Dr. Schweitzer," *The Diapason,* August 1949, p. 1.

[4] Albert Schweitzer. *Out of My Life and Thought,* 2nd. ed. (1949; rpt. New York: Mentor Books, 1964), p. 64.

[5] Personal interview with Ruth Scott, 11 September 1974.

[6] "America in Tribute to Dr. Schweitzer," p. 1.

[7] Personal interview with Francois Paradis, Spring 1969.

[8] Aubrey Thompson-Allen, "Information Given, Part IV," *Music, The AGO-RCCO Magazine,* 7, no. 1 (January 1973), p. 42.

[9] Letter received from John J. Bolten, 24 October 1975.

CHAPTER 21

Loneliness and Despair
1951–1956

NOW THAT Ernest Skinner was at last retired from the organ business he had more time to share with his wife Mabel. Many hours were occupied by playing chess, one of Ernest's favorite pastimes, especially during his later years. Mabel loved to play bridge, but she could never manage to interest Ernest in the game. Mabel was an excellent chess player and proved to be a formidable opponent for her husband. According to Eugenia Shorrock, Mabel always beat Ernest in the chess games which they played every night during his retirement, and it made him mad. Ruth Scott seemed to think her parents were fairly evenly matched in their chess-playing skills, and said that "they'd each have their streaks."[1]

In the summer Ernest and Mabel continued to go to their camp at Alton Bay where they would often sit by a front window overlooking Lake Winnipesaukee and play an animated game of chess or quietly enjoy each other's company. Eugenia Shorrock could recall her parents occasionally sitting in her Alton Bay gift shop shed, wrapped in blankets and holding hands.

Because of kidney disease, Mabel was afflicted with high blood pressure and, late in life, had several strokes. One of these strokes occurred at Alton Bay during the night when Ernest was not with her. Fortunately, her daughter Eugenia was there and was able to drive her into town for medical help. Not many days after Mabel's stroke she and Ernest showed up outside of the Shorrocks' gift shop, much to Eugenia's consternation. Ernest had practically carried Mabel all the way from their camp, and, eternal romantic that he was, he was taking her out for a good dinner, neither of them realizing that Mabel was in no condition to be going out.

In March of 1951 *The Diapason* congratulated Ernest Skinner on attaining his eighty-fifth birthday on 15 January of that year and printed a brief autobiography, written by the veteran organ builder upon that publication's request. That same month, on 29 March 1951, Ernest and Mabel celebrated their fifty-eighth wedding anniversary. Ned Hastings recalls that "up until the very end of her life, her memory was fantastically good."[2] In spite of having had several strokes in recent years, Mabel's mind was as sharp as ever on the evening of 14 April, as she and her husband played their usual nightly game of chess. That evening she beat Ernest at both of the two games they played before going to bed.[3] Those two chess games were to be the last Ernest would ever play with Mabel, for she died in her sleep that night.[4]

Toward the end of her life Mabel had attended church quite regularly. While they lived in Reading she went to the Unitarian Church which was just around the corner from the house at 30 Prospect Street. It was in this church that Mabel's funeral service was held. She was buried in the Woodland Cemetery in Bethel, Maine, in a family plot given to Ernest and Mabel by her father about fifty years before and "endowed for good care permanently."[5]

Ernest missed Mabel intensely after she died, and he was lost without her. In a letter written by Ned Hastings to Joseph Dzeda on 12 April 1972, we learn just how important a role Mabel played in Ernest's mercurial life:

> In her quiet way . . . she provided the kind of stability he so sorely needed. In every sense of the word she was the rock on which his life was built, and her death left him utterly bereft. In those later years I never saw him when he wasn't speaking of her, reminiscing about their years together, missing her. Every summer he made several trips to Bethel from Alton Bay, N. H. just to visit her grave.

The cemetery at Bethel, about a one-and-one-half mile drive from the center of town, is situated in a hilly land, lightly wooded with pines and a scattering of maple trees. Ernest was enchanted with this cemetery because it had a "natural landscape."[6] For all of his love of its natural beauty, he never stayed long when he went there to "call on Mabel." He would simply go to her grave—nothing else—and then leave for home after about a moment. His car was in such bad shape by then that, on the way back to the village green in the center of Bethel, he would just barely make it up the hill.[7]

After Mabel's death Ernest took her wedding ring and had it enlarged to fit his ring finger. He wore this ring for the rest of his life. He moved from his own small bedroom on the north side of the house to the bright spacious south-east room Mabel had slept in. Ernest was to spend most of his nights in that room for the remainder of his stay at 30 Prospect Street.

Somehow, life manages to go on, even in the midst of grief. Toward the end of 1951 someone had the audacity to call Ernest Skinner's organs "romantic atrocities" and, predictably, Ernest was back to defending his ideas in the editorial pages of *The Diapason*. He was already planning to attend the next convention of the American Guild of Organists, which was to be held in San Francisco the following year. In the December 1951 issue of *The Diapason,* Ernest writes:

> I intend to go to the convention of the A.G.O. to be held in San Francisco next June, by automobile, and to take some pictures en route, at the Yosemite, the Yellowstone and the Grand Canyon. If there are a few who would like to share that trip with me I would be glad of word from them addressed to me at Reading, Mass.[8]

Ernest's driving capabilities were well known, and it would appear that eastern conventioneers were not rushing to take him up on his offer, for by 25 February 1952, he wrote Catharine Crozier:

> ... I'm not yet sure I'll go to the convention as 6000 odd miles is a bit much, if I fail to enveagle anyone into going with me. I know of one who is going, but he is staying several months, which means I return alone, as probably all easterners will have return tickets, which are not good in a Dodge touring car.[9]

During the years following Mabel's death Ernest alleviated his loneliness somewhat by visiting with friends. According to his daughter Eugenia, he would take off to see his friends on impulse. If it so happened that no one was at home, he would look up another acquaintance in the area and drop in for a visit. Bill Deveau, then curator of organs at West Point Military Academy, recalls that his former employer would take off from home any time, unpredictably. Bill and his wife never knew when Ernest would show up at their West Point home.[10] The Deveaus would always put him up overnight and he would be on his way again the next day, perfectly happy. Mrs. Deveau, a Swede, often made Swedish meat balls which Ernest liked very much.

One day she was in the kitchen preparing this dish when, first thing she knew, there was Ernest in the kitchen, with absolutely no warning! Fortunately, Bill added, they never happened to have any other overnight guests when Ernest made one of his unannounced visits.

Science and technology, responsible for both the blessing of polio vaccine and the curse of the atom bomb, were the dominating forces shaping the social, political, economic, and cultural climate of the 1950s. The preoccupation with science which characterized that decade also undeniably made its mark on the cultural world of that time. Form now clearly took precedence over aesthetic appeal in the realm of the fine arts. Sentiment, warmth, and beauty for their own sakes were now considered old-fashioned and definitely undesirable.

The musical arts were no less affected by the technological climate of the decade. Warmth and any trace of subjectivity were clearly frowned upon by the musical elite. The one art which had served to express the most deep, lofty, and heartfelt emotions of man through the ages was now becoming a cold, clinical science. Form and precision were all-important in music, and any show of personal feeling in its performance almost amounted to heresy. This was particularly true in regard to sacred music. Music worthy to present to the Lord Almighty could not be debased by any vulgar display of honest human emotion. Bach, the master of musical form, was not only being idolized, exploited, and emasculated by a new breed of organists whose imagination could not (or dared not) go beyond the bare printed notes on the music page, but was now being played on organs which were supposedly patterned after the kind of organ that Bach himself played and which were shrill, harsh, cold, and perfectly suited to this new style of playing. These organists out-baroqued the original baroque organists in the name of authenticity, but that did not matter. This was the composer's intent—according to the musical authorities—and that was that!

Needless to say, organists of the 1950s thoroughly disapproved of the type of organ which Ernest Skinner had given his entire life to creating. For the most part, the neo-classicists had contented themselves with a few additions and changes in some of Ernest's smaller instruments during the preceding two decades. They now launched on a seemingly wholesale destruction of his largest and most famous creations in quest of attaining the all-important virtue of clarity.

In addition to the radical change in musical tastes, the widespread affluence of the 1950s undoubtedly was equally responsible for the drastic redesigning and discarding of many of Ernest Skinner's finest instruments. Church attendance increased considerably during that decade, and now that offering plates were overflowing on Sunday mornings, organists in prominent churches had no difficulty in persuading church authorities to "up-date" and clarify their "tubby" old 1920s vintage organ or replace it with a "modern" baroque instrument.

The first major casualty of the times was the organ at Symphony Hall, Boston, the installation of which Ernest had supervised in 1900 while he was working with George Hutchings. The destruction of this instrument actually predated the 1950s by several months, since the new Aeolian-Skinner organ, resulting from a drastic reconstruction of the old Hutchings instrument, was installed in late 1949.[11] Ned Hastings recalls that in the process of rebuilding this organ, "they threw out the 32' pedal stop. Ernest was infuriated and wrote nasty letters to various publications at the time."[12] Ernest never got over the rebuilding of his Boston Symphony Hall organ, nor did he ever forgive G. Donald Harrison for doing such a thing.

In 1951 the large Skinner installed in Kilbourn Hall, Eastman School of Music, was completely rebuilt by the Aeolian-Skinner Organ Company.[13] In October of 1952 it was announced in *The Diapason* that the Skinner organ in the Cathedral of St. John the Divine, New York City, was to be rebuilt and redesigned by G. Donald Harrison and Joseph S. Whiteford, president and vice-president of the Aeolian-Skinner Company, in consultation with Norman Coke-Jephcott, organist and choirmaster at the Cathedral. By August of 1953 a contract had been signed with the Aeolian-Skinner Organ Company for a large instrument to be installed in Finney Chapel at Oberlin College, incorporating some of the pipework from the old 1915 Ernest M. Skinner organ.[14] Also by this time Harrison had obtained contracts to rebuild the Ernest Skinner organs at St. Paul's Chapel, Columbia University, and Sage Chapel, Cornell University, throwing out the Pedal 32' Diapason in both instances, an act Ernest termed "vandalism."[15]

According to his daughter, Ruth, Ernest was "insulted" that anyone would rebuild his instruments. He was deeply offended when his friend Thomas Webber, organist at Idlewild Presbyterian Church, Memphis, Tennessee had the Möller Organ Company replace his 1927 Skinner console, equipped with a completely self-contained combination action, with a console which had remote combination action. Ernest could not stand to have one of his organs desecrated by "that intolerably clumsy remote control botch work."[16] On 1 March 1952 Ernest wrote William Deveau, "I have sort of soured on Tommy Webber of Memphis . . . as he has had Moller make him a new console, which seems wrong to me as I got him his job there."

Ernest Skinner's reaction to seeing so many of his instruments redesigned during the 1950s went far deeper than mere indignation. According to Carl Bassett, who took over Ernest's business when he retired, it actually made him ill. Mr. Bassett could recall Ernest practically crying on his shoulder at one time, over an organ of his which had recently been rebuilt. Ernest had put so much of himself into the instruments he had designed and built over the years that it apparently was as though a part of himself was being destroyed each time an Ernest Skinner organ was rebuilt or replaced. By 1954 he was becoming so alarmed over what was now happening to his creations that he was moved to comment: "I suppose when I have been dead for fifty years all my organs will be as dead as I am."[17]

During the early part of the 1950s Ernest Skinner continued to write for publication, mostly in *The Diapason*. In an article (July 1952) and an editorial letter (April 1953), Ernest discusses his principles of tone production and tonal design. Most of the material in these writings was probably derived from his forthcoming book, *The Composition of the Organ,* which still had not been published. Another writing of his, in the September 1953 issue of *The Diapason*, advocated the encouragement of American composers and musicians. Aside from the opinions expressed in this last editorial, most of Ernest's ideas were unfortunately received with contempt by the highly intellectual organists who now dominated the organ scene. William H. Barnes recalls:

> I saw Skinner about ten years before he died at one of the National Conventions of the A.G.O. He was a sad figure, from being the focus of attention among the organists, he was looking for someone to talk with. He was like the fond mama who saw her son marching in the parade and remarked that everyone was out of step but her son. Skinner thought all the organists were out of step as they admired Harrison's work more than Skinner's. Mr. Skinner still knew that he was "right," and he would not change any of his New England "positive notions" and jump on the band-wagon and join the crowd.[18]

According to Eugenia Shorrock, her father was everlastingly writing letters after he retired because he did not have much else to do. In mid 1954 Ernest wrote an extensive series of letters to Alexander McCurdy regarding an article McCurdy was writing about him for the *Etude* magazine. (This article appeared in the October 1954 issue). Between 18 May and 26 August Ernest wrote over forty letters to his friend, occasionally writing two or three letters in the same day. In one of those letters, dated 15 June, he remarks, "I shaved off my moustache some weeks ago which in the opinion of my family and friends completely destroys my natural beauty . . ." This moustache had been a trademark of his appearance most of his life, even as a young man in his twenties. His daughter Eugenia thought that he spoiled his looks by shaving it off. To her recollection he never let it grow back again.

In his letters to Alexander McCurdy, Ernest reveals his awareness of the increasing limitations of being old and expresses his frustration over these limitations. A postscript to his letter dated 19 June 1954 reads: "Please don't find it too boresome if I say the same thing several times. It is really very inconvenient to be 88. It makes ones [sic] faculties so unreliable."

In his lengthy correspondence with McCurdy, Ernest would be despairing over the rebuilding of his famous organs and expressing his sense of loneliness one time, and in the next letter he might be in a whimsical mood, fairly exploding with jokes, limericks, and miscellaneous bits of humor. In earlier days, his humor and wit had made him the center of attention when he was in the midst of his friends and admirers at organists' gatherings. Now, with his whole world tumbling down about him and most of his admirers in the organ world having given way to adherents of the so-called baroque school of music and organ design, his humor was a much needed analgesic, easing the many hurts which life was inflicting upon him and which threatened to completely overwhelm him.

By late June of 1954 Ernest had gone to his camp at Alton Bay for the summer. It was there, with only a cat for company, that loneliness seemed to become the dominating theme of his life. On 28 June, Ernest writes:

> It is raining cats and dogs up here today and the paper says it is to continue tomorrow, so I guess I'll be alone for some hours except at meal times. I go down to the town to my daughters for lunch and dinner . . .
>
> . . . since my Blessed one went to sleep everything is sort of empty and somehow I cannot get used to being alone and there [are] a few other conditions which don't help much.

In his letter dated 30 June, we read:

> Well Alexander, I have reached the stage now where I don't know who is to live the longest, me or the cat, but I feel fine and have no evidence that the cat doesn't but when either of us croaks I suppose it will be a catastrophy.
>
> I have not, nor shall I ever get relief from the loss of the dear one who died April 14, 1951 and with whom I lived for fifty eight years

> ... She sleeps in a beautiful spot given us by her father over fifty years ago ... I am going to call on her soon.

A few days later on "July 2th" Ernest writes:

> It is very lovely up here at my camp but I miss my television and my library and I don't like being so far away from my youngest daughter who lives in Duxbury Mass. and who has two beautiful kids both of whom play chess with me when I visit them.

On 16 July Ernest seems momentarily to be in a more light-hearted and rather rakish mood, and then reverts to the darker state of mind which prevailed during that summer:

> Tell me Alexander does anybody else ever open your mail when you are not there for instance, or when you are, a secretary for instance there *[are]* some funny things I might write to you but only for you, such as this.

Ernest then tells his somewhat naughty story about the lady and the young man who mowed her lawn (see chapter 8), after which he continues:

> Well Alec. that is my limit in stories told *[by]* letter and I hope you will forgive me if it is too bad and I'll never tell another. I hope the air is "still fresh."
> Alec, I am deadly sick of being alone. I do not at the moment know just where my book is nor when my son will be back so I am in a condition of suspense and will be 'till my son returns. So please write me soon and send the article *[which McCurdy wrote about Ernest]* and then it wont be a "breath of fresh air" but a garden of flowers, for ME.[19]

Ernest continues to grieve for his departed wife in his letter to McCurdy written on 22 July:

> Somehow it is terribly lonesome and tiresome now up here at camp and without my lost Mabel. I am going up to Bethel Me. early in August to visit her and see how the little pines are gowing, which we planted where she sleeps. Well I'm 88 now and I suppose we will be together again before many years.

And then on the first day of August, Ernest writes: "Wish you and Flora could be up here for a time this Summer as I am constitutionally lonesome since my dear blessed Damozelle died."

Loneliness and Despair (1951-1956)   235

In a few of the letters Ernest wrote to McCurdy that summer the reader is provided with a rare glimpse of Ernest's religious beliefs. In his letter dated 19 June 1954, Ernest states: "You cannot find living conditions as we know them, anywhere in the world without finding the Christian Religion right there behind it as a foundation." He then goes on to tell about his dream-vision, experienced as a young man of twenty, which so profoundly influenced his whole life (see chapter 1). On 6 July, Ernest writes:

> ... I think the most authentic lunkhead on the face of the earth is the atheist. If I were to show an atheist a house and tell him it built itself he would call me a blankety blank fool, but how infinitely complicated is a human being in comparison, which the atheist says just happened or whatever it is they say about it. I couldn't be an atheist if I wanted to and I hate the idea.

In his letter written on 22 July Ernest asks Alexander McCurdy,

> ... what do you think of that line in the Lord's Prayer which says, "lead us not into temptation." I think that carries a fearful implication against the Most High and I never use it. I say "deliver us from temptation and from evil."[20]

Ned Hastings had this to say about his Uncle Ernest's religious beliefs:

> ... he was deeply religious, though I don't think he had much in the way of a specific creed—nor did he attend church regularly. He believed firmly in a life after death, once claimed to have had a dream of heaven, and found it similar to that depicted in Christina Rossetti's poem "Paradise." This was a favorite poem of his ... .[21]

Ruth Scott stated that, although her father had no formal religious beliefs and did not attend church, he was a very religious man. Ruth continues:

> He was a queer mixture. He *never* went to church. If anyone went, my mother did. But he never went—wouldn't dream of going to church ... he felt self-sufficient ... I think he made up his own mind, and that was that ... .[22]

In a letter dated 10 December 1974, Harold Gleason writes: "I do not know what Mr. Skinner's religious beliefs were, if any. I really feel that he was a religious man, even though neither my wife or I ever heard him say anything about it." A story told by Dr. Gleason in another letter, dated 23 March 1974, would strongly indicate that Ernest lived according to the Christian ethic:

> My wife *[Catharine Crozier]* told me about a time when she was playing a recital at Philips Exeter and the organ pedals were *very* dirty and sticky. E.M. came early to her recital and when he heard about the pedals he came up and got to work on them with a cleaner and rag! Just like him.

One of Ernest's favorite anecdotes was the one about a lady who grudgingly gave a slice of bread to a hungry tramp (see chapter 8). Ernest may have had a certain amount of contempt for "super-religious" people who self-righteously obeyed all the laws of their faith and paid lip service to its creeds, but had little in the way of love or charity in their hearts.

Ernest Skinner considered music to be just as important as the spoken word in worship services. Ernest himself evidently worshipped primarily through the ministry of music. During the 1940s he had this quotation from Bruno Walter's autobiography in one of his advertisements:

> The church knows why it calls upon the power of music at its most solemn functions. Music's wordless gospel proclaims in a universal language, what the thirsting soul of man is seeking beyond this life!

Some of Ernest Skinner's detractors thought of him as being egotistical, self-centered, and anything but religious. Yet *love,* the one outstanding virtue of Christianity, was something Ernest possessed to an unusual degree and which he gave freely, in spite of the fact that people often took advantage of him. The following letter, written in the early 1950s to the newborn son of his former employee, Bill Deveau, illustrates Ernest's warm and affectionate nature:

> Dear Eric William Deveau;
> I am very glad to meet you. I have known your progenitors for some time and knowing them as I do, I can say in all confidence that you were inevitable, sooner of later, or I am no judge of anything.
> Did you ever hear the riddle, what is the difference between a stoic and a cynic? Answer; a synic *[sic]* is where you wash the dishes and a stoic is the bird what brings the babies.
> Well be good now because you have been loved for some time even before your arrival, 'tho you may not believe that, but it is true. Speaking of pants, did you ever hear of the man who slit his dogs

tongue so he would have creases in his pants? I wonder if it worked. Well dont get out of tune as it wont do any good, as your dad is a tuner and he will tune you in again in no time and I know from a photo I have that your mother will hold keys for dad to tune you up again.

Well Eric I will come and see you sometime soon as I am sure that Bylleigh or Ingrid will give me an introduction and I look forward to seeing you at Alton Bay this Summer anyhow, if I dont manage to get to you before that. Tell your Mama that you are delighted to see her as soon as you learn a few language, as I know she would be delighted to hear this. Tell Billy too so he wont be jealous.

I know Billy and Ma think it wonderful to be a Pa and Ma, but look at me, I'm a Pa, a Grand pa and a great Grandpa. Isn't that loading me up somewhat?

Well write soon and tell me how your dear mother is, wont you. I wanted the honor of being the first to write you a letter. Hope no one beat me to it. I got your letter one minute before I started this letter to you.[23]

God bless you and keep you as long as he has me and longer if possible. I'll be 87 my next birthday. Give my love to Ma and Dad and remember I'll stay put, hi ope *[sic]* for some time yet.

With love from
(signed) Ernest M.

Even though Ernest seemed to be in a world of his own much of the time, he was actually quite sensitive to other people and their feelings, as evidenced by these lines from a letter written by him to organ enthusiast John Van V. Elsworth, Watertown, N.Y., on 9 March 1933:

> You have a very fine organist there in the person of Mr. Cox. I am inclined to think he feels a little bit depressed that so few people speak to him about his music in Trinity Church, so if you find yourself in the mind to do so, I think it would cheer him up some to have you speak well of his music.

In the series of letters written to Alexander McCurdy in mid-1954, Ernest, in a letter dated 6 July, contemplates the not-too-distant approach of his own death and remarks: "I wonder if my doing everything I could to beautify the service in the house of worship will earn approval for me from the Most High."

Ernest was not afraid of death during these years, but actually almost seemed to be looking forward to being re-united with his "blessed Damozelle" who had left him on 14 April 1951. He more feared annihilation of the Skinner organ, which he had labored all his life to create and which was now dying little by little as his finest instruments continued to be rebuilt, one after another. He was desperate to get his book, *The Composition of the Organ,* published so that the Skinner organ would not completely die with him, even if every instrument he designed and built were wiped off the face of the Earth. In his letter to McCurdy written on 26 May 1954 we read:

> Did I tell you why I want that book published? Well it isn't as financial in reason as some may imagine. It is because it is an attempt to save my developments in organ tone and mechanism from passing out when I do and I'll be ninety in 18 months. I think I wrote you this and it is a good reason, as tone is as personal as handwriting and with all I can do to save my tone I know full well that much of it will be lost . . .[24]

Ernest's daughter Eugenia and her family were often away from home, leaving him alone at 30 Prospect Street a great deal of the time. For that reason, it was arranged that he would go to live with his wife's cousin Stella Bartlett. Upon leaving Alton Bay at the end of the summer, 1954, Ernest Skinner moved into Miss Bartlett's home at 22 Lyndhurst Street in Dorchester.[25] He was to live there almost until the very end of his life.

G. Donald Harrison was not the only builder to make tonal changes in Ernest Skinner's organs during the 1950s, but he seemed to acquire the majority of contracts for rebuilding Ernest's most famous and important instruments—especially those in the eastern part of the country. In one organ after another Ernest's warm, gentle, unforced brilliance was transformed into a comparatively cool, brittle, and somewhat forced brilliance which was typical of Harrison's instruments during that decade. In 1954 the Aeolian-Skinner Organ Company completed an extensive rebuild of the Skinner organ in Princeton University Chapel. This involved a new Great diapason chorus and a new flue chorus in the Choir. All the stops in the Solo division were discarded, with the exception of the Tubas, and a Positiv division was installed in their place.[26] Ernest was very upset upon receiving news of this work, for he considered this instrument to be "one of [his] very best organs."[27]

At about this same time Aeolian-Skinner rebuilt the Skinner organ in Hill Auditorium at University of Michigan. Former University Organist Robert Noehren recalls:

> During the 50s when we rebuilt the Hill organ at the University I exchanged some correspondence with Mr. Skinner and still have

several rather long letters from him in my files... In these letters to me, he tried to persuade us at the University to let him rebuild the Hill organ, and he reflected his bitterness toward Mr. Harrison who had already changed so many of his original instruments. At the time of these letters he was 87 years old and driving across the country alone! He was still trying to keep in the organ business as well. He was indeed a remarkable man.[28]

In a letter written to Mr. Noehren on 7 October 1952, Ernest states:

> To me Harrison is destitute of musical feeling. If you doubt this listen to that most heard of all organs (Radio) the organ in the Germanic museum, Harvard College.
> Well I am to blame for the presence of Harrison in America. I hope I'll be forgiven, but never by myself.

Later that same month on 21 October, apparently after receiving word that there were plans to rebuild his big organ at Hill Auditorium, Ernest writes:

> Dear Robert Noehren;
> I am sending you the "rumor" I received about the Ann Arbor organ. I do not know for what reason the writer could have for making such statements as I have marked in said letter, but the moment I read you were a pupil of Palmer Christian I *[knew]* that I had nothing to worry about...
> ... If you will pay me two cents per mile to go to Ann Arbor, I will give my time without any charge whatever to go and examine the organ and give you a written report of its condition...
> ... I am sufficiently interested in what I consider to *[be]* one of the best organs, to be more than willing to go to Ann Arbor free gratis for nothing without charge for my time...
> If you desire competition I suggest you try Casavant of Canada to whom I have given my remote control drawings. Also most of my original reed stops...
> But unless you have some objection to me, what is the matter with my doing it myself here in Reading where I have some very competent men...
> If it happens that you want me to come but funds for milage are lacking... I expect I would come at my own expense if I am really needed. In three years I'll be ninety, so if you happen to really want old man Skinner for the nonce (whatever that is) I'll come on my own. I would love to see that organ again and do you know why? Well I doubt if another such organ will ever be built in your life time nor mine, as stop costs averaged about $400. when that organ was built,

if my memory is aproximately *[sic]* correct, but now the average cost is eleven hundred per stop . . .

A year and a half later, on 21 April 1954, Ernest writes:

Dear Mr. Noehren;
    If material restoration is to be made in the organ I built for you what is wrong with my doing it personally. I sold my business to my former foreman and have been doing nothing except write letters for something over three years and I am deadly sick of what might be called a purposless existence. I will go and do this work for you for my expenses and whatever else you happen to think concomitant the service . . .[29]

Needless to say, Ernest Skinner's generous offer to Robert Noehren was not accepted.

In 1955 Ernest learned that Harrison had been engaged to rebuild one of his most famous organs, the one in St. Thomas Episcopal Church in New York City. This was also one of Ernest's favorite organs. Because it was across the street from the old Skinner Company's Fifth Avenue studio, he had taken many well-known visiting musicians to hear and play the instrument. Ernest had made numerous additions and improvements to the St. Thomas Church Skinner as his knowledge of tonal design had grown and matured. Since Dr. Noble's retirement in 1943, Möller had made some changes in this organ, but they were exceedingly small when compared with what was yet to come under Harrison's direction.[30]

Of course, Ernest was greatly upset over the proposed redesigning of his St. Thomas Church organ. His reaction to the news of this rebuild is well illustrated in a story told by Joseph Dzeda, as related to him by William Self, then organist at that church:

He *[Self]* said that about the time the rebuild was announced, old EMS, in his late '80's, came to him and asked if Self would hold off on the proposed work until EMS was dead. Self refused. Then EMS asked Self to store the pipes for his organ in the church basement, on the condition that if the new organ was not up to Self's hopes, EMS would return and re-install his old organ.[31]

After having failed in persuading Self to postpone the rebuilding of the St. Thomas Church organ, Ernest wrote the following letter, dated 7 October 1955, to the rector of that church:

Loneliness and Despair (1951-1956) 241

> Dear Sir;
> I am the builder of the original organ in the above Church *[St. Thomas]*, which I understand is to be discarded and replaced by another to be build *[sic]* by a builder who for some reason is obliged to use my name, but who was formerly in charge of sending out men on maintenance work for Willis, the famous London organ builder.
> If it happens that your good people do not like the organ after its rebuilding and I suppose revoicing, and wish to remake it, to be more as it was originally I will be very glad to restore it at the lowest possible cost, which implies no sacrifice or compromise whatever. I will be glad to do it, for as it happens this organ as originally built has brought me more opportunities to build organs and for more Churches than any other of the one thousand organs I have built since the beginning . . .

After naming more than a dozen of the best known organs he had built, Ernest continues:

> So now I will conclude by saying that if the anticipated improvements in the St. Thomas organ are not regarded as improvements by your good people, I suggest the above remedy, which I sincerely hope will not be desired, nor necessary.

In a postscript, Ernest adds: "I received word that Mr. Candlyn, your former organist, became what might be termed grief stricken, when he heard that organ was to be done over . . ."

The Aeolian-Skinner rebuild, which Ernest felt to be the crowning insult, was barely completed when, on 14 June 1956, G. Donald Harrison died of a heart attack in his New York City home.[32] Even though his St. Thomas Church organ was gone forever, Ernest, now ninety years old, was left with the meager satisfaction of having outlived his adversary of twenty-seven years, to whom death had come at the comparatively young age of sixty-seven.[33]

Harrison's destruction of the Ernest Skinner organ did not stop with his demise. Shortly before he died, Harrison drew up the design for the proposed rebuild of Ernest's masterpiece, his great organ at the Washington National Cathedral, to be executed upon completion of the nave of the Cathedral.[34] This reconstruction would be accomplished in the mid-1970s under the direction of one of Harrison's former associates. So it was that even Ernest's ultimate achievement was not to survive another two decades. Even without G. Donald Harrison, Aeolian-Skinner and other builders continued their ever-accelerating destruction of the Skinner organ. Announcements of these rebuilds appeared with increasing frequency in the pages of *The Diapason* and, as the decade wore on, there seemed to be no end in sight.

FOOTNOTES

[1] Personal interview with Ruth Scott, 11 September 1974.
[2] Edward H. Hastings, Letter to Joseph F. Dzeda, 12 April 1972.
[3] Ernest M. Skinner, Letter to Alexander McCurdy, 30 June 1954.
[4] "Mrs. Ernest M. Skinner Dies at Home in Reading, Mass.," *The Diapason,* May 1951, p. 1.
[5] Ernest M. Skinner, Letter to Alexander McCurdy, 30 June 1954.
[6] Personal interview with Ruth Scott, 10 October 1972.
[7] Personal interview with Edward H. Hastings, 12 October 1972.
[8] Ernest M. Skinner, " 'Romantic Atrocities' Found Buyers," *The Diapason,* December 1951, p. 18.
[9] Ernest M. Skinner, Letter to Catharine Crozier, 25 February 1952 (courtesy of Harold Gleason).
[10] When the position of curator of organs at West Point Academy became available in 1948, Ernest, in anticipation of his own retirement, wanted William Deveau to be assured of a good job and therefore arranged to have him interview for the position.
[11] "Boston Symphony Organ is Designed," *The Diapason,* September 1949, p. 1.
[12] Edward H. Hastings, Letter to Joseph F. Dzeda, 15 September 1966.
[13] "Noted Eastman Organ Scheme is Revised," *The Diapason,* November 1951, p. 4.
[14] "Aeolian-Skinner to Build Large Organ for Oberlin," *The Diapason,* August 1953, p. 1.
[15] Ernest M. Skinner, Letter to Robert Noehren, 7 October 1952.
[16] Ernest M. Skinner, Letter to Robert Noehren, 21 October 1952.
[17] Ernest M. Skinner, Letter to Alexander McCurdy, 7 June 1954.
[18] Letter received from William H. Barnes, December 1974.
[19] Ernest's son Richmond had been trying to find a publisher for Ernest's second book and, at that time, was in the hospital for surgery.
[20] Ernest M. Skinner, Letters to Alexander McCurdy, 28 June, 30 June, 2 July, 16 July, 22 July, 1 August, 19 June, and 6 July 1954 (courtesy of Alexander McCurdy).
[21] Letter received from Edward H. Hastings, 11 June 1974.
[22] Personal interview with Ruth Scott, 11 September 1974.
[23] This letter, dated 3 April 1952, was, according to Bill Deveau, written before Ernest had received word of Eric Deveau's birth, which took place on 1 April 1952. This was, in fact, the first letter written to Eric Deveau.
[24] Ernest M. Skinner, Letter to Alexander McCurdy, 26 May 1954 (courtesy of Alexander McCurdy).
[25] Ernest M. Skinner, Letter to Alexander McCurdy, 26 August 1954.
[26] "Organ at Princeton Chapel is Remodeled," *The Diapason,* November 1954, p. 1.
[27] Ernest M. Skinner, Letters to Alexander McCurdy, 7 June 1954 and 26 May 1954.
[28] Letter received from Robert Noehren, 14 September 1973.
[29] Ernest M. Skinner, Letters to Robert Noehren, 7 October 1952, 21 October 1952, and 21 April 1954 (courtesy of Robert Noehren).
[30] M. P. Möller Organ Company advertisement, *The Diapason,* March 1949, p. 5.
[31] Letter received from Joseph F. Dzeda, 21 July 1975.
[32] "G. Donald Harrison Dies of Heart Attack," *The Diapason,* July 1956, p. 1.
[33] Ironically, Harrison's 1956 rebuild of the St. Thomas Church Skinner, considered by many organists to have been Harrison's masterpiece, was, in turn, drastically altered in tonal design before another decade passed.
[34] Personal interview with Robert Schunemann, January 1975.

CHAPTER 22

Ernest's Last Years 1956-1960

THE OCCASION of Ernest Skinner's ninetieth birthday warranted front page notice in the January 1956 issue of *The Diapason*. Along with a reprint of his autobiography, which first appeared in the March 1951 issue of that publication, it was stated that "the veteran craftsman still enjoys good health and takes a lively interest in musical matters." Up to this time, Ernest had been traveling by car all over New England and beyond, attending concerts and dropping in to visit his friends. However, his mobility was to be severely reduced before 1956 was half over, for by May of that year Ernest was no longer allowed to drive. He was very unhappy about this, and in a letter written to Alexander McCurdy on 9 May 1956, remarked, "The commissioner of motor vehicles has deprived me of my drivers license so now I have no car and that to me is a mild form of death."

Unknown to Ernest Skinner, his daughter Ruth had worked for two years to have his driver's license taken away from him—for his own good, and for everyone else's. Ruth Scott recalls:

> I refused to let my children ride with him . . . I don't think he was always a lousy driver. I think that came with old age, because he never used to have accidents. But the last fifteen years of his life . . . it was one accident after another. And the only way he kept his license was that he paid for it himself out of his own pocket to get the car fixed. He never could afford it for the insurance company.
>
> . . . I finally, through a friend (he never knew it, it would have

244   *The Life and Work of Ernest M. Skinner*

>killed him), got his license away from him. But it took me two years with the registrar to do it. I was afraid he'd kill himself or kill somebody else.
>
>... I know it was *[a mild form of death to him]*, and I was so scared he'd find out that I'd done it. But I still think it was a smart thing to do.
>
>You see, he didn't even have a bad record because he got all *[his auto repairs]* ... fixed himself... That was my trouble.[1]

After losing his driver's license Ernest still managed to participate in local musical events for a while. But even these activities were curtailed by mid-1957, after he suffered a severe fall over a small podium in a church aisle while attending a meeting of the Boston Choir Director's Guild. The June 1957 issue of *The Diapason* reported:

>X-ray examination at the Newton-Wellesley Hospital revealed that he had fractured his right shoulder. After some ten days in the hospital, Mr. Skinner has now been moved to the Plymouth Nursing Home, Plymouth, Mass., where he will be staying for at least the next month.

Once he had recovered from this accident Ernest returned to 22 Lyndhurst Street. Now that he was almost entirely confined to his home there was little he could do to occupy his time outside of writing letters, reading, and watching television. Ned Hastings, who lived fairly close by, helped keep his Uncle Ernest entertained when he could by playing the piano for him in the daytime and by taking him out to movies in the evening. Ned also took him to visit the John Hayes Hammond Museum so he could see and hear the organ there.

Ernest loved company but unfortunately seldom had any during those years because his instruments and his opinions on music and organ building no longer found favor with the organists of that day. By that time, moreover, many people did not even realize that Ernest was still alive. Barbara Owen was one of the few visitors who called on him during the late 1950s. She recalled that Ernest was deteriorating physically by then, but was still mentally sharp and quick-witted, continuing to be so almost until the end of his life. According to Barbara, "He had all his marbles," but did tend to wander off the subject, toward the end.[2]

Ernest had not yet succeeded in getting his book, *The Composition of the Organ,* published by 1957. Ned Hastings relates:

>The saga of that manuscript is a long and dreary one. Always an opinionated man, Uncle Ernest grew worse in this respect as the

years went by . . . Frank Campbell Watson of Associated Music Publishers accepted it for publication and gave it to an editor for revision. There is no question that editing was necessary. I read most of the thing in manuscript and, as an English professor, could only wince at the quantity of questionable grammar and downright repetition which it contained.

The idea of someone editing his work was anathema to Uncle Ernest. He carefully crossed out all recommendations and fought every criticism bitterly. I tried my darndest to calm him down, for I knew what would happen if he didn't give at least a little. What I had feared came to pass; Campbell Watson tired of the whole mess and returned the manuscript . . .[3]

Ernest refers to dealings with Frank Campbell Watson in a letter to Alexander McCurdy, written on 18 May 1954, so the above episode apparently took place in the early to mid-1950s. Eugenia Shorrock recalled that her father was still trying to get the book published on his own after he moved in with Mabel's cousin on Lyndhurst Street. In a letter to Barbara Owen dated 16 April 1957, Ernest writes:

I gave this book (manuscript) to my son hoping he might find a publisher but no luck, so I applied to an English publisher and they immediately said, send it along. So now I have an Ernest hope that I shall see it published soon even if I am ninety one, plus.[4]

In another letter, written a year earlier to Alexander McCurdy, Ernest remarked that when his book was published, he would "feel completed." Ernest was never to see his book in print.[5]

The following letter from Ernest Skinner, dated 23 November 1958, was printed in the January 1959 issue of *The Diapason*:

Dear Sir:

I read a letter in *The Diapason* for September which says that with the electro key action "you lose the direct sensitive control of the instrument."

By this process of reasoning I suppose if I want to get a word of importance to a friend a letter will arrive more promptly than a telegram.

Well, as I once heard, "It's a queer world and few of us get out of it alive."

Very truly,
Ernest M. Skinner

These were the last known words of Ernest to appear in print.

In the December 1959 issue of *The Diapason,* which marked the fiftieth anniversary of the founding of that publication, William H.

Barnes wrote an article expressing his appreciation of Ernest Skinner and his work. In this article, Barnes reminisces about the Skinner organs at the Cathedral of St. John the Divine and St. Thomas Episcopal Church, both of which had been rebuilt by the Aeolian-Skinner Organ Company in recent years. After reviewing some of Ernest's tonal contributions to the American organ, Barnes concludes with these paragraphs:

> Naturally as interest has increased in the classic organ ensemble, and the music written for it, it has waned with regard to the orchestral voices. In small and medium sized organs built to-day, ensemble voices come first, and the orchestral voices are relegated to the luxury and non-essential class. With organs costing three times as much as in Mr. Skinner's heyday every voice must really justify itself to gain a place in the stoplist.
>
> The many fine organs built twenty-five to fifty years ago, in a great many parts of the country, still proclaim the artistry of Ernest M. Skinner in the matter of lovely orchestral voices—flute celestes, kleine erzählers, tuba mirabilis—and a certain mild but very beautiful type of chorus reeds. Many organists and congregations were (and still are, for that matter) supremely happy with the sound of these voices. They were the best examples of this phase of American organ building. Such voices are still invaluable in adapting to organ accompaniment extended choral works originally written for orchestral accompaniment.
>
> With all of the marvelous orchestral recordings of practically all of the standard literature available on hifi and radio there is surely no longer any need for orchestral transcriptions on the organ. This was not true fifty years ago and some of the greatest organists of this period—W. T. Best, Alexandre Guilmant, Edwin H. Lemaire—arranged and played many such works. It was the only opportunity for many people to hear these great works played.
>
> Mr. Skinner's influence exists today on organ building in America not by what is now being used of his inventions in organ tone but in the tradition he established with regard to the kind of material, workmanship and artistic appreciation that went into his organs. Certainly no more colorful nor distinguished figure has graced American organ building in the twentieth century. When we are remembering back fifty years we must all bow respectfully to the deans' dean of organ builders and give thanks that Ernest M. Skinner came on the organ building scene in an important way just when he did . . .[6]

This warm tribute was probably of little comfort to its subject. Those "non-essential" orchestral voices, which were now relegated to the "luxury" class, were still supremely important to Ernest Skinner. Moreover, many of his finest organs were already gone, with the certainty of continuing destruction of his creations in the years to come. Now that his ideas on organ building and tonal design were largely rejected by most organists and organ builders, Ernest Skinner's indomitable will was slowly breaking down as the Skinner organ died, little by little, and it became increasingly apparent that he and his ideas had outlived their day.

On 15 January 1960, Ernest Skinner attained his ninety-fourth birthday. Little is known about this final year of his long and eventful life. We do know that he spent the summer at Alton Bay, staying at the old farm house of his daughter Eugenia, who came up there every year to tend her gift shop. By mid-Autumn Mabel's cousin Stella Bartlett was becoming too old and frail to care for Ernest, so he then went to live with his other daughter, Ruth Scott, in Duxbury, Massachusetts. Ruth recalls that her father's mind was clear right up to the end of his life, but his memory was very bad. If he was told something, he was likely to forget it the next minute. Ernest still desired his independence and, during those last years, would get impatient with members of the family when they would try to prevent him from doing things which were harmful or unwise. In mid-November, after Ernest had been staying with Ruth for perhaps two or three weeks, she found she could no longer cope with caring for him, so she put him in a nursing home in nearby Plymouth.[7]

Ernest was not at all happy in this new environment. In spite of the fact that he was older than most of the other residents of the nursing home, he disliked being with all those "old fogies" and refused to speak to any of them. Independent soul that he was, he hated having his meals served to him in bed. Fortunately, he was not to remain in the nursing home for long.

On Sunday morning, 27 November 1960, ten days after Ernest had been admitted to the nursing home, Ruth Scott was awakened at 3:00 a.m. by a phone call notifying her that her father had died that night in his sleep. Eugenia was in New Hampshire at the time and was informed of his death by a phone call from her sister.

According to his death certificate, Ernest Skinner died of cardiac arrest due to arteriosclerotic heart disease, which was due to generalized arteriosclerosis. His daughter Ruth said that he died of "old age." But there also are those who maintain that Ernest died of a broken heart because the world no longer seemed to appreciate the beauty which he had brought into being and to which he had devoted his entire life. With the announcement of his death to the organ world in the January 1961 issue of *The Diapason,* the editor of that publication wrote these words about Ernest Skinner:

> The America that was, the exciting country in which many of us grew up, the essentially pioneer land which was changed forever by the depression of the thirties and the second great war is nowhere better typified in the organ world than by Ernest Skinner. Born in a typical small village in the state long known as "the cradle of presidents" he became, as a result of his own energy, creative force and individuality, a towering figure in a field where towering is uncommon. His tastes, his preferences intimately affected the builders, the players, even the composers of his time.
>
> Though most of Ernest Skinner's organs were built for churches, colleges and great halls in America, much of the mushroom development of the theater organ got its impetus from him. His love for lush orchestral color in the organ, his experiments with higher wind pressures and his developments in electric action all contributed . . .
>
> Few of Mr. Skinner's masterpieces—and masterpieces of their time and taste they surely were—still remain in their original design. The quality of a striking personal expression which they all had made a complete swing of the pendulum in the other direction natural. A whole generation of organists, though, regretted that Mr. Skinner had to live to watch it happen. But the mid-century was that kind of a time: great men all saw their worlds crumble about them!

The funeral service for Ernest Skinner was held on Tuesday morning at ten o'clock at the Unitarian Church in Reading, the same church where his beloved Mabel's funeral had been held nine years earlier.[8] Among those who went to Ernest's funeral were William Bunch, formerly associated with the Aeolian-Skinner Organ Company, and "a number of the old-timers who knew [Ernest] well."[9] Other than by these men, the service was attended mainly by relatives. According to Eugenia Shorrock, none of the famous people whom Ernest had befriended over the years showed up at his funeral because there was too little time between the appearance of his death notice in the newspapers and the day of the funeral.

Ned Hastings was asked to play for his Uncle Ernest's funeral, something he "found very hard to do." The organ, not a Skinner, was "a two-manual monstrosity with several dead notes and one persistent cipher."[10] Ned finally ended up removing the offending pipe just before the service. He played about forty minutes of music for the prelude, which included two Purvis chorales; the Transformation Scene from "Parsifal"; the Bach chorale prelude "O God Be Merciful to Me"; "Berceuse," from Vierne's 24 Pieces in Free Style; and "Air," by

William Churchill Hammond. Just before the actual service, as he was playing the prelude music, Ned broke down and wept as he realized that all of the pieces he was playing were Ernest's favorites.

For many years Christina Rossetti's poem "Paradise" had had a special significance for Ernest (see chapter 21). At Ned Hastings' suggestion the minister read the poem as part of the funeral service. Ernest was laid to rest in the Woodland Cemetery in Bethel, Maine, alongside his wife Mabel. Eugenia Shorrock recalls that it was raining while they were on their way to the cemetery that day. In addition to the dismal weather, they had two flat tires en route.

Much thought and effort went into the selection of a monument for the family plot in Bethel, and likewise into determining what to put on Ernest's grave marker. After a great deal of research and visiting many cemeteries, Eugenia decided on a monument with the likeness of church windows on either side of the Skinner name, an appropriate choice, since her father had worked most of his life to "beautify the service in the house of worship."[11] Eugenia asked many people for suggestions as to what epitaph should be placed on her father's grave marker. After much deliberation, she had it inscribed:

ERNEST MARTIN SKINNER
GREAT AMERICAN ORGAN BUILDER

FOOTNOTES

[1] Personal interview with Ruth Scott, 11 September 1974.
[2] Telephone interview with Barbara Owen, 29 April 1976.
[3] Edward H. Hastings, Letter to Joseph F. Dzeda, 15 July 1965
[4] Ernest M. Skinner, Letter to Barbara Owen, 16 April 1957 (courtesy of Barbara Owen).
[5] Ernest M. Skinner, Letter to Alexander McCurdy, 9 May 1956. Skinner's book, *The Composition of The Organ,* was finally published by Melvin Light, curator of organs at University of Michigan, in 1981.
[6] William H. Barnes, "Appreciation of Ernest Skinner Voiced by Barnes," *The Diapason,* December 1959, p. 39.
[7] It was most likely that Ernest was, at this time, put in the Plymouth Nursing Home, the same one where he had recuperated from a broken shoulder several years earlier.
[8] "Ernest M. Skinner, 94, Dies," *The Boston Globe,* 28 November 1960, p. 25.
[9] Letter received from William Bunch, 7 July 1978.
[10] Edward H. Hastings, Letter to Joseph F. Dzeda, 15 July 1965.
[11] Ernest M. Skinner, Letter to Alexander McCurdy, 6 July 1954.

CHAPTER 23

Epilogue

ERNEST M. SKINNER has been called a "genius of a man *[who]* was also a man of great mystery."[1] He also has been described as being "a curious man in many respects and sometimes hard to understand."[2] Ernest possessed a personality of many facets which often seemed contradictory. He was gregarious and loved the company of other people, but also was the introspective dreamer. He was a flamboyant and aggressive man who could be very sensitive and vulnerable. Ernest could, at times, be impossibly stubborn and resistant to change and yet be quite receptive to new concepts and ideas when they struck his fancy. He was a man who could be very irritating to those who opposed his ideas, but still, as Ned Gammons expressed it, "You couldn't help but love him."[3]

Ernest was regarded by a few individuals as being temperamental and egotistical, but most of those who were close to him esteemed him as a good and generous man who would give his friends "the shirt off his back." Harold Gleason writes: "I always found E. M. to be friendly, even when we had our moments of disagreement. I think he was like most of us . . . who, under presure, sometimes had moments of bad conduct."[4] Notwithstanding Ernest's reputation for being argumentative, Bill Deveau recalls that he had only one fight with his former employer in all the seventeen years he worked for him.[5]

Ernest was a man who thoroughly enjoyed life. Yet he was also a man of great spirituality who deeply believed in the Christian ethic as a way of life. The Skinner organ fully reflects this duality of Ernest's nature in that its tone is at once rather sensual and yet profoundly mystical in character. Ernest's creations also convey an irresistable warmth which was so much a part of his personality.

During the late 1930s Ernest, in one of his advertisements, stated that "emotion is the vitalizing factor of all art."[6] Throughout his long career Ernest faithfully applied this principle to his art, building instruments which appealed to the emotions through the beauty and variety of their tone. When the classical emphasis of objective form over subjective content came into vogue during the mid-twentieth century, it was precisely this quality of emotion to which more recent generations of organists and organ builders objected.

In 1916, with the dedication of his instrument at First Universalist Church (Church of Our Father) in Detroit, Michigan, Ernest Skinner made this statement of prophetic significance:

> . . . the voice of the organ is full of appeal, and if it falls indifferently upon the ear of this generation, it will find recognition in another, and help to make our day to become ancient.[7]

The passage of time revealed a curious twist to the fulfillment of this prophecy. Ernest's own generation, with their fondness for orchestral transcriptions, received the highly orchestral Skinner organ readily and with great enthusiasm. It was the succeeding generation which rejected his instruments. Today, however, there is a renewed interest in the Skinner organ. Increasing numbers of the present generation of organists are developing an appreciation of these instruments and are becoming concerned with saving the few of them which still exist in their original tonal design.

In view of his effort to create the perfect medium on which *all* music could be played effectively and with infinite tonal variety, Ernest may have been, in some respects, ahead of his time. Of course, the concept of an "all-purpose" organ was anathema to the classical "purists" who emerged on the scene in the 1930s ad 1940s, since they insisted upon *absolute* authenticity in the performance of early music and advocated a return to the ancient baroque instruments for the "correct" interpretation of this music. G. Donald Harrison and a few more recent organ builders have attempted to produce instruments which blended the various schools of organ building, using the same general idea as that which Ernest Skinner had in mind—an organ suitable for the performance of all types of music. Usually, the result in these attempts was, at best, a bad compromise. Moreover, in the opinion of this writer, none of these builders succeeded in equaling the refinement, warmth, and charm possessed by Ernest's creations.

In a way, the ability to create the Skinner organ may well have died with Ernest Skinner. It is for this reason: Even if an instrument were built today with the same stop list, pipe scaling, metal composition and thickness, wind pressures, etc., there would be no guarantee that the finished product would have that indefinable something that only Ernest's personal sensitivity and taste could provide. All we can do to preserve the beauty of true Skinner tone is to faithfully restore and preserve those creations of his which do yet remain.

As mentioned at the beginning of this chapter, Ernest Skinner was a many-faceted personality. Above all else he was a romantic in every sense of the word—an unmitigated romantic who "suffered from an unrequited love of music" and who lived life with all the depth, intensity, and passion that the word implies. He gave himself to life and to his chosen work without reservation, even though it meant personal sacrifice. In a letter of 3 June 1954 to Alexander McCurdy, Ernest stated: "The office of art is to create beauty and I have followed that principal [sic] from the beginning and for which I make no apology." Indeed, he was dedicated to creating all the beauty he could through his instruments, expressing the hope late in life that the "Most High" would approve of his work in beautifying the service of worship.[8] A quotation, found in the May 1940 issue of *The Diapason*, defines the legacy of Ernest Skinner with these words:

> He gives the world through his organs a taste of real beauty and spiritual uplift, provided, of course, that a kindred soul is playing upon one of his instruments.

It is unlikely that anyone living today knows the details of that dream-vision which Ernest Skinner experienced as a young man of twenty. But, the vision is not entirely lost to us as long as a single Skinner organ exists. It is present in the tone of every pipe of the magnificent instruments he built, coming alive every time they are played, speaking to the very depths of the soul its wordless message which only the receptive heart can understand.

FOOTNOTES

[1] Letter received from William Francis Vollmer, 6 August 1974.
[2] Letter received from Harold Gleason, 10 December 1974.
[3] Personal interview with Edward B. Gammons, 3 May 1976.
[4] Letter received from Harold Gleason, 14 March 1975.
[5] Personal interview with William Deveau, 3 May 1973.
[6] Ernest M. Skinner & Son Company advertisement, *The American Organist*, 20, no. 5 (1937), p. 149.
[7] Dedication Recitals Program, First Universalist Church (Church of Our Father), 26 & 27 April 1916 (courtesy of Barbara Owen).
[8] Ernest M. Skinner, Letter to Alexander McCurdy, 6 July 1954.

Organ Specifications

Ernest M. Skinner's Ideal Organ (1894) 254
South Congregational Church, New Britain, Conn. (1897) 255
Symphony Hall, Boston (1900). 256
Unitarian Church, Ludlow, Vermont (1902). 257
First Dutch Reformed Church, Kingston, N.Y. (1903) 257
Old Cabell Hall, University of Virginia, Charlottesville, Va.
   (1906) 258
Great Hall, City College of New York (1906) 259
Williams College, Williamstown, Mass. (1911). 260
First Universalist Church, Detroit, Mich. (1915) 262
Portland Municipal Auditorium, Portland, Oregon (1916) 264
Second Congregational Church, Holyoke, Mass. (1921). 265
Robert Law Residence, Port Chester, N.Y. (1922) 267
Capitol Theatre, Boston, Mass. (1922). 268
Cossitt Avenue School, La Grange, Ill. (1923) 269
Baptist Temple, Charleston, West Va. (1925) 270
Jefferson Avenue Presbyterian Church, Detroit, Mich.
   (1925). 271
St. Joseph's Episcopal Church, Detroit, Mich. (1926). 273
First Presbyterian Church, Concord, N.C. (1927). 274
Our Lady of Mount Carmel R.C. Church, Chicago, Ill.
   (1928). 275
Cathedral Church of Our Lady, Queen of the Holy Rosary,
   Toledo, Ohio (1930) 276
First Presbyterian Church, Newburgh, N.Y. (1937). 277
Resurrection Chapel, Washington National Cathedral,
   Washington, D.C. (1938). 278
Washington National Cathedral, Washington, D.C. (1938) 278
St. Martin's Church, New York City, N.Y. (1940). 280

Ernest M. Skinner's Ideal Organ, 1894

GREAT
- 16' Open Diapason
- 8' Open Diapason, American type
- 8' Open Diapason, English type
- 8' Open Diapason Small
- 8' French Horn
- 8' Harmonic Flute (large scale)
- 8' Violoncello
- 8' Gemshorn
- 4' Octave
- 4' Harmonic Flute
- 2 2/3' Quinte Flute
- 2' Fifteenth
- IV Mixture
- 8' Trumpet

SWELL
- 16' Gedeckt
- 16' Contra Salicional
- 16' Contra Dulciana
- 8' Open Diapason
- 8' Geigen Principal
- 8' Stopped Diapason
- 8' Concert Flute
- 8' Quintadena
- 8' Spitzflöte
- 8' Viole d'Orchestra
- 8' Salicional
- 8' Voix Celeste
- 8' Dulciana
- 8' Aeoline
- 4' Octave
- 4' Flute d'Amour
- 4' Flauto Traverso
- 4' Violina
- 4' Salicet
- 2' Piccolo
- IV Dolce Cornet
- 16' Contra Fagotto
- 8' Cornopean
- 8' Oboe
- 8' Clarinet
- 8' Saxophone
- 8' Orchestral Oboe
- Tremolo

CHOIR
- 16' Gedeckt (Sw)
- 16' Contra Salicional (Sw)
- 16' Contra Dulciana (Sw)
- 8' Open Diapason (Sw)
- 8' Geigen Principal (Sw)
- 8' Stopped Diapason (Sw)
- 8' Concert Flute (Sw)
- 8' Quintadena (Sw)
- 8' Spitzflöte (Sw)
- 8' Viole d'Orchestra (Sw)
- 8' Salicional (Sw)
- 8' Voix Celeste (Sw)
- 8' Dulciana (Sw)
- 8' Aeolina (Sw)
- 4' Octave (Sw)
- 4' Flute d'Amour (Sw)
- 4' Flauto Traverso (Sw)
- 4' Violina (Sw)
- 4' Salicet (Sw)
- 2' Piccolo (Sw)
- IV Dolce Cornet (Sw)
- 16' Contra Fagotto (Sw)
- 8' Cornopean (Sw)
- 8' Oboe (Sw)
- 8' Clarinet (Sw)
- 8' Saxophone (Sw)
- 8' Orchestral Oboe (Sw)
- Tremolo

ECHO
playable on Great manual
- 8' Quintadena
- 8' Echo Flute
- 8' Echo Voix Celeste (II)
- 8' Vox Humana
- Tremolo

PEDAL
- 32' Bourdon
- 16' Open Diapason
- 16' Bourdon
- 16' Violone
- 16' Dulciana
- 10 2/3' Quinte
- 8' Flute
- 8' Gedeckt
- 8' Dulciana

COUPLERS
Pedal:
- Pedal to Pedal 4'
- Great to Pedal 8'
- Swell to Pedal 8'
- Choir to Pedal 8'

Manual:
- Swell to Great 8'
- Swell to Great 4'

Choir to Great 16'
Choir to Great 8'
Great Separation
Great off, Echo on
Swell to Swell 4'
Swell to Choir 8'

REVERSIBLES
Great to Pedal
Full Organ

COMBINATIONS
Great: 3 non adjustable
Great: 2 adjustable
Swell: 6 adjustable
Choir: 6 adjustable

MECHANICALS
Balanced Swell Pedal
Balanced Crescendo Pedal
All couplers (hitchdown)

Source: E. M. Skinner, "An Ideal Organ," *The Organ,* 2, no. 12 (April 1894), 290, quoted in Homer D. Blanchard, "The Organ in the United States: A Study in Design, Part II," *The Tracker,* 25, no. 1 (Fall 1980), 37.

George S. Hutchings Organ, 1897
South Congregational Church, New Britain, Connecticut

GREAT
  16' Open Diapason 61
  8' First Open Diapason 61
  8' Second Open Diapason 61
  8' Doppel Flute* 61
  8' Gross Flute 61
  8' Gross Gamba* 61
  8' Gemshorn 61
  4' Octave* 61
  4' Flute Harmonique* 61
  2 2/3' Octave Quinte* 61
  2' Super Octave* 61
  IV Mixture* 244
  16' Ophicleide* 61
  8' Trumpet* 61
  4' Clarion* 61

*Stops enclosed in Choir Swell Box

SWELL
  16' Bourdon Treble 61
  16' Bourdon Bass
  8' Open Diapason 61
  8' Stopped Diapason 61
  8' Spitz Flöte 61
  8' Salicional 61
  8' Vox Celestis 49
  8' Aeoline 61
  8' Unda Maris 49
  4' Octave 61
  4' Flauto Traverso 61
  4' Salicet 61
  2' Flageolet 61
  V Dolce Cornet 305
  16' Contra Fagotto 61
  8' Cornopean 61
  8' Oboe 61
  8' Vox Humana 61
  4' Saxophone 61

Tremolo #1
Tremolo #2

CHOIR
Enclosed in separate Swell Box
  16' Contra Gamba 61
  8' Open Diapason 61
  8' Geigen Principal 61
  8' Concert Flute 61
  8' Quintadena 61
  8' Dolcissimo 61
  8' Vox Angelica (prepared for)
  4' Fugara 61
  4' Flute d'Amour 61
  2' Piccolo Harmonique 61
  8' Orchestral Oboe 61
  8' Clarinet 61 (Clarinet Bass)
  Tremolo

SOLO Augmented, Accessory to Great Organ-Heavy Wind
  16' Bombarde (Tuba)
  8' Tuba Mirabilis 85
  4' Trumpette (Tuba)

PEDAL Augmented
  32' Contra Bourdon (Bourdon)
  16' Open Diapason 42
  16' Bourdon 54
  16' Violone 42
  16' Lieblich Gedackt (Sw)
  16' Dulciana 42
  10 2/3' Quinte (Bourdon)
  8' Octave (Open Diapason)
  8' Gedackt (Bourdon)
  8' Gamba (Violone)
  8' Orchestral 'Cello 30 (Tuned with a wave)
  8' Violoncello (Dulciana)

4' Super Octave 30
16' Trombone 42
16' Bassoon (Sw)
8' Tromba (Trombone)

Ranks: 58
Stops: 63
Pipes: 3454

COUPLERS
Pedal:
  Swell to Pedal
  Great to Pedal
  Choir to Pedal
Unison:
  Swell to Great
  Choir to Great
  Swell to Choir
  Great Organ off
  Solo Organ off
Octaves:
  Swell to Great 4'
  Choir to Great 16'
  Swell to Swell 4'
  Swell to Swell 16'

REVERSIBLES
Great to Pedal
(piston & pedal)

COMBINATIONS by pistons & pedals
Great: 5
Swell: 7
Choir: 5
General: 4
General release
(Combinations indicated by an electric annunciator.)

MECHANICALS
Balanced Swell Pedal
Balanced Great & Choir Pedal
Balanced Crescendo Pedal
Sforzando Pedal
Sostenuto

Source: *Specification of the Organ*, a brochure contemporary to completion of the organ, furnished by Barbara Owen. The date 1897 is given in T. Scott Burhman, "Mr. Ernest M. Skinner's Record," *The American Organist,* 19, no. 4 (1936), 126; the date 1896 is given in Homer D. Blanchard, "The Organ in the United States: A Study in Design, Part II," *The Tracker,* 25, no. 1 (Fall 1980), 40. Neither source specifies the date as being of the contract, the installation, or the dedication.

George S. Hutchings Organ, 1900
Symphony Hall, Boston, Massachusetts

GREAT
  16' Open Diapason
  8' First Open Diapason
  8' Second Open Diapason
  8' Gross Flute
  8' Gross Gamba
  8' Stopped Diapason
  8' Gemshorn
  4' Octave
  4' Gross Flute
  2 2/3' Twelfth
  2' Fifteenth
  VI Mixture
  IV Scharff
  16' Trumpet
  8' Trumpet
  4' Clarion

SWELL
  16' Bourdon
  8' Open Diapason
  8' Stopped Diapason
  8' Concert Flute
  8' Salicional
  8' Voix Celeste
  8' Spitz Flute
  8' Aeoline
  4' Octave
  4' Violina
  4' Flute Harmonic
  2' Flautino
  V Mixture
  16' Contra Fagotto
  8' Cornopean
  8' Oboe
  8' Vox Humana
  Tremolo

CHOIR
  16' Contra Gamba
  8' Open Diapason
  8' Geigen Principal
  8' Melodia
  8' Dolcissimo
  4' Fugara
  4' Flauto Traverso
  2' Piccolo
  8' Clarinet
  Tremolo

PEDAL
  32' Diapason
  16' First Diapason (Wood)

Organ Specifications 257

16' Second Diapason (Metal)
16' Violone
16' Bourdon
16' Dulciana
10⅔' Quinte
 8' Octave
 8' Flute
 8' Gedackt
 8' Cello
 4' Super Octave
16' Trombone
 8' Tromba

COUPLERS
Pedal:
 Swell to Pedal
 Great to Pedal
 Choir to Pedal
Unison:
 Swell to Great
 Choir to Great
 Swell to Choir
 Great to Swell

Octave:
 Swell to Swell 16'
 Swell to Swell 4'
 Choir to Great 16'

REVERSIBLES
Great to Pedal (pedal)

COMBINATIONS
Pistons:
 Great & Pedal: 5 & release
 Swell & Pedal: 6 & release
 Choir & Pedal: 4 & release
 General release
 Pedal release
Pedals:
 Generals: 4
 Great: 4 & release
 Swell: 4 & release

MECHANICALS
Balanced Swell Pedal
Balanced Crescendo Pedal

Source: *The Symphony Hall Organ,* a brochure dated 1900, furnished by Homer D. Blanchard.

First Ernest M. Skinner Organ, 1902
Unitarian Church, Ludlow, Vermont

GREAT
 8' Diapason
 8' Melodia
 8' Gedackt (Sw)
 8' Dulciana (Sw)
 4' Flute 8' (Sw)

SWELL
 8' Gedackt
 8' Salicional
 8' Vox Celestes

 8' Dulciana
 4' Flute
 Tremolo

PEDAL
 16' Bourdon
 8' Gedackt

MECHANICALS
4 Couplers
Swell expression pedal
Tubular-pneumatic action

Source: "A New Church," *The Vermont Tribune,* Friday, 18 July 1902, quoted in E. A. Boadway, *The Boston Organ Club Newsletter,* January and February 1978, p. 9. This source establishes the completion date as 1902.

E. M. Skinner Organ (rebuild), 1903
First Dutch Reformed Church, Kingston, New York

GREAT
 16' Double Open Diapason
 8' Open Diapason
 8' Melodia
 8' Gamba
 8' Dulciana
 4' Principal
 4' Flute
 2⅔' Twelfth

 2' Fifteenth
 III Mixture
 8' Trumpet

SWELL
 16' Bourdon
 8' Open Diapason
 8' Stopped Diapason
 8' Quintadena

8' Salicional
8' Voix Celestes
8' Aeoline
4' Principal
4' Flauto Traverso
4' Violina
III Cornet
8' Cornopean
8' Oboe
Tremolo

PEDAL
16' Open Diapason
16' Bourdon
16' Second Bourdon
8' Violoncello
8' Flute
8' Gedackt

COUPLERS
Swell to Pedal
Great to Pedal
Swell to Great
Swell to Great 16'
Swell to Great 4'

COMBINATIONS, Pistons
Great: 4 & release
Swell: 3 & release
General release

MECHANICALS
Swell expression pedal
Crescendo pedal
Sforzando pedal
Great to Pedal reversible
Tubular-pneumatic action

Source: "Boston Builders' Contracts," *The Music Trades*, 31 January 1903, furnished by E. A. Boadway. This source establishes the contract signing as having occurred January 1903.

E. M. Skinner Organ, Opus 127, 1906
Old Cabell Hall, University of Virginia
Charlottesville, Virginia

GREAT
16' Diapason 61
8' Diapason 61
8' Gross Floete 61
8' Gamba 61
8' Gedackt (Sw)
8' Erzähler 61
4' Octave 61
2' Fifteenth 61
8' Cornopean (Sw)

SWELL
16' Bourdon 61
8' Diapason 61
8' Salicional 61
8' Voix Celestes 61
8' Gedackt 61
8' Dulciana (Ch)
4' Flute (Ch)
4' Violin 61
2' Piccolo (Ch)
III Cornet 183
8' Cornopean 61
8' Oboe (Ch)
Tremolo

CHOIR
8' Melodia 61
8' Geigen Principal 61
8' Dulciana 61
8' Unda maris 49
4' Flute 61

2' Piccolo 61
8' Clarinet 61
8' Oboe 61

PEDAL
16' Diapason 30
16' First Bourdon 42
16' Second Bourdon (Sw Bourdon)
8' Floete (1st. Bourdon)
8' Gedackt (Sw Bourdon)
8' 'Cello (Sw Salicional & Voix Celestes)

Ranks: 27
Stops: 35
Pipes: 1585

COUPLERS
Pedal:
  Swell to Pedal
  Great to Pedal
  Choir to Pedal
Unison:
  Swell to Great
  Choir to Great
  Swell to Choir
  Great to Swell
Octave:
  Swell to Swell 16'
  Swell to Swell 4'
  Swell to Great 16'
  Swell to Great 4'
  Choir to Choir 16'

COMBINATIONS
Swell & Pedal: 5
Great & Pedal: 3 & release
Choir & Pedal: 2 & release
MECHANICALS
Swell & Choir expression pedal

Crescendo pedal
Great to Pedal reversible

Electro-pneumatic action
All-electric movable console

Source: Examination by the author. According to a letter written by Lynn T. McRae to the author on 21 July 1976, the contract for the organ was signed in May, 1906, installed in early 1907, and dedicated 18 and 19 March, 1907. The organ is extant, restored in 1983, and in its original tonal and mechanical design.

E. M. Skinner Organ, Opus 135, 1906
Great Hall, College of the City of New York

GREAT 6" wind
  16' Diapason 61
  16' Bourdon 61
  8' First Diapason 61
  8' Second Diapason 61
  8' Third Diapason 61
  8' Gross Floete 61
  8' Gamba 61
  8' Gedackt 61
  8' Erzähler 61
  4' Octave 61
  4' Flute 61
  2' Fifteenth 61
  16' Tuba (Solo)
  8' Tuba (Solo)
  8' Trumpet 61
  4' Tuba (Solo)

SWELL 6" wind
  16' Bourdon 61
  8' First Diapason* 61
  8' Second Diapason 61
  8' Gross Floete 61
  8' Gedackt 61
  8' Spitz Floete 61
  8' Viol d'Orchestre 61
  8' Voix Celestes 61
  8' Salicional 61
  8' Aeoline 61
  4' Octave 61
  4' Flute 61
  4' Salicet 61
  2' Flautino 61
  III Cornet 183
  16' Trumpet* 61
  8' Cornopean* 61
  8' Horn* 61
  8' Oboe 61
  8' Vox Humana 61
  4' Clarion* 61
  Tremolo

CHOIR 6" wind
  16' Dulciana 61
  8' Diapason 61
  8' Gamba 61
  8' Concert Flute 61
  8' Quintadena 61
  8' Dulciana 61
  8' Unda Maris 61
  4' Flute 61
  4' Violino 61
  2' Piccolo 61
  16' Fagotto 61
  8' Clarinet 61
  8' Orchestral Oboe 61
  Tremolo

SOLO 10" wind
  8' Stentorphone 61
  8' Philomela 61
  8' Gamba (Ch)
  8' Dulcet (II) 122
  8' Concert Flute (Ch)
  8' Quintadena (Ch)
  8' Dulciana (Ch)
  4' Flute 61
  4' Flute (Ch)
  16' Tuba (8' Tuba)
  16' Fagotto (Ch)
  8' Tuba Mirabilis***85
  8' Tuba**85
  8' Clarinet (Ch)
  8' Orchestral Oboe (Ch)
  4' Tuba (8' Tuba)

PEDAL 6" wind
  32' Diapason (16' Diapason)
  16' First Diapason* 56
  16' Second Diapason 44
  16' Violone 44
  16' First Bourdon (Gt)
  16' Second Bourdon (Sw)
  16' Dulciana (Ch)

10 2/3' Quint 32
    8' First Flute 16' (1st. Diapason)
    8' Second Flute (16' 2nd. Diapason)
    8' Viola (16' Violone)
    8' Gedackt (Gt Bourdon)
    8' Cello (Sw Voix Celestes)
    4' Flute 32
    32' Bombarde (Solo Tuba Mir.)
    16' Ophicleide (Solo Tuba Mir.)
    16' Trombone (Solo Tuba)
    8' Tromba (Solo Tuba Mir.)

  *10" wind
 **15" wind
***25" wind

Ranks: 61
Stops: 84
Pipes: 3672

COUPLERS
Pedal:
   Swell to Pedal
   Great to Pedal
   Choir to Pedal
   Solo to Pedal
   Swell to Pedal 4'
   Choir to Pedal 4'
   Solo to Pedal 4'
Unison:
   Swell to Great
   Choir to Great
   Solo to Great
   Great to Swell
   Solo to Swell
   Swell to Choir
   Solo to Choir
   Great to Solo
   Swell to Solo
   Choir to Solo

Octave:
   Swell to Swell 16'
   Swell to Swell 4'
   Swell to Great 16'
   Swell to Great 4'
   Choir to Choir 16'
   Choir to Choir 4'
   Choir to Great 16'
   Choir to Great 4'
   Solo to Solo 16'
   Solo to Solo 4'
   Solo to Great 16'
   Solo to Great 4'

COMBINATIONS
Pistons:
   Full Organ: 4 & release
   Great (Couplers & Pedal): 5 & release
   Swell (Couplers & Pedal): 6 & release
   Choir (Couplers & Pedal): 4 & release
   Solo (Couplers & Pedal): 4 & release
   Pedal: 3 & release

Pedals duplicating manual pistons:
   Great: 5
   Swell: 6
   Choir: 4

MECHANICALS
Swell expression pedal
Choir expression pedal
Solo expression pedal
Crescendo pedal
Sforzando pedal
Great to Pedal reversible
Swell to Pedal reversible
Electro-pneumatic action
All-electric movable console

Source: "City College Organ," *The American Organist,* I (1918), 83; *Organ in the College of the City of New York,* pamphlet published by the Ernest M. Skinner Organ Company, furnished by Barbara Owen. According to "The Skinner and Aeolian-Skinner Opus List," *Boston Organ Club Newsletter,* this organ was installed in 1906 and rebuilt numerous times.

E. M. Skinner Organ, Opus 195, 1911
Grace Chapin Hall
Williams College, Williamstown, Massachusetts

GREAT
   16' Diapason 61
   16' Bourdon 61
   8' First Diapason 61
   8' Second Diapason 61
   8' Philomela (Ped. Diapason)
   8' Grosse Floete 61
   8' Melodia 61
   8' Gamba 61

   8' Gemshorn 61
   4' Octave 61
   4' Wald Floete 61
   2' Fifteenth
   III Mixture 183
   16' Trombone (Solo)
   8' Tuba (Solo)
   8' Trumpet 61
   4' Clarion (Solo)

Organ Specifications

SWELL
- 16' Bourdon 73
- 8' First Diapason 73
- 8' Second Diapason 73
- 8' Claribella 73
- 8' Gedackt 73
- 8' Spitz Floete 73
- 8' Salicional 73
- 8' Vox Celeste 73
- 8' Aeoline 73
- 8' Vox Angelica 61
- 4' Octave 73
- 4' Flauto Traverso 73
- 4' Salicet 73
- 2' Flautino 61
- III Solo Mixture 183
- 16' Trumpet 73
- 8' Cornopean 73
- 8' Oboe 73
- 4' Clarion 73
- Tremolo

CHOIR
- 16' Contra Gamba 73
- 8' Geigen Principal 73
- 8' Quintadena 73
- 8' Concert Flute 73
- 8' Flauto Dolce 73
- 8' Dulciana 73
- 8' Unda Maris 61
- 8' Dulcet (II) 146
- 4' Flute d'Amour 73
- 2' Piccolo Harmonique 61
- 16' Fagotto 73
- 16' English Horn 73
- 8' Orchestral Oboe 73
- 8' Vox Humana 73
- Carillons
- Tremolo

SOLO
- 8' Stentorphone 73
- 8' Philomela (Ped. Diapason)
- 8' Viol d'Orchestre 73
- 8' Viol Celeste 73
- 16' Trombone (Tuba)
- 16' English Horn (Ch)
- 8' Tuba 85
- 8' French Horn 73
- 8' Corno d'Bassetto 73
- 8' Clarinet 73
- 8' Orchestral Oboe (Ch)
- 8' Vox Humana (Ch)
- 4' Clarion (Tuba)
- Carillons
- Tremolo

ECHO
- 8' Fern Flute 73
- 8' Dulcet (II) 146
- 4' Rohr Floete 73
- 8' Vox Humana 61
- Cathedral Chimes
- Tremolo

PEDAL
- 32' Diapason (16' 1st, Diapason)
- 32' Contra Bourdon (16' Bourdon)
- 16' First Diapason 44
- 16' Second Diapason (Gt)
- 16' Violone 32
- 16' Bourdon 68
- 16' Gedackt (Sw Bourdon)
- 16' Contra Gamba (Ch)
- 8' Octave (16' 1st. Diapason)
- 8' Flute (16' Bourdon)
- 8' Gedackt (Sw Bourdon)
- 8' Flauto Dolce (Ch)
- 8' 'Cello (Sw Salicional & Voix Celeste?)
- 4' Flute (16' Bourdon)
- 16' Trombone (Solo Tuba)
- 8' Tuba (Solo Tuba)
- 4' Clarion (Solo Tuba)

Ranks: 66
Stops: 84
Pipes: 4479

COUPLERS
Pedal:
- Swell to Pedal
- Great to Pedal
- Choir to Pedal
- Solo to Pedal
- Echo to Pedal
- Swell to Pedal 4'
- Choir to Pedal 4'
- Solo to Pedal 4'

Unison:
- Swell to Great
- Choir to Great
- Solo to Great
- Great to Swell
- Solo to Swell
- Swell unison off
- Swell to Choir
- Solo to Choir
- Choir unison off
- Great to Solo
- Swell to Solo
- Solo unison off
- Solo off; Echo on
- Echo unison off

Octave:
  Swell to Swell 16'
  Swell to Swell 4'
  Swell to Great 16'
  Swell to Great 4'
  Swell to Choir 16'
  Swell to Choir 4'
  Choir to Choir 16'
  Choir to Choir 4'
  Choir to Great 16'
  Choir to Great 4'
  Solo to Solo 16'
  Solo to Solo 4'
  Solo to Great 16'
  Solo to Great 4'
  Echo to Echo 16'
  Echo to Echo 4'

COMBINATIONS
Adjustable at the console, and visibly operating the draw stop knobs
Pistons:
  Great: 6
  Swell: 7
  Choir: 5
  Solo: 6
  Pedal: 6
  General cancel
  Pedal cancel
Pedals:
  Generals: 3

MECHANICALS
Swell expression pedal
Choir expression pedal
Solo & Echo expression pedal
Crescendo pedal
Sforzando pedal
Great to Pedal reversible
Solo to Great reversible
Solo to Pedal reversible
Hitchdown pedal for all expression pedals to Solo pedal.
Horizontal crescendo pedal indicator with graduated scale.
Electro-pneumatic action
All-electric movable console

Source: "Four Manual for Williams College," *The Diapason*, October 1912, p. 2. According to "The Skinner and Aeolian-Skinner Opus List," *Boston Organ Club Newsletter*, the organ was installed in 1911. According to "Four-Manual for Williams College," the instrument was under construction in 1912. On 11 September 1969, Joseph Dzeda wrote the author that this instrument had "been unplayable for 10 years" and that it was vandalized and "ruined beyond restoration."

E. M. Skinner Organ, Opus 232, 1915
First Universalist Church (Church of Our Father) Detroit, Michigan

GREAT
  16' Bourdon (Ped. Bourdon)
  8' First Diapason 61
  8' Second Diapason 61
  8' Philomela (Ped. 16'Diapason)
  8' Waldflöte 61
  8' Erzähler 61
  8' Gedackt (Sw)
  8' Aeoline (Sw)
  4' Flute (Sw)
  8' Tuba (Sw Cornopean)

SWELL
  16' Bourdon 61
  16' Dulciana 61
  8' Diapason 61
  8' Gedackt 61
  8' Spitzflöte 61
  8' Flute Celeste 49
  8' Salicional 61
  8' Voix Celestes 61
  8' Aeoline 61
  8' Unda Maris 49
  4' Octave 61
  4' Flute 61
  2' Flautino 61
  III Solo Mixture 183
  16' Contra Posaune 61
  8' Cornopean 61
  8' Flügel Horn 61
  8' Vox Humana 61
  Tremolo

CHOIR
  8' Diapason 61
  8' Concert Flute 61
  8' Dulciana 61
  8' Kleine Erzähler (II) 110
  4' Flute 61
  16' Fagotto 61
  8' Clarinet 61
  8' Orchestral Oboe 61
  8' Harp Sub (Harp)
  4' Harp 61 bars
  Tremolo

SOLO
  8' Philomela (Ped. 16' Diapason)
  8' Gamba 61

8' Gamba Celeste 61
8' Tuba Mirabilis 61
8' French Horn 61
8' English Horn 61
8' Clarinet (Ch)
8' Orchestral Oboe (Ch)
Tremolo

ECHO
8' Diapason 61
8' Quintadena 61
8' Viol d'Orchestre 61
8' Concert Flute 61
8' Cor de Nuit 61
8' Vox Angelica (II) 122
4' Flute 61
8' Flügel Horn 61
8' Vox Humana 61
Cathedral Chimes
Tremolo

PEDAL
32' Resultant (16' Diapason & 16' Bourdon)
16' Diapason 44
16' Violone 32
16' Bourdon 44
16' Dulciana (Sw)
16' Lieblich Gedeckt (Sw Bourdon)
8' Octave (16' Diapason)
8' Cello (Solo Gamba)
8' Gedeckt (16' Bourdon)
8' Still Gedeckt (Sw Bourdon)
32' Bombarde (Sw Contra Posaune)
16' Contra Posaune (Sw)
16' Fagotto (Ch)
8' Tromba (Sw Contra Posaune)

Ranks: 52
Stops: 70
Pipes: 3037

COUPLERS
Pedal:
　Swell to Pedal
　Great to Pedal
　Choir to Pedal
　Solo to Pedal
　Swell to Pedal 4'
　Choir to Pedal 4'
　Solo to Pedal 4'
Unison:
　Swell to Great
　Choir to Great
　Solo to Great
　Swell to Choir
　Solo to Choir
　Great to Solo
Octave:
　Swell to Swell 16'
　Swell to Swell 4'
　Swell to Great 16'
　Swell to Great 4'
　Choir to Choir 16'
　Choir to Choir 4'
　Solo to Solo 16'
　Solo to Solo 4'
　Solo to Great 16'
　Solo to Great 4'
　Great to Great 4'

COMBINATIONS
Visibly operating the draw stop knobs and adjustable at the console
Manual Pistons:
　Swell: 6
　Great: 6
　Choir: 6
　Solo & Echo: 6
　Pedal: 6
　Universal: 3
Toe Pistons:
(duplicating manual pistons)
　Swell: 6
　Pedal: 6

Pedal combinations to manual, On & off: Swell, Great, Choir, Solo & Echo.
Pedal combination to operate Great combinations when Great combinations operate Pedal combinations.

MECHANICALS
Swell expression pedal
Choir, Solo, Echo expression pedal
Crescendo pedal
Sforzando (hitchdown pedal)
Great to Pedal reversible pedal

Source: examination by the author. According to "The Skinner and Aeolian-Skinner Opus List," *Boston Organ Club Newsletter,* this organ was installed in 1915; "The Dedication Recitals Program," furnished by Barbara Owen, states that it was dedicated on 26 and 27 April 1916, in recitals played by Gaston M. Dethier. The instrument is extant and in its original tonal design.

E. M. Skinner Organ, Opus 265, 1916
Municipal Auditorium, Portland, Oregon

GREAT
- 16' Diapason 61
- 8' First Diapason 61
- 8' Second Diapason 61
- 8' Philomela (Ped. Diapason)
- 8' Claribel Flute 61
- 8' Erzähler 61
- 4' Octave 61
- 4' Flute 61
- 2' Fifteenth 61
- III Mixture 183
- 16' Euphonium (Solo)
- 8' Tuba (Solo)
- 4' Clarion (Solo)
- Cathedral Chimes

SWELL
- 16' Bourdon 73
- 8' Diapason 73
- 8' Clarabella 73
- 8' Gedeckt 73
- 8' Salicional 73
- 8' Voix Celestes 73
- 8' Spitz Floete 73
- 8' Flute Celestes 61
- 4' Octave 73
- 4' Flute 73
- 2' Flautino 61
- III Mixture 183
- 16' English Horn 73
- 8' Cornopean 73
- 8' Flügel Horn 73
- 8' Vox Humana 73
- 4' Clarion 73
- Tremolo

CHOIR
- 16' Gamba 73
- 8' Diapason 73
- 8' Quintadena 73
- 8' Concert Flute 73
- 8' Dulcet (II) 146
- 4' Flute 73
- 2' Piccolo 61
- 8' Clarinet 73
- 8' Celesta Sub (Celesta)
- 4' Celesta 61 bars
- Tremolo

SOLO
- 8' Stentorphone 73
- 8' Philomela (Ped. Diapason)
- 8' Gross Gamba 73
- 8' Gamba Celeste 73
- 16' Euphonium (8' Tuba)
- 8' Tuba Mirabilis 73
- 8' Tuba 85
- 8' French Horn 73
- 8' Orchestral Oboe 73
- 4' Clarion (8' Tuba)
- Tremolo

PEDAL
- 32' Diapason 16' (Diapason)
- 16' Diapason 68
- 16' Bourdon 44
- 16' Violone 32
- 16' Gamba (Ch)
- 16' Echo Lieblich (Sw Bourdon)
- 8' Octave (16' Diapason)
- 8' Gedeckt (16' Bourdon)
- 8' Cello (Ch)
- 8' Still Gedeckt (Sw 16' Bourdon)
- 4' Super Octave (16' Diapason)
- 32' Bombarde (16' Trombone)
- 16' Trombone 68
- 16' English Horn (Sw)
- 8' Tuba (Solo)
- 8' Tromba (16' Trombone)
- 4' Clarion (16' Trombone)

WIND PRESSURES
Pedal: 6"
Great & Choir: 7½"
Swell: 10"
Solo: 10", 15", & 25"
Bombarde: 15"

Ranks: 50
Stops: 68
Pipes: 3378

COUPLERS
Pedal:
    Swell to Pedal
    Great to Pedal
    Choir to Pedal
    Solo to Pedal
    Swell to Pedal 4'
    Choir to Pedal 4'
    Solo to Pedal 4'
Unison:
    Swell to Great
    Choir to Great
    Solo to Great
    Swell Unison Release
    Swell to Choir
    Choir Unison Release
    Solo to Choir
    Great to Solo

Octave:
    Swell to Swell 16'
    Swell to Swell 4'
    Swell to Great 16'
    Swell to Great 4'
    Choir to Choir 16'
    Choir to Choir 4'
    Choir to Great 16'
    Choir to Great 4'
    Solo to Solo 16'
    Solo to Solo 4'
    Solo to Great 16'
    Solo to Great 4'
    Great to Great 4'

COMBINATIONS
(Visibly operating the draw stop knobs and adjustable at the console)
Manual Pistons
    Swell: 7
    Great: 7
    Choir: 7
    Solo: 7
    Pedal: 7
    Generals: 3
Toe Piston:
    (duplicating manual pistons)
    Swell: 7

REVERSIBLES
    Great to Pedal (piston & pedal)
    Swell to Pedal (piston & pedal)
    Choir to Pedal (piston only)
    Solo to Pedal (piston & pedal)
    Swell to Great (pedal only)

MECHANICALS
    Swell expression pedal
    Choir expression pedal
    Solo expression pedal
    Crescendo pedal
    Sforzando (hitchdown pedal)

Source: "Portland, Oregon Organ," *The American Organist,* I (1918), 309. According to "Portland, Oregon, Award to Skinner," The Diapason, October 1916, p. 1, the contract was signed 13 September 1916; "The Skinner and Aeolian-Skinner Opus List," *Boston Organ Club Newsletter,* dates its installation as 1916, and notes that it was "sold in 1971 to Alpenrose Dairy, Portland."

E. M. Skinner Organ, Opus 322, 1921
Second Congregational Church, Holyoke, Massachusetts

GREAT
    16' Diapason 61
    16' Bourdon 61
    8' First Diapason 61
    8' Second Diapason 61
    8' Claribel Flute 61
    8' Wald Flute 61
    8' Erzähler 61
    4' Octave 61
    4' Flute 61
    2²/₃' Twelfth 61
    2' Fifteenth 61
    8' Tromba 61
        Cathedral Chimes 25 tubes

SWELL
    16' Bourdon 73
    8' First Diapason 73
    8' Second Diapason 73
    8' Clarabella 73
    8' Gedeckt 73
    8' Spitz Flute 73
    8' Flute Celeste 61
    8' Gamba 73
    8' Salicional 73
    8' Voix Celeste 73
    8' Aeoline 73
    8' Unda Maris 61
    4' Octave 61
    4' Flute 61
    4' Unda Maris (II) 122
    2' Flautino 61
    III Mixture 183
    16' Posaune 73
    8' Cornopean 73
    8' French Trumpet 73
    8' Flügel Horn 73
    8' Vox Humana 73
    4' Clarion 61
        Tremolo

CHOIR
    16' Gamba 73
    8' Diapason 73
    8' Concert Flute 73
    8' Kleine Erzähler (II) 110
    8' Gamba (mild) 73
    4' Flute 61
    2²/₃' Nazard 61
    2' Piccolo 61
    1³/₅' Tierce 61
    1¹/₇' Septième 61
    16' English Horn 73
    8' Clarinet 73
    8' Orchestral Oboe 73
    8' Celeste Sub (Celesta)
    4' Celesta 61 bars
        Tremolo

SOLO
- 8' Gross Gedeckt 73
- 8' Gamba 73
- 8' Gamba Celeste 73
- 4' Hohl Pfeife 61
- 16' Fagotto 73
- 8' Tuba Mirabilis 73
- 8' French Horn 73
- 8' Corno di Bassetto 73
- 8' Heckelphone 73
- 8' Musette 61
- Tremolo

ECHO
- 8' Diapason 73
- 8' Quintadena 73
- 8' Night Horn 73
- 8' Tromba 73
- 8' Vox Humana 61
- Chimes (Gt)
- Tremolo

PEDAL
- 32' Bourdon (16' Bourdon)
- 16' Diapason 44
- 16' Violone 44
- 16' Bourdon 68
- 16' Gamba (Ch)
- 16' Echo Lieblich (Sw Bourdon)
- 10 2/3' Quint (16' Bourdon)
- 8' Octave (16' Diapason)
- 8' Cello (16' Violone)
- 8' Gedeckt (16' Bourdon)
- 8' Still Gedeckt (Sw 16' Bourdon)
- 4' Flute (16' Bourdon)
- 3 1/5' Tierce (16' Bourdon)
- 2 2/7' Septieme (16' Bourdon)
- 32' Bombarde (16' Trombone)
- 16' Trombone 68
- 16' Posaune (Sw)
- 16' Fagotto (Solo)
- 16' English Horn (Ch)
- 8' Tromba (16' Trombone)
- 4' Clarion (16' Trombone)

Ranks: 71
Stops: 88
Pipes: 4707

COUPLERS
Pedal:
- Swell to Pedal
- Great to Pedal
- Choir to Pedal
- Solo to Pedal
- Swell to Pedal 4'
- Choir to Pedal 4'
- Solo to Pedal 4'

Unison:
- Swell to Great
- Choir to Great
- Solo to Great
- Swell to Choir
- Solo to Choir
- Great to Solo

Octave:
- Swell to Swell 16'
- Swell to Swell 4'
- Swell to Great 16'
- Swell to Great 4'
- Swell to Choir 4'
- Choir to Choir 16'
- Choir to Choir 4'
- Choir to Great 16'
- Solo to Solo 16'
- Solo to Solo 4'
- Solo to Great 16'
- Solo to Great 4'

COMBINATIONS, adjustable
- Swell: 8
- Great: 5
- Choir: 6
- Solo & Echo: 8
- Pedal: 6
- General cancel

Pedal combinations to manual, on & off:
  Swell, Great, Choir, Solo & Echo.

REVERSIBLES, piston & pedal
- Great to Pedal
- Swell to Pedal
- Choir to Pedal
- Solo to Pedal
- Sforzando

MECHANICALS
- Swell expression pedal
- Choir expression pedal
- Solo & Echo expression pedal
- Crescendo (with indicator)
- Octave couplers off
- All swells to swell

Source: Dedication Recital Program, 27 Jaunary 1922, furnished by Barbara Owen; "Organ of 84 Stops for Holyoke Church," *The Diapason*, January 1921, p. 1. The article sets the contract signing date as late 1920. The inaugural recital program is dated 27 January 1922. The program was played by William Churchill Hammond.

E. M. Skinner Organ, Opus 357, 1922
Robert Law Residence, Port Chester, New York

MANUAL I (GREAT)
- 16' Bourdon 73
- 8' Diapason 73
- 8' Gedeckt 73
- 8' Salicional 73
- 8' Voix Celeste 73
- 8' Flauto Dolce 73
- 8' Flute Celeste 61
- 8' Unda Maris (II) 134
- 4' Unda Maris (II) 146
- 8' Harp (Celesta)
- 4' Celesta 61 bars
- Tremolo

MANUAL II (SWELL)
- 8' Diapason 73
- 8' Chimney Flute 73
- 8' Voix Celeste (II) 146
- 4' Flute 61
- 8' Tuba 73 (on high wind)
- 8' French Horn 73 (on high wind)
- 8' Clarinet 61
- 8' English Horn 61
- 8' Vox Humana
- Chimes 25 tubes
- Tremolo I
- Tremolo II (Tuba & French Horn)

MANUAL III (SOLO)
- 16' Bourdon (Gt)
- 8' Diapason (Gt)
- 8' Diapason (Sw)
- 8' Gedeckt (Gt)
- 8' Chimney Flute (Sw)
- 8' Salicional (Gt)
- 8' Voix Celeste (Gt)
- 8' Voix Celeste (II) (Sw)
- 8' Flauto Dolce (Gt)
- 8' Flute Celeste (Gt)
- 8' Unda Maris (II) (Gt)
- 4' Unda Maris (II) (Gt)
- 4' Flute (Sw)
- 8' Tuba (Sw)
- 8' French Horn (Sw)
- 8' Clarinet (Sw)
- 8' English Horn (Sw)
- 8' Vox Humana (Sw)
- 8' Harp (Gt)
- 4' Celesta (Gt)
- Chimes (Sw)

MANUAL III (ECHO)
- 8' Chimney Flute 61
- 8' Chimney Flute Celeste 49
- 8' Vox Humana 61
- Tremolo

PEDAL
- 16' Bourdon 44
- 16' Echo Lieblich (Sw Bourdon)
- 8' Gedeckt (16' Bourdon)
- 8' Still Gedeckt (Sw 16' Bourdon)
- 16' Trombone 44
- 8' Tromba (16' Trombone)

Ranks: 26
Stops: 51
Pipes: 1720

COUPLERS
Pedal:
- Swell to Pedal
- Great to Pedal
- Solo to Pedal
- Swell to Pedal 4'

Unison:
- Swell to Great
- Solo to Great
- Swell to Solo
- Swell Unison Release
- Great Unison Release
- Solo Unison Release

Octave:
- Swell to Swell 16'
- Swell to Swell 4'
- Swell to Great 16'
- Swell to Great 4'
- Great to Great 16'
- Great to Great 4'
- Solo to Solo 16'
- Solo to Solo 4'
- Solo to Great 16'
- Solo to Great 4'

COMBINATIONS, adjustable
- Swell: 5
- Great: 5
- Solo: 5
- Pedal: 3

MECHANICALS
- Manual I expression pedal
- Manual II expression pedal
- Echo expression operating from Manual I expression pedal.
- Crescendo pedal
- Manual I to Pedal reversible
- Sforzando (by man. & toe piston)
- Harp Dampers on & off

PLAYER
Ventil
Semi-Automatic

Full-Automatic
Re-Roll

Source: "The Robert Law Organ Specifications," *Stop, Open, and Reed*, 2, no. 1 (January 1924), 19. According to "The Skinner and Aeolian-Skinner Opus List," *Boston Organ Club Newsletter,* this instrument was installed in 1922, and "junked in 1958."

E. M. Skinner Organ, Opus 369, 1922
Capitol Theatre, Boston, Massachusetts

GREAT
- 8' Diapason 73
- 8' Major Flute 73
- 8' Gedeckt 73
- 8' Violoncello 85
- 8' Viole Celeste 73
- 8' String Organ (IV) 292
- 8' Dolce Celeste (II) 134
- 4' Unda Maris (II) 122
- 4' Orchestral Flute 61
- 16' Trumpet (8' Trumpet)
- 8' Harmonic Trumpet 85
- 8' Vox Humana 61
- 4' Clarion (8' Trumpet)
- 8' Harp (Celesta)
- 4' Celesta 61 bars
- Tremolo

SWELL
- 16' Bourdon 73
- 8' Diapason (Gt)
- 8' Major Flute (Gt)
- 8' Gedeckt (Gt)
- 8' Violoncello (Gt)
- 8' Viol Celeste (Gt)
- 8' String Organ (IV) (Gt)
- 8' Dolce Celeste (II) (Gt)
- 4' Unda Maris (II) (Gt)
- 4' Orchestral Flute (Gt)
- 16' Trumpet (Gt)
- 8' Harmonic Trumpet (Gt)
- 8' Corno d'Amour 73
- 8' Vox Humana (Gt)
- 4' Clarion (Gt)
- 8' Harp (Gt)
- 4' Celesta (Gt)
- Tremolo

ORCHESTRAL
- 8' Doppel Floete 73
- 8' Concert Flute 73
- 8' String Organ (IV) 292
- 8' Orchestral Strings (II) 146
- 4' Violina 61
- 4' Orchestral Flute 61
- 2 2/3' Nazard 61
- 2' Piccolo 61
- 1 3/5' Tierce 61
- 1 1/7' Septième 61
- 16' Bassoon 73
- 8' Clarinet 61
- 8' English Horn 61
- 8' French Horn 61
- 8' Musette 61
- 8' Physharmonica 61
- Tremolo

SOLO
- 8' Doppel Floete (Orch)
- 8' Concert Flute (Orch)
- 8' String Organ (IV) (Orch)
- 8' Orchestral Strings (II) (Orch)
- 4' Violina (Orch)
- 4' Orchestral Flute (Orch)
- 2 2/3' Nazard (Orch)
- 2' Piccolo (Orch)
- 1 3/5' Tierce (Orch)
- 1 1/7' Septième (Orch)
- 16' Bassoon (Orch)
- 8' Orchestral Tuba 73
- 8' Clarinet (Orch)
- 8' English Horn (Orch)
- 8' French Horn (Orch)
- 8' Musette (Orch)
- Cathedral Chimes 20 tubes
- Tremolo

PEDAL
- 32' Resultant (16' Diapason & 16' Bourdon)
- 16' Diapason 44
- 16' Violone (Gt 8' Violoncello)
- 16' Bourdon 44
- 16' Lieblich Gedeckt (Sw Bourdon)
- 8' Octave (16' Diapason)
- 8' Violoncello (Gt)
- 8' Gedeckt (16' Bourdon)
- 8' Still Gedeckt (Sw 16' Bourdon)
- 8' String Organ (IV)
- 16' Double Trumpet (Gt 8' Trumpet)
- 16' Bassoon (Orch)
- 8' Trumpet (Gt 8' Trumpet)
- 8' Bassoon (Orch 16' Bassoon)
- Chimes (Solo)

Ranks: 41
Stops: 80
Pipes: 2706

TRAPS
Enclosed with Great:
Snare Drum
Bass Drum
Chinese Block
Tamborine
Cymbal
Tympani
Auto Horn
Bird Song
Orchestral Bells (metal hammers repeating on Celesta)
Enclosed with Orchestral:
Xylophone 49 bars

COUPLERS
Pedal:
   Swell to Pedal
   Great to Pedal
   Orches. to Pedal
   Solo to Pedal
   Swell to Pedal 4'
   Solo to Pedal 4'
Unison:
   Swell to Great
   Orches. to Great
   Solo to Great
   Swell to Orches.
   Solo to Swell
   Great to Solo

Octave:
   Swell to Swell 16'
   Swell to Swell 4'
   Swell to Great 16'
   Swell to Great 4'
   Swell to Orches. 16'
   Swell to Orches. 4'
   Orches. to Orches. 16'
   Orches. to Orches. 4'
   Orches. to Great 16'
   Orches. to Great 4'
   Solo to Solo 16'
   Solo to Solo 4'
   Solo to Great 16'
   Solo to Great 4'
   Great to Great 16'
   Great to Great 4'

COMBINATIONS, adjustable
Swell: 6, 2nd. touch to bring on all couplers to Swell.
Great: 6, 2nd. touch to bring on all couplers to Great.
Orchestral: 6, 2nd. touch to bring on all couplers to Orchestral.
Solo: 6, 2nd. touch to bring on all couplers to Solo.
Pedal: 6
Full: 1, 2, 3, 4 to operate 3, 4, 5, 6 of Swell, Great, Orchestral, Solo and Pedal, and on 2nd. touch bring on couplers.
General Cancel

Source: "The Capitol Theatre Organ, Boston, Mass.," *Stop, Open, and Reed,* 1, no. 4 (December 1922), 15. "The Skinner and Aeolian-Skinner Opus List," *Boston Organ Club Newsletter,* dates installation in 1922, and states that the organ was stored as of 1972 in St. Mary's, Quincy, Ma., and the theater was demolished.

E. M. Skinner Organ, Opus 405, 1923
Cossitt Avenue School, La Grange, Illinois

GREAT
  8' Diapason
  8' Clarabella
  8' Erzähler
  4' Octave
  8' French Horn (Enclosed in Sw)
     Chimes

SWELL
 16' Bourdon
  8' Diapason
  8' Gedeckt
  8' Salicional
  8' Voix Celeste
  8' Aeoline

  4' Flute Harmonique
 III Mixture (15-19-22)
  8' Cornopean
  8' Flügel Horn
  8' Vox Humana
     Tremolo

CHOIR
  8' Concert Flute
  8' Dulciana
  4' Flute Harmonique
  8' Clarinet
  8' Harp (Celesta)
  4' Celesta
     Tremolo

270   *The Life and Work of Ernest M. Skinner*

PEDAL
  16' Diapason
  16' Bourdon
  16' Echo Bourdon (Sw Bourdon)
  8' Octave (16' Diapason)
  8' Bourdon (16' Bourdon)
  8' Still Gedeckt (Sw 16' Bourdon)
  Chimes

Ranks: 24
Stops: 30

COUPLERS
Pedal:
  Swell to Pedal
  Great to Pedal
  Choir to Pedal
  Swell to Pedal 4'
  Great to Pedal 4'
Unison:
  Swell to Great
  Choir to Great
  Swell to Choir
Octave:
  Swell to Swell 16'
  Swell to Swell 4'

Swell to Great 16'
Swell to Great 4'
Choir to Choir 16'
Choir to Choir 4'
Choir to Great 16'
Choir to Great 4'
Great to Great 4'

COMBINATIONS, adjustable
Swell: 6
Great: 4
Choir: 3
Pedal: 4
Cancel

Pedal combinations to manual, on & off:
  Swell, Great, Choir.

REVERSIBLES
Great to Pedal
Sforzando

MECHANICALS
Swell expression pedal
Choir expression pedal
Crescendo pedal

Source: When this organ was for sale a decade ago, the author's husband took the specification by telephone from an unidentified caller. The *Boston Organ Club Newsletter* dates the organ as 1923.

E. M. Skinner Organ, Opus 467, 1925
Baptist Temple, Charleston, West Virginia

GREAT
  8' Diapason 73
  8' Clarabella 73
  8' Gedeckt (Sw)
  8' Aeoline (Sw)
  4' Flute (Sw)
  8' Cornopean (Sw)
  8' Flügel Horn (Sw)
  Chimes (Echo)

ECHO playable on Great manual
  8' Viole Aetheria 61
  8' Vox Angelica 49
  8' Vox Humana 61
  Chimes 20 tubes
  Tremolo

SWELL
  16' Bourbon 73
  8' Diapason 73
  8' Gedeckt 73
  8' Salicional 73
  8' Voix Celeste 73
  8' Aeoline 73
  4' Flute 73

  8' Cornopean 73
  8' Flügel Horn 73
  8' Vox Humana 73
  Tremolo

CHOIR
  8' Concert Flute 73
  8' Dulciana 73
  4' Flute d'Amour 73
  8' Clarinet 73
  Tremolo

PEDAL
  16' Diapason 44
  16' Bourdon 44
  16' Echo Bourdon (Sw 16' Bourdon)
  8' Octave (16' Diapason)
  8' Gedeckt (16' Bourdon)
  8' Still Gedeckt (Sw 16' Bourdon)
  Chimes (Echo)

Ranks: 21
Stops: 32
Pipes: 1427

COUPLERS
Pedal:
  Swell to Pedal
  Great to Pedal
  Choir to Pedal
  Swell to Pedal 4'
Unison:
  Swell to Great
  Choir to Great
  Swell to Choir
Octave:
  Swell to Swell 16'
  Swell to Swell 4'
  Swell to Great 16'
  Swell to Great 4'
  Choir to Choir 16'
  Choir to Choir 4'
  Choir to Great 16'
  Choir to Great 4'
  Great to Great 16'
  Great to Great 4'

COMBINATIONS
Swell: 4 (man. pistons only)
Great: 4 (man. pistons only)
Choir: 3 (man. pistons only)
Pedal: 4 (toe pistons only)
Pedal combinations to Great, on & off.
Cancel

REVERSIBLES
Great to Pedal (pedal)
Sforzando (pedal)

MECHANICALS
Swell expression pedal
Choir & Echo expression pedal
Crescendo pedal
Great on-Echo off,
Echo on-Great off,
Both (Echo & Great on)

Source: examination by the author. According to "The Skinner and Aeolian-Skinner Opus List," *Boston Organ Club Newsletter,* the Organ was installed in 1924. It was replaced by a Holtkamp organ in 1969, and is now in the home of the author.

E. M. Skinner Organ, Opus 475, 1925
Jefferson Avenue Presbyterian Church, Detroit, Michigan

GREAT
  16' Diapason 73
  8' First Diapason 73
  8' Second Diaspason 73
  8' Claribel Flute 73
  8' Erzähler 73
  4' Octave 73
  4' Flute 73
  2 2/3' Twelfth 61
  2' Fifteenth 61
  16' Ophicleide (Solo)
  8' Tromba 73
  8' Tuba (Solo)
  4' Clarion 73
  4' Tuba Clarion (Solo)
  Chimes (Echo)

SWELL
  16' Bourdon 73
  8' First Diapason 73
  8' Second Diapason 73
  8' Clarabella 73
  8' Gedeckt 73
  8' Gamba 73
  8' Voix Celeste (II) 146
  8' Flauto Dolce 73
  8' Flute Celeste 61
  8' Aeoline 73
  8' Unda Maris 61
  4' Octave 73
  4' Flute Triangulaire 73
  4' Unda Maris (II) 122
  2' Flautino 61
  V Mixture
    (15-19-22-26-29) 305
  16' Posaune 73
  8' Cornopean 73
  8' Flügel Horn
  8' Vox Humana 73
  4' Clarion 73
  Tremolo

CHOIR
  16' Gamba 61
  8' Diapason 61
  8' Concert Flute 61
  8' Kleine Erzähler (II) 110
  4' Flute 61
  2 2/3' Nazard 61
  2' Piccolo 61
  8' Clarinet 61
  8' Orchestral Oboe 61
  8' Harp (from Celesta)
  4' Celesta 61 bars
  Tremolo

SOLO
  8' Stentorphone 73
  8' Gamba 73

8' Gamba Celeste 73
16' Ophicleide 73
8' Tuba Mirabilis 73
8' Tuba 73
8' French Horn 73
8' English Horn 73
4' Tuba Clarion 73
   Tremolo

ECHO
  8' Diaspason 61
  8' Chimney Flute 61
  8' Voix Celeste (II) 122
  4' Flute 61
  8' Tromba 61
  8' Vox Humana 61
    Chimes 25 tubes

PEDAL
  16' Diapason 56
  16' Diapason (Gt 16' Diapason)
  16' Violone 44
  16' Gamba (Ch 16' Gamba)
  16' Bourdon 68
  16' Echo Lieblich (Sw 16' Bourdon)
  8' Octave (16' Diapason)
  8' Gedackt (16' Bourdon)
  8' Cello (16' Violone)
  8' Still Gedeckt (Sw 16' Bourdon)
  4' Super Octave (16' Diapason)
  4' Still Flute (16' Bourdon)
  2' Piccolo (16' Bourdon)
  32' Bombarde (16' Trombone)
  16' Trombone 68
  16' Posaune (Sw 16' Posaune)
  8' Tromba (16' Trombone)
  16' Clarion (16' Trombone)
    Chimes (Echo)

Ranks: 68
Stops: 82
Pipes: 4548

COUPLERS
Pedal:
  Swell to Pedal
  Great to Pedal
  Choir to Pedal
  Solo to Pedal
  Swell to Pedal 4'

Choir to Pedal 4'
Solo to Pedal 4'
Unison:
  Swell to Great
  Choir to Great
  Solo to Great
  Swell to Choir
  Solo to Choir
  Swell to Solo
  Great to Solo
Octave:
  Swell to Swell 16'
  Swell to Swell 4'
  Swell to Great 16'
  Swell to Great 4'
  Swell to Choir 4'
  Choir to Choir 16'
  Choir to Choir 4'
  Choir to Great 16'
  Choir to Great 4'
  Solo to Solo 16'
  Solo to Solo 4'
  Solo to Great 16'
  Solo to Great 4'
  Great to Great 4'

COMBINATIONS adjustable
Swell: 8 (man. pistons only)
Great: 6 (man. pistons only)
Choir: 6 (man. pistons only)
Solo & Echo: 8 (man. pistons only)
Pedal: 6 (toe pistons only)
General: 6 (man. pistons only)
General Cancel
Pedal combinations to manual, on & off:
  Swell, Great, Choir, Solo & Echo.

REVERSIBLES
Great to Pedal (man. piston & pedal)
Swell to Pedal (man. piston only)
Choir to Pedal (man. piston only)
Sforzando (man. piston & pedal)

MECHANICALS
Choir expression pedal
Swell expression pedal
Solo & Echo expression pedal
Crescendo pedal (with light indicator)
Octave Couplers Off (man. piston)
all Swells to Swell (hitchdown pedal)

Source: examination by the author. *The Detroit Presbyterian* 10 April 1924, sets the contract signing in early 1924; an unsigned copy of a letter to Mr. John R. Russell, Augusta, Georgia, dated 24 March 1926 and found in miscellaneous stored papers at the church, indicates that the installation, final finishing, and tuning were completed by late March, 1926. The church bulletin of 4 April 1926 announces the opening recital by Palmer Christian on 8 April 1926. It was restored in 1976 with original design intact.

E. M. Skinner Organ, Opus 623, 1926
St. Joseph's Episcopal Church, Detroit, Michigan

GREAT
  16' Bourdon (Ped.)
  8' First Diapason 61
  8' Second Diapason 61
  8' Claribel Flute 61
  8' Gedeckt (Sw)
  8' Flute Celeste (Sw)
  4' Octave 61
  4' Flute Triangulaire (Sw)
  III Mixture (15-19-22) 183
  8' Tromba 61

SWELL
  16' Bourdon 73
  8' Diapason 73
  8' Gedeckt 73
  8' Salicional 73
  8' Voix Celeste 73
  8' Flauto Dolce 73
  8' Flute Celeste 61
  4' Octave 73
  4' Flute Triangulaire 73
  IV Mixture (15-19-22-26) 244
  16' Waldhorn 73
  8' Cornopean 73
  8' Flügel Horn 73
  8' Vox Humana 73
  Tremolo

CHOIR
  8' Concert Flute 73
  8' Cello 73
  4' Flute 73
  2' Piccolo 73
  8' Clarinet 61
  8' Harp (Celesta)
  4' Celesta 61 bars
  Tremolo

SOLO
  8' Flauto Mirabilis 73
  8' Gamba 73
  8' Gamba Celeste 73
  8' Tuba 73
  8' French Horn 73
  8' English Horn 73
  Tremolo

PEDAL
  16' Major Bass 44
  16' Bourdon 61
  16' Echo Bourdon (Sw 16' Bourdon)
  8' Octave (16' Major Base)
  8' Still Gedeckt (Sw 16' Bourdon)
  16' Trombone 44
  16' Waldhorn (Sw 16' Waldhorn)
  8' Tromba (16' Trombone)

Ranks: 39
Stops: 46
Pipes: 2609

COUPLERS
Pedal:
  Swell to Pedal
  Great to Pedal
  Choir to Pedal
  Solo to Pedal
  Swell to Pedal 4'
  Solo to Pedal 4'
Unison:
  Swell to Great
  Choir to Great
  Solo to Great
  Swell to Choir
  Solo to Choir
  Great to Solo
Octave:
  Swell to Swell 16'
  Swell to Swell 4'
  Swell to Great 16'
  Swell to Great 4'
  Swell to Choir 16'
  Swell to Choir 4'
  Choir to Choir 16'
  Choir to Choir 4'
  Choir to Great 16'
  Solo to Solo 16'
  Solo to Solo 4'
  Solo to Great 16'
  Solo to Great 4'

COMBINATIONS, adjustable
Swell: 6 (man. pistons only)
Great: 5 (man. pistons only)
Choir: 5 (man. pistons only)
Solo: 5 (man. pistons only)
Pedal: 5 (toe pistons only)
Cancel
Pedal combinations to manual, on & off:
  Swell, Great, Choir, Solo.

REVERSIBLES
Great to Pedal (man. piston & pedal)
Swell to Pedal (man. piston only)
Choir to Pedal (man. piston only)
Swell to Pedal 4' (man. piston only)
Solo to Pedal 4' (man. piston only)
Swell to Great (man. piston only)
Solo to Great (man. piston only)

Swell to Choir (man. piston only)
Sforzando (man. piston & pedal)
MECHANICALS
Choir expression pedal
Swell expression pedal
Solo expression pedal
Crescendo pedal (with dial indicator)
Manual 16′, on & off

Source: examination by the author. Installation is dated as 1926 by the *Boston Organ Club Newsletter*. The Solo organ was installed in 1927, according to the business manager at the church, now called St. Matthew's-St. Joseph's Episcopal Church. The organ has had some tonal changes.

E. M. Skinner Organ, Opus 632, 1927
First Presbyterian Church, Concord, North Carolina

GREAT
   16′ Bourdon (Ped.)
   8′ Diapason
   8′ Clarabella
   4′ Octave
   4′ Flute
   2′ Fifteenth
   8′ Tromba
   8′ French Horn
   Chimes

SWELL
   16′ Bourdon
   8′ Diapason
   8′ Gedeckt
   8′ Salicional
   8′ Voix Celeste
   8′ Aeoline
   4′ Flute
   2′ Harmonic Piccolo
   8′ Cornopean
   8′ Oboe d'Amore
   8′ Vox Humana
   Tremolo

CHOIR
   8′ Concert Flute
   8′ Dulciana
   4′ Flute
   8′ Clarinet
   8′ Harp (Celesta)
   4′ Celesta
   Tremolo

PEDAL
   32′ Resultant
   16′ Subbass
   16′ Bourdon
   16′ Echo Lieblich (Sw 16′ Bourdon)
   8′ Octave (16′ Subbass)
   8′ Gedeckt (16′ Bourdon)
   8′ Still Gedeckt (Sw 16′ Bourdon)

Ranks: 24
Stops: 33

COUPLERS
Pedal:
   Swell to Pedal
   Great to Pedal
   Choir to Pedal
   Swell to Pedal 4′
Unison:
   Swell to Great
   Choir to Great
   Swell to Choir
Octave:
   Swell to Swell 16′
   Swell to Swell 4′
   Swell to Great 16′
   Swell to Great 4′
   Choir to Choir 16′
   Choir to Choir 4′
   Choir to Great 16′
   Choir to Great 4′
   Great to Great 4′

COMBINATIONS, adjustable
Swell: 6 (man. pistons only)
Great: 4 (man. pistons only)
Choir: 3 (man. pistons only)
Pedal: 4 (toe pistons only)
Cancel
Pedal combinations to manual, on & off:
   Swell, Great, Choir.

REVERSIBLES, manual piston & pedal
Great to Pedal
Sforzando

MECHANICALS
Choir expression pedal
Swell expression pedal
Crescendo pedal

Source: Letter to Kenneth H. Holden from Robert Stigall, organ consultant, 14 November 1974. The organ was replaced by a Flentrop.

E. M. Skinner Organ, Opus 719, 1928
Our Lady of Mount Carmel Roman Catholic Church
Chicago, Illinois

GREAT
- 16' Diapason 73
- 8' First Diapason 73
- 8' Second Diapason 73
- 8' Harmonic Flute 73
- 4' Octave 73
- 4' Flute 73
- 2 2/3' Twelfth 61
- 2' Fifteenth 61
- III Harmonic (17-19-22) 183
- 8' Tromba 73
- 4' Clarion (8' Tromba)

SWELL
- 8' Diapason 73
- 8' Rohrfloete 73
- 8' Salicional 73
- 8' Voix Celeste 73
- 8' Flauto Dolce 73
- 8' Flute Celeste 61
- 4' Octave 73
- 4' Flute Triangulaire 73
- 2' Flautino 61
- V Mixture (15-19-22-26-29) 305
- 16' Waldhorn 73
- 8' Trumpet 73
- 8' Oboe d'Amore 73
- 8' Vox Humana 73
- 4' Clarion 73
- 8' Harp (Choir)
- 4' Celesta (Choir)
- Tremolo

CHOIR
- 16' Gamba 73
- 8' Concert Flute 73
- 8' Gamba 73
- 8' Gamba Celeste 73
- 8' Dulciana 73
- 4' Gambette 73
- 4' Flute 73
- 2 2/3' Nazard 61
- 8' Tuba Mirabilis 73
- 8' French Horn 73
- 8' Clarinet 73
- 8' Orchestral Oboe 73
- 8' Harp (Celesta)
- 4' Celesta 61 bars
- Tremolo

PEDAL
- 16' Diapason 32
- 16' Diapason (Gt 16' Diapason)
- 16' Contrabass 56
- 16' Bourdon 44
- 16' Gamba (Ch 16' Gamba)
- 8' Octave (16' Contrabass)
- 8' Cello (Ch 16' Gamba)
- 8' Gedeckt (16' Bourdon)
- 4' Super Octave (16' Contrabass)
- 16' Trombone 44
- 8' Tromba (16' Trombone)

Ranks: 47
Stops: 53
Pipes: 3159

COUPLERS
Pedal:
 Swell to Pedal
 Great to Pedal
 Choir to Pedal
 Swell to Pedal 4'
 Choir to Pedal 4'
Unison:
 Swell to Great
 Choir to Great
 Swell to Choir
Octave:
 Swell to Swell 16'
 Swell to Swell 4'
 Swell to Great 16'
 Swell to Great 4'
 Swell to Choir 16'
 Swell to Choir 4'
 Choir to Choir 16'
 Choir to Choir 4'
 Choir to Great 16'
 Choir to Great 4'

COMBINATIONS
Swell: 7
Great: 6
Choir: 6
Pedal: 6
General: 4
General Cancel
Pedal combinations to manual, on & off:
 Swell, Great, Choir.

REVERSIBLES
Great to Pedal
Swell to Pedal
Choir to Pedal
Sforzando

Mechanicals
Choir expression pedal
Swell expression pedal
Crescendo pedal

Source: William H. Barnes, "The Organ," *The American Organist*, 12, no. 5 (1929), 287; also, examination by the author. The article gives the dedication date as 24 March 1929, with the opening concert by Palmer Christian. The instrument was in its original tonal design in 1975. The installation date given by the *Boston Organ Club Newsletter's* "The Skinner and Aeolian-Skinner Opus List is 1928.

E. M. Skinner Organ, Opus 820, 1930
Cathedral Church of Our Lady, Queen of the Holy Rosary
Toledo, Ohio

GREAT
  16' Double Diapason 61
  8' First Diapason 61
  8' Second Diapason 61
  8' Third Diapason* 61
  8' Harmonic Flute 61
  8' Gedeckt* 61
  8' Erzähler 61
  8' Viola* 61
  4' Octave 61
  4' Flute* 61
  2⅔' Twelfth 61
  2' Fifteenth 61
  IV Mixture (19-22-26-29) 244
  IV Harmonics (17-19-21-22) 244
  16' Trumpet 61
  8' Tromba 61
  4' Clarion 61

*stops enclosed in Choir box

SWELL
  16' Melodia 73
  8' Diapason 73
  8' Rohrflöte 73
  8' Salicional 73
  8' Voix Celeste 73
  8' Flute Celeste (II) 134
  8' Echo Gamba 73
  4' Octave 73
  4' Flute Triangulaire 73
  2' Flautino 61
  V Mixture (15-19-22-26-29) 305
  16' Waldhorn 73
  8' Trumpet 73
  8' Oboe d'Amore 73
  8' Vox Humana 73
  4' Clarion 73
  Tremolo

CHOIR
  16' Gamba 73
  8' Diapason 73
  8' Concert Flute 73
  8' Gamba 73
  8' Kleine Erzähler 73

  8' Kleine Erzähler Celeste 61
  4' Gemshorn 73
  4' Flute 73
  2⅔' Nazard 61
  2' Piccolo 61
  III Carillon (12-17-22) 183
  16' Fagotto 85
  8' Flügel Horn 73
  8' Clarinet 73
  8' Harp (Celesta)
  4' Celesta 61 bars
  Tremolo

SOLO
  8' Flauto Mirabilis 73
  8' Gamba 73
  8' Gamba Celeste 73
  4' Orchestral Flute 73
  16' Corno di Bassetto
    (8' Corno di Bassetto)
  8' Tuba Mirabilis 73
  8' French Horn 73
  8' Corno di Bassetto 85
  8' English Horn 73
  Tremolo

PEDAL
  32' Major Bass (16' Diapason)
  16' First Diapason 68
  16' Second Diapason (Gt 16' Diapason)
  16' Bourdon 44
  16' Melodia (Sw 16' Melodia)
  16' Dulciana 44
  16' Gamba (Ch 16' Gamba)
  8' Octave (16' Diapason)
  8' Gedeckt (16' Bourdon)
  8' Still Gedeckt (Sw 16' Melodia)
  8' 'Cello (16' Dulciana)
  4' Super Octave (16' Diapason)
  IV Mixture (17-19-21-22) 128
  32' Fagotto (Ch 16' Fagotto)
  16' Trombone 44
  16' Waldhorn (Sw 16' Waldhorn)
  16' Fagotto (Ch 16' Fagotto)
  8' Tromba (16' Trombone)

Ranks: 72
Stops: 76
Pipes: 4884
COUPLERS
Pedal:
   Swell to Pedal
   Great to Pedal
   Choir to Pedal
   Solo to Pedal
   Swell to Pedal 4'
   Choir to Pedal 4'
   Solo to Pedal 4'
Unison:
   Swell to Great
   Choir to Great
   Solo to Great
   Swell to Choir
   Solo to Choir
   Solo to Swell
   Great to Solo
Octave:
   Swell to Great 16'
   Swell to Great 4'
   Swell to Choir 16'
   Swell to Choir 4'
   Choir to Great 16'
   Choir to Great 4'
   Solo to Great 16'
   Solo to Great 4'
Octave: (In stop jambs)
   Swell to Swell 16'
   Swell to Swell 4'
   Choir to Choir 16'
   Choir to Choir 4'
   Solo to Solo 16'

Solo to Solo 4'
Solo Reeds to Great
COMBINATIONS, adjustable
Swell: 10 & Cancel (2nd. touch for Pedal Combination to manual)
Great: 10 & Cancel (2nd. touch for Pedal combination to manual)
Choir: 10 & Cancel (2nd. touch for Pedal combination to manual)
Solo: 5 & Cancel (2nd. touch for Pedal combination to manual)
Pedal: 8 & Cancel (toe pistons only)
General: 6
General Cancel
REVERSIBLES
Great to Pedal (man. piston & pedal)
Swell to Pedal (man. piston & pedal)
Choir to Pedal (man. piston only)
Solo to Pedal (man. piston only)
Choir to Great (man. piston only)
Solo to Great (man. piston only)
Swell to Choir (man. piston only)
Solo to Choir (man. piston only)
All Swells to Swell pedal (man. piston & pedal)
Sforzando (man. piston & pedal)
MECHANICALS
Choir expression pedal
Swell expression pedal
Solo expression pedal
Crescendo pedal (with light indicators)
Manual 16' stops on & off
Pedal 32' stops on & off
All couplers on & off crescendo

Source: examination by the author. The installation date given by the *Boston Organ Club Newsletter* is 1930; "Description of the New Organ in the Queen of the Holy Rosary Cathedral," *New Cathedral Festival* (Rededication Program), June 1931, furnished by Hugh L. Murray, places the completion and dedication in June 1931. The instrument is in its original tonal design in 1984.

Ernest M. Skinner & Son Organ, 1937
First Presbyterian Church, Newburgh, New York

GREAT
  16' Gemshorn (Ped. 16' Gemshorn)
   8' Diapason 61
   8' Principal Flute 61
   8' Erzähler 61
   4' Octave 61
  2 2/3' Twelfth 61
   2' Fifteenth 61
   8' French Horn
     (in Choir box) 61
     Chimes 25 tubes

SWELL
  16' Bourdon 73
   8' Diapason 73
   8' Gedeckt 73
   8' Salicional 73
   8' Voix Celestes 73
   8' Flute Celeste (II) 134
   4' Octave 73
   4' Violina 73
   2' Fifteenth 61
  IV Mixture 244

278   *The Life and Work of Ernest M. Skinner*

16′ Flugel Horn 85
8′ Cornopean 73
8′ Cor d'Amour 73
8′ Vox Humana 61
8′ Celesta Sub (Ch)
4′ Celesta (Ch)
Tremolo

CHOIR
8′ Diapason 73
8′ Concert Flute 73
8′ Viola 73
4′ Flute 73
2 2/3′ Nazard 61
8′ Clarinet 61
8′ Celesta Sub (Celesta)
4′ Celesta 61 bars
Tremolo

PEDAL
16′ Diapason 44
16′ Gemshorn 61
16′ Echo Lieblich (Sw 16′ Bourdon)
8′ Octave (16′ Diapason)
8′ Principal (16′ Gemshorn)
8′ Still Gedeckt (Sw 16′ Bourdon)
5 1/3′ Quinte (16′ Gemshorn)
32′ Fagotto (Sw 16′ Flügel Horn)
16′ Flugel Horn (Sw 16′ Flügel Horn)
8′ Tromba (Sw 8′ Cornopean)
Chimes (Gt)

Ranks: 33
Stops: 43
Pipes: 2188

Source: "Organ at Newburgh Opened by Dr. Noble," *The Diapason,* January, 1938, p. 1. According to the article, the dedication was played by T. Tertius Noble on 5 December 1937.

Ernest M. Skinner & Son Organ, 1938
Resurrection Chapel, Washington National Cathedral
Washington, D.C.

GREAT
8′ Diapason
8′ Gedeckt (Sw)
8′ Salicional (Sw)
8′ Voix Celeste (Sw)
4′ Flute (Sw)
III Mixture (Sw)
8′ Flügel Horn (Sw)

SWELL
8′ Gedeckt
8′ Salicional
8′ Voix Celeste
4′ Flute
III Mixture
8′ Flügel Horn
Tremolo

PEDAL
16′ Gedeckt
8′ Gedeckt (16′ Gedeckt)
5 1/3′ Quinte (16′ Gedeckt)

Ranks: 10
Stops: 16

COUPLERS
Swell to Pedal 8′
Great to Pedal 8′
Swell to Great 16′
Swell to Great 8′
Swell to Great 4′
Swell to Swell 16′
Swell to Swell 4′

Source: examination by the author

Ernest M. Skinner & Son Organ, 1938
Washington National Cathedral, Washington, D. C.

GREAT ORGAN
16′ Diapason 61
8′ First Diapason 61
8′ Second Diapason 61
8′ Third Diapason 61
   Muted String Ensemble (four 8′ and one 4′ rank)
8′ Principal Flute 61

8′ Clarabella 61
8′ Viola 61
8′ Erzähler 61
5 1/3′ Quint 61
4′ Octave 61
4′ Principal 61
4′ Harmonic Flute 61
2 2/3′ Twelfth 61

Organ Specifications 279

2′ Fifteenth 61
VII Plein Jeu (15-19-22-26-29-33-36) 427
IV Harmonics (17-19-21-22) 244
III Cymbale 183
16′ Posaune 61
8′ Tromba 61
8′ Trumpet 61
4′ Clarion 61

SWELL ORGAN
16′ Bourdon 73
16′ Dulciana 73
8′ First Diapason 73
8′ Second Diapason 73
8′ Claribel Flute 73
8′ Gedackt 73
8′ Viol d'Orchestre 73
8′ Viol Celeste 73
8′ Salicional 73
8′ Voix Celeste 73
8′ Flauto Dolce 73
8′ Flute Celeste 61
   Muted String Ensemble
8′ Aeoline 73
8′ Unda Maris 73
4′ Octave 73
4′ Harmonic Flute 61
4′ Gemshorn 73
4′ Violin 73
4′ Unda Maris (II) 122
2 2/3′ Twelfth 61
2′ Fifteenth 61
V Full Mixture (15-19-22-26-29) 305
V Cornet (1-8-12-15-17) 305
III Carillon (12-17-22) 183
16′ Posaune 73
8′ Trumpet (light wind) 73
8′ Cornopean 73
8′ Flügel Horn 73
8′ Vox Humana 73
4′ Clarion 61
   Tremolo

CHOIR ORGAN
16′ Gemshorn 73
8′ Diapason 73
8′ Concert Flute 73
8′ Gemshorn 73
8′ Viol d'Oechestre 73
8′ Viol Celeste 73
8′ Kleiner Erzähler (II) 134
4′ Harmonic Flute 73
4′ Gemshorn 73
4′ Violin 73
2 2/3′ Nazard 61
2′ Piccolo 61

1 3/5′ Tierce 61
1 1/7′ Septieme 61
III Carillon (12-17-22) 183
16′ Orchestral Bassoon 61
8′ Trumpet (small orchestral type) 73
8′ Clarinet 61
8′ Orchestral Oboe 61
   Celesta 61
   Celesta Sub 61
   Tremolo

SOLO ORGAN
8′ Flauto Mirabilis 73
8′ Gamba 73
8′ Gamba Celeste 73
4′ Orchestral Flute 61
VII Compensating Mixture
     (8-12-15-17-19-21-22) 427
16′ Ophicleide 73
16′ Corno di Bassetto 12
8′ Tuba Mirabilis 73
8′ Trumpet 73
8′ French Horn 61
8′ Cor d' Amour 61
8′ English Horn 61
8′ Corno di Bassetto 61
4′ Clarion 73
   Tremolo

PEDAL ORGAN
32′ Diapason 12
32′ Violone 12
16′ Diapason 32
16′ Diapason (metal) 32
16′ Contra Bass 32
16′ Violone 32
16′ Bourdon 32
16′ Echo Lieblich (Sw)
16′ Gemshorn
16′ Dulciana (Sw)
8′ Octave 12
8′ Principal (metal) 12
8′ Gedackt 12
8′ Still Gedackt (Sw)
8′ Cello 12
8′ Gemshorn (Ch)
5 1/3′ Quinte (Ch)
4′ Super Octave 32
4′ Still Flute 32
4′ Still Gedackt (Sw)
V Mixture (15-19-22-26-29) 160
IV Harmonics (17-19-21-22) 128
32′ Bombarde 12
32′ Fagotto 12
16′ Trombone 32
16′ Fagotto 32

8' Tromba 12
8' Fagotto 12
4' Clarion 12
4' Fagotto 12

COUPLERS
Unison:
  Swell to Great
  Choir to Great
  Solo to Great
  Swell to Choir
  Solo to Choir
  Great to Solo
  Swell to Solo
Octave:
  Swell to Swell 4'
  Swell to Swell 16'
  Swell to Great 4'
  Swell to Great 16'
  Swell to Choir 4'
  Swell to Choir 16'
  Choir to Choir 4'
  Choir to Choir 16'
  Choir to Great 4'
  Choir to Great 16'
  Choir to Great 5 1/3'
  Solo to Solo 4'
  Solo to Solo 16'
  Solo to Great 4'
  Solo to Great 16'
Pedal:
  Swell to Pedal

Great to Pedal*
Choir to Pedal
Solo to Pedal
Swell to Pedal 4'
Choir to Pedal 4'
Solo to Pedal 4'

*Also by reversible piston

COMBINATIONS
Adjustable at the console; moving knobs
Swell: 1-2-3-4-5-6-7-8-9-10
Great: 1-2-3-4-5-6-7-8-9-10
Choir: 1-2-3-4-5-6-7-8-9
Solo: 1-2-3-4-5-6-7-8-9
Pedal: 1-2-3-4-5-6-7-8-9-10
Full: 1-2-3-4-5-6-7-8-9-10-11-12
Couplers: 1-2-3-4
General Cancel to include crescendo and sforzando
Coupler Cancel

MECHANICALS
Swell expression with tremolo control
Choir expression with tremolo control
Solo expression with tremolo control
Crescendo
Sforzando by pedal and piston reversible
16' manual stops off
32' Pedal stops off
All Swells to Swell
3 Reversibles for 32' stops

Source: Program for *The Office for the Dedication of the Great Organ,* 10 November 1938 (courtesy of Frank H. Taylor).

Ernest M. Skinner & Son Organ, 1940
St. Martin's Church, New York City, New York

GREAT
  16' Bourdon (Ped. Bourdon)
  8' First Diapason 61
  8' Second Diapason 61
  8' Waldflöte 61
  4' Octave 61
  4' Flute 61
  2' Fifteenth 61
  III Mixture 183
  8' Tromba 61
      Chimes (Solo)

SWELL
  16' Bourdon 73
  8' Diapason 73
  8' Gedeckt 73
  8' Salicional 73
  8' Voix Celeste 73
  8' Flute Celeste (II) 134
  4' Octave 73
  4' Flute Triangulaire 73
  2' Piccolo 61
  V Mixture 305
  16' Waldhorn 73
  8' Cornopean 73
  8' Oboe 73
  8' Vox Humana 61
  4' Clarion 73
      Tremolo

CHOIR
  16' Dulciana 73
  8' Concert Flute 73
  8' Gamba 73

Organ Specifications 281

8' Dulciana 73
4' Gemshorn 85
4' Flute Harmonique 73
2⅔' Nazard (4' Gemshorn)
2' Fifteenth (4' Gemshorn)
1⅗' Tierce (4' Gemshorn)
1⅐' Septième (4' Gemshorn)
8' Clarinet 61
8' Harp (Celesta)
4' Celesta 61 bars
    Tremolo

SOLO
8' Orchestral Flute 61
8' Gamba 61
8' Gamba Celeste 61
8' Tuba 61
8' French Horn 61
8' English Horn 61
    Chimes 25 tubes
    Tremolo

PEDAL
32' Resultant Diapason
16' Major Bass 44
16' Bourdon 61
16' Dulciana (Ch 16' Dulciana)
16' Echo Lieblich (Sw 16' Bourdon)
8' Octave (16' Major Bass)
8' Gedeckt (16' Bourdon)
8' Still Gedeckt (Sw 16' Bourdon)
4' Flute (16' Bourdon)
16' Trombone 32
16' Waldhorn (Sw 16' Waldhorn)
8' Tromba (Sw 16' Waldhorn)
    Chimes (Solo)

Ranks: 46
Stops: 58
Pipes: 2988

Source: "Four-Manual Placed in St. Martin's New York," *The Diapason,* June 1941, p. 4. The dedication concert was played by Roy Tibbs on 27 April 1941 according to the article.

Bibliography

BOOKS AND PAMPHLETS

Audsley, George Ashdown. *Organ Stops and Their Artistic Registration.* 2nd. ed. New York: The H. W. Gray Co., 1941.
Barnes, William H. *The Contemporary American Organ.* 3rd. ed. New York: J. Fischer & Bro., 1937.
Barnes, William H., and Edward B. Gammons. *Two Centuries of American Organ Building.* Melville, N.Y.: Belwin-Mills Publishing Corp., 1970.
Editors of Time-Life Books. *This Fabulous Century.* Vols. I, II, & III.
Flint, Edward W. *The Great Organ in the Methuen Memorial Music Hall.* Methuen: Methuen Memorial Music Hall, Inc., 1954.
———. *The Newberry Memorial Organ at Yale University.* New Haven: Yale University Press, 1930.
Ochse, Orpha. *The History of the Organ in the United States.* Bloomington & London: Indiana University Press, 1975.
Organ in the College of the City of New York. Pamphlet published by the Ernest M. Skinner Organ Company.
Schweitzer, Albert. *Out of My life and Thought.* 2nd. ed. 1949; rpt. New York: Mentor Books, 1964.
Shafer, Chet. *The Pipe Organ Pumper.* New York: Greenberg, 1926.
Skinner, Ernest M. *The Modern Organ.* 6th. ed. New York: H. W. Gray Co., 1945.
The Skinner Organ. A brochure published by the Skinner Organ Company.
The Skinner Residence Organ. A brochure published by the Skinner Organ Company, 1927.
Sumner, William Leslie. *The Organ.* 2nd. ed. London: Macdonald & Co., Ltd., 1955.
Truette, Everett. Scrapbooks. Unpublished collection in the Boston Public Library.

ARTICLES

"Additions to Skinner Organ Library." *Stop, Open, and Reed,* 2, no. 1 (January 1924), 21.
"Aeolian-Skinner to Build Large Organ For Oberlin." *The Diapason,* August 1953, p. 1.
"Alexander McCurdy at Organ in Serlo Hall." *The Diapason,* December 1931, p. 3.
"Alice F. Skinner, Church Founder, Dies at 94." newsclipping (name and date of original source unknown). Scrapbook of Mabel Hastings Skinner.
"America in Tribute to Dr. Schweitzer." *The Diapason,* August 1949, pp. 1–2.
"Army Medical Center Organ Work in the Walter Reed Hospital in Washington." *The American Organist,* 15, no. 7 (1932), 439.
"Arthur Hudson Marks Taken Off Suddenly." *The Diapason,* June 1939, p. 1.
"Arthur Hudson Marks." *The American Organist,* 22, no. 6 (1939), 197–198.
Barnes, William H. "Appreciation of Ernest M. Skinner Voiced by Barnes." *The Diapason,* December 1959, p. 39.
———. "The Organ." *The American Organist,* 12, no. 5 (1929), 286–287.
———. "The Organ." *The American Organist,* 15, no. 5 (1932), 282–284.
———. "Trinity College." *The American Organist,* 16, no. 7 (1933), 364–365.
———. "University Organs." *The American Organist,* 12, no. 1 (1929), 22–23.
Barton, Dan. "A Genius Who Failed . . . Why?" *The Bombarde,* 3, no. 1 (Spring 1966), 3, 4, 6.
"Big Addition to Organ at St. Bartholomew's." *The Diapason,* August 1927, p. 8.
"Big Work Completed in New York Church." *The Diapason,* December 1929, p. 3.
Blanchard, Homer D. "The Organ in the United States: A Study in Design, Part II." *The Tracker,* 25, no. 1 (Fall 1980), 13–51.
"Boston Builders' Contracts." *The Music Trades,* 31 January 1903.
"Boston Music Hall Organ Shrine Center." *The Diapason,* March 1931, p. 4.
"Boston News." *The American Organist,* 14, no. 12 (1931), 751.
"Boston Symphony Organ is Designed." *The Diapason,* September 1949, p. 1.

"Brick Church, New York." *The American Organist*, 1, no. 11 (1918), 562–565.
"Broadcasting the Skinner Organ." *Stop, Open, and Reed*, 2, no. 1 (January 1924), 9–11, 21.
Bruening, Herbert D. "Inveterate Recital Goer Remembers Five Decades." *The Diapason*, December 1959, p. 47.
"Bruton Parish Church." *The American Organist*, 22, no. 10 (1939), 335–336.
"Bruton Parish Church Will Add to its Organ." *The Diapason*, April 1942, p. 13.
Buhrman, T. Scott. "Clarity and its Development." *The American Organist*, 20, no. 2 (1927), 47–50.
———. "A Comparison." *The American Organist*, 15, no. 10 (1932), 610.
———. "Ernest M. Skinner: Organ Builder." *The American Organist*, 8, no. 5 (1925), 173–185.
———. "Mr. Ernest M. Skinner's Record." *The American Organist*, 19, no. 4 (1936), 125–126.
———. "The St. Mary Festivities." *The American Organist*, 16, no. 2 (1933), 97–99.
"Build 9170 Organs in 1931, Census Reveals." *The Diapason*, December 1932, p. 1.
"Builders of the Future." Article from unidentified newspaper. Scrapbook of Mabel Hastings Skinner.
"The Capitol Theatre Organ, Boston, Mass." *Stop, Open, and Reed*, 1, no. 4 (December 1922), 15–16.
"Carnegie Music Hall Will Have New Organ." *The Diapason*, March 1917, pp. 1, 10.
"Cathedral of St. John the Divine." *The Diapason*, October 1952, p. 1.
"Chandler Goldthwaite Dies after Nine Years' Illness." *The Diapason*, June 1946, p. 1.
"Chicago Organ is Finished." *The Diapason*, June 1914, p. 1.
"Chicago University Opens Great Organ." *The Diapason*, December 1928, pp. 1, 12.
"Cleveland Orchestra Will Have a Skinner." *The Diapason*, February 1930, p. 1.
"Congratulations." *The Diapason*, March 1951, p. 20.
"Convention Echos." *The Diapason*, October 1928, p. 39.
Covell, William K. "Donald Harrison's Work in America." *Organ Quarterly*, 24 (1944–1945), 139–140.
"Dean of Church Musicians Retires From Brick Church." *The Diapason*, August 1960, p. 21.
The Detroit Presbyterian, 10 April 1924. Newsclipping from scrapbook in the Archives of Jefferson Avenue Presbyterian Church.
"Dickinson Opens New Brick Church's Organ." *The Diapason*, January 1941, p. 4.
Diggle, Roland. "Southern California News." *The Diapason*, February 1926, p. 20.
Downes, Ralph. "The Baroque Organ." *Organ Quarterly*, 23 (1943–1944), 140–141.
"Dr. Carl Presides at New Four-Manual." *Stop, Open, and Reed*, 1, no. 3 (July 1922), 6–7.
"Dr. Francis W. Snow of Trinity Church, Boston." *The Diapason*, March 1946, p. 4.
"Dr. Miles Farrow, Former N. Y. Cathedral Organist, Dies." *The Diapason*, August 1953, p. 2.
"Dr. T. Frederick H. Candlyn." *The Diapason*, July 1954, p. 17.
"The Educational Value of a Skinner Organ." *Stop, Open, and Reed*, 1, no. 4 (December 1922), 6.
"Edwin Arthur Kraft Who Retires After 51 Years." *The Diapason*, July 1959, p. 1.
"E. M. Skinner & Co. in New York." *The Music Trades*, New York, 8 November 1902.
"E. M. Skinner is Guest of Guild in New York." *The Diapason*, November 1942, p. 2.
"Englewood, N. J. Organ Work of E. M. Skinner." *The Diapason*, December 1946, p. 1.
"E. Power Biggs." *The Diapason*, June 1943, p. 13.
"Eric Delamarter Chosen." *The Diapason*, May 1914, p. 2.
"Ernest Douglas Recovering and Skinner Back at Work." *The Diapason*, February 1941, p. 2.
"Ernest M. Skinner and Our Organ." *First Parish Church News* (Taunton, Mass.), February 1961, p. 2.
"Ernest M. Skinner Breaks Rib." *The Diapason*, February 1915, p. 10.

"Ernest M. Skinner Factory in Methuen, Mass., Burned." *The Diapason,* July 1943, p. 1.
"Ernest M. Skinner Joins Schantz Staff." *The Diapason,* February 1947, p. 1.
"Ernest M. Skinner, Ninety-Four, Dies." *The Boston Globe,* 28 November 1960, p. 25.
"Ernest M. Skinner Takes a Partner." *The Music Trades,* New York, 4 October 1902.
"Ernest M. Skinner, Who Announces New Plans." *The Diapason,* February 1936, p. 3.
"Ernest M. Skinner Will be 90 Years Old." *The Diapason,* January 1956, p. 1.
"Ernest Skinner Suffers Broken Shoulder in Fall." *The Diapason,* June 1957, p. 20.
"Events Forecast." *The American Organist,* 15, no. 5 (May 1932), 314.
"Example in Placing Organ Successfully." *The Diapason,* May 1926, p. 3.
"Famous Old Church Welcomes New Organ." *The Diapason,* April 1924, pp. 1–2.
"Finish Organ Orders; Change to War Work." *The Diapason,* April 1942, p. 1.
Fitter, Harold W. "Annual Meeting Marked by Reports for the Year; Honor Ernest M. Skinner." *The Diapason,* July 1948, p. 8.
"Four-Manual for Williams College." *The Diapason,* October 1912, p. 2.
"Four-Manual in St. Martin's New York." *The Diapason,* June 1941, p. 4.
"Fourth Church Post to Barrett Spach." *The Diapason,* March 1936, p. 7.
"Four Well Known American Organists." *Stop, Open, and Reed,* 1, no. 3 (July 1922), 3.
"Freak Accident Wrecks Organ in Norfolk Church." *The Diapason,* December 1957, p. 1.
"Gala Days of Music at Portland, Oregon." *The Diapason,* October 1917, p. 1.
"G. Donald Harrison." *The Diapason,* July 1933, p. 13.
"G. Donald Harrison Dies of Heart Attack." *The Diapason,* July 1956, p. 1.
"G. Donald Harrison Heads Organ Concern." *The Diapason,* May 1940, p. 1.
"G. Donald Harrison, Newly-appointed Technical Director and Chief of the Aeolian-Skinner Staff." *The Diapason,* August 1933, p. 5.
"Goldthwaite Goes Abroad. Organist Will Be Associate With Skinner Company." *The Diapason,* June 1923, p. 3.
"Good Prospects For New Year." *The Music Trades,* 16 January 1904.
"Gordon Balch Nevin Joins Skinner Force." *The Diapason,* October 1917, p. 11.
"Great Organ Built in Course of 20 Years." *The Diapason,* April 1942, p. 2.
"Great Organ Opened in Capital Cathedral." *The Diapason,* December 1938, p. 1.
"Great Skinner Organ is Opened at Detroit." *The Diapason,* December 1915, p. 1.
"Guilmant Organ School." *The American Organist,* 25, no. 8 (1942), 231.
Gunn, Glenn Dillard. *The Washington Herald.* Quoted in "Builders of the Future." Newsclipping (name and date of source unknown). Scrapbook of Mabel Hastings Skinner.
Holden, Dorothy J. "The Tonal Evolution of the E. M. Skinner Organ, Part I." *The Diapason,* July 1977, pp. 1, 4, 5.
———. "The Tonal Evolution of the E. M. Skinner Organ, Part II." *The Diapason,* February 1978, pp. 16–19.
———. "The Tonal Evolution of the E. M. Skinner Organ, Part IV." *The Diapason,* March 1979, pp. 12–14.
"Hymn Society Honors Noble." *The Diapason,* June 1943, p. 11.
"Inventions and Tonal Developments of Ernest M. Skinner." *The Diapason,* February 1946, p. 17.
"Joseph Bonnet Dead; End Career in Canada." *The Diapason,* September 1944, p. 1.
"Joseph Bonnet." *The Diapason,* September 1954, p. 20. Reprinted from *The Diapason,* September 1944.
Judd, Wilber Webster. "The St. Paul Auditorium Organ." *St. Paul Pioneer Press.* Quoted in *Stop, Open, and Reed,* 1, no. 1 (January 1922), 7.
Karlson, Karl. "Group Hopes it Can Break Spell on 'Sleeping' Skinner Organ." *St. Paul Dispatch,* 15 September 1973, p. 5.
Knight, George L. "Clarence Dickinson: A Retrospect." *The Diapason,* October 1969, pp. 16–17.
Kraege, Elfrieda. "The Early Organs of the Fifth Avenue Presbyterian Church." *The Tracker,* XVIII, no. 2 (Winter 1974), 8–10.

Kraft, Edwin Arthur. "S.O.S. Organists." *The American Organist,* 15, no. 4 (April 1932), 249.
"Large Four-Manual for Jackson, Miss." *The Diapason,* February 1940, p. 2.
"Large Organ Designed for Harvard Chapel." *The Diapason,* May 1932, pp. 1–2.
"Large Organ is Dedicated in Jackson, Miss. Church." *The Diapason,* January 1941, p. 2.
"Large Organ Opened at Girard College." *The Diapason,* June 1933, p. 3.
"Large Skinner For Cleveland Church." *The Diapason,* October 1930, pp. 1–2.
"The Law Organ." *Stop, Open, and Reed,* 2, no. 1 (Janaury 1924), 2.
"Looking Back into the Past." *The Diapason,* January 1956, p. 22
"Lynnwood Farnam." *The American Organist,* 14, no. 1 (1931), 23–27.
"Marie Simmelink Kraft Takes Cleveland Position." *The Diapason,* May 1949, p. 32.
Marks, Arthur Hudson. "An Autobiography." *Stop, Open, and Reed,* 2, no. 1 (January 1924), 5–7.
———. "A Biography of Ernest M. Skinner." *Stop, Open, and Reed,* 1, no. 4 (December 1922), 2–5.
———. "The Skinner Residence Organ." *Stop, Open, and Reed,* 3, no. 1 (1925), 13–16.
Martin, Ralph G. "Did Edward Mourn Vanished Power?" *The Detroit Free Press,* 1 March 1975, p. 14C.
McCurdy, Alexander. "An Organ Builder's Opinions." *Etude,* 72, no. 10 (October 1954), 24, 64.
"Michigan Dedicates Its Great New Organ." *The Diapason,* June 1928, pp. 1–2.
"Michigan University to Have Large Organ." *The Diapason,* September 1927, pp. 1, 44.
"Miss Skinner as Heroine." *Boston Post,* 11 August 1914. Quoted in *The Diapason,* September 1914, p. 5.
"Mrs. Ernest M. Skinner Dies at Home in Reading, Mass." *The Diapason,* May 1951, p. 1.
"A New Church." *The Vermont Tribune,* Friday 18 July 1902. Quoted in E. A. Boadway, *The Boston Organ Club Newsletter,* January & February 1978, p. 9.
"New Concern Starts Well." *The Music Trades,* New York, 1903 (exact date unknown).
"New Honolulu Organ is Opened by Carruth." *The Diapason,* September 1924, p. 3.
"New Oberlin Organ to Be Skinner Work." *The Diapason,* October 1927, p. 2.
"New Order Permits Use of Tin in Organs." *The Diapason,* January 1946, p. 1.
"News and Notes." *The American Organist,* 4, no. 5 (May 1921), 143–144.
"News and Notes." *The American Organist,* 5, no. 9 (September 1922), 410.
"News Brevities." *The American Organist,* 10, no. 10 (October 1927), 263.
"New Scheme of Stops of Great Yale Organ." *The Diapason,* November 1928, p. 3.
"The New Skinner Organ for 'Old Trinity'." *Stop, Open, and Reed,* 2, no. 1 (January 1924), 25.
"The New Skinner Organ in St. Luke's." *Stop, Open, and Reed,* 1, no. 4 (December 1922), 11–12.
"New Skinner Organs That Have Been Completed and Installed During the Past Two Years." *Stop, Open, and Reed,* 3, no. 1 (1925), 41–45.
"News Record and Notes." *The American Organist,* 7, no. 1 (January 1924), 55.
"New York." *The American Organist,* 18, no. 11 (November 1935), 433.
"Night Falls for a Giant." *The Diapason,* January 1961, p. 22.
"No Meal for the Lice: Organ is of Mahogany." *The Diapason,* June 1926, p. 22.
"Noted Eastman Organ Scheme is Revised." *The Diapason,* November 1951, p. 4.
"Novel Piano Pedal Board." *The Diapason,* January 1923, p. 19.
"Nunc Dimittis." *The Diapason,* September 1969, p. 21.
"Oberlin College Orders of Skinner." *The Diapason,* July 1914, p. 1.
"Organ at Newburgh Opened by Dr. Noble." *The Diapason,* January 1938, p. 1.
"Organ at Princeton Chapel is Remodeled." *The Diapason,* November 1954, p. 1.
"Organ Builder and Player Meet." *The Christian Science Monitor,* 1 August 1911, p. 5.
"Organ Builder Hitchcock Dead at 91." *The Diapason,* April 1967, p. 38.
"Organ Builder Retains Youth by Love of Music." *Richmond News Leader,* 27 November 1944.

"Organ Building Stops July 31 by War Order." *The Diapason,* July 1942, p. 1.
"Organ For Medical Center." *The Diapason,* June 1930, p. 1.
"Organ is Dedicated in Severance Hall." *The Diapason,* April 1931, p. 6.
"Organists as Guests Hear Princeton Organ." *The Diapason,* November 1928, pp. 1–2.
"Organists in Convention at the National Capital." *The Diapason,* July 1941, p. 2.
"Organ of 84 Stops for Holyoke Church." *The Diapason,* January 1921, pp. 1–2.
"Organ Opened in Dome of St. Bartholomew's." *The Diapason,* January 1931, p. 1.
"The Organs at Washington Cathedral." (courtesy of Barbara Owen)
"Organ Stoplists." *The American Organist,* 10, no. 8 (1927), 200.
"Organ Union is Enjoined." *The Diapason,* May 1930, p. 2.
"Painesville, Ohio, Lake Erie College." *The American Organist,* 18, no. 8 (August 1935), 308–309.
"Patent for New Way of Transmitting Organ Music by Radio Granted to Arthur H. Marks." *Stop, Open, and Reed,* 4, no. 1 (1927), 23–25.
"Pipe Organ a Patient." *Kansas City Star,* 8 July 1949.
"Pitman-Chest Action." *The American Organist,* 19, no. 6 (1936), 199.
"Pittsburgh Sessions of N.A.O. are Inspiring . . . Organists and Builders Meet." *The Diapason,* September 1919, p. 6.
"Pneumatic Reed-Control." *The American Organist,* 22, no. 2 (1939), 54–55.
"A Pneumatic Swell Pedal." *The Organ,* 1, no. 7 (November 1892), 164.
"Portland, Oregon, Award to Skinner." *The Diapason,* October 1916, pp. 1–2.
"Princeton Dedicates Beautiful Chapel." *The Diapason,* July 1928, p. 4.
"Princeton Will Have Large Skinner Work." *The Diapason,* July 1927, pp. 1–2.
"Raises Capital to $250,000." *The Diapason,* April 1920, p. 13.
"Rebuild Grace Church Organ." *The Music Trades,* New York, 2 August 1902.
"Recent Skinner Organ Installations." *Stop, Open, and Reed,* 1, no. 3 (July 1922), 2.
"R. H. Skinner." *The American Organist,* 17, no. 4 (April 1934), 177.
Richards, Emerson. "An American-Classic Organ Arrives." *The American Organist,* 26, no. 5 (May 1943), 105.
"Richmond H. Skinner." *The Diapason,* July 1941, p. 15.
Rizzo, Jeanne. "Lynnwood Farnam." *The Diapason,* December 1974, pp. 1, 3–6.
"R. Kenneth Holt." *The Diapason,* July 1945, p. 4.
"The Rückpositiv Reappears." *The American Organist,* 16, no. 12 (December 1933), 597.
"The St. Joseph's Cathedral Organ." *Stop, Open, and Reed,* 2, no. 1 (January 1924), 2–3.
"St. Paul Out to Hear New Municipal Organ." *The Diapason,* October 1921, p. 1.
"St. Paul's Successful Organ Campaign." *The American Organist,* 3, no. 6 (1920), 215–216.
"Schenley High School Organ Being Built by the Skinner Co." *The American Organist,* 7, no. 5 (1924), 296.
Scherer, Mary Grace. "Organ Builder Retains Youth by Love of Music." *Richmond News Leader,* 27 November 1944.
Searl, Helen Hulett. "Wizard of the Pipes." *Christian Science Monitor,* 5 June 1943, pp. 6, 14.
"Serlo Organ Program Broadcasts Through WBZ." Article from unidentified newspaper. Everett Truette Scrapbooks. Unpublished collection in the Boston Public Library.
"Sigfried Karg-Elert Arrives in U.S. January 4." *The Diapason,* January 1932, p. 3.
Simmons, Morgan. "Fourth Presbyterian Church." *Music: The A.G.O.-R.C.C.O. Magazine,* 5, no. 2 (February 1971), 28–29.
"Skinner." *The American Organist,* 11, no. 7 (July 1928), 259.
"Skinner." *The American Organist,* 11, no. 12 (December 1928), 572.
"Skinner and Aeolian Companies to Merge." *The Diapason,* January 1932, pp. 1–2.
"Skinner and Ernest Douglas Severely Injured in Crash." *The Diapason,* January 1941, p. 1.
"Skinner and Steere Companies Combine." *The Diapason,* April 1921, p. 1.
"Skinner Building Three Large Organs." *The Diapason,* April 1915, pp. 1–2.
"Skinner Company Host to its Factory Staff." *The Diapason,* May 1921, p. 3.

"Skinner Company Leases Space." *The Diapason,* October 1921, p. 20.
"Skinner Company Starts on New Era." *The Diapason,* November 1919, p. 1.
Skinner, Ernest M. "An Ideal Organ." *The Organ,* 2, no. 12 (April 1894), 290–291.
———. " 'Authentic' Tone and 'Synthetic' Defined by Ernest M. Skinner." *The Diapason,* April 1953, p. 22.
———. "The Capitol Theatre Organ, Boston, Mass." *Stop, Open, and Reed,* 1, no. 4 (December 1922), 15–16.
———. "Cinema Music." *The American Organist,* 1 (1918), 417–418, 421.
———. "Communications." *Pianist and Organist,* 3, no. 11 (November 1897), 283.
———. "Details of Mr. Skinner's Offer." *The Diapason,* October 1929, p. 31.
———. Editorial. *The Organ,* 23, no. 132 (April 1954), 199.
———. Editorial. *Stop, Open, and Reed,* 4, no. 1 (1927), 4.
———. "Ernest M. Skinner on 'Classic Organ' and Modern Advance." *The Diapason,* November 1932, p. 8.
———. "Ernest M. Skinner on Fine Organ Tone Versus 'Ritualism'." *The Diapason,* August 1933, p. 21.
———. "Ernest M. Skinner Recalls the Past on 85th. Birthday." *The Diapason,* March 1951, p. 4.
———. "Features in Cleveland Organ." *The Diapason,* April 1921, p. 12.
———. "G. Donald Harrison." *The Diapason,* January 1928, p. 2.
———. "Interesting Light on Life and Work of Sigfried Karg-Elert." *The Diapason,* December 1933, p. 24.
———. "Karg-Elert." *The American Organist,* 15, no. 3 (March 1932), 175.
———. "Modern Organ Ahead as Compared with Old." *The Diapason,* November 1941, p. 22.
———. "Mr. Skinner in Rebuttal." *The Diapason,* September 1949, p. 25.
———. "Mr. Skinner Suggests Programs." *The Diapason,* May 1946, p. 26.
———. "Mr. Skinner Traces Rise of Organ Playing to Highest Pinnacle." *The Diapason,* November 1944, p. 11.
———. "Mr. Skinner Writes of Console and Tone; Also Standardization." *The Diapason,* January 1933, p. 29.
———. "Mr. Skinner Writes of His Latest Work, and Other Matters." *The Diapason,* April 1928, p. 35.
———. "Organ Builder Soars Above Clouds." *The Diapason,* December 1917, p. 6.
———. "Organ Building as a Fine Art." *Stop, Open, and Reed,* 3, no. 1 (1925), 3–5.
———. "Plea for American Composers." *The Diapason,* September 1953, p. 40.
———. "Principles of Tonal Design Are Outlined by a Noted Builder." *The Diapason,* July 1952, p. 28.
———. "Programs That Will Not Bore." *The Diapason,* February 1933, p. 17.
———. "Recitals That Will Make Organ Popular." *The Diapason,* February 1946, p. 30.
———. " 'Romantic Atrocities' Found Buyers." *The Diapason,* December 1951, p. 18.
———. "The Slider Chest." *The American Organist,* 22, no. 6 (1939), 205.
———. "Thoughts on the Organ Pipe." *The American Organist,* 15, no. 12 (December 1932), 725–726.
———. "Transcriptions Bad? Why Not Translation?" *The Diapason,* March 1942, p. 12.
———. "A Trip Abroad." *Stop, Open, and Reed,* 3, no. 1 (1925), 30–34.
———. "A Trip Abroad at Home." *Stop, Open, and Reed,* 4, no. 1 (1927), 14–17.
———. "Visible as Against Dead Combinations." *The Diapason,* June 1913, p. 1–2.
———. "Word from Ernest Skinner." *The Diapason,* January 1959, p. 20.
"Skinner Factory is Ready." *The Diapason,* February 1914, p. 1.
"Skinner Forces at Annual Dinner." *The Diapason,* May 1928, p. 35.
"Skinner Forces at Dinner." *The Diapason,* June 1926, p. 8.
"Skinner Four-Manual For Memphis Church." *The Diapason,* March 1927, p. 4.
"1921 Skinner Installations." *Stop, Open, and Reed,* 1, no. 1 (January 1922), 6.
"Skinner Opening in Yale." *The American Organist,* 13, no. 1 (1930), 40–41.
"Skinner Opens Big Year." *The Diapason,* January 1927, p. 1.

"Skinner Organ for Girard College." *The Diapason*, October 1931, p. 1.
"The Skinner Organ in Colony Theatre, New York City." *Stop, Open, and Reed*, 3, no. 1 (1925), 7.
"The Skinner Organ in Kilbourn Hall." *Stop, Open, and Reed*, 1, no. 3 (July 1922), 4–6.
"Skinner Organ in Ogden Hall, Hampton Institute, Hampton, Va." *Stop, Open, and Reed*, 2, no. 1 (January 1924), 20.
Skinner, Richmond H. "Facts and Fancies." *The American Organist*, 17, no. 4 (April 1934), 173.
"The Skinner Small Residence Organ." *Stop, Open, and Reed*, 1, no. 3 (July 1922), 11–13.
"Skinner Will Build Organ For St. Paul." *The Diapason*, April 1920, pp. 1–2.
"Skinner Wins Order For Cleveland Organ." *The Diapason*, February 1921, pp. 1–2.
Smith, Rollin. "Dupré in the Twenties." *The Diapason*, June 1971, pp. 26–27.
"Speaking of Mr. Skinner." *The Diapason*, April 1928, p. 30.
"Specification of Skinner in St. Joseph's Cathedral." *Stop, Open, and Reed*, 2, no. 1 (January 1924), 16.
"Stoplists." *The American Organist*, 40, no. 12 (December 1957), 406.
"The Story of Robert Hope-Jones." *Theater Organ*, VI, no. 1 (Spring 1964), 22–24.
"The Superb Four-Manual Skinner at Grove Park Inn." *The Diapason*, December 1927, p. 9.
"Thirty Per Cent Cut in Organ Construction." *The Diapason*, May 1918, p. 1.
Thompson-Allen, Aubrey. "Information Given, Part III." *Music: The A.G.O.-R.C.C.O. Magazine*, 6, no. 1 (January 1972), 33–36.
———. "Information Given, Part IV." *Music: The A.G.O.-R.C.C.O. Magazine*, 7, no. 1 (January 1973), 36–42.
"Those Were the Days." *The Diapason*, April 1965, p. 24.
"Those Were the Days." *The Diapason*, March 1968, p. 18.
"Thousands at St. Paul Hear New City Organ." *The Diapason*, November 1921, p. 3.
"To Rebuild St. Thomas' Organ in New York." *The Diapason*, July 1945, p. 5.
"Trinity Concerts are Off." *The Diapason*, February 1918, p. 22.
"T. Tertius Noble Stays in America." *The Diapason*, February 1913, p. 3.
Tusler, Robert L. "A Concert Organ for Royce Hall, U.C.L.A." *The Diapason*, April 1972, pp. 6, 7, 23.
"Twenty Thousand Hear Opening Recital By Kraft on the New Skinner Organ in the Cleveland Public Auditorium." *Stop, Open, and Reed*, 1, no. 4 (December 1922), 9.
"Two Record Metropolitan Installations." *The American Organist*, 7, no. 7 (1924), 398–405.
Tyler, Abram Ray. "Detroit." *The American Organist*, 11, no. 7 (1928), 262.
———. "Detroit." *The American Organist*, 13, no. 6 (1930), 372.
"A Typical Radio Program." *Stop, Open, and Reed*, 2, no. 1 (January 1924), 13.
Unidentified newsclipping. 1947. Scrapbook of Ernest M. Skinner.
Unidentified newsclipping. Scrapbook of Mabel Hastings Skinner.
Unidentified newsclipping. January 1905 (?). Scrapbook of Mabel Hastings Skinner.
Untitled. *The Music Trades*, New York, 11 May 1901.
Untitled. *The Music Trades*, New York, 16 June 1904.
"Up 78 Per Cent, Aeolian-Skinner Company Reports Excellent Condition." *The American Organist*, 15, no. 8 (August 1932), 494.
Valentine, Ralph B. "An Answer for Mr. Ditewig." *The American Organist*, 49, no. 5 (May 1966), 3.
"Vierne to make U.S. Tour." *The Diapason*, August 1926, p. 1.
"Vierne to Sail in January." *The Diapason*, October 1926, p. 1.
Ward, Herbert Ralph. "Why Not Please Your Audiences?" *The Diapason*, May 1940, p. 21.
Washington Herald, 11 November 1938. Quoted in "Great Organ Opened in Capital Cathedral." *The Diapason*, December 1938, p. 1.
"Washington Organ's Design is Announced." *The Diapason*, March 1937, pp. 1–2.

"What They Say About Recent Skinner Organs." *Stop, Open, and Reed,* 1, no. 1 (January 1922), 4–5.
"Wilkes-Barre Organ Will Be Remodeled." *The Diapason,* March 1941, p. 1.
"William E. Zeuch Joins the Skinner Company." *The Diapason,* January 1917, p. 3.
Willis, Henry. "A Footnote by Henry Willis." *Musical Opinion,* no. 947 (August 1956), p. 673.
"The Wise Selection of a Skinner Organ Was Made by these Educational Institutes." *Stop, Open, and Reed,* 1, no. 4 (December 1922), 6.
"With the Builders." *The American Organist,* 10, no. 2 (February 1927), 45.
"Year is Good for Skinner." *The Diapason,* January 1928, p. 1.
Zeuch, William E. "An Appreciation of the Work of G. Donald Harrison." *The American Organist,* 16, no. 9 (September 1933), 438–439.

MISCELLANEOUS

"Alden, John." *Encyclopedia Americana.* 1966 ed.
Anderson, William. Testimonial. Early 1942. Quoted in Ernest M. Skinner & Son Company advertisement. *The Diapason,* March 1942, p. 15.
Boadway, E. A. "The Skinner and Aeolian-Skinner Opus List." *The Boston Organ Club Newsletter,* July & August 1972, pp. 2–8; September 1972, pp 4–8; October 1972, pp. 5–7; November 1972, pp. 3–6; December 1972, pp. 2–4; January 1973, pp. 5–8.
Church Bulletin. Jefferson Avenue Presbyterian Church, Detroit, Michigan. 4 April 1926 (Easter Sunday).
Dedication Recitals Program. First Universalist Church (Church of Our Father), Detroit, Michigan. 26 & 27 April 1916.
"Description of the New Organ in the Queen of the Holy Rosary Cathedral." *New Cathedral Festival* (Rededication Program). June 1931.
Dupré, Marcel. Testimonial in Skinner Organ Company advertisement. *The Diapason,* October 1929, p. 7.
Koch, Caspar P. Letter to Ernest M. Skinner. 11 April 1925. Quoted in *Stop, Open, and Reed,* 3, no. 1 (1925), 35.
List of Mixtures of the Skinner Organ Company.
McCurdy, Alexander. Recital Program. 22 June 1932. Everett Truette Scrapbooks. Unpublished collection in the Boston Public Library.
Moss, B. S. Letter Dated 26 January 1922. Quoted in *Stop, Open, and Reed,* 1, no. 2 (April 1922), 10.
Organ Dedication Recital Program. First Methodist Church, Wilkes-Barre, Pa. 26 February 1942.
Patent no. 500,040. *Specifications and Drawings of Patents.* 20 June 1893.
Patent no. 595,660. *Specifications and Drawings of Patents.* 14 December 1897.
Patent no. 663,368. *Specifications and Drawings of Patents.* 4 December 1900.
Patent no. 667,039. *Specifications and Drawings of Patents.* 29 January 1901.
Patent no. 715,307. *Specifications and Drawings of Patents.* 9 December 1902.
Patent no. 807,510. *Specifications and Drawings of Patents.* 19 December 1905.
Patent no. 1,076,069. *Specifications and Drawings of Patents.* 21 October 1913.
Patent no. 1,169,687. *Specifications and Drawings of Patents.* 25 January 1916.
Patent no. 1,192,005. *Specifications and Drawings of Patents.* 25 July 1916.
Phillipi, Daniel. Letter to the Skinner Organ Company. 27 October 1924. Quoted in *Stop, Open, and Reed,* 3, no. 1 (1925), 37.
Skinner, Ernest M. Program for the dedication of the C. H. K. Curtis Memorial Organ, Christ Church, Philadelphia. 29 May 1935.
——. *Who's Who in America.* vol. 19, 1936.
——. *Who's Who in America.* vol. 30, 1947.
"Stokowski, Leopold." *Music Lover's Encyclopedia.* 1954 ed.
Straus, Ernst G. "Einstein, Albert." *Encyclopedia Americana.* 1966 ed.

INDEX

Stoplists in bold type

Accenting piano player, 25, 26
Aeolian Company, 96, 156-158
Aeolian-Skinner Organ Company
  mentioned, 156-158, 175, 178, 181-183, 191, 195, 231, 238, 241
  merger, 156-158
  rebuild of Skinner organs by, 178, 231, 238-242
Alden, John, 1, 2
Alfring, W. H., 157
All-purpose organ, 13, 16, 111, 114, 251
American Academy of Arts and Letters, New York City, 141
"American classic" organ, first, 160-161
American Guild of Organists, 46-47, 72, 84, 105, 106, 150, 151, 196-197, 223-224, 229, 232
Ancestry, Skinner, 1, 2
Anderson, William, 191
Appleton Chapel, Harvard University, 60, 84, 144
Arkansas Organ Company, 216-217
Armature valve, 17
Arno, Ruth Barrett, 213
Audsley, George Ashdown, 34
Augmented pedal, 33

Bankruptcy of Ernest M. Skinner & Son Co., 210-211
Banks, Harry, 159
Baptist Church, Taunton, Mass., 5, 6
Baptist Temple, Charleston, W. Va., **270**
Barker lever, 16
Barnes, Edward Shippen, 139
Barnes, William H., 131-132, 159, 245-246
Baroque organ, 230, 251
Barrow, Robert, 186-188
Bartlett, Stella, 238, 247
Bassett, Carl, 214, 226, 232
Bassoon, 16' Orchestral, 62, 184
Beckett, Wheeler, 72, 78, 118, 159-160, 198, 221
Bellows pumper, employment as, 5
Bethany Congregational Church, Foxboro, Mass., 183
Bibliography, 284
Biggs, E. Power, 150
Bingham, Seth, 139
Birth of E. M. Skinner, 1, 2
Bombarde, 32', 39, 115-116, 160
Bonnet, Joseph, 112, 135, 143, 208

Boston Music Hall organ, 14-16, 147, 149-151, 212
Boston Symphony Hall organ, 25, 40, 231, **256**
Brett, Alice Francis, (see: Skinner, Alice F.)
Brett, Otis, 1
Brick Presbyterian Church, New York City, 60, 111, 185, 192
Brother of E. M. Skinner, (see: Skinner, Harry Clifford)
Bruton Parish Church, Williamsburg, Va. 210-211
Bunch, William, 248

Calloway, Paul, 153
Candlyn, T. Frederick H., 213, 241
Capitol Theatre, Boston, Mass., 92, 93, 94, 111, **268**
Carl, William C., 84
Carnegie Free Library & Hall, North Side, Pittsburgh, Pa., 113
Cathedral Church of Our Lady, Queen of the Holy Rosary, Toledo, Ohio, 141-142, **276**
Cathedral of St. John the Divine, New York City, 31, 43, 44, 192, 231
Catlin, George, 156-158, 173-174
Cavaillé-Coll, Aristide, 21, 22, 110, 122, 224, influence, 142, 213
Celesta, 41, 43
Celeste, 4', 60, 62, 63
Central Methodist Church, Detroit, Mich., 58, 59
Central Union Church, Honolulu, Hawaii, 100, 215
Chateau de Cande, Monts, France, 132-133
Chorus reeds
  Harrison, 160-163, 165
  Skinner, 18, 22, 25, 59, 127-128, 141-142, 191-192, 213, 217
  Willis, 21, 22, 25
Christ Church, Hartford, Conn., 29
Christ Episcopal Church, Philadelphia, Pa., 180
Christian, Palmer, 106, 113, 127, 128
Church of Christ, Congregational Church, Norfolk, Conn., 42
Church of the Ascension, Pittsburgh, Pa., 113
Church of the Convenant, Cleveland, Ohio, 141-142

Church of the Holy Communion, New York City, 116
Church of the Holy Trinity, Brooklyn, New York, 116
City College of New York, Great Hall, 39, 44, **259**
Clarion, Pa., 1
Classic revival, 121-122, 150, 161, 168, 178-179, 191-192, 230-231, 251
Cleveland, Mrs. Grover, 208
Cleveland Municipal Auditorium, Cleveland, Ohio, 81-83, 106, 111
Cleveland Museum of Art, 179
Clinic organ, 214-215
Coke-Jephcott, Norman, 231
Cole, James, 28, 29
Colgate University, 84
Colony Theatre, New York City, 94, 111
Columbia University, St. Paul's Chapel, 231
Combination action, 46, 47
Composition of the Organ, The, by E. M. Skinner, 173, 180, 219, 232, 238, 244-245
Console, 18, 32, 33, 37, 45, 46, 94
Contract, five-year, 148-149, 162, 165-166, 180
Contrafagotto, 32′, 130
Coolidge, Calvin, 76
Cor d'Amour, 43
Cor de Nuit, 59
Cornell University, Sage Chapel, 40, 43, 231
Corno d'Amour, 43
Corno di Bassetto, 44, 45
Corno di Bassetto, 16′, 142
Cossitt Avenue School, LaGrange, Ill., **269**
Coupler action, 17, 18, 45
Courboin, Charles M., 130, 131, 208
Covell, William King, 191
Cram, Ralph Adams, 57
Crawford, Jesse, 103-104
Crescendo pedal, 16, 17
Crozier, Catharine, 196-197, 236
Cuba, Holy Trinity Episcopal Cathedral, Havana, 116-117
Curtis, C. H. K., residence organ, 180

Davison, Archibald T., 60
Death of E. M. Skinner, 247
De Lamarter, Eric, 106, 128
Del Castillio, Lloyd, 151
Depression, 139, 144, 148, 156
Deveau, William, 193, 229-230, 236-237, 250

Diapasons
  American, 1920s, 110
  English, 112
  Harrison, 130, 160-161
  Hope-Jones, 33, 34
  Skinner, 18, 33, 34, 37, 59, 114, 169, 184, 191-192
Diapason chorus (see: Ensemble and Upperwork)
  American, early 1920s, 110
  Audsley, 34
  Cavaillé-Coll, 110
  Cole, 28
  Harrison, 130, 160-161, 167
  mentioned, 28, 37, 59, 99, 110-114, 122, 130, 131-132, 142, 161, 218
  Skinner, 16, 18, 28, 38, 59, 92, 99, 111-112, 113, 114, 122, 131-132, 141-142, 191-192, 218
  Willis, 110, 112-113
Diaphone, 33, 34, 89, 93
Dickinson, Clarence, 105, 192
Dorchester, Mass., factory, 58
Double primary, 145
Douglas, Ernest, 193-194, 211
Downes, Ralph, 130-131
Dream-vision, 4, 5, 235, 252
Dulcet, two-rank, 39
Duplex chest, 27
Dupré, Marcel, 112, 132-134, 143
Dutch Reformed Church, Flatbush, Brooklyn, 19

East Liberty Presbyterian Church, Pittsburgh, Pa. 158-159
Eastman School of Music, Rochester, N.Y., Kilbourn Hall, 69, 84-86, 111, 231
Easton, Georgia B., 75
East Side High School, Cincinnati, Ohio, 84
Einstein, Albert, 208
Electric action
  history, 16
  mentioned, 16-19, 28, 37, 45
  Skinner, 17-19, 28, 37, 45
Electro-pneumatic action, 19, 45, 75, 145
Elmwood Theater, Buffalo, N.Y., 89
E. M. Skinner & Co., 1904, 29
England
  travel to, 1898, 19-22
  travel to, 1924, 110, 111-112
English Horn, 41-43, 115
English influence, 20-22, 25, 27, 28, 38, 39, 44, 111-113, 114-115, 121-124, 127, 130, 141, 142, 213

Ensemble (see: Diapason chorus and Upperwork)
American, 1860s, 15
American, early 1890s, 16
American, early 1920s, 110
Audsley, 34
European, early 1800s, 13
European, mid-1800s, 14
Harrison, 122, 130, 160-161, 167
mentioned, 89, 112, 114, 121-124, 127-128, 131-132, 142-143, 161, 169, 181, 184, 187
Skinner, 16, 18, 25, 38, 59, 111-112, 113, 114, 127-128, 131-132, 141-142, 181, 184, 187, 191-192
Ernest M. Skinner & Co., 1902, 27
Ernest M. Skinner & Son Co.
history, 148-149
mentioned, 148-149, 180-181, 215-216
opening of, 180-181
termination of, 215-216
Ernest M. Skinner Company, 1905, 30
Erzähler, 29, 128, 214
Evangelical Lutheran Church of the Holy Trinity, New York City, 29
"Experimental" organ, 159-160

Factory
Dorchester, 58
Methuen, 147-149, 180, 181, 211-212
Reading, 212
South Boston, 26
Farnam, Lynnwood, 101, 104, 105, 131, 139
Farote, Fay Leone, 101
Farrow, Miles, 104-105
Father, Washington Martin Skinner, 1-6, 54, 186
Federlein, G. H., 101
Fifth Avenue Presbyterian Church, New York City, 40, 41
First Baptist Church, Jackson, Miss., 192-193
First Church of Christ, Scientist, Boston, Mass., 213
First Church of Northampton, Northampton, Mass., 183
First Congregational Church, Brewer, Maine, 28
First Congregational Church, Los Angeles, Calif., 159
First Dutch Reformed Church, Kingston, N.Y., 27-28, **257**
First Methodist Church, Reading, Mass., 183

First Methodist Church, Wilkes-Barre, Pa., 193, 201
First Methodist Episcopal Church, Atlantic City, N.J., 28
First Presbyterian Church, Concord, N.C., **274**
First Presbyterian Church, Englewood, N.J., 217-218
First Presbyterian Church, Newburgh, N.Y., 185, **277**
First Presbyterian Church, New York City, 84
First Skinner electric action, St. Bartholemew's Church, New York City, 17
First Skinner factory, South Boston, 26
First Skinner organ, Unitarian Church, Ludlow, Vt., 26
First Universalist Church, Detroit, 58, 65, **262**
Five-year contract, 148-149, 162, 165-166, 180
Flauto Dolce, 42
Flauto Mirabilis, 128
Flint, Edward W., 139
Flügel Horn, 43
Flute Celeste, 41, 42, 59, 63
Flute, Harmonic, 8', 142
Flute, Harmonic, 4', 184
Flute, Orchestral, 63
Flute Triangulaire, 114
Ford, Henry, 135-136
Fourth Presbyterian Church, Chicago, Ill., 40, 45, 106
Fox, Virgil, 105
France
Chateau de Cande, Monts, 132-133
travel to, 1898, 21, 22
travel to, 1924, 110, 111, 112
French Horn, 44
French influence, 38, 43, 112, 122, 127, 142-143, 213, 217
French Trumpet, 43, 217

Gamba Celeste, 43
Gammons, Edward B., 144, 204-205, 250
Garabrant, Maurice, 101
Garden, Charlotte Lockwood, 75, 153
Germani, Fernando, 131
Girard College, Philadelphia, Pa., 158, 159, 173
Gleason, Harold, 85, 86, 101-102, 143, 250
Goldsworthy, W. A., 101
Goldthwaite, Chandler, 81, 82, 101, 106, 131
Goss-Custard, Reginald, 112

Grace Cathedral, San Francisco, Calif., 173
Grace Church, New York City, 27, 44, 52
Grace Covenant Church, Richmond, Va., 212
Grand Avenue Methodist Temple, Kansas City, Mo., 224
Greenfield Village, Dearborn, Mich., 135
Grosse Gedeckt, 60
Grove Park Inn, Asheville, N.C., 69, 76, 106

Hammond, John Hayes, 209, 226, 244
Hampton Institute, Hampton, Va., R. C. Ogden Auditorium, 99
Harp (see: Celesta)
Harrison, G. Donald
  death of, 241
  feud with E. M. Skinner, 139, 143-145, 160-168, 172-175, 239-241
  mentioned, 122-127, 129-130, 132, 138, 139, 143-145, 150, 159, 160-168, 172-175, 178-179, 191, 210, 231, 238-242, 251
  rebuild of Skinner organs by 178-179, 231, 238-242
  tonal concepts, 122, 130, 160-161, 167-168, 238, 251
Harvard University, 60, 84, 144, 160
Hastings, D. S., 9
Hastings, Edward H., 51, 72, 73, 77, 78, 88, 151, 153, 154, 205-206, 228, 235, 244-245, 248-249
Hastings, Mabel, (see: Skinner, Mabel H.)
Haven Street shop, Reading, Mass., 212
Hawaii, Central Union Church, Honolulu, 100, 215
Heckelphone, 69, 70
Hershey Auditorium, Hershey, Pa., 158, 159
High school installations
  East Side High School, Cincinnati, Ohio, 84
  McLain High School, Greenfield, Ohio, 84
  Schenley High School, Pittsburgh, Pa., 84
Hill Auditorium, University of Michigan, Ann Arbor, Mich., 121, 127-129, 131, 238-240
Hitchcock, William, I., 26
Holt, R. Kenneth, 215
Holy Trinity Church, Pawling, N.Y., 185
Holy Trinity Episcopal Church, Havana, Cuba, 116-117

Holtkamp, Walter, 179
Hope-Jones, Robert
  mentioned, 19, 20, 30-34, 37, 89, 90
  tonal concepts, 33
Hospital installations
  St. Luke's, New York City, 81
  Walter Reed General Hospital, Washington, D.C., 141
Hutchings, George S., employment with, 7, 17-19, 22, 24-26

Ideal organ, 13, 16, 17, 111-112, 114, 251, **254**
Idlewild Presbyterian Church, Memphis, Tenn., 121, 231
Income Tax Amendment, 16th, 65
Incorporation of Ernest M. Skinner Company, 30

Japan, Cathedral, Tokyo, 40
Jefferson Avenue Presbyterian Church, Detroit, Mich., 113-114, 127, **271**
Jepson, Harry B., 139, 143
Jones, I. L., 210
Jordan Hall, New England Conservatory, Boston, Mass., 69

Karg-Elerg, Sigfrid, 152-153
Kellogg, W. K., 194-196
Kilbourn Hall, Eastman School of Music, Rochester, N.Y., 69, 84-86, 111, 231
Kimball, Wallace, 182
Kleine Erzähler, 45, 209
Koch, Caspar, 113, 182
Kraft, Edwin Arthur, 83, 106
Kraft, Mrs. Edwin Arthur, 106

Labor unions, 70, 71, 140
Lake Erie College, Painesville, Ohio, 121
Lakewood Mortuary Chapel, Minneapolis, Minn., 185
Lang, Edith, 75
Largest Skinner organ (see: Woolsey Hall, Yale University; Washington National Cathedral)
Lasell Junior College, Auburndale, Mass., 186
Law, Robert, residence, **267**
Lockwood, Charlotte, 75, 153

Magnets, 17, 18, 45, 145
Main Street Baptist Church, Saco, Maine, 28
Maitland, Rollo, 131

Marks, Arthur Hudson, 66, 67, 81, 100-101, 107-108, 124, 144-145, 148-149, 157, 160, 161-167, 173-174, 191
Marriage of E. M. Skinner and Mabel Hastings, 10
Martin, A. Perry, 107
Mass production, 80
McCurdy, Alexander, 139, 150-151
McLain High School, Greenfield, Ohio, 84
Mechanical action, 15, 16, 40, 135
Melody-coupler, 116
Methuen factory
  acquisition of, 147
  fire, 211-212
  mentioned, 147-149, 180-181, 182, 183, 211-212
Methuen Organ Company, 147-149, 180
Michell, Carlton, 22, 28, 34
Mixtures
  Carillon, 142
  mentioned, 14, 16, 18, 33, 34, 37, 59, 110-115, 122-124, 126-128, 141-142, 161, 184, 187, 191-192, 213, 217
  Willis, 112-115
Modern Organ, The, by E. M. Skinner, 60, 173
Möller Organ Co., 231, 240
Mother, Alice Francis Brett Skinner, 1, 2, 4, 54, 190-191
Mount Calvary Lutheran Church, Charlotte, N.C., 218, 223
Mount Carmel Roman Catholic Church, Chicago, Ill, 132, **275**
Mount Holyoke College, South Hadley, Mass., 185
Muck, Karl, 40
Multiple wound magnets, 17, 18
Municipal auditorium installations
  Cleveland, Ohio, 81-83, 106, 111
  Portland, Oregon, 59, **264**
  St. Paul, Minn., 69, 81, 82
Mutations, 14, 33, 85, 92, 99, 111, 112, 124, 128, 142, 160, 213, 218

National Association of Organists, 72, 131, 150, 168, 178
National City Christian Church, Washington, D.C., 141
Nevin, Gordon Balch, 61
New England Conservatory of Music, Boston, 27, 69
New Old South Church, Boston, 58, 111
Noble, T. Tertius, 104, 185, 186, 213, 240
Noehren, Robert, 238-240
Nold, Raymond, 160-161, 162

Oberlin College, Oberlin, Ohio
  Finney Chapel, 58, 111, 231
  mentioned, 84
  Warner Hall, Oberlin Conservatory of Music, 121, 127
Old First Presbyterian Church, New York City, 178
Old Trinity Church, New York City, 99-100
Orchestral Oboe, 38, 39
Orchestral Trumpet, 86
Orchestrator
  four colors, 61-63
  mentioned, 70
  seven colors, 159-60
Organ Builders' Association of America, 71
Our Lady of Mount Carmel Church, Roman Catholic, Chicago, Ill., 132, **275**
Owen, Barbara, 42, 244

Palace of the Legion of Honor, San Francisco, Calif., 117
Paradis, Francois, 225-226
Park Church, Elmira, N.Y., 31-33
Pedal board
  piano, 116
  radiating-concave, 27, 46
Philomela, 34
Piano accenting device, 25, 26
Pitman action, 19
Player, organ
  action, 28, 61, 95, 159-160
  mentioned, 63, 65, 70, 95-97, 100, 158
Plymouth Church, Brooklyn, N.Y., 29, 30
Plymouth Church, Minneapolis, Minn., 185
Pneumatic starter, 32' reeds, 115-116
Portable console, 17, 45
Portland Municipal Auditorium, Portland, Oregon, 59, **264**
Princeton University Chapel, Princeton, N.J., 129-131, 238
Purvis, Richard, 201-202

Radio broadcasts, New York studio, 100-101
Reading shop, 212
Reed chorus, 18, 59, 99, 110-111, 127, 130, 131, 141-142, 161, 191-192, 213, 217
Register crescendo, 16, 17
Religious beliefs, 4, 5, 54, 160, 235-238, 250
Residence organs
  installations, 28, 96, 97

mentioned, 28, 60, 61, 65, 94-97, 156
  small, 97
Retirement of E. M. Skinner, 226
Richards, Senator Emerson, 168
Robert Law residence, Port Chester, N.Y., **267**
Rockefeller Chapel, University of Chicago, Chicago, Ill., 129, 131
Romanticism, influence on E. M. Skinner, 13-16
Rosary Cathedral, Toledo, Ohio, 141-142, 276
Royce Hall, U.C.L.A., 143
Russell, Alexander, 129-130
Russian Symphonic Choir, 117-118, 152
Rutgers College, 84
Ryder, Charles A., 27
Ryder, George H., employment with, 6, 7

Sage Chapel, Cornell University, 40, 43, 231
St. Bartholemew's Church, New York City, 17, 60, 121, 140-141
St. George's School, Newport, R.I., 192
St. John's Church, Washington, D.C., 127, 193
St. John's Episcopal Church, Stamford, Conn., 191-192
St. John's Evangelical Lutheran Church, Allentown, Pa., 186
St. Joseph's Cathedral, Columbus, Ohio, 60, 99, 106, 111
St. Joseph's Episcopal Church, Detroit, Mich., **273**
St. Luke's Church, Evanston, Ill., 84
St. Luke's Church, Germantown, Pa., 22 (see also: Michell, Carlton)
St. Luke's Hospital Chapel, New York City, 81
St. Martin's Church, New York City, 193, **280**
St. Mary the Virgin, New York City, 158, 160-162
St. Matthew's Church, Worcester, Mass., 218
St. Paul's Chapel, Columbia University, 231
St. Paul's Church, Albany, N.Y., 192
St. Paul's Episcopal Church, Rochester, N.Y., 116
St. Paul Municipal Auditorium, St. Paul, Minn., 69, 81, 82
St. Peter's Episcopal Church, Beverly, Mass., 210
St. Stephen's Church, Providence, R.I., 186

St. Thomas Church, New York City, 45, 59, 104, 186, 213-214, 240-241
San Salvador Church, Broome Street, New York City, 27
Schantz, John A., 218
Schantz Organ Co., Orrville, Ohio, 218-219
Schenley High School, Pittsburgh, Pa., 84
Schweitzer, Albert, 224-225
Scott, George, 78, 154
Scott, Ruth, 48, 51, 52, 74, 76-78, 117, 118, 154, 247
Scottish Rite Cathedral, Detroit, Mich., 115, 116
Searles, Edward F., 147
Sears, Montgomery, 19
Second Congregational Church, Holyoke, Mass., 69, 111, **265**
Seibert, Henry F., 101
Self, William, 240-241
Senator Emerson Richards, 168
Serlo Hall
  acquisition of, 147
  mentioned, 147-151, 154, 211-212
Seventh United Presbyterian Church, Philadelphia, Pa., 192
Severance Hall, Cleveland, Ohio, 141
Sforzando, 17
Shofar, 115
Shorrock, Ernest, 63
Shorrock, Eugenia, 11, 49, 50, 53-56, 63, 74, 75, 106, 221, 222, 225-226, 227, 229, 233, 238, 247, 248, 249
South Boston factory, 26
Single contact coupler action, 17, 18
Skinner, Alice F., 1, 2, 4, 54, 190-191
Skinner & Cole Organ Co., 28, 29
Skinner, company names
  E. M. Skinner & Co., 29
  Ernest M. Skinner & Co., 27
  Ernest M. Skinner & Son Co., 148-149, 180, 181, 215
  Ernest M. Skinner Co., 30
Skinner, Cornelia Otis, 75
Skinner, Ernest M.
  ancestry, 1, 2
  begins apprenticeship, 5, 6
  begins own business, 25-27
  birth of, 1, 2
  death of, 247
  death of wife, Mabel, 228-229
  leaves Aeolian-Skinner, 180-181
  marriage to Mabel Hastings, 10
  retirement from organ business, 226
  travel to England and France, 19-22, 110, 111-112

Skinner, Eugenia, (see: Shorrock, Eugenia)
Skinner, Harry Clifford, 2, 3
Skinner, Mabel H.
  birth and childhood, 9
  death of, 228-229
  marriage to E. M. Skinner, 10
  mentioned, 9-12, 49-53, 55, 64, 74, 75-79, 117, 118, 148, 153-155, 181, 222, 227-229, 233-234
Skinner, Nathan, 1
Skinner Organ Company, 69-71, 183
Skinner, Richmond H., 12, 54, 55, 64, 107-108, 148-149, 154, 180-181, 186, 209, 212, 215-216
Skinner, Ruth Alden, (see: Scott, Ruth)
Skinner, Washington Martin, 1-6, 54, 186
Smallest Skinner organ (see: Greenfield Village; Clinic Organ)
Snow, Albert, 104
Snow, Francis, 151
South Congregational Church, New Britain, Conn., 17-19, 28, 44, **255**
Stambaugh Auditorium, Youngstown, Ohio, 115
Steere Organ Company, Westfield, Mass., 80, 81
Stenberg, John, 70
Stokowski, Leopold, 106
Stop action, 17
Stop, Open, and Reed, 100-101, 103
Strauss, Richard, 44, 62, 69, 203, 205-206
Strikes, 70, 71, 140
Studio, Dorchester, 63, 70
Studio, New York City, 100-103, 157
Studio organ, Dorchester, 61-63, 70
Studio organ, New York City, 100
Sub-Bass, 32', 45
Swell pedal, 15-17, 45
Swell pedal action
  electro-pneumatic, 45
  pneumatic, 17, 45
"Symphonic" organ, 61-63, (see: Orchestrator)
Symphony Hall, Boston, Mass., 25, 40, 231, 256

Taft, Frank, 157
Temple Emanu-El, San Francisco, Calif., 115, 117
Temple Methodist Episcopal Church, San Francisco, Calif., 141
Theater organs, 32, 88-94
Themodist, 25, 26
Thompson-Allen, Aubrey, 124-125, 226
Tibia, 89

Tokyo, Japan, 40
Toledo Museum of Art, Toledo, Ohio, 45
Tompkins Avenue Congregational Church, Brooklyn, N.Y., 39
Tonal concepts
  Audsley, 34
  Harrison, 122, 130, 160-161, 167-168, 238, 251
  Hope-Jones, 33, 34
  Skinner, 13, 16, 18, 19, 25, 30, 33, 34, 37, 38, 59, 60, 91-13, 111-112, 113, 114, 115-116, 127, 131-132, 142, 167-173, 184, 187, 191-192, 213, 217-218, 238, 250-251
Town Hall, New York City, 178
Townsend, Paul W., 161
Tracker action, 15, 16, 40, 135
Tracker organs, Skinner, 40, 135
"Tracker" touch, 46
Travel to England and France (see: England; France)
Trinity Cathedral, Cleveland, Ohio, 31
Trinity Chapel, Hartford, Conn., 160
Trinity Episcopal Church, Boston, Mass., 115, 185, 217
Trinity Episcopal Church, Toledo, Ohio, 40-42
Trombone, 16' (Willis) 22, 25
Trumpet family, 21, 25, 27, 43, 44, 86, 131, 160, 165, 184, 187, 191-192, 213, 217
Trumpet, Orchestral, 86
Trompette, 160
Tuba Mirabilis, 27, 44
Tubular-pneumatic action, 16, 27, 28, 116
Tubular-pneumatic organs, Skinner, 27, 28

U.C.L.A., Royce Hall, 143
Unda Maris, 4', 62, 63
Unification, 32, 33, 89-92, 94
Union Church, North East Harbor, Maine, 28
Unions, 70, 71, 140
Unitarian Church, Dedham, Mass., 186
Unitarian Church, Ludlow, Vermont, 26, 27, **257**
Unitarian Church, Taunton, Mass., 5, 224
Universalist Church (Church of Our Father), Detroit, Mich., 58, 65, **262**
University of Chicago, Chicago, Ill., Rockefeller Chapel, 129, 131
University of Florida, Gainesville, Fla, 115
University of Michigan, Ann Arbor, Mich., Hill Auditorium (see: Hill Auditorium)

University of Minnesota, Minneapolis, Minn., 158, 160, 162
University of Virginia, Charlottesville, Va., Old Cabell Hall, 37, 38, 258
Upperwork (see: Diapason chorus and Ensemble)
  American, 1860s, 15
  American, early 1890s, 16
  American, early 1920s, 110
  Audsley, 34
  European, early 1800s, 13
  European, mid-1800s, 14
  Harrison, 122, 160-161, 167
  mentioned, 13-16, 33, 34, 124, 127-128, 161
  Skinner, 16, 18, 34, 38, 59, 92, 111-114, 127-128, 141-142, 187, 191-192, 213, 217-218

Vierne, Louis, 21, 134-135
Violette, 4', 60
Violone, 32', 43
Vollmer, William Francis, 210

Walcker organ, Boston Music Hall (see: Boston Music Hall)
Walter Reed General Hospital, Washington, D.C.
  chapel, 141
  clinic organ, 214-215
Washington National Cathedral, Washington, D.C.
  Chapel of St. Joseph of Arimethea, 185
  Great Organ, 183-185, 186-188, 196-197, **278**
  Resurrection Chapel, **278**
  temporary organ, 186
Webber, Thomas, 192, 231
Welte, M., and Sons, Inc., 65
Whiteford, Joseph S., 231
Wife, Mabel Hastings Skinner (see: Skinner, Mabel H.)
Williams College, Williamstown, Mass., Grace Chapin Hall, 44, 84, **260**
"Whiffle-tree" swell engine, 45
Willis
  Henry, father, 21, 22, 39, 110, 112
  Henry, Jr., 21, 22
  Henry III, 112, 122-125, 167
  Henry IV, 125
  influence, 21, 22, 25, 27, 38, 39, 44, 112-113, 114-115, 142, 213
Wind pressure, 15, 61, 19, 21, 25, 32, 33, 37, 40, 43, 44, 89, 90, 114, 140, 160, 169, 193
Wind supply, 15, 16, 83
Woodberry, Jesse, employment with, 7
Woolsey Hall, Yale University, 138-139, 143
World War I, 58, 63-65
World War II, 208-209, 211, 212, 214-218
Wurlitzer Organ Co., 32, 89, 90, 94

Yale University, Woolsey Hall, 138-139, 143
York, Francis L., 58
Young, Walter E., 27, 28

Zeuch, William E., 60, 63, 67, 101, 128, 151, 175

We, the undersigned officers, councillors and members of the

American Guild of Organists

wish to record our high esteem and sincere affection for our fellow member

Ernest M. Skinner

whose friendship and jovial personality hold an enduring place in our professional relations.

For many years, in all his work, he has distinguished himself by ever placing art as his chief goal, and we are happy to honor him as an artist whose achievements will leave lasting impressions on the art of organ-building.

Our warmest personal greetings are hereby extended to our honored friend, with continuing good wishes.

May 24, 1948

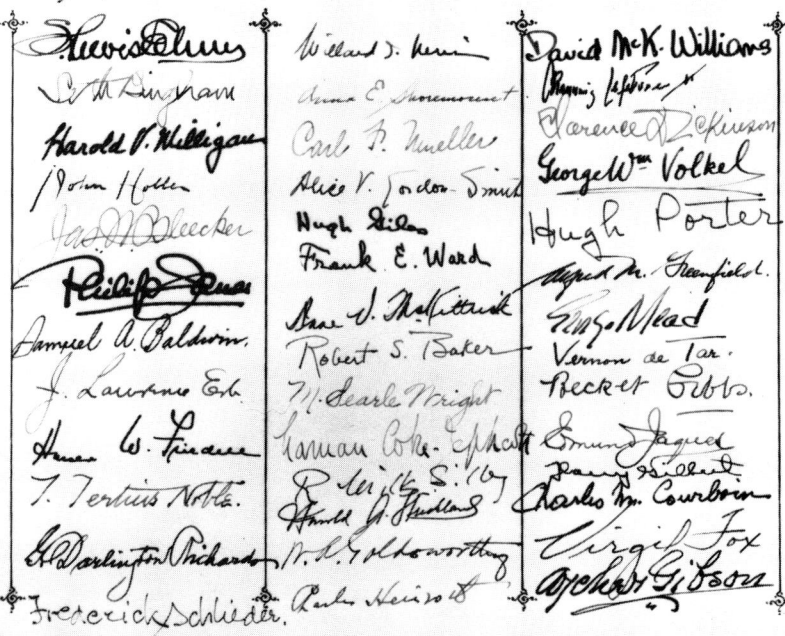

This certificate was presented to Ernest M. Skinner by the American Guild of Organists on May 24, 1948. Photographs appearing in this section were supplied by Eugenia Shorrock unless otherwise noted.

Sitting on the front steps of their home at 7 Evandale Terrace, Dorchester, circa 1903, Ernest and Mabel photographed each other with their children, Eugenia and Richmond. *In the top oval at the left* is their first child, Eugenia, and below is their second, Richmond Hastings Skinner. *In the larger oval,* Mabel Hastings Skinner appears as a young wife. *At the immediate left,* she holds Ruth Alden Skinner, their youngest child.

Ernest as a young man

Ernest prepares for an outing in his first automobile, a 1907 Winton Touring Car. Mabel holds baby Ruth in the back seat.

Mabel Hastings Skinner in her wedding dress.

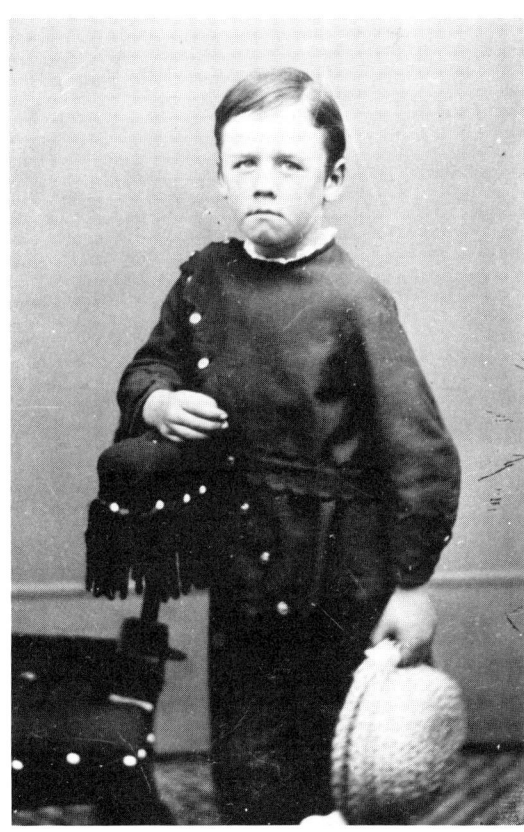

At the left are three residences, from the top: The Skinners' second home, 7 Evandale Terrace, Dorchester, Massachusetts; their third home, 130 Beacon Street, Chestnut Hill, Massachusetts; and their Alton Bay cottage with Ernest seated in the water. *Near left,* Ernest is seen as a child. *Below* are Ernest's mother and father, Alice Frances Brett Skinner and Washington Martin Skinner.

At the right, Ernest is seen in his middle years. *Below,* he is seated before the organ in the Dorchester studio. *Further below,* he poses with his French horn reed pipe and its orchestral counterpart.

Ernest called this widely-published picture of him his "Lloyd George" photograph.

The first Skinner factory, 387 East Eighth Street, South Boston, formerly the Hale Rubber Works.

The second Skinner factory, Crescent Avenue and Sydney Street in Dorchester, occupied in 1914.

Serlo Hall and the adjoining organ factory, Methuen, purchased by Ernest in 1929.

The last location of the Ernest M. Skinner & Son workshop was on the third floor in the Lyceum Building at the left in the picture, 179 Haven Street in Reading.

This picture of Ernest Skinner, left, and Henry Willis, right, was published in 1927 and supplied courtesy E. A. Boadway.

Ernest works in his experimental voicing room in the Dorchester factory. Courtesy of Ruth Scott.

A 32′ Bombarde stands in the erecting room.

The Skinner at the Colony Theater, New York.

Console for Opus 150, Cathedral of St. John the Divine, New York.

The Skinner studio at 677 Fifth Avenue in New York City was equipped with a roll-playing instrument. Photo courtesy Barbara Owen.

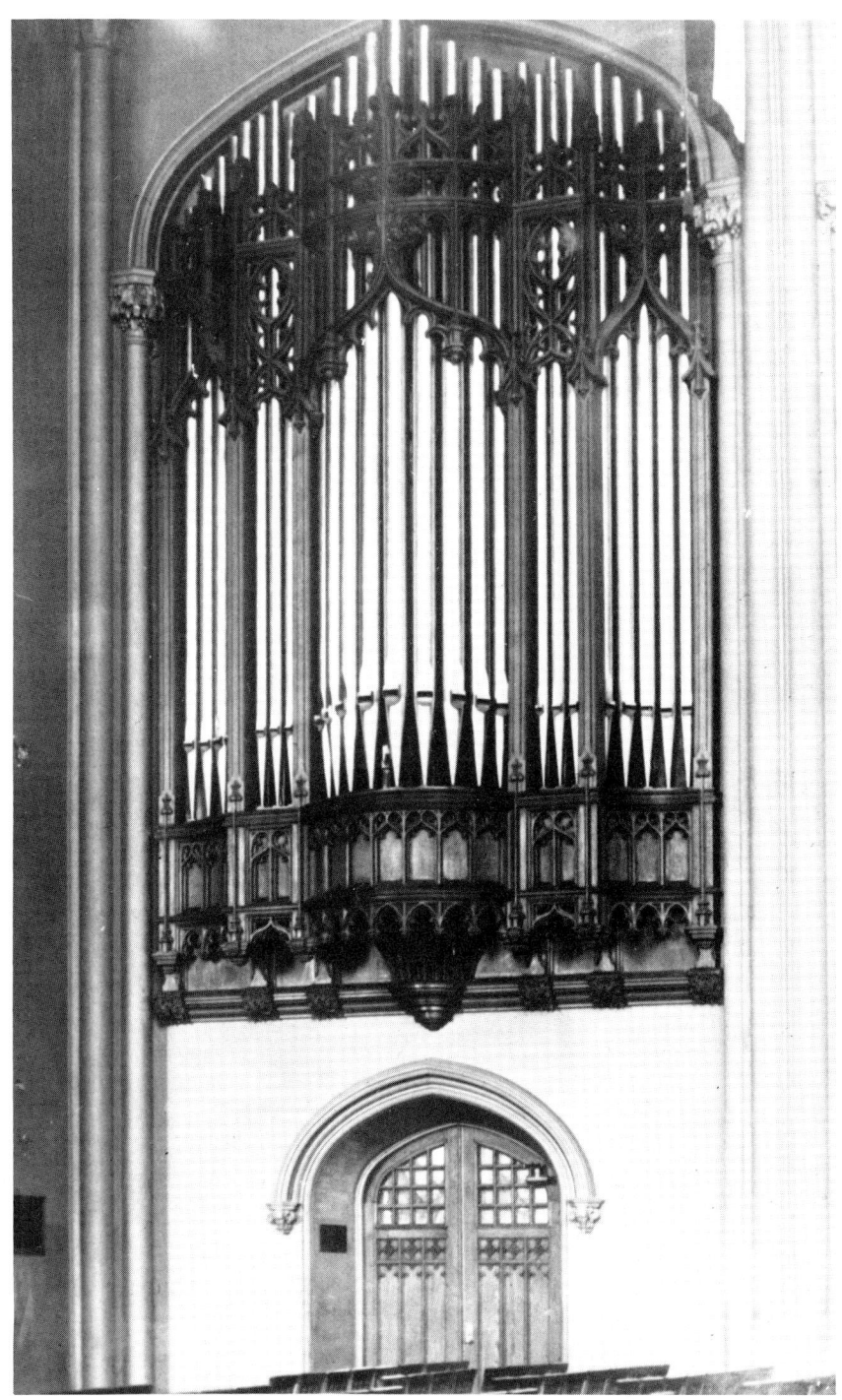

Facade of Opus 135, built in 1906 for the Great Hall, City College of New York. Photograph courtesy of Henry Karl Baker.

Above, the facade of Opus 233, a four-manual of 1915 built for Central Methodist Church, Detroit. *At the right, above:* Ernest Skinner reeds from left to right are Orchestral Oboe, English Horn, Flugel Horn, and French Horn. *At the far right* is his revised version of the English Horn. *Below, right:* E. M. Skinner holds the register crescendo pedal action that he patented in 1897.

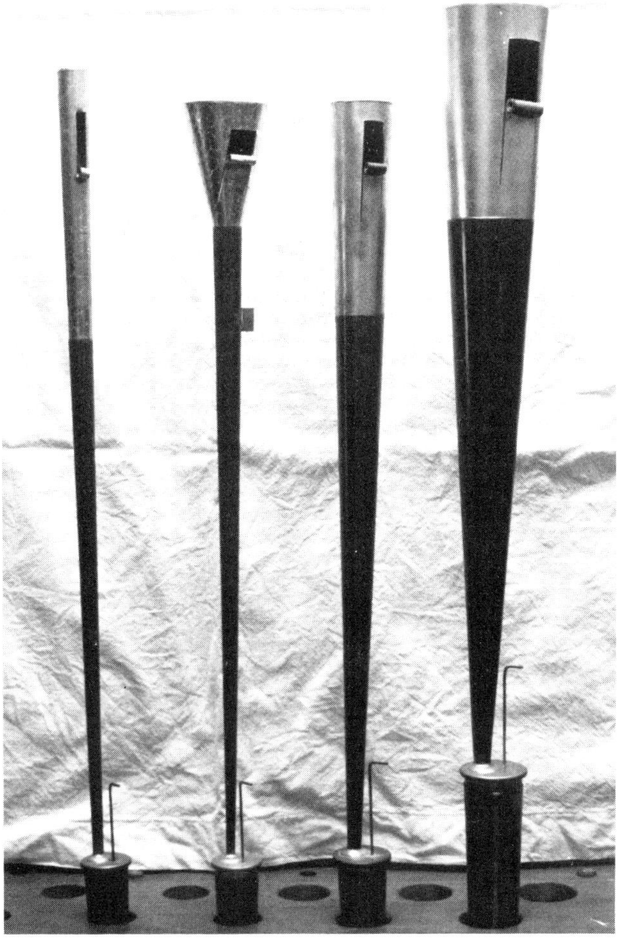

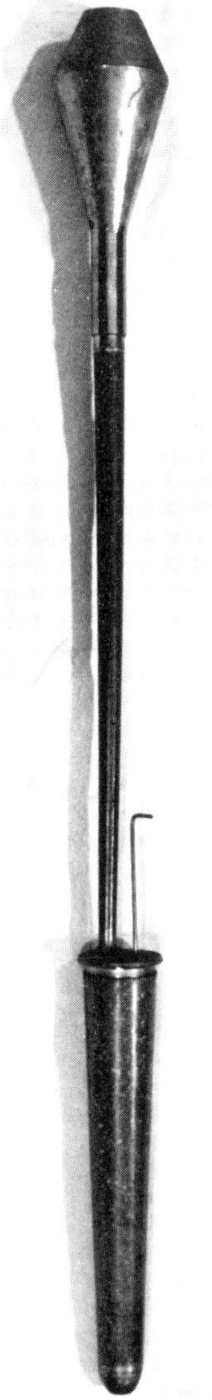

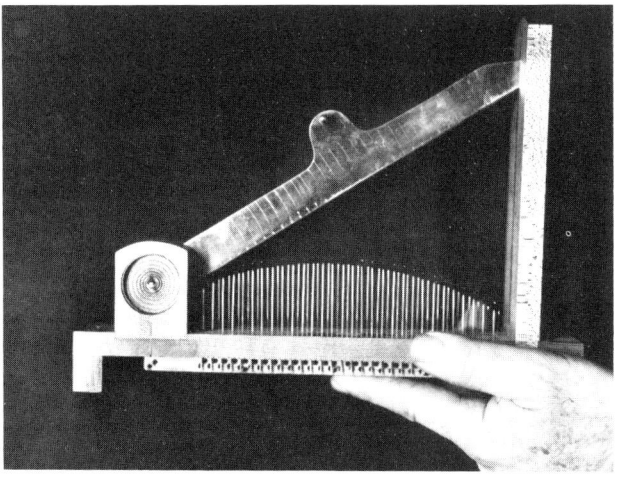

Views of Opus 190 of 1910 in the Grand Avenue Methodist Temple, Kansas City, Missouri, photographed by Mark McGuire, are seen below. The front Swell chest, at the bottom, shows the Cornopean and Clarion ranks in the foreground. *At the right,* pipes in the Swell division of Opus 475 of 1924 at Jefferson Avenue Presbyterian Church in Detroit are, left to right: portion of Mixture V, 2′ Flautino, 8′ Gedeckt, 4′ Flute Triangulaire, and 8′ Flauto Dolce.